SAND-BURIED RUINS OF KHOTAN

SAND-BURIED RUINS OF KHOTAN

PERSONAL NARRATIVE OF A JOURNEY OF ARCHAEOLOGICAL AND GEOGRAPHICAL EXPLORATION IN CHINESE TURKESTAN

BY
M. AUREL STEIN

CHEAPER EDITION
WITH A MAP FROM ORIGINAL SURVEYS AND NUMEROUS ILLUSTRATIONS

GYAN

Published by

Gyan Publishing House
5, Ansari Road
Daryaganj, New Delhi-110002
Phone: 011-47034999, 9811692060
E-mail: books@gyanbooks.com

Distribution Network
gyanbooks.com
India, USA, Canada, UK, Australia, France

ISBN : 978-81-212-3981-3 (PB)
First Published, 1904

2nd Impression 2020

Printed at: Gyan Press, Delhi.

Sand-Buried Ruins of Khotan
Author: M. Aurel Stein

SAND-BURIED RUINS OF KHOTAN

PERSONAL NARRATIVE OF A JOURNEY OF ARCHÆOLOGICAL AND GEOGRAPHICAL EXPLORATION IN CHINESE TURKESTAN

BY

M. AUREL STEIN

CHEAPER EDITION

WITH A MAP FROM ORIGINAL SURVEYS AND NUMEROUS ILLUSTRATIONS

LONDON
HURST AND BLACKETT, LIMITED
13, Great Marlborough Street
1904

TO THE MEMORY

OF

MY BROTHER

WHOSE LOVING CARE EVER FOLLOWED ME THROUGH LIFE.

THIS ACCOUNT OF MY JOURNEY,

FIRST RECORDED FOR HIM

IS INSCRIBED

IN UNCEASING AFFECTION AND SORROW

INTRODUCTION.

THE journey described in these pages was carried out in the year 1900–01, under the auspices of the Government of India. Its main object was the systematic exploration of ancient remains about Khotan and in the adjoining parts of the great desert of Chinese Turkestan. The fresh materials thus brought to light for the study of the early history and culture of those regions were so extensive that my full scientific report must, by reason of its bulk and cost, necessarily remain beyond the reach of the general public. I have therefore gladly availed myself of the permission accorded to me to publish independently the present narrative, which is intended to record for a wider class of readers my personal experiences and observations, as well as the main facts concerning my antiquarian discoveries.

I have spared no trouble to render my account of the latter accurate in its details and yet thoroughly intelligible to the non-Orientalist. It has been my hope to attract his interest to a fascinating chapter of ancient history which witnessed interchange between the civilisations of India, China, and the Classical West in that distant part of Central Asia, and which seemed almost completely lost to us. If this hope is fulfilled, and if at the same time these pages convey adequate impressions of the strange scenes and conditions amidst which I passed that year of trying but happy toil, I shall feel repaid for the additional labour involved in the preparation of this narrative.

The circumstances which induced me to form the project of these explorations, and the arrangements by which I was enabled to carry it into execution, have already been explained in my "Preliminary Report on a Journey of Archæological and Topographical Exploration in Chinese Turkestan," published in 1901 under the authority of the Secretary of State for India. Hence a succinct notice of them may suffice here. The idea of archæological work about Khotan first suggested itself to me in the spring of 1897, in consequence of some remarkable antiquarian acquisitions from that region. Among the papers left by the distinguished but ill-fated French traveller, M. Dutreuil de Rhins, were fragments of ancient birch-bark leaves, which had been acquired in the vicinity of Khotan. On expert examination they proved to contain a Buddhist text in an early Indian script and language, and were soon recognised as the oldest Indian manuscript then known, going back to the first centuries of our era.

About the same time the "British collection of Central-Asian antiquities" formed at Calcutta through the efforts of Dr. A. F. Rudolf Hoernle, C.I.E., received from the same region notable additions, consisting of fragments of paper manuscripts, pieces of ancient pottery, and similar relics. They had been sold to representatives of the Indian Government in Kashgar, Kashmir and Ladak as finds made by native "treasure-seekers" at ancient sites about Khotan. Similar purchases had reached public collections at St. Petersburg through the Russian Consul-General at Kashgar and others. A curious feature of all these acquisitions made from a distance was that, besides unmistakably genuine documents in Indian and Chinese writing, they included a large proportion of texts displaying a strange variety of entirely "unknown scripts," which could not fail to arouse suspicion. While the materials thus accumulated, no reliable information was ever forthcoming as to the exact origin of the finds or the true character of the ruined sites which were supposed to have furnished them. No part of Chinese Turkestan had then been explored from an archæological point of view, and it struck me that, however much attention these and other future discoveries might receive from competent Orientalists in Europe, their full historical and antiquarian value could never be realised without systematic researches on the spot.

The practicable nature of the project was proved in the meantime by the memorable march which Dr. Hedin made in the winter of 1896 past two areas of sand-buried ruins in the desert north-east of Khotan. Though the distinguished explorer, during his necessarily short halt at each place, was unable to secure any exact evidence as to the character and date of the ruins, this discovery (of which the first account reached me in 1898) sufficed to demonstrate both the existence and the comparative accessibility of ancient sites likely to reward excavation.

It was only in the summer of 1898 that I found leisure to work out the detailed plan of my journey and to submit it with Dr. Hoernle's weighty recommendation to the Indian Government, whose sanction and assistance were indispensable for its execution. Generously supported first by Sir Mackworth Young, K.C.S.I., late Lieutenant-Governor of the Punjab, and subsequently on my temporary transfer to Bengal by the late Sir John Woodburn, K.C.S.I., the lamented head of that administration and a zealous friend of Oriental learning, my proposals met with favourable consideration on the part of Lord Curzon's Government. In July, 1899, the scheme, in which Sir Charles Rivaz, K.C.S.I., then Member of the Viceregal Council and now Lieutenant-Governor of the Punjab, had from the first shown kind personal interest, received the final sanction of the Government of India. A resolution in the Department of Revenue and Agriculture provided for my deputation on special duty to Chinese Turkestan, during a period of one year. At the same time a grant of Rs. 9,000 (£600), partly from Imperial resources and partly from contributions by the Local Governments of the Punjab and Bengal, was placed at my disposal to meet the estimated expenditure on the journey and explorations.

That, notwithstanding the great distances and physical obstacles to be overcome and in spite of all the uncertainties attending an enterprise in a new field, I succeeded in accomplishing the whole of my programme strictly within the sanctioned estimates of time and expense, is a fact which from a practical and quasi-administrative point of view I feel proud to record. How much anxious thought, calculation and effort its attainment cost me, need scarcely be detailed here. Considering the nature and extent of the ground covered by my travels, and the difficulties of work in the desert, the relatively low expenditure involved in my explorations has since been noted with surprise by brother archæologists and others.

Long experience of marching and camping gained on Indian ground certainly helped in restricting the cost. But even thus the expenses of my expedition would certainly have been higher, had not the Survey of India Department liberally offered its assistance. Previous antiquarian tours in Kashmir, the Punjab, and on the Afghan Frontier had taught me the importance of exact topographical observation as an adjunct of my researches. The necessity of fixing accurately the position of ancient sites and generally elucidating the historical geography of the country was bound to bring surveying operations in Chinese Turkestan into the closest connection with my immediate task. But in addition I was anxious from the first to utilise whatever opportunities the journey might offer for geographical work of a more general character in regions which had hitherto remained without a proper survey or altogether unexplored.

Colonel St. George Gore, R.E., C.S.I., Surveyor-General of India, proved most willing to further this object. He kindly agreed to depute with me one of the native Sub-Surveyors of his Department, and to provide the necessary equipment of surveying instruments, together with a special grant of Rs. 2,000 (£133), in order to cover the additional expenses. Of the excellent services rendered by Babu Ram Singh, the Sub-Surveyor selected, my narrative gives ample evidence. With his help a continuous system of surveys, by plane-table, astronomical observations and triangulation, was carried on during the whole of my travels in Chinese Turkestan. The results of these surveys, which in the mountains I was able to supplement by photogrammetric survey work of my own, and the direction and supervision of which throughout claimed much of my time and attention, are now embodied in maps published by the Trigonometrical Branch of the Survey of India. From these the small scale map was prepared which, with the kind permission of the Royal Geographical Society, has been reproduced for the present volume.

For the generous consideration and aid of the Indian Government that alone enabled me to undertake the scientific enterprise I had planned, I shall ever retain the feeling of deep and sincere gratitude. Through it, I had secured at last the long and eagerly sought chance to serve, in a new field and with a measure of freedom such as had never fallen to my share, those interests of Oriental research which had claimed me from the commencement of my student days, and which had brought me to India.

The twelve years since passed, mainly in the service of the Punjab University, had taught me fully to appreciate the importance of both time and money in regard to archæological labours. Though placed tantalisingly near to the ground which by its ancient remains and historical associations has always had a special fascination for me, I had rarely been able to devote to antiquarian work more than brief intervals of hard-earned leisure.

The fact that my administrative duties had no direct connection with my scientific interests, might well have made me feel despondent about the chance of ever obtaining the means needed for systematic archæological explorations, even on well-known ground and in easily accessible regions. For with, I fear, the majority of fellow-workers I had failed to profit by the example of the late Dr. Schliemann, who, before attempting to realise his grand projects at Troy and Mykene, had resolutely set himself to assure that safest base of success, personal independence and an ample reserve of funds.

The exceptional help which the Indian Government, inspired by Lord Curzon's generous interest in the history and antiquities of the East, had accorded to me, for a time removed the difficulties against which I had struggled, and brought the longed-for opportunity within my reach. But remembering the circumstances under which it had been secured, I could not prevent anxious thoughts often crossing my mind in the course of my preparations and after. Would Fate permit the full execution of my plan within the available time, and would the results prove an adequate return for the liberal consideration and aid that the Government had extended to me?

I knew well that neither previous training and experience, nor careful preparation and personal zeal, could guarantee success.

The wide extent of the region to be searched and the utter insufficiency of reliable information would alone have justified doubts as to how much those sand-buried sites would yield up during a limited season. But in addition there was the grave fact that prolonged work in the desert such as I contemplated would have to be carried through in the face of exceptional physical difficulties and even dangers. Nor was it possible to close my eyes to the very serious obstacles which suspicions of the local Chinese administration and quasi-political apprehensions, however unfounded, might raise to the realisation of my programme.

When I now look back upon these anxieties and doubts, and recognise in the light of the knowledge since gathered how much there was to support them, I feel doubly grateful to the kindly Destiny which saved my plans from being thwarted by any of those difficulties, and which allowed my labours to be rewarded by results richer than I had ventured to hope for. In respect of the efforts and means by which these results were secured, no remarks seem here needed ; the reader of my present narrative, whatever his knowledge of Central Asia and its historical past may be, can safely be left to judge of them for himself. But in regard to the scientific value of the results similar reticence would scarcely be justified, however much personal feelings might make me incline towards it.

It is impossible to overlook the fact that archæological research in great fields like India and Central Asia, which lie beyond the stimulating influence of Biblical associations, has not as yet succeeded in gaining its due share of sympathy and interest from the wider public. In consequence the latter has so far had little opportunity of learning to appreciate the great historical problems which are involved in those researches. In the absence of such preparatory information the non-Orientalist could not be expected to form for himself a correct estimate of the importance of the discoveries resulting from my explorations without the guidance of expert opinion. I must therefore feel grateful that the generous attention paid to my labours by the most representative body of qualified fellow-scholars permits me to supply expert opinion in a clear and conclusive form.

The International Congress of Orientalists, assembled at Hamburg in September, 1902, before which I was privileged to give an account of my journey and excavations, adopted the following resolution, proposed by Professor Henri Cordier, the representative of the French Government, and Dr. A. A. Macdonell, Boden Professor of Sanskrit at Oxford, and recommended by the combined Indian, Central-Asian, and Far-Eastern Sections :—

"The XIIIth International Congress of Orientalists held at Hamburg beg to express their thanks to His Excellency the Viceroy and the Government of India for the great encouragement they have extended to Oriental learning and research by granting to Dr. M. A. Stein the necessary leisure and means for the prosecution of his recent explorations in Eastern Turkestan. They desire at the same time to express their appreciation of the highly important results which have rewarded the labours of the scholar selected by the Government of India, and which represent an ample return for the outlay incurred, owing to the practical nature of the operations conducted by him. They would also venture to express the hope that facilities will be given to him for completing the publication and elaboration of the results obtained, and that the Government will be pleased to sanction any necessary extension for this purpose of Dr. Stein's present deputation. Finally, they venture to express the hope that, when circumstances permit, the interests of archæological research will be allowed to benefit by Dr. Stein's special experience and previous knowledge, which are likely to facilitate considerably the further explorations which it is desirable should be entrusted to him in the interests of India."

As far as the space and the limited means of illustration available in this personal narrative would permit, I have endeavoured to explain to my readers the significance of the mass of antiquarian materials brought to light by my excavations—whether in the form of objects of ancient art and industry; or in those hundreds of old manuscripts and documents which the desert sand has preserved in such surprising freshness; or finally in the many curious observations I was able to make on the spot about the conditions of every-day life, etc., once prevailing in those sand-buried settlements. But of the great historical questions which all these finds help to illuminate, it was impossible to show more than the bare outlines, and those only in glimpses. This cannot be the place for their systematic discussion. But I may at least indicate here the main directions in which those discoveries are likely to open new vistas into obscure periods of Central-Asian civilisation.

The early spread of Buddhist teaching and worship from India into Central Asia, China and the Far East is probably the most remarkable contribution made by India to the general development of mankind. Chinese records had told us that Buddhism reached the "Middle Kingdom" not directly from the land of its birth, but through Central-Asian territories lying northward. We also knew from the accounts left by the devoted Chinese pilgrims who, from the fourth century A.D. onwards, had made their way to the sacred Buddhist sites in India, that Sakyamuni's creed still counted numerous followers in many of the barbarian "Western Kingdoms" they passed through. But these Chinese travellers, best represented by the saintly "Master of the Law," Hiuen-Tsiang, our Indian Pausanias, had their eyes fixed on subjects of spiritual interest, on holy places and wonder-working shrines, on points of doctrine and monastic observance. Of the many things of this world about which their observations would have been of far greater interest for the historical student, they have rarely chosen to inform us even within the sacred bounds of India. Hence their brief notices of Central-Asian countries, visited merely *en route*, fail to supply definite indications of the extent to which Indian culture, language and art had spread with Buddhist propaganda across the Himalaya and the Hindukush.

That such influences had been at work there for long centuries, and sometimes penetrated even much further to the East, occasional references in the Chinese Annals and elsewhere had led us to suspect. But of those indigenous records and remains which might enable us to reconstruct that bygone phase of civilisation in its main aspects, all trace seemed to have vanished with the Muhammadan conquest (tenth-eleventh century).

Chance finds of ancient manuscripts, in Sanskrit and mostly Buddhistic, which commenced in 1890 with Captain (now Colonel) Bower's famous birch-bark leaves from Kucha, were the first tangible proof that precious materials of this kind might still be preserved under the arid soil of Chinese Turkestan. The importance of these literary relics was great, apart from their philological value; for they plainly showed that, together with Buddhism, the study of the classical language of India also found a home in that distant land beyond the Himalaya. But on the cultural *entourage* in which this far transplanted Indian learning had flourished, such chance acquisitions, of uncertain origin and unaccompanied by archæological evidence, could throw little light.

For systematic excavations, which alone could supply this evidence, the region of Khotan appeared from the first a field of particular promise. In scattered notices of Chinese records there was much to suggest that this little kingdom, situated on the important route that led from China to the Oxus Valley and hence to India as well as to the West, had played a prominent part in developing the impulses received from India and transmitting them eastwards. The close connection with ancient Indian art seemed particularly marked in whatever of small antiques, such as pottery fragments, coins and seals, native agency had supplied from Khotan. And fortunately for our researches, archæology could here rely on the help of a very effective ally—the moving sand of the desert which preserves what it buries. Ever since human activity first created the oases of Khotan territory, their outskirts must have witnessed a continuous struggle with that most formidable of deserts, the Taklamakan: while local traditions, attested from an early date, told of settlements that had been abandoned before its advance.

The ruined sites explored by me have more than justified the hopes which led me to Khotan and into its desert. Scattered over an area which in a straight line extends for more than three hundred miles from west and east, and dating back to very different periods, these ruins throughout reveal to us a uniform and well-defined civilisation. It is easy to recognise now that this bygone culture rested mainly on Indian foundations. But there has also come to light unmistakable evidence of other powerful influences, both from the West and from China, which helped to shape its growth and to invest it with an individual character and fascination of its own.

The origin and history of the culture that once flourished in Buddhist Khotan, are faithfully reflected in the remarkable series of sculptures and paintings which the ancient shrines and dwelling places, after long centuries of burial beneath the dunes, have yielded up. Exact archæological evidence enables us to determine the various periods at which these settlements were invaded by the desert sand. Though these periods range from the third to the close of the eighth century of our era, yet the preponderance of Indian art influences is attested by the latest as well as by the earliest of these finds. The rich statuary of the Rawak Stupa Court, and the decorative wood carvings of the ancient site beyond Niya, reproduce with astonishing fidelity the style and motives of that fascinating 'Græco-Buddhist' art which, fostered by Hellenistic-Roman influences grew up and flourished in Gandhara (the present Peshawar Valley) and other neighbouring tracts in the extreme North-West of India, during the centuries immediately preceding and following the commencement of our era. Yet when we turn from those remains to the frescoes on the walls of the small Buddhist shrines at Dandan-Uiliq, dating some five hundred years later, we recognise with equal distinctness the leading features of ancient Indian pictorial art as preserved for us in the Ajanta Cave paintings.

The records of the Chinese Annals plainly showed us that for considerable periods under both the Later Han and the Tang dynasties China had maintained effective political control over the kingdom of Khotan. My excavations have confirmed these records, and from the finds of Chinese documents on wood or paper, Chinese coins, articles of manufacture, etc., it has become abundantly clear that Chinese civilisation no less than political ascendency asserted there a powerful influence. Seeing how close for centuries were the relations between Khotan and the great empire eastwards in matters of administration, trade and industrial intercourse, we cannot feel surprised to find a connection in art also attested by manifest traces. It is China which in this direction appears the main borrower; for besides such distinct historical evidence as the notice about a scion of the royal house of Khotan, whom the Annals name as the founder of a new pictorial school in China in the seventh century A.D., there is much to suggest that the Indian element which so conspicuously pervades the whole Buddhist art of the Far East had to a very large extent found its way thither through Khotan. Yet a careful analysis of the composition and drawing in more than one of the frescoes and painted panels of Dandan-Uiliq will show that Chinese taste also had its influence on the later art of Khotan.

For us still greater interest must attach to the convincing evidence disclosed as to the question how far into Central Asia the classical art of the West had penetrated during the first centuries of our era. We see its triumphant advance to Khotan half-way between Western Europe and Peking, strikingly demonstrated by the remarkable series of classical seals, impressed on clay and yet preserved in wonderful freshness, which still adhere to a number of the many ancient documents on wood discovered at the sand-buried site beyond Niya. As explained in Chapter XXV., where I have discussed and illustrated some of these important finds, we cannot make sure in each case where the well-modelled figures of Greek deities, such as Pallas Athene and Eros, or the classically treated portrait heads that appear in these seals, were actually engraved. But it is certain that the seals themselves were currently used by officials and others resident within the kingdom of Khotan, and that classical models greatly influenced the work of local lapidaries and die-sinkers. The remarkable diversity of the cultural influences which met and mingled at Khotan during the third century A.D. is forcibly brought home to us by these records from a remote Central-Asian settlement, inscribed on wooden tablets in an Indian language and writing and issued by officials with strangely un-Indian titles, whose seals carry us to the classical world far away in the West.

The imitation of early Persian art of which, five centuries later, we find unmistakable traces in some of the paintings of sacred Buddhist subjects recovered from the ruins of Dandan-Uiliq, is a curious parallel, and from an historical point of view almost equally instructive.

The dwelling places, shrines, etc., of those ancient settlements had, no doubt, before the desert sand finally buried them, been cleared by the last inhabitants and others of everything that possessed intrinsic value. But much of what they left behind, though it could never tempt the treasure-seekers of succeeding ages, has acquired for us exceptional value. The remains of ancient furniture such as the wooden chair reproduced on p. 356; the shreds of silks and other woven fabrics; the tatters of antique rugs; the fragments of glass, metal and pottery ware; the broken pieces of domestic and agricultural implements, and the manifold other relics, however humble, which had safely rested in the sand-buried dwellings and their deposits of rubbish—these all help to bring vividly before our eyes details of ancient civilisation that without the preserving force of the desert would have been lost for ever.

But however interesting and instructive such details may be, they would, by themselves, not permit us with any degree of critical assurance to reconstruct the life and social organisation which once flourished at these settlements, or to trace the historical changes which they have witnessed. The hope of ever elucidating such questions was dependent on the discovery of written records, and it is fortunate indeed that, at the very sites which proved richest in those relics of material culture, the finds of ancient manuscripts and documents were also unexpectedly ample and varied. The Sanskrit manuscripts excavated at Dandan-Uiliq acquaint us with that class of canonical Buddhist literature which we may assume to have been most cherished in the monastic establishments of ancient Khotan. The series of Chinese documents discovered in ruins of the same site is of particular historical interest. The exact dates recorded in them (781–790 A.D.), in combination with other evidence, clearly indicate the close of the eighth century as the time when the settlement was deserted, while their contents throw curious side-lights on the economical and political conditions of the territory immediately before Chinese suzerain power finally abandoned these regions to Tibetan invasion. Sanskrit manuscripts and records in Chinese mark foreign imports in the culture of Khotan. All the more interest attaches to the numerous documents and fragmentary texts from the same site which show an otherwise unknown language, manifestly non-Sanskritic yet written in Indian Brahmi characters; for it appears very probable that in them we have records of the tongue actually spoken at that period by the indigenous population of Khotan.

We see Sanskrit, Chinese and the same non-Sanskritic language similarly represented among the literary finds from the ruined temple of Endere, in the extreme east of the territory explored. But here in addition there appears Tibetan, as if to remind us of the prominent part which Tibet too has played in the history of Central Asia. A curious Chinese graffito found on the wall of the Endere temple clearly refers to the Tibetans, and gives a date which, since its recent examination by Sinologists, can be safely read as 719 A.D. It is probable that these finds of Tibetan manuscripts are directly connected with that extension of Tibetan power into Eastern Turkestan which the Chinese Annals record for that very period.

But much older and of far greater importance than any of these finds are the hundreds of Kharoshthi documents on wood and leather brought to light from the ruined houses and the rubbish heaps of the ancient settlement discovered beyond the point where the Niya River now loses itself in the desert. Their peculiar writing material (so much older than the paper of my other literary finds), their early Indian script and language, and the surprisingly perfect state of preservation of many among them would alone have sufficed to invest these documents with special interest. But their exceptional historical value is derived from the fact that they prove to contain records written as early as the third century of our era, and dealing with a wide range of matters of administration and private life.

In Chapter XXVI. I have endeavoured to indicate the varied nature and abounding interest of the information which this mass of official reports and orders, letters, accounts, and miscellaneous "papers" (to use an anachronism) is bound to reveal to us. The results already obtained have opened new and far-reaching vistas. It is no small discovery to find the old local tradition of a colonisation of Khotan from the extreme

North-West of India confirmed by the use, in ordinary practical intercourse, of an Indian language and a script peculiar to the very region from which those Indian immigrants were believed to have come.

The thought of the grave risks with which nature and, still more, human activity threaten all these relics of antiquity, was ever present to my mind, and formed an urgent incentive to unwearied exertion, however trying the conditions of work might be. On the one hand I had ample occasion in the desert to observe the destructive effect of erosion by wind and sand on whatever of ancient remains is left exposed to its slow but unrelenting power. On the other I could not fail to be impressed by the warnings of impending destruction through the hand of man: there were the evident traces of the mischief done by Khotan "treasure-seekers" at the more accessible sites, and also, alas! a vivid remembrance of the irretrievable loss which the study of Indian art and antiquities has suffered through "irresponsible digging" carried on until recent years by, and for, amateur collectors among the ruined Buddhist shrines of the North-West Frontier of India.

Though the climate of the Turkestan desert is not inferior in conserving capacity to that of Egypt, yet neither Khotan nor any other territory bordering on that desert could ever compare with the land of the Pharaohs in wealth of antiquarian remains awaiting exploration. "Ancient cities," complete with palaces, streets, markets, etc., such as are pictured by Turkestan folklore, and also by indiscriminating European imagination, as lying submerged under the sand-dunes through a kind of Sodom and Gomorrah catastrophe, are certainly not to be looked for. The sites where settlements abandoned in early times could be located, with ruins still capable of excavation, were few in number, and even those among them which, being further removed from the present inhabited area, had so far escaped the ravages of the "treasure-seekers," could not be expected to remain safe much longer. The time seems still distant when Khotan will see its annual stream of tourists. Yet the extensive industry of forged "old books" which had grown up in Khotan during recent years, and which I was able to trace and expose in detail (see Chapter XXXI.), sufficiently shows how dangerous a factor "collecting" has already become even in Chinese Turkestan.

In the face of such difficulties as work in the Taklamakan presents I could never have made my explorations sufficiently extensive and thorough without the active co-operation of the Chinese administrators of the districts from which I had to draw guides, labour, supplies—in fact, whatever was needed during my winter campaign in the desert. I had the good fortune to find in the Ambans Pan-Darin and Huang-Daloi, then in charge of Khotan and Keriya, reliable friends, thoroughly interested in my work and ever ready to help me with all that was in their power. I look back to the invariable kindness and attention I received from these amiable Mandarins with all the more gratitude as it was shown at a time when, as they well knew, the conflict with the European powers was convulsing their empire. They were fully aware, too, that the services rendered to my scholarly enterprise could earn them neither material advantages nor honours.

The true historical sense innate in educated Chinese and the legendary knowledge I found to prevail among them of Hiuen-Tsiang, the great Buddhist pilgrim, whom I claimed as my guide and patron saint, certainly helped me in explaining the objects of my explorations to my Chinese friends and enlisting their personal interest. But I cannot doubt that the sympathetic attitude adopted from the first by the provincial administration towards my work was directly due to the efforts made on my behalf by Mr. G. Macartney, C.I.E., the representative of the Indian Government at Kashgar, whose personal influence among all Chinese dignitaries of the province is as great as it is well deserved. My narrative shows the manifold benefits I derived from the unfailing care of this kind and accomplished friend, who from afar never ceased to follow my explorations with watchful interest. For the important help he thus rendered towards their success, and for all his personal kindness, I am anxious to record here the expression of my sincere gratitude.

The *résumé* given above of the aims and results of my archæological work will, I hope, help to account for the character of my present narrative and the labour involved in its preparation. The interests of science obliged me to concentrate my efforts on a series of well-defined tasks and to avoid whatever might interfere with their carefully prepared execution. Mine was not a journey leaving much range for those chance incidents which may at times lead to exciting personal experiences, but are far more likely to cause loss in substantial results through waste of time, energy and means. I can only hope that my book may reach readers ready to find compensation in the thought that long-continued study of the ancient East and familiarity with modern India and its northern borderlands permit me to offer them guidance in regard to much that is of general human interest both in the present conditions and the historical past of the regions traversed.

The critical standards to which I am pledged by my work as a scholar would not allow me to compile a narrative by the mere reproduction of those diary leaves which were intended to convey the first records of my personal experiences and impressions to dear eyes since closed for ever by Death. Though my account was intended for a wider public than that of Orientalist or antiquarian scholars, yet I felt it incumbent to take every care that it should neither contain statements which further scrutiny might require to be modified in my scientific Report, nor pass over unnoticed any essential facts connected with my archæological discoveries.

The preparation of my narrative on these lines has implied far more labour than may, perhaps, appear on the surface. It would, in fact, have been impossible to accomplish it with the scanty leisure left from official duties as Inspector of Schools in the Punjab, to which I had to return on the conclusion of my explorations, in the autumn of 1901. Fortunately, however, the Government of India, on the proposal of the Punjab Government and with the concurrence of the Secretary of State for India, granted to me in the following year a period of deputation to England in order that I might be enabled to elaborate the results of my journey with the help of the original finds temporarily deposited in the British Museum.

For the generous consideration thus shown to me I feel it my duty to record here my deep sense of gratitude to His Excellency the Viceroy and the Indian Government. Just as my explorations were rendered possible only through their powerful aid, so, too, I owe to their liberality the temporary freedom for scholarly labour which has permitted me to complete the present narrative. I feel confident that its contents will be found in more than one respect a necessary complement to my Detailed scientific Report which is still under preparation. On the other hand, I must refer my readers to the latter publication for many illustrations of antiquities, ruins, scenery, etc., which to my regret it was found impossible, on account of technical difficulties and other reasons, to provide here.

It remains for me to record my grateful acknowledgments for the manifold assistance which I have received while preparing this volume. To none do I feel more indebted than to my artist friend, Mr. Fred. H. Andrews, who ever since my return from Chinese Turkestan has furthered my labours with enthusiastic devotion. His wide knowledge of ancient Indian art, acquired in his late post as Principal of the School of Art and Curator of the Museum at Lahore, and his own high artistic abilities, have rendered his co-operation in the arrangement and description of my collection of antiquities of the utmost value. He has never wearied in giving me the full benefit of his expert advice in questions affecting the technical aspects of my finds, and he has spared no trouble to make the illustrations of this book as effective as their number and the available means of reproduction would permit.

Beside drawings and diagrams embodied in these pages I owe to his skill the design reproduced on the cover of this volume and the Black and White drawing for the Vignette which adorns the title-page. This represents a restored yet faithfully conceived enlargement of the figure of Pallas Athene as seen in several of the ancient seal impressions on clay excavated by me from the desert sand. I could scarcely have wished for my narrative to issue under a more felicitous emblem.

Dr. A. F. Rudolf Hoernle, the eminent Indologist, who from the first had shown the warmest interest in my explorations, was kind enough to place at my disposal valuable information in respect of the ancient manuscripts in Brahmi characters, the publication of which has been undertaken by him; he has further rendered me the great service of reading a revision of this book. I owe a similar debt of gratitude to my friend Mr. E. J. Rapson, of the British Museum, who not only charged himself with the care of my collection while I was absent in India, but has also allowed me to benefit at all times by the results of the most painstaking researches he has devoted to the decipherment of the ancient Kharoshthi documents. To Dr. Percy Gardner, Professor of Archæology in the University of Oxford, I am indebted for most competent guidance in respect of the objects of classical art contained in my collection, and for much kind encouragement besides.

For the interpretation of my important Chinese records I must consider myself particularly fortunate in having enjoyed the assistance of such distinguished Sinologist experts as Dr. S. W. Bushell, C.M.G., and Professors É. Chavannes and Douglas. The complete translation and analysis of those documents with which Professor Chavannes, of the Collège de France, has favoured me for publication in my Detailed Report, has already proved of very great value for the study of Chinese influence in Turkestan. Dr. Bushell and Professor Douglas, of the British Museum, have never failed to help me with learned advice on questions concerning Chinese lore.

If I have left it to the last to mention my obligations to my friends Mr. J. S. Cotton, late editor of the *Academy*, and Mr. P. S. Allen, of Corpus Christi College, Oxford, it is only because theirs was the help benefiting more directly the Western or modern aspect of the work now presented. The former did me the great favour of revising my manuscript with special regard to the requirements of the general reader, a task for which he was exceptionally qualified by his literary experience; while the other kind friend cheerfully charged himself with a revision of my proofs and greatly helped me by its thoroughness. To his kind offices and the generous mediation of Mr. Cuthbert Shields, I owed the peaceful retreat for scholarly work which the hospitality of the President and Fellows of Corpus Christi College assured to me during the summer of 1902. With those inspiriting precincts, full of great memories from Erasmus to Ruskin, I shall always associate the recollection of the pleasantest part of my work in England.

* * * * * * * *

The narrative here presented still leaves me far from the conclusion of the labours which the antiquities and observations brought back from Chinese Turkestan have entailed upon me. Yet even thus I cannot prevent my eyes from looking beyond towards other fields of archæological exploration, no less closely linked with the sphere of Indian historical interests and equally likely to yield a rich harvest. On some my thoughts had been fixed long before I was able to visit India; but the years which have since passed by, though as full of scholarly labours as other duties would permit, have seemingly not brought me nearer to the longed-for chance of exploring them.

Life seems short where the range for research is so vast as in the case of ancient India and the regions through which it communicated with the classical West. But life must appear shorter still when the chosen tasks cannot be done in the study, when they call for the exertions of the scholar and explorer combined, such as are readily faced only while the optimism of comparative youth and physical vigour endures. To Fate—and to those who dispense it—I offer due thanks for having allowed me to work on Indian ground and at last, after years of toil, to attain for a time freedom and the means to serve science. Yet when I look back upon all the efforts that had to precede this opportunity, I am tempted to regret that I cannot share the Indian belief in those 'future births' which hold out promise of appropriate reward for 'merits,' spiritual and other. For on the strength of such a belief I might feel more hopeful of meeting yet with that reward for my work at Khotan which I should prize highest—the chance of repeating it elsewhere.

M. AUREL STEIN.

BRITISH MUSEUM,
April 16, 1903.

CONTENTS.

INTRODUCTION.

CHAPTER I.

CALCUTTA TO KASHMIR.

CHAPTER II.

TO ASTOR AND GILGIT.

CHAPTER VI.

ON MUZTAGH-ATA.

CHAPTER VII.

THROUGH THE GEZ DEFILE TO KASHGAR.

CHAPTER VIII.

STAY AT KASHGAR.

CHAPTER IX.

KHANUI AND ORDAM-PADSHAH.

CHAPTER X.

YARKAND AND KARGHALIK.

CHAPTER XI.

ON THE ROAD TO KHOTAN.

CHAPTER XII.

ARRIVAL IN KHOTAN.

CHAPTER XIII.

TO THE HEADWATERS OF THE YURUNG-KASH.

CHAPTER XIV.

OVER THE KARA-KASH RANGES.

CHAPTER XV.

ANTIQUARIAN PREPARATIONS AT KHOTAN.

CHAPTER XVI.

YOTKAN, THE SITE OF THE ANCIENT CAPITAL.

PAGE

CHAPTER XXI.

THROUGH THE DESERT TO KERIYA.

CHAPTER XXII.

TO NIYA AND IMAM JAFAR SADIK.

CHAPTER XXIII.

FIRST EXCAVATION OF KHAROSHTHI TABLETS.

CHAPTER XXIV.

EXCAVATION OF ANCIENT RESIDENCES.

CHAPTER XXXII.

LAST DAYS IN KHOTAN OASIS.

CHAPTER XXXIII.

FROM KHOTAN TO LONDON.

LIST OF ILLUSTRATIONS.

Sand-buried Ruins of Khotan.

CHAPTER I.

CALCUTTA TO KASHMIR.

MOHAND MARG, KASHMIR.

It, was from the Alpine plateau of Mohand Marg, my beloved camping-ground for three Kashmir summers, that I had in June, 1898, submitted to the Indian Government the first scheme of the explorations which were to take me across the great mountain barriers northward and into the distant deserts of Khotan. Almost two years had passed when I found myself, early in May, 1900, again in Kashmir and within sight of Mohand Marg. With a glow of satisfaction I could look up to the crest of the high spur, some 10,000 feet above the sea and still covered with snow, on which my tent had stood, and where my plans had been formed. It had taken two years, and bulky files of correspondence; but at last I had secured what was needed—freedom to move, and the means requisite for my journey.

In the meantime official duty, and minor archæological tours to which I devoted my vacations, had taken me over widely different parts of India. From Lahore, where during eleven long years, amidst the worries and cares of University office work, I had ever felt the refreshing touch of the true East and the fascination of a great historical past, I had been transferred to Calcutta. With its strangely un-Indian conditions of life, its want of breathing space, and its damp heat, the "city of palaces" appeared to me like a tropical suburb of London. From there I had visited Sikkim, that strange half-Tibetan mountain-land where true Alpine scenery is invaded by the luxuriant vegetation of the tropics. I had wandered in South Bihar, the ancient Magadha, tracing the footsteps of Hiuen-Tsiang, the great Chinese pilgrim, among the ruins of the sacred Buddhist sites which he had seen and described more than twelve hundred years ago. Also the fascinating tracts along the Indus and the North-West Frontier, where the influence of classical art has left its witnesses in the ancient "Græco-Buddhist" sculptures of so many a ruined monastery and shrine, had seen me once more on a flying visit.

The thought of the task which was drawing me beyond the Himalaya had followed me everywhere. But it was only when the final sanction for my proposals reached me on a sultry monsoon night down in Calcutta that I had been able to start some of the multifarious preparations which the journey demanded. Busy as I was with official duties and literary work that had to be concluded before leaving India, I managed to arrange for the supply of many articles of equipment, both personal and scientific. The tents which I had ordered from the Cawnpore Elgin Mills; the galvanised iron water-tanks, made at Calcutta workshops, that were to serve in the desert; the stores of condensed food, the photographic outfit, and the semi-arctic winter clothing which I had indented for from London

—all were slowly moving up to Srinagar, whence my little expedition was to start.

But only in Kashmir itself, and not in over-civilised Calcutta, was it possible to complete my practical preparations. So I could not entirely suppress a feeling of unholy joy when an increase of plague, or rather the fear of it, caused Calcutta colleges to be closed some weeks in anticipation of the usual summer vacation. On the 10th of April I was free to escape northward. It was a source of satisfaction to me that on the day of my departure I was able personally to take leave of the late Sir John Woodburn, Lieutenant-Governor of Bengal, and to express my deep gratitude for all the kind help and interest with which he had furthered my undertaking.

The week I spent in Lahore in order to pick up various portions of my outfit and to supervise their despatch passed rapidly amid old friends and surroundings dear to me. After Calcutta the Punjab spring appeared still comparatively cool. All the same I enjoyed as keenly as ever the invigorating change to the fresh air of the hills when the Tonga carried me from Rawalpindi first to the fir-covered heights of Murree, and then along the Jhelam Valley up towards Kashmir. Often had I done this journey along the ancient Hydaspes, where it rushes down towards the plains in an almost uninterrupted succession of rapids and cataracts, but never so early in the year. Whether it was the sight and fragrance of the shrubs still in blossom along the road, or the glittering caps of snow still lying on many of the higher spurs, or simply the prospect of a year's explorations, never had this drive of nearly two days appeared to me so enjoyable.

On the 25th of April I passed once more into the Kashmir Valley by the gorge of Baramula, now as in ancient days the "Western Gate of the Kingdom." The snow still lay low down the mighty Pir Pantsal range which forms the southern rampart between Kashmir and the outer world. But the great riverine plain which opens out just beyond Baramula was decked in all the gay colours of a Kashmir spring, blue and white irises growing in profusion over village cemeteries and other waste spaces. At Baramula, where my servants, sent ahead with the heavy baggage, awaited me, I took to boats for the remaining journey to Srinagar; for old experience had shown me the convenience and attractions of river communication in Kashmir. The day I spent gliding in my comfortable "Dunga" through the limpid water of the great lagoons which fringe the Volur Lake, and along the winding course of the Jhelam, gave delightful repose such as did not again fall to my share for many months. Familiar to me as are *quæ loca fabulosus lambit Hydaspes*, there was plenty to feast my eyes upon. The floating meadows of water-lilies and other aquatic plants which cover the marshes; the vivid foliage of the great Chinar trees which shade all hamlets and Ghats along the river banks; the brilliant snow-fields on the Pir Pantsal, and the higher ranges to the north over which my road was soon to lead—these and all the other splendours of Kashmir spring scenery will never lose their charm for me.

During the second night the boat passed the winding reaches in which the river traverses Srinagar, and the next morning found me once more in the Chinar Bagh, my old camping-ground in the Kashmir capital. With the increasing crowd of European visitors from the Indian plains, the shady grove by the side of the "Apple Tree Canal" has long ago ceased to be a place suited for work or even quiet enjoyment. But haunted as it is at all hours of the day by the versatile Kashmir traders and craftsmen who provide for the Sahibs' camping requirements, it was just the place adapted for the purpose of my first stay at Srinagar. There were plenty of orders to give for mule trunks and leather-covered baskets or "Kiltas," in which stores, instruments, etc., were to be packed. Fur coats and warm winter clothing of all sorts had to be provided to protect myself and my followers against the cold of the Pamirs and the Turkestan winter; bags to carry provisions, and all the other paraphernalia which my previous experience showed to be necessary for a protracted campaign in the mountains. Clever and intelligent as the Kashmir craftsman ordinarily is, it requires protracted interviews to ensure that the work he is going to execute is really that intended. So what with endless particulars to be explained, and all the bargaining which local custom renders indispensable, there remained little time during these busy days to collect information on the important questions affecting the first part of my journey.

The Government of India in the Foreign Department had granted me permission to use the Gilgit-Hunza route for my journey to Kashgar. The special conditions prevailing along the "Gilgit Transport Road" made it necessary to give timely and exact intimation as to the amount of transport required, the number of followers, etc., all the more as the time I had fixed for my start, the end of May, was in advance of the regular transport season. Luckily, Captain G. H. Bretherton, D.S.O., Assistant Commissary-General for Kashmir, to whom I had to apply in the matter of these arrangements, proved exceptionally able and willing to afford information. Guided by his experience, I was soon in a position to prepare with fair accuracy my estimates as to the time, means of transport, and supplies needed not only up to Hunza, but also beyond towards the Chinese frontier. It was no small advantage to obtain quickly a clear working plan of these practical details. For upon the exact information which I could send ahead to Gilgit and Kashgar depended my hope of securing, without loss of time, all that was needful for the onward journey.

I was heartily glad when I succeeded within five busy days in disposing of these preliminaries. The few weeks which remained to me in Kashmir were none too long for the literary tasks that had to be completed before my departure. For over ten years past I had devoted whatever leisure I could spare from official duties to work connected in one form or another with Kalhana's "Chronicle of the Kings of Kashmir." The Sanskrit text of the great poem, the only record of a truly historical nature that exists in the classical literature of India, and one full of interest for the student of Indian antiquities, religion, geography, etc., had long ago been edited by me. But my translation and commentary required protracted researches into all that has survived of ancient Kashmir in records, traditions, and antiquarian lore, and the two stout quarto volumes which they filled in print were only now approaching completion. The introduction which was to give an account of these labours still remained to be written, and in order to complete it in time, together with some minor tasks of a similar kind, seclusion was indispensable.

"To go into Purdah," as our Lahore phrase ran, within Srinagar or its immediate environs, was well-nigh impossible, and Mohand Marg, my mountain retreat of former seasons, was still covered with snow. My knowledge of Kashmir topography, however, stood me in good stead, and after a short search at the debouchure of the great Sind Valley over which Mohand Marg rises, I found near the hamlet of Dudarhom a delightfully quiet grove by the river-bank where I could pitch my tents. There under the shade of majestic Chinars and within view of the snow-covered spurs of Mount Haramukh, I was soon hard at work from morning till evening. It was not an easy task to sum up and review the results of labours that had extended over so long a period and over so wide a field. Yet I felt grateful that I was able to bid farewell to them, while having that Alpine scenery before my eyes with which I shall ever associate the happiest recollections of my Kashmir researches. But still more cheering, perhaps, was the thought of the new field of exploration that awaited me northward, far beyond the ranges I had viewed from my 'Marg.' Undisturbed by intrusion of any kind, these three short weeks afforded leisure for concentrated work which, after the preceding "rush," seemed almost as enjoyable as if it had been a period of rest.

On the 23rd of May I completed the last of the tasks for the sake of which I had retired to my peaceful camping-ground. The date fixed for my start was drawing near, and with it came the necessity for returning to bustling Srinagar for the last preparations. Thanks to the convenient water-way provided by the Anchar Lake and the ancient Mar Canal, a single night passed in boats sufficed to bring me into the Kashmir capital. I found the grounds usually occupied by European visitors more crowded than I had ever seen them. Lines of house-boats along the river-banks and endless rows of tents in all the 'Baghs' seemed to leave no room for a new arrival. Fortunately, in years gone by I had had ample occasion to study the topography of Srinagar, in its modern as well as its ancient aspects, and thus I discovered at last a spot for my camp, on the narrow strip of ground which lines the west foot of the Takht-i-Sulaiman hill towards the Dal Lake. Hidden behind willow plantations and "floating gardens" peculiar to the lake, the little Bagh of Buchvor offered the needed quiet to complete my arrangements.

Busy indeed were the days I passed there. All details of the camp outfit had to be revised; the freshly arrived stores to be sorted and packed into loads for pony transport; surveying and other instruments to be tested and protected against damage; and amid these preparations there were accounts to be settled and farewell visits to be received. Numerous were the questions of my Pandit friends which I had to answer as to the place and object of my journey. More conversant though they are with mythical than with real geography, yet I found that my reference to the "Uttarakurus" (the Ultima Thule of Indian mythology) as the land for which I was about to set out, did not altogether satisfy their curiosity.

Ram Singh, the Gurkha Sub-Surveyor, whose services Colonel St. George Gore, R.E., the Surveyor-General of India, had very kindly placed at my disposal, together with a complete outfit of surveying instruments, joined me punctually on the day of my arrival at Srinagar. He had accompanied Captain Deasy in his recent travels near the sources of the Yarkand River and in the Kuen-luen mountains, and the practical acquaintance he had thus gained of the regions I was about to visit proved useful at once in the course of my preparations. With Ram Singh came Jasvant Singh, a wiry little Kangra Rajput, who was to attend to the Sub-Surveyor as cook and personal servant. He too had travelled in Chinese Turkestan as one of Captain Deasy's followers.

On the 28th of May there arrived Sadak Akhun, the Turkestan servant whom Mr. George Macartney, C.I.E., the British representative at Kashgar, had been kind enough to engage for me. He had left his home in the first half of April and came just in time to start back with me. He was to act as cook and 'Karawan-bashi' combined, and was welcomed with no small satisfaction by honest Mirza Alim, my Kokandi servant, whom I had engaged four months earlier in Peshawar for the purpose of my journey. 'Mirza' had been useful to me by giving me the needed opportunity of practising Turki conversation, but willing as he was to pick up the novel art of attending to the wants of a 'Sahib,' his acquirements did not reach far in regard to the kitchen department. His earlier career as a petty trader in Kabul and Peshawar had not been a special preparation for these functions; and yet his straightforward ways made me anxious to retain him. Sadak Akhun's timely arrival relieved both him and his master of all uneasiness as to the future arrangements of the travelling household. For Sadak Akhun had brought with him not only the appearance of a smart 'Karawan-bashi,' but a training in the mysteries of European cuisine amply sufficient for my wants. When he turned up in his fur-lined cap and coat of unstained azure, and red leather top-boots of imposing size, my camp seemed to receive at once a touch of Central-Asian colour.

But it was not only from the Far North that I was anxiously expecting during these days a much-needed complement of my camp. Knowing that no European traveller in the parts I was bound for could wholly refuse the *rôle* of the 'Hakim' forced upon him by popular belief, I had early ordered my medicine case from Messrs. Burroughs Wellcome & Co., the great London firm of "Tabloid" fame. The South African War and other incidents delayed its arrival for months, and even when it had at last been reported by telegram as landed at Calcutta, it seemed doubtful whether it would reach me in time. The Indian Post Office does indeed provide with its usual efficiency for the wants of the distant frontier post of Gilgit. But its power cannot level mountains, and as the transport of heavy articles across the snow-covered passes was not to begin till later in the season, there seemed little chance of that eagerly looked-for case ever catching me up if not received before my start from Srinagar.

Fortune seemed to offer a small mark of favour at least in this direction. For when, on the evening of the 29th of May, the time of departure fixed weeks before, my little flotilla of boats was lying opposite to the Srinagar Post Office, worthy Lala Mangu Mal, the attentive postmaster, triumphantly reported the arrival of the box. When it was at last safely deposited in my hands it was time to set out from the Venice of India. Gliding down the dark river under the seven bridges which have spanned it since early times, and between the massive embankments built with the slabs of ruined temples, I could not fail to be impressed with—

quod mihi supremum tempus in Urbe fuit.

It was midnight before I had seen the last of my old Pandit friends, who were waiting each at the Ghat nearest to his home to bid me farewell.

ANCIENT TEMPLE AT PANDRENTHAN, KASHMIR.

VIEW IN BURZIL VALLEY.

CHAPTER II.

TO ASTOR AND GILGIT.

WHEN I awoke in the morning my boat had just entered the lagoons which fringe on the east the great Volur Lake. A look towards the mountain range which rises above it on the north showed that the heavy rain of the last few days meant fresh snow on the passes I had to cross. Bandipur village, which forms as it were the port for the route connecting Kashmir with Gilgit and the regions beyond, was soon reached. It appeared as I had seen it in 1889 on my march to Skardo, pre-eminently a place

differtum nautis cauponibus atque malignis.

But as regards transport arrangements it was easy to realise a marked change. Since an Imperial garrison was placed in Gilgit and the new "Gilgit Transport Road" was constructed, the Indian Commissariat Department has taken charge of the means of transport on this route. Timely arrangements had been made on my behalf by Captain Bretherton, and a reference to the warrant officer on the spot brought the quick assurance that ponies and coolies would be available whenever wanted. The time when the intending traveller on this route had to press his transport as best he could has passed, let us hope, for ever. If restrictions have to be placed on the number of private visitors in the interest of the commissariat work on which the supplies of the Gilgit garrison depend, the disadvantage is amply compensated by the benefit to the Valley at large. There was a time, still vividly remembered, when the demand for coolies to carry military baggage or supplies moving to Gilgit would spread terror through Kashmir villages. Of the thousands of cultivators used annually for this *corvée*, a large proportion never saw their country again; for, ill-fed and still worse clad, the 'Begaris' succumbed only too readily to the inclemency of climatic conditions or the epidemics favoured by them. All this has changed since Imperial advice and control has made itself felt in Kashmir, and the construction of the new Gilgit road, fit throughout for laden animals, including camels, during three summer months, has rendered the use of human labour altogether superfluous.

On the morning of the 31st of May sixteen ponies were ready to receive the loads which were made up by our tents, stores, instruments, etc. Formidable as this number appeared to me, accustomed as I was to move lightly on my wanderings in and about Kashmir, I had the satisfaction to know that my personal baggage formed the smallest part of these *impedimenta*. When the string of animals had filed off together with the Sub-Surveyor and servants, there were yet imposing indents to sign and bills to pay which the obliging Commissariat Conductor kept ready for me under a group of fine Chinars by the roadside where on sunny days he transacts the business of his office. No transport can move up the road without his permission, and though the procedure he superintends is modern in its ways, yet it seemed to me as if this modest British official had simply taken the place of those "Masters of the Gates" who used in ancient Kashmir to guard all routes leading into the valley.

The road, after leaving the straggling line of wooden huts which form the Bazar of Bandipur, leads for about four miles up the open valley of the Madhumati stream. In the irrigated fields the fresh green of the young rice-shoots was just appearing, while the hamlets on either side were half hidden under the rich foliage of their Chinars and walnut-trees. It was the typical spring scenery of Kashmir to which I here bade farewell. Near the village of Matargom the road turns to the north to ascend in long zigzags the range which forms the watershed between Kashmir and the valley of the Kishanganga. From the spur up which the road winds I had a splendid view of the Volur Lake and the snow-covered mountains to the east which encircle the hoary Haramukh Peaks. At a height of about 9,000 feet a fine forest of pines covers the spur and encloses a narrow glade known as Tragbal. Here the snow had just disappeared, and I found the damp ground strewn with the first carpet of Alpine flowers.

A rude wooden rest-house begrimed with smoke and mould gave shelter for the night, doubly welcome, as a storm broke soon after it got dark. The storm brought fresh snow, and as this was sure to make the crossing of the pass above more difficult I started before daybreak on the 1st of June. A steep ascent of some two thousand feet leads to the open ridge which the road follows for several miles. Exposed as this ridge is to all the winds, I was not surprised to find it still covered with deep snowdrifts, below which all trace of the road disappeared. Heavy clouds hung around, and keeping off the rays of the sun let the snow remain fairly hard. Soon, however, it began to snow, and the icy wind which swept the ridge made me and my men push eagerly forward to the shelter offered by a Dak runners' hut. The storm cleared before long, but it sufficed to show how well deserved is the bad repute which the Tragbal (11,900 feet above the sea) enjoys among Kashmirian passes.

For the descent from the pass I was induced by the 'Markobans' owning the ponies to utilise the winter route which leads steeply down into a narrow snow-filled nullah. Though the ponies slid a good deal in the soft snow of the slope, we did not encounter much difficulty until we got to the bottom of the gorge. Here the snow bridges over the stream which flows from this valley towards the Kishanganga had begun to give way, and the high banks of snow on either side were in many places uncomfortably narrow. At last our progress was stopped at a point where the stream had washed away the whole of the snow vault. To take the laden animals along the slatey and precipitous side of the gorge, which was free from snow, proved impracticable. To return to the top of the gorge, and thence follow the proper road which descends in long zigzags along a side spur, would have cost hours. So the council of my 'Markobans,' hardy hill-men, half Kashmiri, half Dard, decided to try the narrow ledge of snow which remained standing on the right bank of the stream. The first animal, though held and supported by three men, slipped and rolled into the stream, and with it Sadak Akhun, who vainly attempted to stem its fall. Fortunately neither man nor pony got hurt, and as the load was also picked out of the water the attempt was resumed with additional care. Making a kind of path with stones placed at the worst points, we managed to get the animals across one by one. But it was not without considerable anxiety for my boxes, with survey instruments, and similar contents, that I watched the operation. Heavy rain was falling at the time, and when at last we had all the ponies once more on a safe snow-bridge, men and animals were alike soaked. By one o'clock I reached the Gorai rest-house, down to which the valley was covered with snow, having taken nearly seven hours to cover the eleven miles of the march.

The little rest-house, looking doubly bleak in the drizzling rain, held already three 'Sahibs,' officers who were returning from their shooting nullahs to Kashmir and the plains. Refreshed by their hospitality, I decided to push on to the next stage, Gurez, where better shelter and supplies were available. The offer of some Bakhshish, and the hope of a dry and comparatively warm corner for the night, overcame the remonstrances of the 'Markobans,' and the little caravan moved on. Some four miles lower down I reached the main valley of the Kishanganga, and in it the first Dard village. Another ten miles' march up the valley brought me to Gurez, a collection of villages at a point where the valley widens to a little plain, about a mile broad.

Sombre and forbidding the valley looked between its high pine-covered mountains and under a dark, rainy sky. The effect was heightened by the miserable appearance of the rude log-built dwellings scattered here and there along the slopes, and by the dark-coloured sand in the bed of the river. The latter bears, not without good reason, the name of the "Black Ganga" (in Sanskrit, Krishnaganga). The backward state of the vegetation showed that spring had only just commenced in the valley, which here has an elevation of about 8,000 feet above the sea. With its short summer and scanty sunshine it can raise but poor crops of barley and 'Trumba,' and the population is accordingly thin.

The mountain range towards Kashmir marks also a well-defined ethnographic boundary. The Dard race, which inhabits the valleys north of it as far as the Hindukush, is separated from the Kashmiri population by language as well as by physical characteristics. The relation between the language of the Dards and the other Indo-Aryan vernaculars of North-Western India is by no means clearly established. But whatever the linguistic and ethnic affinities of the Dard race may be, it is certain that it has held these valleys since the earliest time to which our historical knowledge can reach back. Herodotus had heard of them in the same region they now inhabit; for he mentions the gold-washing operations still carried on by them within modest limits on the Indus and the Kishanganga.

There is little in the Dard to enlist the sympathies of the casual observer. He lacks the intelligence, humour, and fine physique of the Kashmiri, and though undoubtedly far braver than the latter, has none of the independent spirit and martial bearing which draws us towards the Pathan, despite all his failings. But I can never see a Dard without thinking of the thousands of years of struggle these tribes have carried on with the harsh climate and the barren soil of their mountains. They, like the Afridis, who also are mentioned by the Father of History, have seen all the great conquests which swept over the North-West of India, and have survived them, unmoved as their mountains.

Gurez was once the chief place of a little Dard kingdom which often harassed the rulers of old Kashmir. But I confess, when I approached it at the close of my fatiguing double march, this antiquarian fact interested me less than the comfortable shelter which I found for my men and myself in Mr. Mitchell's new bungalow.

The following day was a halt, for my people needed rest and my baggage drying. There were besides fresh arrangements to be made for the transport ahead. In Srinagar I had been told officially that the Burzil Pass, which had to be crossed between Gurez and Astor, would, owing to the deep snow, be open only for coolie transport. However, from the parties of Dards whom I met on the road, and who had brought their unladen ponies safely across from Astor, I gathered better news. As the use of coolies meant a complete rearrangement of the loads, and still more trouble for the scanty population of the valley, which had already been obliged to furnish a hundred carriers for a survey party ahead of me, I decided to take ponies. These were easily forthcoming, and on the morning of the 3rd of June I set out from Gurez much as I had reached it, except that the more delicate instruments, like theodolite and photographic cameras, were entrusted to the safer backs of coolies.

The weather had cleared at last, and the march from Gurez up the side valley of the stream which comes from the Burzil was most enjoyable. To the south there was the view of the fine snow-covered mountains which divide the Kishanganga Valley from Kashmir, while along the route leading northwards the slopes of the valley refreshed the eyes with their rich green of Alpine meadows and pine forests. Of avalanches which had swept down on the road there were many to cross. But the task of taking the ponies over them was trifling after the Tragbal experiences. I halted for the night at Pushwari, and next morning continued the march in the same direction and amidst similar scenery up to Minimarg

There, at an altitude of nearly 10,000 feet above the sea, the valley widens to a little plain with plenty of grazing and a little collection of huts used by Gujar cattleherds for their summer quarters. The snow had melted here about ten days before, and the meadow land was already covered with young shoots of grass and a variety of hardy Alpine flowers, mostly old acquaintances from my beloved Kashmir 'Marg.' But a glance at the telegraph office placed here to keep watch over the line across the pass was sufficient to show the rigour of the winter season. Raised high above the ground, and enclosed with heavy palisaded verandahs and sheds, the building looked more like a small fort than an office. These precautions are, indeed, necessary in order to make the place inhabitable during the long winters with their heavy snowfall.

At Minimarg the route to the Burzil strikes off to the northwest, and ascending the valley some five miles higher I reached the rest-house at the foot of the pass. The snow began to cover the ground soon after Minimarg was left behind, and at the foot of the pass it was a true winter scenery which met the eye. The sky was of a dazzling blue, and so clear that I felt quite reassured as to the result of taking my laden ponies across the pass.

The only condition to be observed was an early ascent before the snow should become soft. I therefore got up at one o'clock, and an hour later my caravan was plodding up the snow-filled ravine which forms the winter route to the pass. Of the road no trace could be seen. After two hours' steady ascent we arrived at the point where the Burzil defile is met from the north-east by another pass leading down from the high plateau of the Deosai. A telegraph shelter-hut raised on a wooden scaffolding some thirty feet high serves as a guiding-post to the parties of Dak runners who are obliged to carry the Gilgit mail during the winter. The structure was even now some ten feet deep in the snow. Fortunately the temperature was so low that the hard snow offered comparatively good going to the animals. By the time that the first rays of the sun swept across the higher ranges to the east, we had gained safely the summit of the pass, 13,500 feet above the sea. The six miles from the rest-house had taken over three hours. There was no distant view from the pass, which lies between winding spurs, but the glittering snowfields all around, covered with a spotless crust of fresh ice, were a sight not to be forgotten. The temperature was only 35° F. when I took a hurried breakfast under the shelter of the Dak hut.

The descent on the north side was long and tiring. The snow lay for some eight miles from the top of the pass, and as the morning advanced the going necessarily became heavier. The only living beings that inhabit this Arctic waste are big marmots. Sitting on the top of their burrows as if to warm themselves in the sun, they did their best to attract attention by shrill whistling, only to disappear with lightning speed at the approach of danger. It took some time before my little fox-terrier realised this, and refrained from spending his breath in vain attempts to rush the provoking animals. 'Dash,' or 'Yolchi Beg' ("Sir Traveller"), as he had been renamed since I took to Turki with Mirza, proved true to his name. He marched as cheerily over the miles of snow as on earlier wanderings through the dusty dry Punjab plains or in the dripping jungle of Sikkim. My Turki servants soon grew fond of 'Yolchi Beg,' and, being untrammelled by the caste conventions of India, never hesitated to show their affection for my faithful companion.

It was one o'clock when I arrived at Chillum Chauki, the first rest-house on the Astor side of the pass, having left the snow behind about two miles before. All the ponies came in safely except one, the absence of which was soon noticed when I was looking out for breakfast. The pony carrying the kitchen 'Kiltas' had lagged behind, and I became painfully aware that something had gone wrong when hour after hour passed in vain expectation. My Surveyor, who had marched in the rear, brought news of the animal having broken down in the softening snow, and though I at once despatched coolies to its assistance it was not till after six in the evening that Mirza turned up with his charge. As if to console me for the delay in bodily comforts, I got in the evening the cheerful news of the occupation of Pretoria from Mr. M., the road engineer, who arrived at the rest-house from a shooting excursion. News travels fast along the telegraph line, and although there is, apart from the Political Agent at Gilgit, no subscriber to Reuter's messages this side of the Burzil, telegraph masters in Astor and their friends were evidently well informed of what was happening far away in South Africa.

The set of ponies which I had brought from Gurez, and which were the first laden animals that crossed the Burzil this year, were relieved at Chillum Chauki by fresh ones sent up for me from Astor. My march on the 6th of June, down the valley leading to Astor, was recreation after the previous one. Notwithstanding the brilliant colour imparted to the scenery by a blue sky, glittering bands of snow in the ravines, and the green tossing stream at the bottom of the valley, it was easy to realise that the crossing of the water-shed between the drainage areas of the Jhelam and Indus meant the entry into a sterner region. The hillsides were no longer clothed with verdure as in Kashmir and the Kishanganga Valley. On the slopes of bare decomposed rock cedars and a kind of juniper showed themselves only in scanty patches. Cultivation lower down also bore evidence of the unfavourable conditions of soil and climate. All the more cheerful it was to behold, by the side of the little terraced fields of more than one hamlet, an oblong sward carefully marked off with stones—the polo ground of the villagers. Polo is the national game of all Dard tribes; and that even the inhabitants of these poor mountain hamlets make a sacrifice of valuable soil for its sake attests their devotion to this manly pastime.

At Gadhoi, where a march of about seventeen miles brought

me, it was already distinctly warmer than I had felt it since leaving Kashmir, though the aneroid still indicated an elevation of about 9,000 feet. On the 7th of June I continued my journey to Astor, the chief place of the hill district, to which from early times it has given its name. Some miles below Gadhoi there showed themselves above the bare rocky mountains along the valley the icy crests of the great mass of peaks culminating in Nanga Parbat. That giant of mountains (26,600 feet above the sea), the ice-clad pyramid of which I had so often admired from Kashmir Margs, and even from above Murree itself, remained hidden behind lower ranges, though only about ten miles away, as the crow flies. Yet even its bodyguard of minor peaks, ranging between 18,000 and 23,000 feet, was a sufficiently inspiriting sight.

I felt the need of looking up to their glacier walls; for down on the road it got warmer and warmer. From Gurikot onwards where the two branches of the Astor River unite, the road, dusty and hot, winds up the steep scarp on the left side of the valley until at last the group of villages known as Astor came in sight spread out over a mighty alluvial fan. The view that opened here was striking in its ruggedness. For a wall of rocky ridges seems to close the valley to the north, while the deep ravines cut by the mountain torrents into the alluvial plateaus on either side give them a look of fantastic diversity.

I reached at 3 p.m. the bungalow of Astor, situated on a dominating point of the plateau, and felt heartily glad of its shade and coolness. Below me lay the Fort of the Sikhs, now used for the accommodation of a battery of Kashmir Imperial Service troops, while on the south there stretched the orchards and fields of the Astor "capital." The Rajas of Astor have become "mediatised" since the advent of the Sikhs, and their power, such as it was, is now wielded by a modest Tahsildar of the Kashmir administration. Generosity was not a fault of Sikh rule in these mountain regions, and the deposed family of hill chiefs have little left to support the pride of their ancient lineage.

Though Astor lies about 7,700 feet above the sea, the air would have been decidedly oppressive but for a storm which in the evening swept over the valley. It left plenty of clouds behind to screen the sun on the next morning (June 8th) when I resumed the march down towards the Indus. The valley became bleaker and bleaker as the route descended, and the streaks of red, yellow, and grey displayed by the rocky hillsides offered poor compensation for the absence of vegetation. Of flowering shrubs only a kind of wild rose seems to thrive on the barren soil, and being just in full bloom caught the eye by its purple patches. A few green fields perched on the top of small alluvial fans were all the cultivation visible on the fifteen miles' march to Dashkin village, the first stage from Astor.

As I had heard of the arrival at the next stage, Duyan, of Captain J. Manners Smith, whom I was anxious to meet, I decided to push on. The slow rate of progress made by the baggage animals confirmed the objections which my pony-men had raised. But otherwise, this extra march of twelve miles proved a pleasant surprise. The road, rising gradually to about 5,000 feet above the tossing river, took me through a charming forest of pines, which in the shadows of the setting sun looked its best. This forest evidently owes its growth to its sheltered position on the north-east flank of a great ridge, which on its top was still covered with snow. It was a pleasure to behold once more green moss and ferns along the little streams which rush down through the forest. But when this was left behind at the turning of a cross-spur there spread a grander view before me.

Through the gap between the mountains enclosing the Astor Valley there appeared the broad stream of the Indus and beyond it range after range towards the north. Thin clouds hung over the more distant ranges, yet I thought I could recognise rising above the fleecy mist the icy mass of Mount Rakiposhi. Father Indus was greeted by me like an old friend. I had seen the mighty river at more than one notable point of its course, where it breaks through the rocky gorges of Baltistan, where it bursts forth into the Yusufzai plain, and in its swift rush through the defiles below Attock. But nowhere had it impressed me more than when I now suddenly caught sight of it amidst these towering mountain walls. The shadows of evening fell quickly in its deep-cut valley and the glittering vision of the river had vanished when, somewhat tired, I reached the end of my double march.

My stay at Duyan was prolonged in the pleasantest manner. Early on the morning of June 9 Captain J. Manners Smith, V.C., C.I.E., the Political Agent of Gilgit and the adjacent hill tracts, on his return from a shooting excursion, came to see me and kindly invited me to spend the day in his camp. I was most glad to accept the hospitality of the distinguished officer, then acting as "Warden of the Marches" for the mountain region I was about to traverse; and after despatching my party ahead, soon found myself riding on one of his hill ponies up to the mountain-side occupied by his tents. It was a charming spot on a little shoulder of the fir-covered slope, some 1,500 feet above the road, where the ground was carpeted with wild violets, forget-me-nots, and other mountain flowers, and where a bright little stream added to the attractions of the scene. Picturesque, indeed, it was with the well-fitted hill tents of the Political Agent and the motley crowd of his followers hailing from all parts of Gilgit, Chilas, and Hunza.

In the amiable society of my host and Mrs. Manners Smith I passed a day which I shall long remember for its varied enjoyments. Anglo-Indian ladies know how to carry true refinement into camp life even at the most distant points of the Empire, and here Nature had surrounded the tasteful comforts of a well-arranged camp with special glamour. The hours I spent at this delightful spot fled only too fast. Captain Manners Smith, who has been connected with the political administration of this region for the last twelve years, and whose Victoria Cross was earned at one of the most striking incidents of its modern history, the storming of the Hunza fastness beyond Nilth, knows these mountains and their races better probably than any European.

What added to the interest of his varied communications about the old customs and traditions of the people was the illustration which his remarks received from the hillmen attending his camp. The petty headmen from the valleys towards Chilas and from Punyal furnished me with more than one curious fact bearing on the earlier social and religious condition of the tract. Muhammadanism is a comparatively recent growth here, and the traditions as to former worship and rites have survived in many a valley. One grey-bearded village headman from Gor in particular seemed full of old-world lore. He had investigated the relics of an old burial-place near his home, where the burnt bodies of his ancestors in pre-Muhammadan times used to be deposited, and was not shy about relating the drastic punishment which as a boy he had received from his mother when disturbing the spot. In these mountains, as elsewhere throughout the world, it is the women-folk who act as the best guardians of all old lore and tradition.

The close contact with the Far West into which modern political conditions have brought these once secluded valleys was illustrated by the fact that I could read at Captain Manners Smith's table the latest Reuter telegrams just as if it had been in the Club at Lahore. But the presence in camp of my host's pretty little children offered an even more convincing indication how far European influence has penetrated across the mountains. Bright and rosy-cheeked, they were worthy representatives of the British Baby which in the borderlands of India has always appeared to me as the true pioneer of civilization. I have come across it in many a strange place, and its manifest happiness amongst surroundings which often seemed incongruous with the idea of a nursery has ever forced me to admiration. The British Baby has never been slow to follow the advance of British arms in India. Occasionally it has come early enough to see some fighting: witness Fort Lockhart and the Malakand. But on the whole its appearance on the scene marks the establishment of the pax britannica, and for this mission of peace and security it well deserves that thriving condition which it usually enjoys in the mountains around Kashmir.

For afternoon tea my hosts took me to a pretty 'Marg' on the top of the ridge above their camp. From this height the Indus Valley, in its barrenness of rock and sand, could be seen descending far away towards Chilas and Darel. The day will come when this natural route to the Indian plains will be open again as it was in old times. Then the last bit of terra incognita along the Indus, which now extends from Chilas down to Amb, will be accessible, while the difficulties inseparable from a line of transport crossing the great barriers of the Kashmir ranges will no longer have to be faced.

On the morning of the 10th of June I took leave of my kind hosts and hurried down towards Bunji to catch up my camp. As I descended the defile of the Astor River, where the road leads along precipitous cliffs and past shingly ravines, the heat rose in a marked degree. I could well realise what the terrors of this part of the route, known as Hatu Pir, absolutely waterless and exposed to the full force of the sun, must have been for the Kashmiri coolies of old days. On the eleven miles which brought me down to the level of the Indus close to the point where the Astor River joins it, I did not meet with a single traveller. Equally desolate was the ride from Ramghat, where the road crosses the Astor River, to Bunji, some eight miles higher up on the Indus. The broad rocky plain which stretches from the bank of the great river to the foot of the mountains showed scarcely a trace of vegetation. The radiation of the sun's rays was intense, and I was glad to reach by one p.m. the shelter of the Bunji Bungalow. The neighbouring fort is still held by some detachments of Kashmir troops, though the ferry over the Indus which it once guarded has become disused since the construction of the new road. During the hot hours I spent at Bunji there was little to tempt me outside. A hazy atmosphere hung over the valley and deprived me of the hoped-for view of Nangaparbat, which, rising fully 22,000 feet above the level of the Indus, dominates the whole scenery in clear weather. A strong wind blowing down the valley carried the fine sand of the river-bed even into the closed rooms. Bunji altogether seemed by no means a desirable place to spend much time in, and strongly reminded me of the hot days I had once passed in the low hills of Jammu territory.

Fodder is practically not to be got at Bunji, and this accounts for the difficulty I found in procuring a pony that was to take me in the evening to the next stage where my baggage had marched ahead. At last the local Tahsildar had to lend me his mount, but it was already evening before I could set out. A lonely ride across a sandy plain brought me to the imposing suspension bridge which spans the Indus, just as it was getting dark. In the dim light of the moon which was then emerging for a time from the clouds the deep, rockbound gorge of the river looked quite fantastic. And so did the rugged mountains further east through which the Gilgit River comes down to meet the Indus. To ride along the face of the rocky spur which rises in the angle of the two rivers was slow work in the scanty light of a fitful moon, and by the time I had turned fully into the Gilgit Valley, and reached safer ground, rain came on and brought complete darkness. Mile after mile passed without my coming upon the longed-for rest-house where I could rejoin my camp. At last it became clear that I must have passed it by, and I had only the choice of continuing my ride straight into Gilgit or returning to search for the missed bungalow. Dark as it was I preferred the latter course, and ultimately discovered a side path which brought me to the expected shelter fully half a mile away from the main road. It was close on midnight when I sat down to the dinner which my servants had duly kept ready for me, though it had never struck them that I might require a light to show me the way to it.

Pari, where I spent what remained of the night, proved in the morning a desolate spot by the sandy bank of the river, enclosed by an amphitheatre of bare reddish-brown mountains. The scenery remained the same for the next nine miles or so until after rounding one of the countless spurs along which the road winds the open part of the great Gilgit Valley came into view. Minaur is the first village where cultivated ground is again reached, and thereafter every alluvial fan on the left bank was green with carefully terraced and irrigated fields. A few miles further on the valley of the Hunza River opens from the north, and beyond it stretches the collection of hamlets to which the name Gilgit properly applies. It was a cheerful sight to view this expanse of fertile fields and orchards from the height of an old moraine issuing from a side valley. While riding through it I was met by a note from Captain H. Burden, I.M.S., the Agency Surgeon, offering me that hospitable reception for which Captain Manners Smith's kindness had prepared me.

I soon was installed in a comfortable set of rooms, and realised that for my stay at Gilgit I was to be the guest of the officers remaining at the headquarters of the Agency. Small as their number was I found among them most attractive and congenial company. Each of them, whether in charge of the Kashmir Imperial Service troops supplying the local garrisons, or of the Commissariat, the Public Works, or the hospitals of Gilgit, showed plainly that he knew and liked these hills. For each the semi-independence secured by the arrangements of an out-lying frontier tract under "political" management had been a source of increased activity and consequent experience in his own sphere. That the political interests which necessitated the garrisoning of Gilgit with Imperial officers and troops have benefited this region in more ways than one was apparent from a stroll through the little "station." I found there a well-built hospital, neat offices for the various departments of the administration, a clean and airy bazar, and even substantial buildings for a school and a zenana hospital. Small but comfortable bungalows have been built for the European officers on the terraced slopes overlooking the valley, and in their midst there has quite recently risen even a substantial club with an excellent though necessarily select library. It is only some eleven years since the new era set in for Gilgit, and yet it is already difficult to trace the conditions which preceded it. The fort, built of rubble with a wooden framework, after the usual Sikh fashion, alone reminds one of the days when Gilgit was the prey of an ill-paid and badly disciplined soldiery, when years of unabated exactions had laid great parts of the cultivable land waste and driven the now peaceful Dards into violent rebellions.

I had originally intended to stop only one day at Gilgit in order to give my men a much-needed rest and to effect some repairs in the equipment. But difficulty arose about getting fresh transport for the march to Hunza, and my stay was of necessity extended to three days. Ample work and the amiable attention of my hosts scarcely allowed me to notice the delay. Though all Government transport was occupied in out-lying camps, and the local ponies were grazing far away in distant nullahs, Captain E. A. R. Howell, the energetic Commissariat Officer, provided by the third day a train of excellent animals to which I could safely trust my baggage up to Hunza. Little defects in my outfit which the experience of the previous marches had brought to light were easily made good in the interval, since every member of the "station" offered kind help. While the Commissariat Stores supplied what was needed in the way of followers' warm clothing, foodstuffs, etc., Mrs. W., the only lady left in the "station," kindly offered threads of her own fair hair for use in the photo-theodolite. How often had I occasion to feel grateful thereafter for this much-needed reserve store when handling that delicate instrument with half-benumbed fingers on wind-swept mountain-tops!

MIR'S CASTLE AT BALTIT.

CHAPTER III.

THROUGH HUNZA.

On the afternoon of the 15th of June I left Gilgit full of the pleasant impressions from my cordial reception at this last Anglo-Indian outpost. The first march of eighteen miles was to Nomal, a green oasis in the otherwise barren valley of the river which comes from Hunza. The preceding days in Gilgit had been abnormally cloudy and cool, and this weather made marching pleasant enough. Since the little war of 1891, which had asserted British authority in Hunza, the road up the valley has been greatly improved. Nevertheless, it is but a narrow bridle path, and as it winds along precipitous spurs many hundred feet above the stream, it required such a steady hill pony as that kindly lent to me by Major E. J. Medley, of the 17th Bengal Lancers, then Commanding the Force in Gilgit, to ride with any feeling of comfort.

From Nomal and upwards the river has cut its way through a succession of deep gorges, lined often with almost perpendicular cliffs. The path is carried in long zigzags over the projecting cross-ridges, and more than once traverses their face by means of galleries built out from the rock. At Chalt, the end point of my second day's march, I reached the limit of Gilgit territory. Here the valley widens considerably and takes a sharp turn eastwards. As a reminiscence of an earlier state of things the place is garrisoned with a company of Kashmir Imperial Service troops. Their commandant, an aged Subahdar from the Garhwal district, came to call on me soon after I had arrived at the comfortable bungalow of the Military Works Department. In the course of our long conversation he gave me graphic accounts of what Gilgit meant to the Kashmir troops twenty and thirty years ago; of the hardships which the want of commissariat arrangements caused both to the soldiers and the inhabitants. From the description of these sufferings it was pleasant to turn to other aspects of soldiering in the old Dogra service, *e.g.*, the quaint Sanskrit words of command concocted under Maharaja Ranbir Singh, and still in use not many years ago.

On the 17th I intended to make a double march, pushing on straight to the centre of the Hunza valley, where baggage animals were to be left behind and coolies taken for the rest of the journey to the Taghdumbash Pamir. After leaving Chalt the road crosses to the left bank of the river by a fine suspension bridge, hung like the rest of the more important bridges on the route from Kashmir, from ropes made of telegraph-wires. This mode of construction, first tried in these parts by Colonel Aylmer, of the Royal Engineers, has proved everywhere a signal success; its advantages are easily appreciated in a country where other suitable materials could scarcely be carried to the spot.

It was after rounding a long massive spur which causes a great bend in the river-bed that I first beheld the ice-clad peaks of Mount Rakiposhi in their glory. The weather had been too cloudy during the preceding days to see much of this giant of mountains while I was marching in the valleys which flank it to the south and west. Now that I had got to its north side a day of spotless clearness set in, and the dazzling mass of snow and ice stood up sharp against the blue sky. Rakiposhi, with its towering height of over 25,500 feet, commands completely the scenery in the Upper Hunza Valley. Though several peaks run it close in point of elevation, none can equal it in boldness of shape and noble isolation. All day long I revelled in this grand sight, hidden only for short distances by the spurs which Rakiposhi sends down into the valley. Between them lie deep-cut side valleys through which the streams fed from the glaciers of Rakiposhi make their way to the main stream. The ample moisture supplied by the eternal snows of the higher slopes has not only brought verdure to the cultivated terraces in the valley. High above the walls of bare rock which bound the latter, patches of pine forest and green slopes of grazing land can be seen stretching up to the edge of the snow line. Glaciers, of spotless white on their higher parts, but grey with detritus below, furrow the flanks of the mountain mass and push their tongues almost down to the level of the main valley which here rises from six to seven thousand feet above the sea.

At Nilth, some eight miles above Chalt, the first Nagir village is reached. It was the scene of the notable fight which decided in 1891 the fate of Hunza and Nagir. The two little hill states which divide between them the right and left sides of the valley jointly known as Kanjut, had stoutly maintained their independence against all Dogra attempts at conquest. No wonder that people to whom their own mountains offer so scanty room and sustenance proved troublesome neighbours. Slave raiding into the lower valleys had for a long time been a regular source of revenue for the chiefs or Mirs of Hunza. The plundering expeditions of the sturdy Kanjutis were feared by caravans far away on the

Pamirs and on the trade routes towards the Karakorum. Across the great glaciers which stretch along the flanks of the Muztagh range parties of Kanjuti freebooters used to break into the valleys of Baltistan. I well remember the rude towers near the mouth of the great Biafo glacier which I saw on my visit to the Braldo Valley eleven years before. They plainly showed that even in that forbidding region raids from Hunza had to be guarded against.

All this has changed with the brilliant little campaign which began and ended at Nilth. The graphic accounts of Mr. Knight, who accompanied the small force from Gilgit as correspondent of the *Times*, has made all the incidents well known. From the shady little Bagh in front of Nilth where I halted for breakfast, I could conveniently survey the fortified village which Colonel Durand's force stormed, and the precipitous gorge behind, which stopped his further progress for nearly three weeks. The sangars which had crowned the cliffs on the opposite side and from which the men of Nagir had offered so stout a resistance, were already in ruins. But of their defenders, several joined me in a friendly. chat, and pointed out all the important positions.

Nothing speaks more for the policy and tact of the victors than the good feeling with which the people of the valley remember the contest. The men of the local "Levies" who showed me the precipitous cliffs of conglomerate over 1,000 feet high, seen on the left of the accompanying photograph, which Captain (then Lieutenant) Manners Smith scaled with his handful of Dogras and Gurkhas, seemed almost as proud of the daring exploit that had won that gallant officer his Victoria Cross as if it had been done by one of themselves. The explanation lies probably in the fact that all interference with the habits of the people and their traditional rulers has been scrupulously avoided. The small garrison of Kashmir Imperial Service Troops which was quartered in the centre of the valley for a few years has been removed. The British Political Officer who was left to advise the chiefs of Hunza and Nagir, has now also been withdrawn, and of the visible effects of the conquest there now remains nothing in the valley but a well-made road and absolute security for the traveller. The zeal and bravery which the Kanjuti levies displayed when called to aid in the Chitral campaign are the best proof of the loyal spirit with which the changed situation has been accepted. Yet this population of brave mountaineers, small as it is, has to

CLIFFS OF NILTH GORGE, NAGIR.

struggle harder than ever to maintain itself amidst these gorges bound by rock and ice, now that the days of raiding are gone.

From Nilth onwards the road leads over a succession of highly cultivated plateaus, separated by deep-cut glacier ravines. Everywhere there were little clumps of fruit trees, of which the mulberries were just ripening. The villages which I passed were distinctly picturesque, being all enclosed with walls of rough stone and square loop-holed towers. Their position, which is usually on the very edge of the plateau, falling off in precipitous banks towards the river, also shows that safety was a consideration. Old are these sites in all probability, but the only remains of antiquity that I could see or hear of above ground are those of a small Buddhist Stupa or relic tower passed on the road close to the hamlet of Thol. Built of solid masonry, it rises on a base of ten feet square to a height of nearly twenty feet, and is remarkably well preserved. The only damage done is at the corner, where the masonry of the base has been knocked off to save the detour of a few feet to the road which passes by the side of the monument. It is evident that even at so remote a spot the "Public Works" of modern India involve the same danger to ancient monuments which they have unfortunately proved throughout the peninsula.

While the Nagir side of the valley shows a cheerful succession of villages, the opposite side, which belongs to Hunza, is here for the most part a rocky waste. The difference is easily accounted for by the increased supply of water which Rakiposhi provides. Among the people of Nagir no marked difference from the Dard type is noticeable. Shina, the language of Gilgit, seems to be spoken in most of the lower villages, though Burisheski, the language of Hunza, is also understood. The latter has no apparent connection with either the Indian or the Iranian family of languages, and seems an erratic block left here by some bygone wave of conquest. In its stock of words it shows no resemblance to the Turki dialects, but is closely allied to the Wurshki tongue spoken in the northern valleys of Yasin. How the small race which speaks the language of Hunza has come to occupy these valleys will perhaps never be cleared up by historical evidence. But its preservation between the Dards on the south and the Iranian and Turki tribes on the north is clearly due to the isolated position of the country. It was curious to me to watch the rapid inroads which Hindustani has made in this linguistic area during the last few years. The few hundred men placed in garrison along the valley and the passage of the convoys bringing their supplies have sufficed to spread a knowledge of

Hindustani, or rather Punjabi, among the villagers, which considering the brief time is quite surprising. In view of this experience the rapid spread of Arabic and Persian words on

STUPA OF THOL, NAGIR.

the line of early Muhammadan conquest throughout Asia becomes more easily intelligible.

The constant ups and downs of the road seemed to spread out considerably the distance of twenty-six miles between Chalt and Aliabad, the end of my march. Below the fort village of Tashsot the route crosses the rock-bound bed of the river by a bold bridge, and then continues along absolutely barren slopes of rock and shingle for several miles. In the light of the evening the steep walls of rock rising on either side fully five or six thousand feet above the river, with the icy crests of Rakiposhi in the background, formed a picture worthy of the imagination of Gustave Doré. By the time I had cleared the worst parts of the road along sliding beds of detritus it had got quite dark. For two hours more the road wound round deep side-valleys from the north until I emerged on the open plateau which bears the village and lands of Aliabad. Here a little fort had been erected during the temporary occupation of Hunza, and close to it stands the bungalow of the Political Officer. Though Captain P. J. Miles, the rightful occupant, was absent on leave, I was able to find shelter under its hospitable roof. Cheerful enough the little luxuries of this frontier-officer's home appeared to me. His servants too, sturdy Hunza men, knew how to help a belated Sahib to an early meal and rest.

When I awoke in the morning a view of unexpected grandeur greeted me. Rakiposhi, seen now from the north-east, reared its crown of ice and snow more imposingly than ever, and without a speck of cloud or mist. To the north mighty peaks, also above 25,000 feet in height, frown down upon the valley, while eastwards I could see the range along which my onward route was to lead. The two days which I had saved by the double marches between Gilgit and Hunza, were used for a short halt at Aliabad. I required it in order to distribute my baggage into loads suitable for coolie transport, and also to dispose of arrears of correspondence, etc. Hunza, it is true, does not boast as yet of a post office. But a "Political Dak" connects it every second day with Gilgit, and in view of the long journey before me it seemed right to utilise to the full this last link of regular postal communication.

The first morning brought the Mir's Wazir, who came to assure me of the arrangements that had been made for the onward journey. Wazir Humayun is no small personage in the Hunza State, being the chief adviser and executive officer

MOUNT RAKIPOSHI SEEN FROM ALIABAD.

of the Mir, which rank he holds by hereditary right. He is a tall, well-built man of about fifty years, with an imposing beard, and makes a striking appearance, even in the semi-European costume he has chosen to adopt, evidently as a mark of his progressive ideas. It must have been different in former years, when the Wazir led Kanjuti raids into Sarikol. Gilgit, and Baltistan. A pleasant fire lit up his eyes as he talked to me of his expeditions to Tashkurghan and into the Braldo Valley. Now that the days of fighting are gone he evidently does his best to develop the internal resources. It is no easy task, for the cultivable land is far too limited to provide for the increase of population. Only by elaborate irrigation can produce be wrung from the rock-strewn slopes of the valley, and the long courses of 'kuls' (water-channels) winding along the foot of the mountains often in double and treble tiers, show how carefully the available supply of water from the glacier-fed streams of the side valleys has been utilised.

Curious, too, was the information about the relations of Hunza with the Celestial Empire. Hunza people have for a long time back occupied valleys like that of the Oprang stream draining into the Yarkand River; and their continued occupation of these tracts, which plainly fall within the natural boundaries of Chinese Turkestan, is probably the reason why the further periodical transmission of presents to the Kashgar authorities has been acquiesced in even after the enforcement of British sovereign rights. On the other hand Hunza enjoys the benefit of Chinese return "presents" considerably in excess of those sent, an arrangement manifestly representing the blackmail which the Chinese had to pay to safeguard their territory between Sarikol and the Karakorum from Kanjuti raiding. On my enquiring after records of the relations with the Chinese authorities, the Wazir informed me that a quantity of documents, mostly Chinese, with Persian or Turki translations, had been removed from the Mir's residence at Baltit to Simla, after the occupation in 1891. It would be interesting to ascertain from these or from the Chinese archives, what official status was accorded by Chinese diplomacy to the Kanjuti chiefs.

Though British supremacy in Hunza, very different from Chinese fictions, is a thing of manifest reality, it is maintained without material force. The little fort built in the open fields of Aliabad is now mainly used as a commissariat "Godown," and guarded only by a few local levies raised among the neighbouring villagers. Yet these levies, of whom there are about one hundred and eighty in the state, proved useful during

HUNZA COOLIES, BEFORE START FROM ALIABAD.

the Chitral campaign. As elsewhere along the North-West border, these local militia supply an excellent instrument for the political management of their own territory. Regular pay and easy service are effective in attaching them to the ruling order of things. The additional advantage which levies on the Afghan border offer for the safe employment of notoriously bad characters that would otherwise be likely to give trouble, need fortunately not be considered in Hunza. The people have been described by those best qualified to judge as thoroughly tractable and obedient to constituted authority, and notwithstanding their old raiding reputation, this description seems fully justified

On the second day of my stay at Aliabad I received the visit of the Mir of Hunza, Muhammad Nazim, who had been installed after the occupation in 1891. He is a man of about thirty-five, of open and manly bearing, and evidently deserves the reputation for intelligence and firmness which he enjoys. Our conversation, carried on in Persian, turned naturally more to the old conditions of the country than to the reforms about which the Mir is said to be energetic. Road-making, vaccination, and similar Western improvements seem strange as objects of genuine interest in the representative of a family for which intrigue and murder were down to the present generation the main incidents of life. This transformation in its rapidity and evident thoroughness is a striking proof of the results of the pax britannica.

Through the Wazir I had engaged two Hunza levies who had been on the Pamir before, to accompany my camp to Sarikol as guides. Muhammad Rafi, the commandant of the Mir's bodyguard, was sent to organise and supervise the transport, represented by sixty coolies. Swelled by these numbers my caravan looked alarmingly large as it moved off on the morning of June 20th. The first march was only a short one, to Baltit, the chief place of Hunza, and the Mir's residence. Rising on a cliff from an expanse of terraced fields and orchards, the Castle of Baltit looks imposing enough with its high walls and towers. Below it, closely packed on the hillside, are the rubble-built houses, some two hundred in number, of the Hunza capital. The newly built bungalow which received me lies immediately below the fine polo ground, offering a cheerful sight with its green turf and shady Chinar trees. On the opposite southern side of the valley a striking view opened on the Sumair glacier with a hoary ice peak behind it.

The visit which I paid to the Mir in the late afternoon, gave me an opportunity to inspect more closely the time-honoured castle of the Hunza rulers (see p. 27). The high, massive walls of the foundation upon which the inhabited quarters are raised, are said to have been the work of Balti workmen who came in the train of a Balti princess, and from whom the place has derived its name, Baltit. From the roof of the castle where I found the Mir with his numerous retainers, a superb view extends over the main portion of the Hunza valley. A newly-built pavilion-like structure where I was

FORT-VILLAGE OF ALTIT.

subsequently entertained to tea and cake, occupies the same elevated position and offers the same delightful prospect. Notwithstanding some European articles of furniture of doubtful taste which had already found their way to this apartment, the whole showed clearly the prevalence of Central-Asian manufacture. Carpets from Yarkand, Chinese silks and gaily-coloured prints from Kashgar could indeed make their way to Hunza far more easily over the Sarikol passes than Indian articles before the opening of the Gilgit route. Even now the latter is open to trade for a far shorter period than the passes from the North.

Returning from my visit to this interesting place I noticed several small mosques constructed of wood, and showing on their beams and posts a good deal of effective carving. Rougher in execution than old Kashmir woodwork, it yet displayed, just like the latter, decorative elements of a distinctly early Indian type, *e.g.*, the double 'Chaitya' ornament, the Sacred Wheel, the Svastika. The work I saw was said to be of comparatively recent date, which makes the survival of these patterns borrowed from the South so much the more curious.

My march on June 21st looked short on the map, but the accounts I had collected of it prepared me for its difficulties. Soon after passing, about two miles above Baltit, the picturesque fort-village of Altit, the valley contracts to a gorge of rugged rocks, almost without a trace of vegetation. A narrow path winds along the cliffs, sometimes close by the swollen river, sometimes several hundred feet above it. A small alluvial plateau, reached some four miles beyond, bears the little village of Muhammadabad. But the track leads far below over the sandy bed of the river. This bed indeed forms the easiest route up the valley, and only when its water is low in the winter can ponies be brought up or down. The frequent crossing of the river which this winter route necessitates is altogether impossible when the snow on the mountains has once begun to melt.

Accordingly a high rugged spur had to be climbed and the débris of an enormous old landslip to be traversed before I could descend again to the riverside and reach the camping-ground of Ataabad. The hamlet which gives this name was scarcely to be seen from below, and shut in by an amphitheatre of absolutely bare rocky heights, our halting-place looked a dismal spot. About half a century ago the Ghammesar landslip, already referred to, is said to have blocked the whole valley, when from Ataabad upwards an enormous lake was formed. The black glacier-ground sand, which the Hunza River brings down and deposits in large quantities, rose in thick dust with the wind which blew down the valley in the evening. Drink and food tasted equally gritty; it seemed a foretaste of the Khotan desert. In so desolate a neighbourhood I felt doubly grateful for the Dak-runner who at nightfall brought a long-expected home mail.

The march of the next day proved a trying experience. A short distance above Ataabad the river passes along a series of cross-spurs which at their foot are almost perpendicular. So the path climbs up their sides, and clings to them where they are too steep by means of narrow galleries. These are carried in parts over branches of trees forced into fissures of the rock and covered with small stones. Elsewhere narrow natural ledges are widened by flat slabs packed over them. In some places these galleries, or 'Rafiks,' as they are locally called, turn in sharp zigzags on the side of cliffs where a false step would prove fatal, while at others again they are steep enough to resemble ladders. To carry loads along these galleries is difficult enough, and for cattle as well as ponies, surefooted as the latter must be in Hunza, they are wholly impassable. At more than one place even 'Yolchi Beg,' my little terrier, had reluctantly to submit to the indignity of being carried,

RAFIK ABOVE ATAABAD.

though on our climbs in Kashmir I had found few rocks that would refuse him a foothold. Scrambles of this kind alternated along the whole march with passages over shingly slopes and climbs over rock-strewn wastes. Only at a few spots the barren grey and yellow of the rocks was relieved by some green shrubs growing where scanty water-courses forced their way down the fissured slopes. After six hours' steady climbing and scrambling it was a relief to see at last the valley widen again, and two hours more brought me to Ghulmit village. It occupies a wide alluvial fan on the flank of a considerable glacier, the white crest of which could be seen from a distance rising above the orchards and fields.

At Ghulmit that part of the Hunza Valley is entered which is known as Little Guhyal. It takes this name from its inhabitants, Wakhi immigrants from Wakhan or Guhyal on the Oxus. It was easy to notice the change of race in the assembly of well-built handsome village headmen which received me some distance from the village. Headed by the Mir's relation, Muhammad Nafiz, who acts as his representative among the villages of this part of the valley, they escorted me in stately procession to the little orchard of apricot trees where my camp was to be pitched. I was delighted to hear at last the language of Wakhan, which had attracted my attention years before I first came to India, as a remarkably conservative descendant of the ancient tongue of Eastern Iran. It seemed strange that I should have first touched the linguistic borders of old Iran, high up in these mountains. The fact was bound to remind me that the Pamirs which I was about to approach, mark the point of contact not only of great geographical divisions, but also of equally great language families and of the races speaking them. Close to the Kilik Pass is the point where the watersheds bounding the drainage areas of the Oxus, Indus, and Yarkand Rivers meet; and it is plain that as far as history can take us back, these areas belonged to the sphere of the dominant races of Iran, India, and Turkestan.

The Wakhis of Little Guhyal, numbering altogether about a thousand souls, are a fine stalwart type, taller than the men of Hunza and usually showing clear-cut and intelligent features. The characteristic eagle-nose of the true Iranian was well represented, and their complexion, too, seemed to me distinctly fair. Many of them talk Persian with more or less fluency, and I was thus able to indulge in short chats. The connection with the people of Wakhan and Sarikol is still maintained by

WAKHI VILLAGERS, GHULMIT.

occasional marriages, and the original immigration from the Oxus Valley is distinctly remembered. How the Hunza people proper, undoubtedly more warlike and so pressed for land, acquiesced in this invasion, seems difficult to explain. The peaceful character of the Wakhis is curiously symbolised by the implement which every respectable householder carries about with him on state occasions. It is a long staff with a small heart-shaped shovel of wood at the end, used for opening and damming up the irrigation courses that bring fertility to the laboriously cleared terrace lands.

Ghulmit cannot have seen many Sahibs, for a large assembly of villagers remained for a long time round the neat little fruit garden where I was encamped. Next morning we made a late start owing to the change of coolies, when time is always lost until every one settles down to the load he fancies. But the

VIEW TO NORTH-EAST OF PASU VILLAGE.

march to Pasu proved short, and after the previous days' experience unusually easy. This does not mean, of course, that the track is as yet fit for perambulators. For a short distance above Ghulmit the Ghulkin glacier comes down close to the river, and the numerous channels in which its ash-grey waters rush forth, are troublesome to cross at this season. But the valley is open, and the stony plateaus along the right riverbank afforded easy going. Just before the end of the march the road passes in front of the Pasu glacier, which comes down with its débris-covered masses of ice from a great peak of over 25,000 feet, also visible from Aliabad and Baltit. An enormous side moraine, which is crossed by the route, shows that the glacier must have advanced further at a former period.

The little village of Pasu, situated immediately to the north of the glacier-head, formed with its green fields and orchards a pleasant contrast to the bleak scenery around. It owes its

BATUR GLACIER, SEEN FROM SOUTH-EAST.

existence to the irrigation cuts which catch some of the water issuing from the glacier. A little orchard in the midst of the few scattered homesteads which form the village, was my cheerful camping-ground for the day. The cooler air and the backward state of the crops of oats and millet were indications of the elevation of the place (circ. 8,000 feet above the sea). The flowers by the side of the fields, scanty as they were, gave the whole a springlike look which was most pleasing.

HUNZA VALLEY BELOW KHAIBÁR.

The march of June 24th brought me first to the huge Batur glacier, some three miles above Pasu. Probably over twenty-four miles long, it fills completely a large side valley which descends from the north-west, and unlike the glaciers previously passed, it advances its frozen walls down to the river-bed. They are covered for miles up the valley with an extraordinary mass of detritus, and thanks to this thick crust of rock and shingle the crossing of the glacier was comparatively easy. All the same it took me nearly an hour to scramble across the mile and half of glacier, and the slippery ground delayed the coolies still longer. There are years when masses of ice pushed down from the unexplored upper reach of the glacier make the crossing far more difficult even for men, and altogether close the route for animals. It is in view of such obstacles, which no skill of the engineer can ever completely overcome, that one realises the great natural defences of the Hunza Valley route against invasion from the North.

Above the Batur glacier the valley contracts and continues between bare walls of rock and shingle to Khaibar, the next inhabited place above Pasu. The river, no longer fed by the glacier streams from the high ranges, is now far smaller in volume, yet still quite unfordable in summer. The mountains on either side culminate in serrated rock pinnacles of fantastic forms, but views of mighty masses of ice and snow no longer meet the eye.

The hamlet of Khaibar, which I reached after a tiring march of six hours, lies on an alluvial fan at the mouth of a narrow side valley. Scanty indeed are the fields of the place, and one wonders how they can support even the half-dozen homesteads. Yet even here where Nature is so harsh, defence against human foes was not so very long ago a necessary condition of existence. The path which leads to the plateau is guarded at a point of great natural strength by a rude gateway or 'Darband,' a necessary precaution seeing that the opposite bank of the river was easily accessible to the people of Nagir, the hereditary enemies of Hunza.

From Khaibar to Misgar there are two routes available, one leading through the hamlet of Gircha by the left bank of the river, and the other through Khudabad on the right. The former, which was said to be easier if the water of the river was not too high, was reported impracticable soon after I had started on the morning of June 25th. Hence the track on the right bank had to be taken. Without offering exceptional difficulties that day, it was trying enough, leading almost the whole length over boulder-strewn slopes and along banks of slatey shingle. Just opposite to the hamlet of Murkhun,

RAFIK NEAR MURKHUN.

where a route to the Shimshal Valley opens eastwards, the path descends over a long Rafik built out in the usual fashion from an almost perpendicular rock face. Curiously enough at one point of the narrow ledge which bears the gallery, there issues a little spring of deliciously clear water, offering welcome refreshment to the wayfarer.

Not far beyond I met, to my surprise, the messenger whom the Wazir of Hunza had despatched to Tashkurghan to notify to the Political Munshi there my approaching arrival. The man had left Hunza on the morning of the 18th, and now he was returning with the Munshi's reply and a considerable load of merchandise which he was bringing back as a private venture. As an illustration of the marching powers of the men of Hunza this feat deserves record. The distance from Hunza to the Kilik is about eighty-one miles, and of the character of the track my experiences so far described will suffice to give an idea. In addition to this and half the return journey, the man had covered twice the route along the Taghdumbash Pamir to and from Tashkurghan, a distance of at least eighty miles each way. Performances of this kind make it easy to understand how the raids of Kanjuti parties could be carried to so great distances, and thanks to the rapidity of their movements, usually with impunity.

At Khudabad, a hamlet of eight houses, my day's march ended. Here I passed once more out of the Wakhi area into that of small Hunza settlements. The fact reminds me of the strange variety of tongues which at that time could be heard in my camp. Apart from Turki conversation with my personal servants, Persian served me as a convenient medium with my Wakhi guides and the more intelligent villagers. My coolies spoke partly Wakhi, partly Burisheski, while the Dard dialect of the Shinas was represented by "Raja" Ajab Khan, a relative of the hill chiefs of Punyal, whose services as an orderly Captain Manners Smith had kindly secured for me, and by his retainer. In addition to these languages there was Hindustani talked between my Sub-Surveyor and Jasvant Singh, his Rajput cook. Had I brought the Kashmiri servant whom I had first engaged before Sadak Akhun joined me from

Kashgar, I should have had an opportunity to keep up my Kashmiri also. Notwithstanding this diversity of tongues things arranged themselves easily, for everybody seemed to know something at least of another's language.

The march from Khudabad to Misgar which I did on the 26th of June had been described to me as the worst bit of the route, and as an Alpine climb it certainly did not fall short of the estimate I had been led to form of it. The Chaparsun River, which comes down from the glaciers near the Irshad

KANJUTIS CARRYING MERCHANDISE

and Chillinji Passes in the north-west, was fortunately low at the early morning hour, and could be forded immediately above Khudabad. A long detour and the use of a rope bridge were thus avoided. But the succession of climbs which followed in the main valley beat all previous experience. Scrambles up precipitous faces of slatey rocks, alternated with still more trying descents to the river-bed ; 'Rafiks' and ladders of the type already described were in numerous places the only possible means of getting over the cliffs, often hundreds of feet above the river. The previous five days, however, had accustomed me somewhat to such modes of progress, and it was in comparative freshness that I emerged at last in the less confined portion of the valley above its junction with the gorge of the Khunjerab River. Some miles before Misgar I was met on a desolate little plateau by the levies of that place, a remarkably striking set of men, and conducted to their village.

After the barren wilderness of rocks and glacier streams through which I had passed, the smiling green fields of Misgar were a delight to the eye. They are situated on a broad plateau some 300 feet above the left river-bank, and amply irrigated by channels fed from a stream of crystal-clear water which issues from a gorge to the east. The millet and 'Rishka' were still in young shoots, since the summer comes late at this the northernmost village of the valley. In the midst of the fields and the scattered homesteads I found an uncultivated spot just large enough for my tent, and enjoyed again the pleasure of camping on a green sward. Close by was the Ziarat of a local saint, Pir Aktash Sahib, a simple enclosure adorned with many little flags which fluttered gaily in the wind, just as if they marked the approach to a Buddhist establishment in Sikkim or Ladak. The open view across the broad valley was most cheerful after the gloomy confinement of the previous camping grounds. Far away to the north-west I even beheld a snowy ridge which clearly belonged to the watershed towards the Oxus. I felt at last that the Pamir was near.

At Misgar I was able to discharge the hardy hillmen who had carried our impedimenta over such trying ground without the slightest damage, and on the morning of June 27th I moved on with fresh transport. This consisted chiefly of ponies, as the route further on is open to baggage animals at all seasons. Though the road no longer offered special difficulties, it was tiring owing to the boulder-strewn wastes it crosses for a great part. At Topkhana, where there stands a half-ruined watchtower amidst traces of former habitations and fields, I was met by a jolly-looking young Sarikoli, whose appearance and outfit at once showed that he came from Chinese territory. It was one of the soldiers of the 'Karaul' or guard kept by the Chinese on the Mintaka Pass who had been sent down to

KANJUTI HILLMEN, DISCHARGED AT MISGAR.

inquire as to my arrival. He carried a long matchlock with the gable-ended rest sticking out beyond it, an indispensable implement of the Celestial soldiery of the old type all through the empire. Ruddy-cheeked and clothed in fur cap, mighty boots, and a series of thick 'Chogas' or coats, the young fellow looked serviceable enough. Less so his matchlock, which had lost its breach-piece, and in the barrel of which a broken ramrod had stuck fast evidently for many a long day. He assured me that the expected yaks and ponies were already waiting for me, and tried to make himself as useful on the rest of the march as if he belonged to my following of Hunza levies.

In reality the frontier line seems of little consequence to the Wakhi herdsmen who live on either side of it. When after a march of over twelve miles I arrived at Murkushi, where the routes to the Kilik and Mintaka diverge, there was a set of picturesque Wakhis from across the border waiting for me. They had left their yaks on this side of the pass, where they found better grazing. It was a pleasure to behold these sturdy fellows in their dresses of Yarkand fabrics showing all colours of the rainbow. Their clear-cut Iranian features, almost European in complexion, seemed to contrast pleasantly with their Kirghiz get-up. Down in the little wood of stunted birch-trees by the river where I camped for the night, it was scarcely as cold as might be expected at an elevation of nearly 12,000 feet. At 6 a.m. on the following morning the thermometer showed 47° F.

A march of four hours brought me on the 28th of June to the high grazing ground known as Shīrin Maidan ("the Milky Plain"), close to the foot of the Ḳilik Pass. Here the change in the temperature due to the great elevation made itself most perceptible. When the sun passed behind light clouds at noon and a fresh breeze blew down the pass it was bitterly cold, and I was glad to get into my fur coat as soon as the baggage arrived.

The range immediately to the north which is crossed by the pass, appeared low by the side of the rugged peaks which show their snowy heads further down in the valley. More imposing than the watershed towards the Taghdumbash, looked a distant glacier-covered ridge visible through a side valley westwards. Behind it lay the sources of the Oxus, or more exactly of the Ab-i-Panja branch.

My Guhyal coolies and Hunza levies had now all been discharged, and I was left to enjoy the change in my camp surroundings. Muhammad Yusuf, the Sarikoli headman, and his seven relatives who brought the yaks that were to take my baggage onwards, were cheerful to look at and talk to. They understood Turki quite well and were most communicative: In their midst I felt that I had passed out of India.

YAKS STARTING FOR KILIK PASS.

CHAPTER IV.

ON THE TAGHDUMBASH PAMIR.

When early on the morning of the 29th of June I struck camp to move over the Kilik or 'Kalik' Pass, as it is called by Kanjutis, the ground was covered with hoar frost and the little streams which came down from the pass were partly frozen. I tried to start early in order to find the snow still hard; but the packing of the baggage on yaks proved a lengthy affair, and it was not till 8 a.m. that the caravan moved off. I had the satisfaction of seeing the servants whom the previous marches had tried a great deal, now comfortably mounted on yaks. The ascent lay northwards through a comparatively open though steep nullah for about an hour. Then the ground widened, and the flat watershed still covered with snow came into view. On the east the pass is flanked by spurs of a rugged peak, which rises to a height of nearly 20,000 feet. On the west two small glaciers stretch down to it from a somewhat lower range, the culminating peak of which seems to mark the point where the drainage areas of the Oxus, Indus, and Yarkand Rivers meet. On the flat plain, about half a mile broad, which forms the top of the Kilik, it was not easy to fix the actually lowest point, the true watershed. When I had ascertained the spot that looked like it, a halt was made to boil the water for the hypsometer. It proved a troublesome business in the bitterly cold wind which

KILIK PASS SEEN FROM KHUSHBEL.

was blowing across, and by the time that I got the readings which gave the height as circ. 15,800 feet, it began to snow. Bleak and shrouded in clouds looked the range to the north, which marks the boundary of the Russian Pamirs, but there was nothing striking in its outlines, nor was the amount of snow as great as on the serrated high peaks towards Hunza. The ride down in the soft snow and in the face of the cutting wind was not a pleasant experience, but the yaks proved most useful as snow-ploughs, and by 1 p.m., after a descent of over two hours,

I found myself at Kök-török ("the Blue Boulder," in Turki) on the flat of the Taghdumbash Pamir.

An imposing cavalcade met me as I approached the place where my camp was to be pitched. Munshi Sher Muhammad, the Political Munshi stationed at Tashkurghan under the orders of Mr. Macartney, had come up from his post to greet me; and attracted, no doubt, by his example, the Sarikoli Begs in charge of the several portions of the country above Tashkurghan, also awaited my arrival. Munshi Sher Muhammad, a fine-looking, active man, introduced himself as an old pupil of the Oriental College at Lahore of which I had held charge so long. The arrangements he had made for my journey down to Tashkurghan were all that could be desired and showed his influence with the local authorities as much as his eagerness to help me. It was bitterly cold during this first day on the Taghdumbash as, soon after my arrival, a strong wind sprung up blowing across the valley from the north-east and bringing light snow at intervals. The observation of Captain Deasy, who had encamped at the same spot in 1897, shows that its elevation is close on 14,000 feet.

On the 30th of June the sun shone brightly when I rose, and though the temperature at 6 a.m. was only 37° F. in the shade, it felt pleasant enough as the air was still. The surrounding ridges, all snow-capped, stood out with perfect clearness against the blue sky. The conditions were exceptionally favourable for the survey work which was to be commenced here, and by 8 a.m. the surveyor and myself were on our way to the top of the Khushbel spur which was to serve as a station. This spur descends from the high range on the east of the Kilik Pass towards the valley, and by its detached position offers an extensive view over the upper portion of the Taghdumbash. We were able to ascend close to its top, 16,820 feet above the sea, by means of yaks—an advantage which, in view of the subsequent work, was not to be despised. The way in which the sure-footed animals carried us and our instruments steadily up, first over steep grassy slopes, then over fields of snow, and finally over the shingly beds of rock, was to me a novel and gratifying experience. It was clear that by a judicious use of the yak the difficulties which the high elevations offer to mountaineering in these regions could be reduced for the initial stages. From the top of Khushbel we were able to identify some peaks both towards the Murghab Valley and Hunza which had been triangulated by Captain Deasy. While Ram Singh was busy with his plane-table, I did my first work with the Bridges-Lee photo-theodolite, an excellent instrument, which was now on its first

SNOWY RANGE SOUTH OF HEAD OF AB-I-PANJA VALLEY.

trial in Central Asia. By noon the wind began to blow again, which seems a regular feature of the atmospheric conditions at this season, and I was glad when by 6 p.m. the shelter of the tent was reached.

Köktörök is so near to the Wakhjir Pass, which marks the watershed between the Oxus and the Yarkand River drainage systems, that I could not resist the temptation of visiting it during the two days which were required for the Sub-Surveyor's work round this camp. It would have weighed on my topographical conscience to have passed by without seeing at least the head of the Wakhan Valley and the glacier which Lord Curzon first demonstrated to be the true source of the Oxus. Accordingly, leaving all heavy baggage with the Sub-Surveyor's party at Köktörök, I set out on the morning of the 1st of July towards the Wakhjir Pass. The road led first up the open valley towards

PHOTO-THEODOLITE VIEW OF OXUS SOURCE GLACIERS.

the west, and then after some five miles turned into a narrower side valley in a south-westerly direction. Large patches of snow and the gradual disappearance of the thick, coarse grass, which was to be seen round Köktörök Camp, marked the higher elevation. I pitched my tent at the point which offered the last bit of comparatively dry ground, circ. 15,300 feet above the sea. Higher up there was snow at the bottom of the valley, or boggy soil where the snow had just melted. In front I had the view of numerous small glaciers, which clothes the slopes of the range south of the pass. My intention of going up to the latter the same day was frustrated by a storm which brought sleet and snow. In the cutting cold my people felt the scarcity of fuel; for even the coarse grass known to the Sarikolis as 'Dildung' and to the Kirghiz as Burse,' the dry roots of which supply the only fuel of this region—

VIEW DOWN AB-I-PANJA VALLEY FROM NEAR WAKHJIR PASS.

apart from dry yak dung was no longer to be found at this altitude.

By the morning of the next day the weather had cleared, and the ascent to the pass could be effected without difficulty. One and a half hour's ride on a yak over easily sloping snow beds and past a small lake brought me to the watershed. It was clearly marked by the divergent direction of the small streams which drained the melting snow; and the hypsometer, which I boiled on a boulder-strewn patch of dry ground close by, gave the height as close on 16,200 feet.

A glacier of pure white ice pushes its tongue to within a few hundred yards from the north. The descent to the west of the pass took me into Afghan territory, but in this mountain solitude there was no need to consider whether this short inroad into His Highness the Amir's dominions was authorized or not. The soft snow impeded my progress for about a mile and a half, but then the ground got clear, and I was able to follow without trouble the stream from the pass down to where it joins the far greater one which drains the glaciers at the true head of the Wakhan Valley. A climb of some eight hundred feet up the mountain-side to the north gave me a splendid view of the valley through which the collected waters of the Ab-i-Panja flow down towards Bozai Gumbaz and Sarhad. The glaciers, too, from which they chiefly issue, were clearly in view. An hour's work with the photo-theodolite enabled me to retain the whole of this impressive panorama. It left no doubt as to Lord Curzon being right in placing here the true source of the great river.

The high ranges which line the valley precluded a view further west towards Wakhan proper and Badakhshan. Yet it was a strange and joyful sensation to know that I stood at last at the eastern threshold of that distant region, including Bactria and the Upper Oxus Valley, which has had a special fascination for me ever since I was a boy. How I wished to have been able to follow the waters of the Oxus on their onward course! All the interests of ancient Iran cluster in one form or the other round the banks of the great stream. Since the earliest times it has brought fertility and culture to the regions which it waters. Here at its source there was only a silent, lifeless waste of rock and ice. Yet I found it hard to leave this desolate scene.

The evening glow was spreading over the valley when I retraced my route to the pass, and it was dark before I returned to camp. I found there to my delight an eagerly-expected home mail, which the attentive Wazir of Hunza had sent by special messenger over the Kilik. With it came a batch of the latest telegrams of Reuter, which were to be forwarded to Mr.

Macartney at Kashgar after perusal. They brought news of the attack on the Peking Legations and of the fighting about Tien-tsin. It was strange to read here at the westernmost extremity of the Chinese Empire of the events which had convulsed its capital in the far East scarcely more than a week before. I thought it fortunate indeed at the time that this disturbing news would probably take months to reach the popu-

KIRGHIZ 'AK-UIS' AT TIGHARMAN-SU.

lation of the outlying province of Kashgar. And I felt still more grateful for the time-honoured decentralisation of the Celestial Empire which made any immediate influence of those troubles on Chinese Turkestan and on my programme of explorations appear distinctly improbable.

On the 3rd of July I marched back to *Köktörök*, and having picked up the Sub-Surveyor and heavy baggage, continued in the broad, grassy valley down to Tigharman-su.

There I camped near two Kirghiz felt huts or 'Ak-uis'

pitched by Muhammad Yusuf's people, who graze their flocks of sheep and yaks here during the summer. On the following morning appeared Karakash Beg, the Sarikoli headman in-charge of the Mintaka route, to escort me further down the valley. We were nearing, after a march of some six miles, the post at the northern foot of the Mintaka Pass, when a report was brought to my guide of a "Russian officer," who had just reached the post viâ the Payik Pass from the north. Having heard nothing before of such a visitor being expected, I rode up with some curiosity, and soon found myself face to face with the reported arrival. It was a young German officer, Lieutenant F., of the Bavarian Foot Guards, who had just travelled down from the head of the Russian railways in Farghana, and was now intending to make his way to Gilgit and India. He knew nothing of the special permission of the Indian Government, without which the Hunza route is closed to European travellers, and was also surprised to hear of the time required for the journey down to Kashmir. Finding that his leave would not suffice for this extension of his trip, Lieutenant F. there and then, while refreshing himself at the breakfast my men had soon got ready for us, made up his mind to visit Kashgar instead. Accepting my invitation to share my camp, he accompanied me to Sarik-Jilga, the end of my march.

On the way, and then at table, my young guest told me much of interest concerning his ten days' ride over the Russian Pamirs. Though far too rapid for close observation, it was a performance highly creditable to his endurance. Of outfit and provisions he had brought scarcely more than is wanted for a few days' outing in the Bavarian Alps, but he had soon been obliged to provide himself against the rigours of a Pamir summer, for which he was little prepared, by purchasing a large fur coat off the back of a Kirghiz. I wondered inwardly how he managed to get rid of the livestock likely to be involved in this transaction. As the Kirghiz had so far been his only hosts except at the Russian fort of Pamirski Post, and as he could not make himself readily understood by them, his bodily wants had found but scant satisfaction. His two ponies were also nearly done up by the hardships of these precipitous marches. On the other hand, there was no need for the two revolvers which he was carrying in his belt, and after our conversation he soon found for them a less prominent receptacle. For, indeed, if the Pamir region does not yet offer inns and rest-houses after the fashion of the Alps, it may boast of an equal degree of security.

Comparing notes from north and south we spent a cheerful

WAKHIS AND KIRGHIZ AT DAFDAR.

evening together. Karakash Beg and his followers shared my satisfaction at this chance meeting. For the assurance that the unexpected arrival was after all not a 'Rus' relieved them of all responsibility. On the 5th of July we rode down together some fifteen miles to Ghujakbai (the 'Ujadbhai' of former maps), where the valley turns to the north and considerably widens. The snow-capped ranges on both sides now receded, and the widening expanse of the valley vividly demonstrated the importance which belongs to the Taghdumbash from ancient times as a great natural thoroughfare over the "Roof of the World." Here my newly-found companion left me in order to hurry onwards to Tashkurghan. He had been fitted out with what was needed in the way of tinned provisions, etc., in order to take him comfortably through to Kashgar; and M. Sher Muhammad, for whom I gave him a letter, subsequently secured for him the change of animals and the passport of the local Chinese commandant which were required for his further progress.

My way on July 6th lay from Ghujakbai first over a broad alluvial plateau which stretches for miles up the valley of the stream coming from the Khunjerab Pass. As it approaches the Taghdumbash Darya it spreads out fan-wise, and resembles most closely the 'Karewa' plateaus which form so characteristic a feature of the Kashmir Valley. A ride of some five miles across this barren waste brought me to Dafdar, where, near a couple of 'Ak-uis,' I found a picturesque assembly of Wakhis and Kirghiz awaiting me. The latter had come from Pisling, a small settlement across the river. By the side of their stalwart and handsome Wakhi neighbours they looked somewhat insignificant; but their cheerful expression and joviality amply made up for the defects of stature and countenance. A short distance below Dafdar I came upon the first traces of cultivation. On the scattered fields which little channels from a side stream irrigate, the crops of oats and barley have evidently a hard struggle. All the same it was a pleasure to meet again with this evidence of permanent habitation. It is only during the last ten years that the latter has become possible, since Kanjuti raids have ceased and order has been secured for the valley.

It was a novel sensation, after the weeks passed in narrow gorges and amidst snow-covered heights, to ride along these broad, smiling slopes gently descending from the foot of the mountains. Wherever water reaches them from the side valleys, the ground was covered with a carpet of flowers and herbs which scented the air quite perceptibly. When about midway of the march I made a short halt on the green meadows of Ghan, a summer grazing-ground, I could easily imagine myself enjoying a bright summer day on a Hungarian "puszta." A troop of ponies turned loose to graze around were lustily enjoying the delights of freedom and rich pasture. To watch their lazy, happy ways was a pleasant distraction.

Light, fleecy clouds hung over the mountains, and it was only in the afternoon when approaching the end of my march of some eighteen miles that I could perceive, rising above them in the north, the glistening mass of a great snowy dome. This was Muz-tagh-Ata, "the Father of Ice Mountains," which I had so long wished to behold. At Yurgal Gumbaz, where I pitched my camp by the side of the river now grey and swollen with the water of glacier streams, it was distinctly warm until the wind began to blow up the valley.

Next morning we were ready for an early start, for the neighbourhood of Tashkurghan and such comforts as it could offer was an attraction for my people no less than myself. Muz-tagh-Ata, still so distant, showed itself in fascinating clearness during the early hours of the morning. Its grand dome of ice filled the vista behind the north end of the valley. After a few miles' ride over a stony level 'Dasht,' my guide, Rashid Beg, the Ming-bashi ("head of a thousand men") of Tashkurghan, broke his usual silence, and indicated a white spot in the far distance as the goal of our march. It was the Fort of Tashkurghan, rising over the western bank of the river. Then I reached a strip of delightfully green sward stretching along the irrigation channel which carries the water of the river to the fields of Tughlanshahr, the collection of hamlets opposite Tashkurghan. For miles the path winds along it, and ultimately reaches the fertile tract where the water spreads itself over carefully-terraced fields.

Whether it was the bright surroundings or the historical interests associated with the place, the sight of the walls of Tashkurghan rising higher and higher above the flat filled me with emotion. I knew that they did not hide imposing structures or special comforts. Yet they marked the completion of a considerable part of my journey and my entry upon the ground which was to occupy my researches. The swollen state of the river prevented the use of the nearest route, and I had to descend almost to the foot of the spur which projects into the valley below Tashkurghan from the eastern range, before a practicable ford was reached. Even here, where the river spreads in about half-a-dozen branches over the flat meadow land, the crossing was no easy matter. For the water reached almost up to the saddles, and flowed with great rapidity. At last, however, though wet to the waist, we got safely across, and leaving the care of the baggage to the village headmen who had assisted me in the passage, I galloped over the rich meadows towards the foot of the cliffs on which the fort stands.

M. Sher Muhammad awaited me near the comfortable Kirghiz 'Yürt' (felt hut), once belonging to Major F. E. Younghusband, which he had pitched for my accommodation, and which in the meantime had proved useful for my fellow-traveller of the previous days. The news that the Chinese Amban of the Sarikol district raised no objection to my proceeding westwards of Muz-tagh-Ata was a welcome piece of intelligence. Less so that Mr. Macartney's Dak for Gilgit, with which I had hoped to post my Europe mail, had already started by the route on the left river-bank, and had consequently missed me. Fortunately it is easier to rectify such postal mishaps in Central Asia than in civilised Europe, and after an evening busily spent in writing, a special messenger rode off with my own mail bag, which was to catch up the Dak courier before he had started from his first night's quarters.

CHINESE FORT WITHIN RUINED TOWN OF TASHKURGHAN.

CHAPTER V.

IN SARIKOL.

THE 8th of July and the day following were given up to a halt at Tashkurghan. There were not only fresh supplies and transport to be arranged for, but also much information to be collected on points of historical and archæological interest. For Tashkurghan, the chief place of the mountain tract known as Sarikol, is undoubtedly a site of considerable antiquity. Its importance reaches back to the days when the traders from the classical West exchanged here their goods for the produce of ancient China. As far as local observations go, everything tends to support the view first expressed by Sir Henry Rawlinson, that Tash-kurghan, "the Stone Tower," retains the position as well as the name of the λίθινος πυργος, which Ptolemy, and before him the great geographer, Marinus of Tyre, knew as the emporium on the extreme western frontier of Serike, *i.e.*, the Central Chinese Dominions. Nature itself has marked the site not only as the administrative centre for the valleys forming the Sarikol region, but also as the most convenient place for trade exchange on an ancient and once important route connecting great portions of Central Asia with the far West and East. From Tashkurghan the road lies open equally to Kashgar and Khotan, and thus to both the great routes which lead from Turkestan into the interior of China. Here also the two best lines of communication across the Pamir converge. The Taghdumbash Valley, giving direct access to the Upper Oxus, is met by the route which crosses by the Naiza-Tash Pass into the Aksu Valley and thence by the Great Pamir leads down to Shighnan and Badakhshan.

At Tashkurghan I had the satisfaction of finding myself once more on the track of Hiuen-Tsiang, the great Chinese pilgrim, whose footsteps I had traced to so many a sacred Buddhist site of ancient India. Travelling about A.D. 649 from Badakhshan to Khotan, he passed through the district of Kie-pan-to, long ago identified by Sir Henry Yule as the modern Sarikol. Examining on the spot the description he and the earlier Chinese pilgrim, Sung-yun (circ. 500 A.D.), give of the old capital of that territory, I found it to agree most closely with the position and remains of Tashkurghan. The ruined town, within which the modern Chinese fort is built, " rests on a great rocky crag and is backed by the river Sita " (*i.e.*, the Taghdumbash branch of the Yarkand River), on the east, exactly as the pilgrims describe it.

A line of massive but crumbling stone walls crowns the edges of a quadrangular plateau of conglomerate cliffs, roughly one-third of a mile in length on each of its faces. A small portion of the area thus enclosed, on the east side facing the river, is occupied by the Chinese fort. Its high and carefully plastered walls of sun-dried bricks stand undoubtedly on far more ancient foundations. Outside them now all is silence and desolation. The rubble-built dwellings, whose ruins fill part of the area, were tenanted as long as the insecure condition of the valley made it impossible for the scanty cultivators to live near their fields. Since peace has come to Sarikol new villages have sprung up near all the cultivated patches of land, and the stronghold has become deserted. When the earthquake of 1895 shook down most of the dwellings, there was no need to rebuild them. The walls of the town had already suffered by earlier earthquakes, and show in many places wide gaps as if they had been breached. Rebuilt undoubtedly again and again after successive periods of neglect, and always of unhewn stone, they cannot afford any distinct criterion of age. But the high mounds of débris over which the extant walls rise, in some places to a height of over 25 feet, show plainly that these fortifications mark the lines of far more ancient ones.

In order to prove my identification of these and other old remains, such as that of a ruined Stupa, just beyond the north wall, an exact survey of the site was essential. To make it required some diplomatic caution, as the Chinese commandant or his subordinates might easily have mistaken its object. M. Sher Muhammad's local experience obviated any trouble on this score. After I had gone over the site with the Sub-Surveyor in an apparently casual fashion, we waited with the surveying until the hours after midday when the whole garrison is wont to take its siesta. When the work continued beyond this safe period, the clever diplomatist went to see the Amban and so skilfully occupied his attention with various representations concerning my journey that he and his underlings had no time to grow suspicious about the work around their stronghold.

What I saw of the Celestial soldiery quartered at this frontier station, showed them as peaceful gardeners or harmless idlers. One or two of the soldiers, clad in blue cotton fabrics, were loitering about my camp to satisfy their curiosity. Neither Persian, Turki, nor Wakhi could draw any conversation from them. According to the Munshi's statement scarcely any of the men, who have now passed close upon eight years in the district, have even an elementary knowledge of the language spoken around them. Considering that the same observation holds good of the few officials, and that the military force at their disposal is really insignificant, the order maintained by the Chinese administration appeared truly admirable. The success may largely be due to the wise arrangement by which all local affairs are left in the hands of local chiefs and headmen. Taxation in these frontier districts is very light, and as the Chinese are anything but exacting masters the people seemed perfectly contented. Facts like these make one appreciate the power which an ancient culture and the political wisdom resulting from many centuries' experience give to the Chinese administration even in these days of apparent political dissolution.

The Amban had just returned from leave in Kashgar in a somewhat ailing condition, and as it seemed doubtful whether he would be able to make the return call demanded by etiquette during the short time available, I had by the Munshi's advice to forego my intended visit, however much I should have liked to profit by the first opportunity to see something of the representatives of the Imperial power. All the local dignitaries, with Karim Beg, the chief of Sarikol, at their head, came, however, to pay their respects, and with M. Sher Muhammad's assistance the little Durbar in my 'Kirgha' or Yürt proved quite a success. The Begs told much that helped me to understand the former condition of Sarikol and the curiously mixed aspect of its population. Among the better-class people it seems difficult to trace any whose families are indigenous to the soil. Some are descended from Wakhi immigrants; a few from Chitrali and Kanjuti refugees; more numerous are those who have come from Shighnan. It seems that Sarikol, exposed to inroads from all sides, has been a kind of happy hunting-ground for adventurous spirits of the neighbouring tracts who for one reason or the other found their own valleys too hot for them. This curious mixture is reflected in the polyglot faculties of the people, who seem all more or less familiar with Sarikoli, closely akin to Wakhi, as well as with Persian and Turki.

M. Sher Muhammad had done his best to explain that I was no 'Hakim.' All the same, the applications for medicines from among my visitors were numerous. I could in conscience do nothing for the aged relative of one of the Begs, whose eyesight had grown dim with his burden of years. Still less was there a remedy in my little medicine-case for the initial stage of leprosy from which the youthful son of another Beg manifestly suffered. "Tabloids" of a sufficiently harmless kind had nevertheless to be prescribed, and as these would not be considered sufficiently efficacious without stringent orders as to diet, etc., I found myself compelled to add verbal prescriptions also on matters of my patient's daily life, which lay quite beyond my ken. Spells, if I could have offered them, would undoubtedly have been still more appreciated.

On the 10th of July I was able to continue my journey, all arrangements for transport and such supplies as the place could offer having been completed. The valley, fully 10,000 feet above the sea, grows only oats and pulse. Vegetables there were none to be had. M. Sher Muhammad, with due forethought of the inhospitable region before me, had all the hamlets ransacked for eggs, and succeeded in furnishing my "chef," Sadak Akhun, with three score of them. This requisition had evidently exhausted local resources; for before I started I was very politely, and with many excuses, asked to favour the Amban with half-a-dozen of these precious eggs, as they were urgently wanted for making up a medicine! Of course, I felt happy to oblige that dignitary.

My route took me first for about three miles down the left bank of the river to the fortified village of Tiznaf. There my attention was attracted by a large cemetery with a number of mud-built domes (Gumbaz), of which the photograph reproduced here gives a view. A short distance further down the Taghdumbash River turns to the east and enters the narrow gorge of Shindah, by which it has forced its way through the meridional range. All the mountains around looked bleak and bare of vegetation, forming a striking contrast to the green fields and meadows of the riverine flat.

The winter route along the Tagharma-su, which joins the Taghdumbash River from the west slopes of Muztagh-Ata, was closed by the depth of the water. So we had to turn off from Tiznaf to the North-West, and make for a low pass over the spur which descends in the angle formed by the two rivers. From the top of the Shush or Kum-Dawan ("the Sandy Pass"), though it scarcely exceeds 12,000 feet in height, there opened an extensive view over the Tashkurghan Valley southwards.

The distant snowy peaks, half-enveloped in clouds, which rose behind it in the South, were the last glimpse I had of the border of India. The view to the North was still more extensive. The great mass of Muztagh-Ata, with its mantle of ice, rose up clearly from the broad valleys which encircle its base on the west

IN THE CEMETERY OF TIZNAF.

and south. Imposing as the great mountain looks from its mass and its crown of glaciers, it did not seem to me from this distance to equal in grandeur and picturesque form those mountain giants of the Himalaya I had seen, Nangaparbat, Mount Godwin Austen (" K. 2"), Rakiposhi, still less Kinchanjanga. The fact that the relative elevation of the highest dome of Muztagh-Ata above the broad, undulating plain of Tagharma at its southern foot is only about 14,000 feet, largely accounts for this; equally, perhaps, also the absence of boldness in its form, and the great height of the permanent snow-line which towards the south does not seem to reach down much below 17,000 feet.

After the world of soaring peaks, glaciers, and deep gorges through which the way from India had taken me, I felt it difficult to believe myself still in an Alpine world in view of the broad, rolling plains before me and of the low-looking ranges which fringe them towards the Pamir. It was a novel type of mountain scenery that greeted me, and I confess it looked somewhat tame by the side of the views which have indelibly impressed themselves on my memory between Kashmir and the Taghdumbash. A descent of about one thousand feet brought me to the irrigated fields of Tagharma, which were clothed in the fresh green of young shoots of oats and barley. Without raising one's eyes to Muztagh-Ata I might have thought myself on the steppe of some northern region. The felt-covered Kirghas scattered over the plain did not dispel this impression; the yaks contentedly grazing on the young grass of the meadows were the sole feature suggestive of the high elevation at which we still moved. Safsgos, where I encamped for the night, is one of the small Sarikoli summer settlements spread over the Tagharma plain. The inhabitants of the three Kirghas, as far as I could see them, the men and children, were all singularly good-looking. Milk and delicious cream were obtainable in plenty.

On the morning of July 11th the air was comparatively still and warm, and only the highest parts of Muztagh-Ata were enveloped in clouds. Riding along the open grassy plain I enjoyed distant views, both to the East and West. In the latter direction the passes of Ghulan, Sarik-tash, and Berjash (or Berdasht), all leading across the range into Russian territory, came consecutively into view. Though snow-covered on the highest shoulders over which they pass, these routes are all evidently easy enough at this season. Near the small hamlet of Sarala, where Sarikolis carry on some cultivation, we passed a little Chinese post, enclosed by loopholed mud walls. It is intended to maintain some control over the small detachments of Sarikoli levies ('Karaulchi,' as they are called) which guard the approaches from the Russian side.

After Sarala cultivation ceased, and the irrigated grassy ground became more and more cut up by patches of sandy soil scantily covered with hardy herbs. The few Yürts we now passed were tenanted by squalid-looking but jovial Kirghiz herdsmen. After Kukyar the route enters a broad stony nullah, enclosed East and West by low walls of conglomerate, which looked like remains of ancient moraines. Above them to the east towered the snow-capped heights of a great spur known as Karakorum, which projects from Muztagh-Ata southwards. By noon a strong wind began to blow down from the north, and I was glad to reach the little Kirghiz settlement of Ghujak, which offered a suitable place for camping. The wind brought light rain soon after the tents were pitched, and as the temperature descended rapidly I was glad to get again into my fur coat, discarded since our entry into the open Sarikol Valleys. The hypsometer showed an elevation of about 11,600 feet.

The next day's march was to be a short one, and accordingly I utilised the morning to ascend with Ram Singh to the top of the steep spur of conglomerate which rose immediately to the East in front of the Karakorum peaks. Light clouds, foreboding a change in the weather, had settled everywhere around the higher ranges. But the view over the great Tagharma Valley, and far beyond it to the peaks South-East of Tashkurghan, was unobstructed, and the plane table work benefited no little by this excursion. To the North, unfortunately, Muztagh-Ata, with its glaciers, hid itself in a thick veil of mist and cloud. After descending again to our last camping-place we resumed the route to the North. A little beyond I passed the mouth of a narrow side valley running to the west, known as Khayindi. It contains a little Mazar or shrine much frequented by the Kirghiz who graze around Muztagh-Ata. A little heap of stones on the road, adorned with horns of Ovis Poli and the wild goat, and a few sticks bedecked with rags of various hues, direct the attention of the wayfarer to the neighbouring shrine. The bits of rag, as throughout the hills of northern India, mark the ex-voto offerings of those who have turned to the saint for help in sickness or some other trouble.

A ride of a little over two hours along the gradually diminishing stream, and between gently sloping ridges of disintegrated rock and gravel, brought me to Kara-su. There I found a small post, or 'Karaul,' enclosed by loopholed mud walls, and my servants comfortably established in the few huts built inside. The garrison, the last on this side subject to the authority of the Tashkurghan Amban, consisted at the time of just three men. Considering that the ramparts of the post are commanded by the rising ground to the West within a hundred yards, the defensive purpose seems to have been less in the mind of those who built it, than the wish to secure a wind-sheltered corner for the garrison. Immediately to the South-West a series of broad, undulating downs leads up to the Kulma Pass, apparently the easiest of all routes which cross the watershed into the valley of the Aksu. A Kirghiz whom I met riding on a heavily-laden pony, some miles below Karasu, had left the Russian outpost on the other side of the pass that very morning.

The meadows round Karasu were carpeted with the few varieties of red and white flowers which had greeted me on the Taghdumbash; else, the scenery looked gloomy enough, for the clouds were hanging still lower than in the morning. The hypsometer gave the elevation as 12,100 feet. Next morning, the 13th of July, the temperature was not as low as I expected, being 46° F. at 6.30 a.m., but the air was full of mist and rain threatened. I left the Sub-Surveyor behind to wait for better weather to continue his work, and marched off by 9 a.m. The ponies seemed to have a presentiment of the bad time before them and gave trouble when their loads were being packed. One of them managed to knock off my travelling bookcase with such impetus that its internal fittings were rudely dislocated. Soon after marching off a violent blast from the pass before us brought icy rain and sleet, and, driving it right into our faces, made progress both slow and disagreeable. As far as I could see the road led between low, bare ridges by the side of a little brook, the head-waters of the Tagharma-su. As, after two hours' marching, we were nearing the summit of the pass, the

Ulugh-Rabat (" High Station "), the rain stopped a little, and soon it was noticeable that this bleak upland was not altogether untenanted. The shrill, whistling voices of the Himalayan marmots were heard all round, and more than half-a-dozen of these brown guardians of the passes, so well known to me from beyond Kashmir, could be seen sitting, with seeming unconcern, on the little mounds over their holes.

At 11.30 a.m. I reached the pass, which seems to be only a slight depression in a broad transverse ridge connecting the Muztagh-Ata *massive* with the so-called Sarikoli range, the eastern brim of the Russian Pamirs. The pass, a little over 14,000 feet above the sea, is marked by a stone heap, the traditional resting-place of some saint. Popular lore about mountain passes does not seem to differ much northwards of the great Himalayan watershed from what I know it to be on the other side. Heavy mist on right and left prevented a view of the higher ranges, but just in front to the North I could look down into the open, flat valley which descends to Subashi and the Little Karakul Lake. I had not far advanced on the small spur over which the path leads steeply downwards, when icy-cold rain, mixed with snow, began to come down again. It was far heavier than before, and by the time I passed the first Aul (herdsmen's camp), called Igrikyök at the bottom of the hill amphitheatre, I felt nearly drenched. However, there was little hope of the weather getting better, and I therefore deemed it best to push on to Su-bashi (" Head of the Waters "), the Chinese post in the valley, where better shelter and supplies could be expected. In the drizzling rain I passed some half-decayed Kirghiz graveyards and a stone-built Gumbaz, evidently the remains of some older structure.

At last, by 2 p.m., the Chinese post came in view, and with heartfelt gratitude I greeted its shelter. Inside a neglected stone enclosure I found, besides a number of tumbledown buildings, a row of mud-built huts, representing the quarters of the garrison. The latter soon emerged in its full strength of eight men, and their commandant, a sort of corporal, hospitably invited me to his state-room. It was, in truth, a poor enough hovel, lighted by a hole in the roof which, closed on account of the rain, admitted only a dim twilight. However, it was dry and warm and it felt cheerful amid the felts and quaint articles of equipment which covered the raised sleeping platform and the walls. A fire was lit under the hole already mentioned, but its smoke drove me into the interior apartment adjoining, long before the tea was ready which it was to warm. Perhaps my little terrier felt happiest, who, shivering with cold and wet, could scarcely wait for the host's good-natured invitation to bury

CHINESE GARRISON OF SUBASHI.

himself in the bundle of quilts marking the bed in one corner of the platform. That he met there a little pet cat without picking a quarrel with it was the surest proof of his usual temper having softened under the influence of exposure.

Whether it was the hospitable reception they gave me or their neat look and get-up, the little Chinese garrison made by no means a bad impression on me. The men were mostly big, well-set fellows, talking Turki more or less fluently, and seemed intelligent enough. When the rain stopped they turned out to be photographed in their parade dress—blue velvet trousers, red cloth tunics, with Chinese letters in black velvet sewn on them, and neat black felt boots. All these articles were in good order, less so their Enfield carbines bearing the "Tower" mark. In the meantime the news of my arrival had been sent on to Karm Shah Beg, the chief of the Kirghiz herdsmen in the valley North of the Ulugh-Rabat, who duly came to welcome me. As the rain had stopped I moved my baggage down two miles from the post of Subashi to where his Kirghas stood. One of them was readily vacated for the accommodation of my servants, while a short break in the rain sufficed for pitching my tent on a dry, sandy spot by the side of one of the numerous branches by which the stream of the Subashi Valley finds its way down to the Karakul Lake. The glittering surface of the latter, one and a half miles further North, could just be seen from my camp.

MUZTAGH-ATA PEAKS SEEN FROM ABOVE YAMBULAK VALLEY.

CHAPTER VI.

ON MUZTAGH-ATA.

THE 14th of July brought no change in the weather, and was by necessity a day of repose. I used it to collect information as to my intended excursion up the western slopes of Muztagh-Ata and to pay off the Sarikolis who had so far supplied my transport. Previously, however, I took the opportunity of effecting anthropometric measurements on them. After Shams Beg, the Yüz-bashi ("Head of a Hundred"), who had escorted me from Tashkurghan, had set the example, they readily submitted to the various operations, each victim in turn affording amusement to his companions.

In the afternoon the rain grew less, and I rode out with Karm Shah Beg to pay a short visit to the Little Kara-kul and the neighbouring tarns of Basik-kul. The detailed descriptions of Dr. Sven Hedin, who studied these little lakes for weeks and with loving interest, have made the readers of his work fully familiar with all aspects of the neighbourhood. Riding round the West shore of Karakul I had a full view of the grand moraine which borders the lower edge of the lake and originally caused its formation. Above it only a mass of cloud indicated the high range which closes the valley to the North-East.

The bleakness of the hills which rise on the West to a height of about four to five thousand feet above the lake and the low mounds of old moraines stretching along the shore, under the grey sky, gave a desolate, sombre look to the little lake. As the glaciers of Muztagh-Ata kept wholly invisible, this impression was not relieved by the grandeur of the more distant surroundings. Mournful, too, looked the still smaller Basikkul basins and wild the confusion of ice-ground mounds of rock and detritus which ancient moraines have left in the narrow space between them. It was evident that the icy splendour of the great range eastwards is required to give to this group of little lakes its true Alpine beauty.

I returned by the east shore of Karakul, past the little bay where Dr. Sven Hedin's camp had been pitched. Considering how long he stopped in the neighbourhood, and how closely acquainted he became with the Kirghiz then encamped there, I was surprised how little my guides could tell me of this distinguished visitor. But the nomadic ways of the Kirghiz fully explain this scant recollection. The families then grazing around Muztagh-Ata have wandered elsewhere. Togdasin Beg, Dr. Hedin's friend, has since died far away on the Russian Pamir, and the other companions of his excursions in these mountains seem also to have scattered to other grazing-grounds. It was instructive evidence how little local tradition can be expected among the wandering tribes that frequent these valleys. The path back to camp took me along the cliffs which run down into the lake from Kara-kir ("Black Ridge"), a bleak height of dark rock rising immediately to the East of it. As soon as camp was reached at six o'clock the rain began to pour heavily again. It plainly meant snow in the higher regions and consequent delay in my excursions. My diary entries for July 15th, which I here transcribe, show that I had not been mistaken in my apprehension.

"It rained and snowed through the whole night, and mist and grey, drizzling rain covered what little I could see of the valley when I got up. There was nothing for it but to sit in the tent and write up notes and letters that were to go down to Tashkurghan to catch the next Dak for India and Europe.

Karm Shah Beg came to pay his respects and to sit in happy disregard of time and weather under the little awning in front of my tent, but what I could elicit from him as to the arrangements for my further journey was far from cheerful. It was easy to notice that the want of instructions from the Chinese at Bulunkul was sorely disturbing his peace of mind. In a tone intended to convey a sense of mystery and secret devotion, he assured me that *he* was ready to render any service—if it were not for the distrustful Chinese. To give me yaks and men for my intended visit to the Yambulak Glacier and the slopes of Muztagh was a thing he could do in safety. But to supply animals for a move to Kashgar might bring down upon him the wrath of the Amban. Even to send a few yaks to my last camp at Karasu for the baggage of the Sub-Surveyor, who was to join me, seemed an act of grave risk. The Beg's faltering excuses gave me a good idea of how well the Chinese manage to keep their roving Kirghiz in hand, but equally little hope of the help I needed for my immediate movements. I accordingly sent the Sarikoli Beg, who had come with me from Tashkurghan, back to Karasu with orders to provide there locally for the transport needed by Ram Singh. At the same time I got Karm Shah Beg to despatch a messenger to Bulunkul who was to show to the Amban the local passport issued to me by his Tashkurghan colleague and to bring back orders for my Kirghiz host.

"In the afternoon the clouds lifted a little and showed the mountain slopes down to a few hundred feet above the level of the valley clad in fresh snow. No encouraging prospect for my Muztagh-Ata excursion, which if to be made at all must be made within the next few days! I used the short interval when the rain stopped in the evening for a visit to the Beg s Yürt. He seemed to appreciate the compliment, and whatever doubts he may feel as to the results of any assistance he may render me, they did not interfere with a display of cordial hospitality. In the middle of the Yürt a big cauldron ('Kazan') of milk was boiling over the fire. One of the Beg's wives, no longer young, but of a pleasing expression and cleanly dressed, was attending to the fire of dwarf juniper ('Teresken').

"While the dish was getting ready, I had time to look about and to examine the homestead. Comfortable it looked in contrast to the misty, grey plain outside. The wicker-work sides and the spherical top of the Yürt are covered with coloured felts, which are held in position by broad bands of neatly-embroidered wool. All round the foot of the circular wall lie bundles of felt rugs and bags of spare clothes, evidently stored for a more rigorous season. A screen of reeds, covered with woollen thread worked in delicate colours and bold but pleasing pattern, separated a little segment of the Yürt apparently reserved for the lady of the house, who again and again dived into it, to return with cups and other more precious implements. The floor all round, except in the centre where the fire blazed, was covered with felts and thick rugs made of yak's hair; for my special accommodation a grey-coloured Andijan carpet was spread on one side. The warm milk, which was offered from the cauldron by the presiding matron, tasted sweet and rich. I had it presented in a large Chinese cup, while the rest of the company, which comprised over a dozen of the Beg's male relatives and neighbours, helped themselves from a number of bowls in wood and iron. Milk is a staple article of food with the Kirghiz, and the healthy look of the men around me, young and old, showed how well it agrees with them.

"Towards the end of my visit Karm Shah Beg produced a big sheep that I was to accept as a token of hospitality and good-will. I should gladly have taken a smaller one, since for weeks past I had occasion to notice that the sheep which my men selected for purchase were as distinguished for toughness as for size. Karm Shah Beg, however, had different notions on this point, and was not to be denied. So I consoled myself with the thought that at least there would be satisfaction among my men. The Kirghiz are a matter-of-fact people, with a keen eye for money. Hence I did not fail to assure my host that his present would be returned by more than its equivalent in value before I left the valley.

"Late in the evening, as I was comfortably settled in my tent and busy writing, Karm Shah Beg turned up with a triumphant mien to announce the arrival of a Chinese officer from Bulunkul who had brought orders to supply me with transport. It was clear that a great load had been taken from the Beg's mind. Glad as I was for this early settlement of the question, I thought it right to treat the news as a mere matter of course. I could not have expected it otherwise! Karm Shah Beg was accordingly told to keep his Chinaman

ICY RANGE, WITH SARGULUK PEAK, TO NORTH-EAST OF KARAKUL LAKE.

and the message he was to deliver until I should find it convenient to receive them on the morrow."

The night brought at last a change in the weather, and when on the morning of the 16th the Beg turned up with the Amban's messenger and the commandant of the Subashi post, I could receive them in the open. I had tea passed round in cups and bowls which my servants procured—I do not know from where—and then received the assurance that whichever way

I should choose for my journey to Kashgar, transport would be forthcoming. There seemed little hope of the shortest route down the valley, by the Gez defile, being available; for the river, swollen by the melting snows, was said to have carried away one if not two bridges, which could scarcely be repaired before the autumn. But there is another, if more difficult, route round by the northern spurs of Muztagh-Ata and over the Karatash Pass, and though this was represented as nearly blocked by snow, I made it clear that if the Amban and his people wished to get rid of me, it would have to be by either of the above two routes. On both of them there was surveying work to be done, which explains my insistence.

When I had finally dismissed my visitors with a clear notion of what I expected from them, I set out for the Karakir Hill, east of the lake, which by its central position promised to be a good station for work with my photo-theodolite. The rain had stopped during the night, but the clouds were still hanging round the peaks, and icy gusts of wind were shifting them continually. The yaks carried me and my instruments easily enough to the long ridge which crowns the hill and is seen in the foreground of the view reproduced on p. 83; but it was only after a long wait, made trying by the cold wind which passed through all my thick clothing, that the clouds lifted sufficiently to permit of satisfactory work. Then glacier after glacier emerged from the great white wall to the north and east formed by a succession of ice-crowned peaks, the worthy rivals of Muztagh-Ata; the deep valley of the Ekkibel-su, which drains Muztagh-Ata from the north, also lifted its veil, and by 3 p.m. the tiring work on the wind-swept height was rewarded by a complete round of accurately fixed views which, I could hope, would prove a useful supplement and check to the plane-table work. That in the midst of the operation the tangent scale of the photo-theodolite broke, and had to be replaced with what primitive tools I managed to procure about my person, was an incident taxing what little I possess of mechanical skill. It was no surprise that my benumbed fingers, while replacing the scale, broke one of the cross-hairs of the camera. But this mishap was repaired too, thanks to the ample supply

MUZTAGH-ATA PEAKS SEEN FROM CAMP SOUTH OF LAKE KARAKUL.

of delicate threads of hair which Mrs. W.'s kindness had provided in Gilgit.

It was bitterly cold by the time I descended, and all the more grateful I felt for the shelter of my little tent. Its warmth was increased by the use of a small "Stormont-Murphy Arctic Stove," burning cakes of compressed fuel, with which I had provided myself from the Military Equipment Co., London. Thus comfortably ensconced within my tent-walls of eight feet square, it was a pleasure to work away till midnight at a mail that was to carry my news to distant friends.

On the 17th of July I awoke to a glorious clear morning. Without a speck of cloud or mist the gigantic mass of Muztagh-Ata towered above my camp. I had counted on this chance for my projected visit to its higher slopes. The rain of the previous days had interfered with the Sub-Surveyor's work, and while he was making up for the delay I could effect my excursion without having to accuse myself of any waste of time. I had soon separated the outfit most needed for this tour from the rest of my baggage. The ten yaks that were to move it and to serve as mounts were also soon procured from among Karm Shah Beg's herd that was grazing near the lake. All surplus stores and baggage not needed were to be left behind in charge of Mirza, my Turki servant from Peshawar, who, not equal to the fatigues of the long journey, seemed manifestly in need of rest. With him I also decided to leave 'Yolchi Beg,' who was to be spared unnecessary climbs in ice and snow. He had so far borne the long marches wonderfully well, and had lost none of his vivacity and high spirits.

It was midday by the time I moved off, accompanied by Sadak Akhun, my Kashgar servant, and the three followers from Hunza and Punyal, who were now to have a chance of showing what they were worth on the mountain-side. The air was delightfully still and warm, and as we rode along the rich grazing land at the bottom of the valley, the fragrance of the flowers and herbs was most perceptible. Passing the Subashi post, which now in full sunshine looked far more dilapidated than when it first offered me its shelter, we turned round the foot of the great spur of Shamalda into the valley leading towards the Yambulak Glacier. The latter descends in a westerly direction from the col connecting the two main peaks of Muztagh-Ata, and is flanked by mighty ridges both to the north and south. From Dr. Sven Hedin's experience, fully detailed in his fascinating volumes, it was clear that the only part of the great mountain from which access might be gained to its higher slopes, if not to one of its summits, was the spur rising above the north edge of the Yambulak Glacier. From a height near the head of the valley, where the fine view reproduced at the head of this chapter lay before me, I surveyed through my small telescope this great ridge as it stretches up in apparently unbroken line to the northern summit. The corresponding ridge on the south side of the glacier could be seen to be coated with a huge crust of old ice, which, furrowed by crevasses up to the very highest summit, manifestly left no chance of ascent. The rocky spur which this mantle of ice covers, rises above the glacier in an almost perpendicular face of cliff several thousand feet high. The rock wall on the opposite, northern side of the Yambulak Glacier, is not only lower, but its slope is less steep and seemed less encrusted with ice. Further to the north the sides of the mountain are far more precipitous and packed with glaciers.

My preliminary examination of the northern ridge which Dr. Hedin had followed in his three attempts to ascend Muztagh-Ata, fully bore out his description, except in one important particular. His ascents in 1894 had taken him along ground that up to a height he estimated at over 20,000 feet, was almost clear of snow. But now I could not fail to note even from a distance that snow of considerable depth covered the identical ridge down to a level of less than 17,000 feet. Satip Aldi, my Kirghiz guide, who had accompanied Dr. Hedin on one of his ascents, was aware of a change which the heavy snow-fall of the last two years had brought about in the condition of this part of the mountain. It was evident that I could not possibly hope to reach the height to which that distinguished explorer's party had ridden up on yaks, in the same convenient manner.

The night from the 17th to the 18th of July was spent in camp near the few Yürts in the upper part of the valley which bears the name of Yambulak. Reckoning with the increased difficulties which deep snow was likely to offer, I decided to obtain spare yaks for myself and the men who were to accompany me. Animals broken for riding were secured after some delay, and it was only by 7 a.m. on the following morning that I was able to move off. An hour later I had reached the foot of the great moraine which flanks the lower portion of the Yambulak Glacier on the north, and with it the last bit of fairly level ground. Leaving my baggage behind with orders to pitch the tents, I then rode up the steep slope of moraine débris and gravel to reconnoitre the ridge above. The point where the baggage was left lay already at an elevation of over 15,000 feet, and the panting of the yaks as they struggled up over the trying slopes of loose stones and shingle showed plainly that these hardy animals felt the effects of the elevation. With their wonderful surefootedness the yaks combine a sluggishness of temper which at all times makes a ride on them a trying mode of locomotion. But I never felt this more than when we had to make our way over these steep and slippery slopes and at the same time to drag along the spare yaks that were to relieve our mounts. Comparatively safe from sticks, the use of which alone could keep the yaks to an upward track, these extra animals were ever and again twisting themselves into the wrong place.

More than an hour passed before we reached the lower end of the rocky ridge above described over which we were to make our way. The ground now became firmer, but with it too we had reached the line of snow. It lay thin at first and did not hamper our progress. But after half a mile of ascent along the crest it became deeper, and at an elevation of about 16,500 feet practically forced us to dismount. It was half-past ten by this time, and the clouds which seemed thin and fleecy in the early morning were now gathering in heavier masses above us. The point to which we had been able to force our yaks seemed the last where we could pitch a camp. The snow which covered the top of the ridge had melted on the slope which descended to the glacier several hundred feet below. The slope was not too steep for tents, but seemed otherwise to offer little advantage. Far above the region where even yaks could secure food, the spot was yet decidedly too low to serve as a convenient starting-point for a long climb on the following day.

Considering the height above us, the selection of a suitable spot for a camp seemed all-important. From where the yaks had brought us nothing was to be seen but a broad slope of snow fringed on its southern edge by precipitous cliffs falling towards the glacier. In order to make sure of the chances for camping higher up I despatched the two Hunza levies on a reconnaissance. They were to examine the conditions of the snow, and to look out for some shelter in the rocks which might enable us to pass a night at a greater elevation eventually without tents. I myself remained behind to use the comparatively clear weather for work with the photo-theodolite. The clouds that were gathering and the high wind that sprang up were a warning not to lose time.

The view which the place of my halt offered, and part of which is shown by the photograph reproduced on p. 90, was grand indeed. It comprised to the west range after range of the Pamirs, from the distant peaks of Wakhan far away to the Alai mountains. The mountains lining the valley below me on the west seemed nowhere higher than my place of observation, for which the hypsometer reading indicated 16,820 feet. From the same point splendid views were obtained up and down the Yambulak Glacier. Compressed between mighty walls of rock the stream of ice seemed in a state of petrified convulsion. From its highest point where its firn filled the space between the twin peaks of Muztagh-Ata down to the opening of its rock-bound gorge, the glacier displayed a bewildering maze of huge crevasses. Their greenish depths contrasted vividly with the spotless white of the snow-crust that covered the surface of the ice. Opposite to us rose the almost perpendicular wall of rock which faces the great ridge ascending straight to the southern and highest peak of Muztagh. Above this rock-wall there showed the thick

VIEW FROM ABOVE YAMBULAK GLACIER LOOKING WESTWARDS.

ice of the glacier-mantle covering that side of the mountain.

Though the sun was hidden only for short periods by light clouds, it felt cold enough in the strong breeze. So it took time to work the delicate apparatus of the photo-theodolite. The two Kirghiz who had come up with us in charge of the yaks had already complained of headache, and by the time I completed my work succumbed to mountain sickness in that most drastic form affecting the digestive organs. To get from them the needed topographical information was for the time quite impossible. I was watching the snow-covered ridge by which my Hunza followers had ascended, with some anxiety as the day wore on, when at last by 5 p.m. they returned. Hardy and born climbers as they are, Wali Muhammad and Ghun looked thoroughly exhausted. They reported that they had climbed in deep snow shoulder after shoulder of the great ridge above until they were stopped by a precipice of sheer rocks descending to a side glacier which separates the ridge they followed from the main mass of the northern peak.

Their account confirmed the doubt which the observation made on the preceding day had left in me as to the continuity of the spur apparently leading to the summit. High up, at an altitude approximately estimated at 22,000 feet, I had noticed what looked like crevassed masses of ice protruding to the north from below one of the buttresses of the ridge. From the description of my men I was forced to conclude that this ice was in reality the end of a transverse glacier hidden from view by the ridge on which we stood. Both men described a descent over the cliffs down into the glacier-filled gorge as wholly impracticable, and the ascent on the opposite face giving access to the summit as of equal difficulty. They complained bitterly of the cold they had experienced in the higher part of their ascent and of the difficulty of breathing. Though they had followed closely the line of the cliffs overlooking the Yambulak glacier, they had found no possible place of shelter among the rocks nor even a spot where a small tent could be pitched. Everywhere the snow was too deep and tolerably level space wholly wanting. This report showed clearly the limits which existing conditions imposed on any attempt at ascending Muztagh-Ata from this side. I realised that without the possibility of camping higher up for one night all that could be aimed at was to penetrate the gorge which had stopped my men. The discovery of this formidable obstacle was in itself an interesting fact; for Dr. Sven Hedin, who in 1894 had ridden on yaks to a height estimated at over 20,000 feet, seemed to have remained wholly unaware of its existence. At the same time the report showed that the ascent up to that point was only a question of endurance and fair weather. I accordingly determined to use the chance of the next day keeping clear for an ascent by the track which my Hunza men had followed.

This chance seemed doubtful indeed, for clouds settled around the summits, and violent gusts of wind made us glad to seek the shelter of the tents below. I found them pitched by the side of the great moraine wall and Ram Singh duly arrived from Karasu. The sky was cloudy when I turned in, and when I rose on the 19th at 3.30 a.m. there was every indication of a storm. It did not take long before the snow, driven by a hard gale, came down. Wrapped in furs I was sorrowfully watching this atmospheric interference with my plans when by 6 a.m. the sky began rapidly to clear. I saw that it had been only one of those short-lived gales which, according to Dr. Hedin's testimony, almost daily visit one or other face of the great mountain. The yaks were kept ready, and when the sun broke through, a little before 7 a.m., I gave the order to start. Instead of the Kirghiz who had proved so useless on the mountain-side, only my Hunza men and Ajab Khan, the Punyali orderly, were to accompany me and the Sub-Surveyor. The latter's instruments were to be carried as far as practicable by honest Hai Bai, a Turki 'Kirakash' (pony-man) from Kökyar, who had accompanied Captain Deasy's caravan to Ladak and Kashmir, and who, anxious to return homewards after a winter's rest, had attached himself to my camp at Srinagar.

This time we were not encumbered by spare yaks for which

no use could be found, and a little over an hour from the time of the start saw us at the point I had reached the day before. The weather kept clear though there was much wind. The yaks toiled on through the snow, which gradually grew deeper, but their progress was slow, and the task of keeping them ahead trying for the riders. More and more frequently we had to dismount and drag the stubborn animals out of the deep snowdrifts into which they had plunged. At last, when an hour's toil had advanced us only some 500 feet above the previous day's station, it became necessary to leave the yaks behind. The snow by this time had increased to an average of five feet in depth, and in many places where some projection of the ridge had favoured the formation of drifts, our alpenstocks altogether failed to strike the rock. The surface snow was crisp and granular, hence so easily shifted by the wind that in most places the footprints left by the men on their ascent the day before could barely be distinguished. The snow along the edge of the rock-wall, which we were careful to follow, seemed at this altitude to have accumulated only during recent winters. Hence it had scarcely yet had time to be compressed by its own weight into ice; and the glittering snow sheet over which we were ascending rested firmly on the rock. Against slips of snow and avalanches we were thus safe enough, while from the opposite side of the glacier where the southern wall of rock was topped by a thick layer of ice, little avalanches would glide down more and more frequently as the day wore on.

It was not easy work to ascend in the soft snow, where we continually sank in for a couple of feet, and where a slight deviation from the track of the front man would land one up to the waist. Though the high elevation we gradually attained caused me neither headache nor any other symptoms of mountain sickness, yet the rarity of the air necessarily imposed slow progress and frequent though short halts. The wind grew stronger as the day advanced, and brought passing showers of snow. Yet more troublesome was the snow which the force of the wind swept up at times from the slope before us. Shortly before midday I reached a point where a few dry rocks at the edge of the spur protruded from the snow. They offered a convenient spot for a halt and refreshment. Immediately below the nearly perpendicular cliffs there stretched the contorted icy surface of the Yambulak Glacier. Contrary to my expectation, the altitude of close on 19,000 feet which we must have reached by this time interfered in no wav with my appetite.

After another short snow squall had passed we resumed our climb, but the Sub-Surveyor and Ajab Khan began to complain of headache and general lassitude. Bichlorate of potash tabloids, with which after Dr. Bellew's advice I had provided myself, proved of little avail, and by 1.30 p.m. Ram Singh had to remain behind. The wind had by this time driven away all clouds that hung over the ranges west and north, and he was thus able to check his plane-table work by rays to a number of distant peaks previously sighted or triangulated. Twenty minutes later Ajab Khan, skilled mountaineer as he is, fell out and received permission to descend. There remained now Wali Muhammad and Ghun, my two Hunza levies, and they without a word of complaint steadily plodded on with me. The snow became still deeper, and the mist that settled on the peaks above us showed clearly that a further ascent would offer no chance of a close survey of the summits. A change in the weather seemed also to threaten, and after due deliberation I fixed upon the buttress of the ridge just before me as the final object of the climb. By 2.30 p.m. I had reached its top and settled down by the side of the precipitous rock wall descending to the glacier.

In the piercing wind it was not easy to boil the water for the hypsometer. By scooping a hole in the snow, however, sufficient shelter was at last secured, and repeated careful readings of the thermometer gave a mean of 177.8° Fahr. as the boiling point. Taking into calculation the temperature of the air, which was 33° Fahr., this corresponds to an elevation of almost exactly 20,000 feet. Our bodily condition would have allowed a further climb, though I as well as my Hunza followers felt the effect of our six hours' ascent through the snow. But neither the state of the weather nor the remaining daylight justified the hope that we could reach this day the end of the spur reconnoitred on the previous day. I accordingly decided to descend and to let a fresh attempt at reaching that point depend on the chance of the weather improving on the next day. The soft snow rendered even the descent by the route we had come a slow and arduous affair; but the grand view which lay before me amply compensated for the delay. To the west the clouds had lifted completely, and the multiplicity of the ranges over which my gaze travelled was the best demonstration of the height we were at.

Straight in front, where the view must have extended practically across the whole breadth of the Pamir region, there were no notable landmarks to attract attention. But this seemingly endless succession of valleys and ranges was perhaps best calculated to impress me with a sense of the vastness of the "Roof of the World." To the south-west there glittered white pinnacles of bolder shape far away on the horizon, and in them I thought I could recognise the mountain-giants that guard the approach to the Indus Valley. They had worthy rivals to the north in some towering masses of ice and snow, which from a reference to the map I could not fail to identify with Mount Kaufmann and other great peaks of the Trans-Alai range. Their highest points were shrouded in fleecy clouds.

The grand spectacle which made me stop again and again, heedless of the cold and wind, also impressed my companions, though from another point of view. Here was a vast region full of rich grazing grounds, greater than the dwellers of the narrow valleys of Hunza could ever imagine. It was not difficult to guess what were the prominent thoughts that passed through my Kanjutis' minds, and a few sympathetic hints soon brought them to their tongues. What a vast field for raids and conquest lay there before the hardy, brave hillmen of Hunza! The old freebooting spirit broke forth again in their talk, together with their contempt for the meek Kirghiz, those willing servants of whoever lets them graze in peace. Wali Muhammad revelled in recollections handed down by his father how the men of Hunza had raided the rich flocks of Tagharma, to the very foot of the great mountain on which we stood. But now the 'Sirkar' has made its will felt, and no Kanjuti dare disturb the peaceful dwellers in these valleys. I could not cheer my plucky guides with promises of a return to those happy days, but I must own to sympathy with their views in my innermost heart. Were it not for the great powers that keep watch from south to north, there is no doubt that little Hunza would with ease sweep across all the valleys from the Oxus to the Kashgar border.

When by 6 p.m. we had descended to that portion of the ridge where the snow had left some patches of bare rock, I was cheered to find the tents pitched on the steep declivities towards the glacier. The place was the best that could be had for the purpose, but the angle of the slope was anything but adapted for a tent. When I retired to its shelter, I felt as if it were a cabin on board a ship rolling badly. With some trouble the nearest approach to a horizontal position was secured for the camp-bed, and as it was the only thing on which it was possible to sit or lie in comfort, I soon succumbed to its attraction. Before, however, I finally got to rest the patients had to be attended to. Ram Singh and Ajab Khan, huddled up in their little tent, still complained of splitting headache and nausea. Outside, undismayed by cold and wind, my hardy Hunza men were feasting in great glee on the big mutton-legs which had been assigned for their refreshment. Their cheery talk, alas! unintelligible to me, was still in my ears when I fell asleep after a frugal dinner. Was it of the pluck and prowess of their little race that they chatted, or of the happy hunting-ground for slaves and sheep which the Pamirs had so long offered to it?

The night brought violent gusts of wind and several light falls of snow. The noise of the avalanches falling over the cliffs on the south side of the Yambulak Glacier woke me at frequent intervals. It was a comfort to think that there was no danger of that kind to fear on the ridge we occupied. When I woke up at 6 a.m. there was fresh snow to a depth of two inches covering the ground. The sky was still cloudy.

There was nothing for it but to wait in patience for a change in the weather. But the change would not come, and as the temperature still kept at freezing-point we felt badly the exposed position of the camp. At last all hope of an ascent that day had to be abandoned, and as to wait for better weather would have meant loss of more time than I could afford, I had by midday reluctantly to give the order for the move to a less inclement region.

On the evening of the 20th of July I camped once more by the side of the Kirghas in the Yambulak Jilga. On the

ICY RANGE WITH PEAKS ABOVE KONGUR-DEBE AND KOKSEL GLACIERS.

following day Ram Singh and myself ascended the high side spur, called Shamalda, which descends from Muztagh-Ata northwards of the Kampar-Kishlak Glacier, for survey work. Icy blasts of wind blew in turn from different directions, and kept now one and now the other side of the mountain shrouded in clouds and mist. Work with the photo-theodolite was trying under such conditions, yet by using the favourable moments views were secured of the valleys and ranges opposite, which from this height—14,570 feet above the sea—showed clear and sharp, as if on a relievo map spread before me. The triangulation, too, was extended to the great peaks north-east of Lake Karakul. After long and trying hours on the wind-swept bleak ridge I was glad to hurry down to my camp, which in the meantime had been moved again to its old place south of the lake. To my pleasant surprise there awaited me a troop of 'Kirakash' men with ten ponies, whom Mr. Macartney, most thoughtfully anticipating my need of fresh transports, had sent from Kashgar to meet me. Through them there came, to my intense joy, a packet of home letters which had reached Kashgar from Europe by the Russian post viâ Samarkand. The latest bore the date of the 24th of June, a proof how near the railway has brought even the slopes of Muztagh-Ata.

On the 22nd of July the weather cleared very suddenly, and the day of rest and quiet work in camp was made doubly enjoyable by a perfect view of the grand mountain. Even the great glacier-clad range to the north-east, dubbed "Kongur" on our maps, but locally bearing neither that nor any other general name, lifted for an hour the veil of clouds from its highest peaks. Those above the glaciers of Kongur-debe and Koksel rise, according to our triangulation, to elevations of 23,600 and 23,470 feet respectively, and thus fairly rival Muztagh-Ata, for which 24,321 feet is the latest ascertained height. All the same I was glad to learn from the Kashgar pony-men that I should not have to force my way through the gap known as the Kara-tash ("Black stone") Pass, which on the south separates that range from the "Father of Ice Mountains." Instead of this difficult route the Gez gorge was reported to be available, though in the flooded condition of the Yamanyar River I had scarcely ventured to hope for this.

START FOR GEZ DEFILE.

CHAPTER VII.

THROUGH THE GEZ DEFILE TO KASHGAR.

THE morning of the 23rd of July found me ready for the start northwards on the way to Kashgar, while Ram Singh, with a small camp, was to move to the north-east to complete the survey up to the Karatash Pass and towards Bulunkul. He was then to follow me to Kashgar a week in the rear. To provide against possible loss of the plane-table work so far done, through accident or Chinese interference, I photographed the section of the map that Ram Singh was to keep. My two Hunza men and Ajab Khan were discharged to their homes, cheered by the prospect of returning to their own mountains and by the substantial rolls of rupees representing their pay. Before I said good-bye to Karm Shah Beg, who in a handsome Bakhshish in cash had found compensation for the revolver he had previously coveted as a "keepsake," I had the satisfaction of seeing my Indian mail arrive from Sarikol. It was a big one, and brought besides welcome letters and papers from home and India eagerly expected little parcels, the result of orders I had sent to Lahore six weeks before from Gilgit, after the first experience had shown me the *lacunæ* of my equipment.

While the baggage marched on to Bulunkul I took the opportunity of completing my photo-theodolite survey from an isolated hill rising due west of Karakul, and about 1,500 feet above it. The panoramic view I enjoyed from the height of Kok-tumshuk Hill was perfect. The lake at my feet glittered in the changing tints of emerald and chrysoprase. Just opposite on the eastern shore the telescope showed Ram Singh working from my former station on Karakir with the theodolite. To the north there lay peacefully the little tarns of Basikkul, deep green in colour, and in the soft clear light even the bleak old moraines around them, with their "cirques" and walls of rocky débris, looked less desolate and dreary. By 3 p.m. I had exposed the last plate and hurried down to where the limpid stream leaves Karakul. Then I marched along the eastern shore of the Lower Basikkul, and realised for the first time the charms of this pretty "eye of the sea" as it would be called in the Carpathians. Sleepy it looked on the quiet summer afternoon, and inviting for rustic repose the grassy strip on its eastern bank. But I had little time to spare for such pleasures, and soon had to tear myself away from this newly discovered attraction.

Beyond, vegetation soon diminished as I marched along the stony 'Dasht' that forms the bottom of the valley further down. The river, swelled by the great glacier stream known as Ekkibel-su, that joins it from the south-east, occupies a gradually broadening bed of rubble and boulders. I crossed it with some little difficulty about four miles below Karakul, its depth there reaching 4 to 5 feet. The rest of the march lay alternately over stony "alluvial fans" spreading in front of the glaciers which descend from the great icy range eastwards, and over narrow strips of rich meadow land fringing here and there the steeply-cut conglomerate banks. The flora seemed more or less the same as about Karakul, but the growth and the scent of the herbs growing in these sheltered nooks was stronger.

It was close on 8 p.m. when I reached my camp pitched near the Chinese post of Bulunkul on the swampy piece of meadow-land that fills a bend of the river. The military Amban of the place is supposed to watch the neighbouring passes which lead across to Rang-kul and adjoining parts of the Russian Pamirs. From the report brought to me he seemed little inclined to help me on my journey. Though he sent fuel and a sheep as a present, Osman Beg, the influential headman of the Kirghiz grazing in the neighbourhood, to whom I had been recommended from Tash-kurghan, found it advisable to pay his visit by stealth and under the cover of darkness. Next morning the attitude of the Amban made itself palpably felt. Karm Shah Beg's men, with their ponies, which had brought part of my baggage from Karakul, had disappeared during the night. To move on with the five Kashgar animals (the rest I had left for Ram Singh's camp) was manifestly impossible. From the Amban, to whom I sent, came nothing but a rude reply, leaving it to my own choice how I should make my way beyond. I thought of Dr. Sven Hedin, who had met with an even worse reception at Bulunkul, and consoled myself with the conjecture that possibly the climate of the place disagrees with the liver of successive Chinese commandants.

Fortunately the Amban's obstructiveness was purely passive. I found little difficulty in persuading his interpreter ('Tolmach') that it was to his material advantage to supply the needful animals. He took the hint, and by 11 a.m., by taking Dak ponies and pressing Kirghiz animals, the needed complement of my transport was made up. The pliable factotum of the Chinese "Warden of the Passes" was for a consideration found ready even to issue in his chief's name an order for the supply of other animals at the Karauls further down the valley. When my little caravan was fairly started I could not deny myself the satisfaction of returning to the Amban the sheep he had sent, as a present that was not acceptable. The Kirghiz, in whose presence I sent my message, were evidently much tickled by the announcement.

The weather had again become cloudy and cold, quite wintry in aspect. With the clouds covering the mountains almost to their foot the wide valley, through which the river beyond Bulunkul spreads in numerous broad branches, looked like a dreary steppe in the autumn. About five miles north of Bulunkul the expanse of muddy glacier water contracts and enters by a sudden bend to the east the long defile known as Gez-Darra. At its entrance we passed a lonely Karaul, square-walled and garrisoned by a dozen Chinese soldiers—scarcely tenable as a defensive work, even in the days of matchlocks. The rest of this day's march lay along the right bank. The gorge kept narrow, and the road almost throughout led over old moraines and stony "fans." By 6.30 p.m. we passed the first serious impasse of the gorge called Janguruk. Great serrated coulisses of rugged rock, several thousand feet in height, descend from the main mountain spurs on both sides. Along the face of one of them the road is carried by a gallery, a true 'Rafik' of Hunza recollection, only that the one here was well built and gave a roadway of at least four feet breadth. It was getting dark between the high mountain walls when this awkward part of the route had been passed. So we had to stop for the night's camp as soon as the necessary bit of level space could be found by the river side. Here amidst sombre Alpine scenery, with snowy heights gleaming up side gorges, I was to be reminded of the very different region that awaited me eastwards. Heavy yellowish clouds overspread the narrow bit of sky, visible between the mountains, and soon the tail end of a duststorm, wafted from the eastern plains swept up the valley. The night, too, was warm for this elevation.

On the morning of the 25th we had to cross to the left of the tossing river a little below the spot of our camp, known as Ilegorum. The river is compressed there by mighty rocks to a width of some 45 feet, and the chasm is spanned by a wooden bridge 6 feet broad, quite a creditable specimen, I thought, of Chinese engineering. The sides were protected by a substantial railing, and the whole painted bright yellow. The opposite bank for more than a mile further down was formed by a high and precipitous wall of rock wholly impassable to man or beast.

After some three miles we recrossed by a similar bridge to the right bank, and could have continued our march there with ease had it not been that the bridge across the swollen glacier-stream from a side-valley to the south had been washed away. The stream was wholly unfordable, and it was necessary to climb up for some three miles to the mouth of the huge Koksel glacier from which it issues. It was a trying detour, for the whole valley is blocked by enormous old terminal moraines. When at last the present end of the glacier was reached, it was with difficulty that we dragged up the ponies to the top of that mass of ice rising in a bank of at least 150 feet above the river. It was fortunately thickly coated with glacier mud and detritus, and in half-an-hour we had safely got the first pony across. From the eastern side moraine the glacier could be seen stretching away for miles up the valley to the slopes of high peaks which were enveloped in clouds. Subsequent surveying showed that the highest summit of this mountain mass is identical with the ice-clad Koksel or Sarguluk Peak (23,470 feet), which rises prominently at the salient angle of the great range north of Muztagh-Ata, and is visible even from Kashgar, in the form of a great truncated cone.

This detour had delayed us much, and it was getting late in the afternoon when the baggage arrived at the little Karaul of Gez, from which the valley takes its name. Fresh animals were to be taken here, but they were said not to have arrived as yet from their grazing-grounds. So we pitched camp among the fantastic conglomerate formations which line the river-bank. The evening brought a fresh duststorm, and notwithstanding the elevation—about 8,000 feet above the sea—it felt oppressively warm. On the morning of the 26th of July I awoke to hear the news that the promised ponies had not arrived, and that the men from Bulunkul together with their animals had decamped during the night. To make matters worse, the 'Karaulchis'—Kirghiz posted at the Karaul for carrying the Chinese Dak—had also for some unknown reason disappeared.

I did not appreciate the prospect of being detained indefinitely at so dreary and desolate a spot, and the hours of weary waiting sorely tried my patience. Amidst the sand and bare rocks the air grew almost hot as the day advanced. Satip Aldi, the Kirghiz I had engaged at Karakul, was despatched to the herdsmen high up the Koksel Valley, but I knew that assistance from that side could not come till nightfall. All the greater was the feeling of relief when by 2 p.m. a party of traders with four ponies came in sight, the first travellers we had met since leaving Karakul. With some persuasion and gentle pressure my men prevailed on the party to unload their animals and to help to take our baggage down to the next Karaul, Kaurük-Kurghan. Heavy loads had to be made up, and we all had to walk—no great sacrifice, for the ten miles down the valley proved exceptionally easy-going. The scenery became less sombre as the valley broadened, and after returning once more to the right bank at Kök-moinak, a picturesque little cross-spur, I was gratified by the first view of cultivated fields. The reception that met me at Kaurük-Kurghan was a cheerful contrast to our Gez experience. The Kirghiz Karaulchis, among them some picturesque old men in padded coats of wonderful hues, turned out for my reception in great style. All the ponies we required for the difficult marches of the next two days were supplied most readily, and the services of extra men offered to help the animals over the difficulties of the track. Kaurük-Kurghan proved a far cooler place than Gez. The evening, after a light shower from the east had sprinkled the ground, was delightful, and I felt refreshed by the scent of the thyme growing profusely about my camping-place.

The ordinary route to the plains below Kaurük-Kurghan runs along the bottom of the river gorge, but this is impassable during the summer months owing to the flood. Then communication can be maintained only by the circuitous track through the mountains, known characteristically as Tokuz-Dawan, "the Nine Passes." The first of these passes was up a steep spur a couple of miles below the Karaul. The hillsides were clothed with plenty of shrubs, and reminded me of the scenery I had seen in Buner and in Hazara, east of the Indus. On the top of the pass a pleasant surprise awaited me. Unexpectedly the path opened on a charming glen with trees and fertile patches of oat-fields. The height was over 9,000 feet. Kaurük-Bel looked a veritable oasis after the stony barrenness of the Gez defile, and might with some imagination be turned into a suitable site for a cosy "hill-station." Unfortunately the glen holds practically no water. For a couple of miles we descended it, and then turned up a narrow side gorge to the north-east.

The scenery had by this time changed considerably. All vegetation disappeared from the gravel-strewn bottom of the gorge, and the sides were formed by bare rocks of reddish-grey tint, worn into fantastic shapes by the influences of climatic extremes. At the bottom of the narrowing gorge, cut into the rock by the action of rain and melting snows, we wound our way onwards, often in the welcome coolness of overhanging cliffs. In a little cul-de-sac of rocks there was a tiny stream of cool water dripping over the stones and losing itself below in the fine sand. Not far from it the Ularlik Jilga contracts to a narrow fissure, some 8 to 10 feet across, closed in by unscalable crags. The large rocks which form the bottom are too steep to be climbed by laden animals. So all the baggage had to be taken off and carried by men for a short distance. Emerging from this gloomy fissure we had fresh trouble in pulling the ponies along a series of rocky ledges and up an exceptionally steep spur. At last the top of the second pass was reached, with a distant view to the snowy peaks south-west and a succession of bare serrated ridges in the foreground looking like lines of petrified waves. Far-advanced decomposition was plainly written on all features of the landscape. Winding round the highest ridges of some neighbouring peak, at an elevation of about 10,500 feet, we reached at last the head of the Khush-kishlak Valley, the only one in this maze of mountains which contains a permanent spring, and where a longer halt is practicable. Dreary and miserable the place looked, which we reached after a descent of some three miles between bare hillsides, apparently sandstone. But there was the spring, fresh and clear, and after the long, hot climb men and beasts were equally grateful for its blessing.

The march of the 28th of July was to bring me right down into the plains to the large oasis of Tashmalik at the entrance of the Gez defile. It was a double march, and we started early. A slight storm had cleared the air remarkably, and when the top of the next pass, the Aktiken-Bel, was reached in the fresh morning air I was surprised by a delightfully distant view. On the west it extended to the great icy peaks which lie between Muztagh-Ata and the Gez-Darra, most prominent among them the glittering cone of Sarguluk. To the east the plains could be seen far away to the green tracts under irrigation round Yangi-Hissar, Opal, and Tashmalik. A light haze of dust that hung over the plain on the pale-blue horizon was all that suggested to the mind the great desert beyond. Immediately before me was a maze of bare rocky ridges. The eye revelled in the bright and wonderfully varied tints which they exhibited. From bluish grey to terra-cotta every shade of colour glistened in the full sunlight. It was a view which will long live in my memory for its vastness and fascinating variety. For a couple of hours it remained before my eyes as I crossed in succession the Talantik, Sarvai-Bel, and Topalu-Bel Passes. The valleys between them were not deep, and progress was easy. Then at last there was a decided descent into the Kizil Jilga (" the Red Valley "), not inappropriately so-called from the reddish-brown hills that enclose it. A six miles' march in the dry bed of the stream that in the spring drains the nullah, brought us at last back again to the bank of the Gez River. It was flowing here over a bed of rubble nearly a mile broad, divided into numerous channels, but as rapid as above.

Only for one and a half miles was there a way along the river-bank. Then a precipitous spur of conglomerate, which is washed at its foot by the current of the river, intervenes, and we had to wend our way again into a tortuous gorge. It felt hot in its still air, though the thermometer in the shade showed only 83° F. At the end of the gorge there was an extremely steep ascent at an angle of over 30°, where the ponies even without their loads had difficulty to scramble up. After crossing this —the Shagildik Dawan—there was once more a descent to the main valley. But our way there was soon blocked by a fresh spur, and instead of emerging on the level plain for which, I confess, I was by this time longing, a last great detour into the wild barren waste of conglomerate hills had to be made. One after the other of the ponies that had come all the way from

Karakul broke down, and I was heartily glad that the forethought of our guides from Kaurük-Kurghan had provided spare animals to shift their loads on to. After a tiring ascent of close on 2,000 feet the Yamala or Kepek Pass, the last obstacle, was surmounted, and I hurried ahead of my caravan to reach Tashmalik if possible before dusk. The plain at the point where I

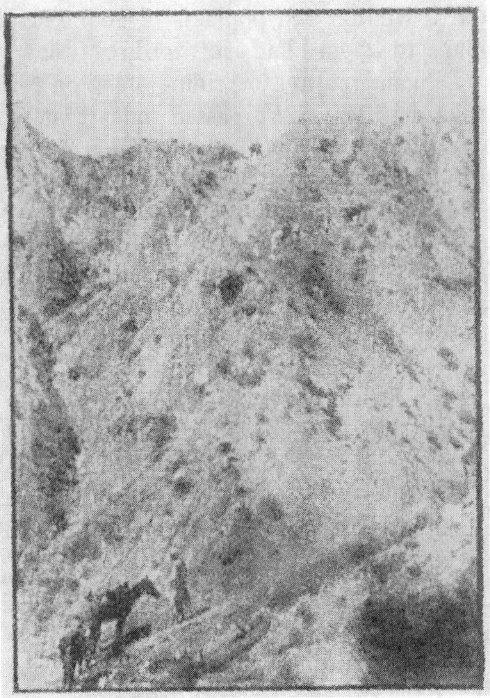

ASCENT OF SHAGILDIK DAWAN.

struck it at last by 6.30 p.m. was a stony waste, but pursuing my way by the side of the river I soon came to a canal and then to fertile irrigated lands. Men were still working in the fields and in all directions rills of water, betokening by its colour its glacier sources, were spreading fertility over the rich soil. It was a picture of life doubly impressive after the stony wilderness from which I had emerged.

It was getting dark when I arrived at the first houses of Tashmalik. Thus the oasis is called, and not "Tashbalik" or "Tashbulak," as, distorted by a sort of "popular etymology," its name appears in almost all maps and books except the records of the old Jesuit Surveyors of the eighteenth century. The mud-walls of the buildings and those enclosing many gardens looked quite imposing in the dim light. The roads were lined with willows and poplars. I enquired at first after the Beg's house, to whom I had sent word regarding fresh ponies. An elderly 'Dihkan' (cultivator) riding along on a lively donkey offered to take me there. We passed miles that seemed to me endless between fields and gardens and little groups of houses. Yet the Beg's place was ever ahead. I had forgotten that in Eastern Turkestan extensive groups of villages or hamlets, spreading over a wide area of cultivated ground, bear a common name, representing in reality that of a little district. When, tired out by a ride and walk of nearly fourteen hours, I arrived at the house, I found to my annoyance that the Beg was away in Kashgar and that whatever arrangements were possible would have to be made at the Karaul. It meant riding back in the darkness for over two miles. But at last I reached the place, though the pony stumbled and nearly broke down with weariness. The baggage, too, turned up at last, and my tent was pitched on a field close to racks of fresh-cut scented 'Beda,' a kind of lucerne. But it was long after ten o'clock before I managed to get a "wash" and close on midnight before I could sit down to a well-earned dinner.

On the 29th of July we were up as soon as the day broke. The vicinity of Kashgar was an irresistible attraction to hurry on, and though the available information allowed me to estimate the distance correctly at close on fifty miles, I was anxious to cover it that day. There was the usual difficulty of getting fresh ponies to replace those hired at Kaurük-Kurghan, whose owners naturally enough would not consent to their going on to Kashgar. But Alia Beg, the 'Dakchi' in charge of the Chinese post, proved more helpful than the Beg's people, and by six a.m. I could start with the most needful loads of baggage packed on a couple of post-horses. The rest of my camp was to follow as soon as the needed animals had been secured. I was glad to leave its encumbrances behind, for I knew that at the other end of my long march a hospitable roof was awaiting me. A greyish haze covered the sky and effaced all view of the higher hills to the west, but to the north I could dimly discern the low broad ridge which is fringed by the cultivated lands of Opal, our immediate goal.

To reach it we had to cross the river from Gez, the Yamanyar as it is here called, which, notwithstanding all the water drawn off for irrigation, still spreads in half-a-dozen broad branches over the plain. The water was 4–5 feet deep in most of them, and the flow so rapid that it required careful guiding of the animals by special men stationed to assist at the fords, to effect a safe passage. After an hour I reached the other side of the broad river-bed, wet above the knees but without damage to the baggage. Then followed a delightful ride through the green grazing land that stretches by the side of the river for several miles. A little Chinese garrison occupies a dilapidated post at the foot of the low plateau which bears the lands of Opal. Outside a circular Karaul we managed to obtain a change of ponies, but the gain in time it was intended to assure was more than compensated by the delay which ensued by a quarrel among the post-men. It was evidently the question who were to accompany me to Kashgar which excited the commotion. Ultimately I found the baggage subdivided into four small loads and a villager perched on the top of each laden animal. I acquiesced in an arrangement which seemed to solve the difficulty, and had no reason to regret it, for the little caravan moved gaily along and never stopped till I reached Kashgar.

Opal is a conglomeration of numerous hamlets spread between fields and irrigated meadows. To ride along its lanes shaded by willows and poplars was a delightful change after the dreary wilderness of stone and sand we had lately passed through. In the fields the melons were ripening, and richly cultivated gardens displayed a profusion of vegetables. Everywhere was the welcome presence of water, irrigation cuts of all sizes following and intersecting the roads. The quantity of reddish mud deposited by these little streams was a notable feature. By the side of one

I made a brief halt to refresh myself with a modest "Tiffin" carried in a saddle-bag and some apples and plums I had bought from a wayside stall. It was the first fruit I had tasted for months.

After an hour and a half we had passed through the whole breadth of the oasis of Opal. On the stretch of sterile sandy plain to be crossed eastwards I gathered my first impressions of the Turkestan desert. Here its look of barren desolation was mitigated by tamarisks and other low scrub growing profusely along the now dry ravines that intersect it. To my surprise the temperature kept comparatively cool even after midday; 93° F. in the sun, with a refreshing breeze from the east, was nothing to complain of. But the glare was trying and soon forced me to protect my eyes with goggles of neutral-coloured glass. As we passed one low sandy dune after the other the pony-men struck up singing, and their tunes, surprisingly melodious, brought life and a feeling of cheeriness into the solitude. By 3 p.m. we left the desert track behind and emerged on the edge of the cultivated lands of Tokuzak. Here by the side of the little Sarai of Saibagh several parties of travellers, with ponies and rude carts, were resting in the shade of a small poplar grove. Water kept ready in big jars and a stock of melons were the refreshments provided at this Turkestan edition of a roadside inn.

The hours of a pleasant ride which followed will long keep fresh in my memory. Hamlet after hamlet was passed, ensconced among green avenues of poplars, mulberry, apricot, and other fruit trees. The mud walls of the houses with their bright yellow and brown looked singularly neat in this setting of gardens and orchards. Here and there a cemetery with tombs of sun-dried bricks and a crumbling mosque or Ziarat built of the same material added a picturesque touch to the rural landscape. The high-pitched songs of my pony-men as we moved at a rapid amble through the lanes always brought the children and women before the doors of their homesteads. The men were busy in the fields, and until we got to the Bazar of Tokuzak I saw scarcely any grown-up person that was not occupied in some way. We had so far suffered little from the dust, for the route we had followed was not the high-road from Tashmalik, but a more circuitous track connecting hamlet with hamlet. But at last we emerged on the road and found it as dusty as it was broad. High lumbering carts or 'Arabas' dragged along by little ponies and droves of donkeys kept up a continuous cloud. I was getting eager to reach the end of the journey and too readily gave credence to Sadak Akhun, who about 5 p.m. assured me that Kashgar was now within one 'Tash's' distance. I had not yet learned that, away from the main caravan roads where the Chinese administration has marked

ROAD TO MR. MACARTNEY'S HOUSE, WITH CITY WALL.

the distances of ten 'Li' (approximately two miles) by small mud-built towers popularly known as 'Tash' (stone), this measure in Turkestan conveys only the vaguest estimate of distance.

It was disappointing when after an hour's ride there was still no sign of the river-bed which I knew we should have to cross before approaching the town. At last at a turn of the road a broad nullah came in sight, with a shallow stream. But beyond it no trace of walls, Minars or other tokens of an Eastern city. The river was not the Kizil-su which flows past Kashgar, but only a branch of it known as Ak-su (" White Stream "), or

Telwichuk. Another three miles or so of endless rice fields seemed a long distance in the failing light and on the tired ponies. But at last they too came to an end, and we forded the truly red water of the Kizil-su (" Red Stream "). Beyond it we wound along dusty suburban lanes where the women with quaint caps of imposing height sat in groups enjoying a chat in the twilight.

It was almost dark when the walls of the city suddenly rose before me. Mud-built as they are, they looked massive and imposing, while the quaint regularity of their battlements and square bastions vividly reminded me of many a picture of mediæval towns seen in old books of travel. Outside the city walls all was quiet and dark. The gates were already closed. At last Sadak Akhun struck off to the left, along a short, poplar-lined avenue, and the light of a lantern showed me the outer gate of Mr. Macartney's residence that was to offer me a home for the next few weeks. Belated as I was, my arrival was not unexpected, and as I descended from the spacious court to the terraced garden I found myself welcomed in the heartiest fashion by Mr. and Mrs. Macartney. Comfortable quarters adjoining the garden were awaiting me, and when after a needful change I joined my hosts in their dining-room, there was every little luxury to favour the illusion that I was in an English home far away from the Heart of Asia.

CHAPTER VIII.

STAY AT KASHGAR.

THE cheerful impressions of that first evening under Mr. Macartney's hospitable roof were a true indication of the happy circumstances under which the busy weeks of my stay at Kashgar were to pass. Busy, indeed, they were bound to be; for numerous and urgent tasks had to be completed before I could set out from the capital of Chinese Turkestan for the proper goal of my explorations. For almost every one of these tasks I stood in need of Mr. Macartney's experience and active help. But great as the facilities were which his official position and local knowledge assured to me, I could scarcely have availed myself of them with full advantage, had not his friendly care surrounded me from the first with all personal comfort and encouragement. After two months of almost incessant mountain travel I felt the need of some bodily rest. Nowhere could I have combined it more pleasantly with active preparations for the long journey before me than in the charming residence to which my kind Kashgar friends welcomed me.

Chini-Bagh had been a simple walled-in orchard with a little garden house, such as every respectable Kashgari loves to own outside the city walls, when Mr. Macartney, more than ten years before my visit, took up the appointment of the Indian Government's Political Representative at Kashgar. Continuous improvements effected with much ingenuity and trouble had gradully changed this tumbledown mud-built garden house into a residence which in its cosy, well-furnished rooms now offered all the comforts of an English home, and in its spacious out-houses and "compound" all the advantages of an Indian bungalow. Built on the very brink of a high loess bank overlooking the broad bed of the Tümen-Darya, the house and the adjoining terraces command a delightfully open view over the fertile belt of village land and gardens which skirt the city to the north. Even through the light dust haze which is so common a feature of a Turkestan summer day, the picturesque outlines of the low hill-range beyond gave a setting to the scene. On repeated occasions when rain had cleared the atmosphere, I enjoyed distinct views of the great ice-crowned range north and north-east of Muztagh-Ata, and also of distant snowy peaks belonging to the Thian-shan mountains.

After the fatigues and daily "rush" of the preceding two months of rapid marching, it was a delightful change to the well-ordered surroundings of my friends' home. Free for a time from the petty cares of camp life, I could enjoy in their genial company all that makes the contact with European ways of life and thought attractive. Yet I felt as safe as before from the bustle and outside interference which seem so difficult to evade during an ordinary European existence. There was ample reason to feel grateful for the peace and leisure thus assured to me; for I needed them badly for the manifold labours that now claimed my attention.

Foremost among them was the organisation of the fresh caravan which was required for my onward journey, and the explorations in the desert. I realised that my chances of success in covering within the limited period allowed the whole of the wide area I desired to visit, depended largely on the careful selection of the men and animals that were to make up my party. It was essential to limit the baggage with a view to rapidity of movement, and at the same time to ensure that all stores and equipment required for travels likely to spread over eight months, and under widely varying conditions of ground and climate, should be kept within easy reach. I found that, including riding animals, eight camels and twelve ponies would be needed for my caravan. The season was not favourable for the purchase of camels, for most of the caravan animals were away engaged on the brisk summer traffic towards the Russian trade-centres of Andijan and Almati. But after lengthy trials and negotiations, in the course of which the local experience and help of Munshi Bahadur Shah and other members of Mr. Macartney's establishment proved of great advantage, the necessary complement of transport and riding animals was gradually secured. The trouble taken about their selection was, as subsequent experience showed, fully rewarded by the result. For notwithstanding the fatigues and hardships implied by travels which covered an aggregate of more than 3,000 miles, none of the animals I brought from Kashgar ever broke down. The average price paid for the camels amounted to 624 Tangas per animal, representing approximately Rs. 91, at the then current rate of exchange. The cost of the ponies varied considerably, an average of 260 Tangas, or 38 rupees, being paid for each of a serviceable lot of baggage animals.

In regard to the personnel, too, of my caravan, it was necessary to exercise careful selection, in order to keep the number of followers down to the minimum indicated by considerations for economy and for facility of supply arrangements. For Mirza Alim, my personal servant from Peshawar, who had proved not quite equal to the fatigues of rough and rapid marching in the mountains, I found a very useful substitute in Muhammad-Ju, a hardy 'Kirakash' of half Yarkandi, half Kashmiri extraction, who from long trading experience on the Karakorum route had acquired much useful knowledge about ponies. Having served Captain Deasy on his return journey to India, he had also learned the indispensable rudiments of the art of looking after a "Sahib's" kit and of serving at table

Niaz Akhun, a Chinese-speaking native of Kashgar,. whom, after several unsuccessful experiments with other individuals, I managed with Mr. Macartney's help to secure for the combined duties of 'Tungchi' (Chinese interpreter) and pony attendant, was outwardly a person of more imposing appearance and of manners to match. He had accompanied Mr. and Mrs. Littledale on their great journey through Tibet and

China, and not unnaturally assumed an air of superiority towards the rest of my Turki followers who had not seen 'Bajin' (Peking) and the other wonders of Cathay. It is only fair to record that they were ever ready to retaliate by artfully conveyed doubts whether he was truly to be reckoned among faithful followers of Islam or not rather among his much-extolled paragons, the heathen Chinese. His relative intelligence made him useful for his particular function, and as an interpreter he served me honestly. Perhaps it was just as well that during the weeks of our stay in the well-ordered surroundings of Chini-Bagh he had no opportunity to display before me those little personal failings, such as his inordinate addiction to opium and gambling, and his strong inclination to qualified looting, which subsequently caused occasional trouble. Two young 'Tugachis,' or camel-men, were engaged with less difficulty through the traders who had sold me the camels. Neither Roza Akhun nor Hassan Akhun had seen much of the world beyond the caravan routes northward. But young as they were they well knew the difficult art of camel management, and prompted perhaps by youthful curiosity and love of adventure, proved readier to face the hardships and supposed risks of desert journeys than their elders. It mattered little that they made up for their cheerfulness and steady conduct on the march through the sand-wastes by an irrepressibly pugnacious disposition whenever the varied temptations of a Bazar were near.

The numerous repairs and additions the camp outfit needed were also among the practical preparations demanding early attention. Saddlery, mule trunks, 'Kiltas' and most other articles of equipment bore marks of the rough wear to which they had been subjected on the long journey from Kashmir. Ever since we emerged from the gorges of Hunza, yaks and Kirghiz ponies seemed to have vied with each other in doing damage by knocking and rubbing their loads against every rock passed on the mountain tracks. The stay at Kashgar seemed none too long for effecting the needful repairs, for the Turkestan artisan has none of the imitative skill of the average Indian craftsman; and finding it apparently easy to make a living, he takes little trouble to accommodate himself to the requirements of the passing European traveller. In view of such leisurely habits of work and the need of constant supervision, I soon ceased to be surprised at seeing Mr. Maçartney's outer courtyard more or less permanently occupied by the few 'Ustads' (masters) who cared to attend to my orders.

The most troublesome operation of all proved to be the preparation of the additional water-tanks which I decided to get made for use in the desert. The pair of galvanised iron tanks which had been specially constructed for me at Calcutta had been safely transported across the mountains. But the total quantity of water which with due regard to the carrying capacity of camels they had been designed to hold, amounted only to seventeen gallons a-piece. The supply of water thus assured would have been, of course, wholly inadequate for the needs of a party such as I proposed to take to sand-buried sites in the desert, and the construction of at least four more tanks proved indispensable. It was found that the only material locally available for this purpose consisted of iron tanks in which kerosene oil is transported into Turkestan from the Transcaspian railway. The adaptation and strengthening of these much-battered "tins," together with the making of the wooden covers needed for their safe transport, was a task that taxed the combined resources of my blacksmith 'Ustads' for weeks.

But luckily the necessity of attending to all these practical arrangements did not prevent me from finding time also for more congenial and equally pressing tasks. Sitting in the cool shade of the poplar groves of Mr. Macartney's garden, I spent long and pleasant hours, refreshing by systematic study my knowledge of the ancient accounts of Eastern Turkestan, such as the Chinese historical Annals, the narratives of old Chinese pilgrims and of the earliest European travellers, have preserved for us. To me it is always a source of pleasure to be able to read such old records on the very soil to which they refer. At Chini-Bagh I enjoyed exceptional advantages for this favourite occupation; for Mr. Macartney, whom long residence and the power of keen observation have made thoroughly conversant with the economic and social conditions of modern Turkestan, was ever ready to allow me to ransack the storehouse of his knowledge for that information without which the ancient accounts of the country cannot be properly understood. Often when matters of Chinese lore were concerned Mr. Macartney would summon to our discussion Sun-Ssu-yieh, the "Chinese Munshi" of the Agency, a literatus thoroughly versed in his classics, and yet keenly alive to the things of this world. As I listened to his vivacious explanations, which Mr. Macartney kindly interpreted, I could not help thinking of my dear old Kashmirian Pandit Govind Kaul, and the converse I used to hold with him in Sanskrit during the long years of common scholarly labour. Bitterly I regretted the great gap in my philological equipment, my ignorance of Chinese. But how should I ever find the leisure to fill it, except perhaps in that "fresh birth" to which, in accordance with the Indian notion, I used to refer my Chinese friends?

It was an important object of my stay at Kashgar to familiarise the officials of the Chinese provincial Government with the purpose of my intended explorations and to secure their goodwill, which I realised would be an indispensable condition for the practical execution of my plans. In this direction too I could not have wished for more effective help than that which Mr. Macartney accorded to me. Already the initial visits which I was able to pay in his company to the Tao-tai, or Provincial Governor, and the other chief dignitaries were under such expert guidance most instructive to me and full of interest. In the course of these visits, followed as they were by "return calls" and other less formal interviews, I was introduced to at least a rudimentary knowledge of the "form" and manners which Chinese etiquette considers essential for polite intercourse. It was no small advantage to receive this instruction through a mentor so familiar with all Chinese notions and ways as Mr. Macartney. Every little act and formality, quaint and strangely contrary to our habits as it often seemed, thus acquired its due significance, until in the end when visiting strange 'Yamens' far away from my

Kashgar friends, I found a comforting assurance in the rigid uniformity of these observances.

It was essential to secure from the Tao-tai the issue of clear instructions to the Amban of Khotan which were likely to assure me all needful assistance in regard to transport, supplies, and labour, as well as full freedom for my movements. In view of the serious difficulties which through a sort of demi-official obstruction Captain Deasy had experienced in the same region only eighteen months earlier, it seemed doubtful at first whether the way would be effectively cleared for my operations, particularly so far as they related to survey work south of Khotan. That the efforts which Mr. Macartney undertook on my behalf proved in the end entirely successful was due largely, I believe, to the personal influence and respect he enjoys among all Chinese officials of rank in the Province. After a series of interviews and a lengthy correspondence the Tao-tai agreed to issue the desired instructions. The result showed that he faithfully carried out his promise, and that Mr. Macartney's representations, coupled with what explanations I could give through him of the historical connection of ancient Indian culture and Buddhist religion with Central Asia, had effectually dispelled any suspicions which might otherwise have been roused by the intended excavations and surveys.

In the course of these interviews my references to the 'Si-yu-ki,' the records of Hiuen-Tsiang's travels, proved singularly helpful. All educated Chinese officials seem to have read or heard legendary accounts of the famous Chinese pilgrim's visit to the Buddhist kingdoms of the "Western countries." In my intercourse with them I never appealed in vain to the memory of the "great monk of the Tang dynasty" (Tang-Seng). Endeavouring as I now was to trace his footsteps through Turkestan as I had done before in more than one part of India, I might well claim that saintly traveller as my special patron in the heaven of Arhats.

Strange enough it seemed to me at the time, this pleasant intercourse with the friendly old Tao-tai, his colleague, the "Hsieh-tai" or General, and the rest of the local Mandarins, when I thought of the great political upheaval far away in the east of the empire. Through the Reuter telegrams transmitted from Gilgit and the news indirectly conveyed to us from Russian sources we knew of the fierce fighting around the legations and the danger surrounding European settlements elsewhere in China. Through the telegraph line from Urumchi to Kashgar the Chinese officials too were receiving accounts of the great conflagration, and apparently fairly correct ones. For while Europe was held in horrified suspense by the false news of a general massacre at Peking, the reports communicated to us from the Yamen, though admitting much fighting, stoutly maintained that the legations kept up their defence and were safe.

Disturbing rumours about the conflict with the European Powers had already in July spread through the Bazars of Kashgar, and just a week before my arrival a feeling of mutual apprehension and distrust threatened for a moment to bring about a collision between the Muhammadan population and the Chinese garrison quartered in the Yangi-Shahr, or "New City." The commotion luckily died away when it was found that the Chinese Commander-in-Chief, whose visit to the "Old City" with an unusual escort had given rise to alarm, had only come to play a harmless game of cards at the Hsieh-tai's Yamen! The recollections of the last great rebellion against Chinese rule (1863–77) have, indeed, not disappeared from the "New Dominions"; but the peaceful cultivators of the oases and the easily cowed petty traders and artisans of the towns have little reason to wish back the times when the turbulent 'Andijanis' carried on their exactions in the name of Islam.

Kashgar, since the days of Sir Douglas Forsyth's mission, has so frequently received the visits of European travellers that I may be excused from attempting within the limited space of this narrative to describe the general features and life of the city. Most of my time was spent in busy work at Chini-Bagh; and to the little oasis of Anglo-Indian civilization which my kind hosts had created around themselves cling my main recollections of Kashgar. There was little contact with the outer world to vary the pleasant round of our daily life. Though the worst of the summer heat of the Turkestan plains had passed, it was still warm enough during the middle part of the day to make the freshness of the morning particularly attractive for work. So I was regularly astir with the break of day, and 6 a.m. found me established beside my books and papers under the tall poplars of the terraced garden.

The fruit season had fully begun. The closely planted apricot-, peach-,. and plum-trees of the orchard occupying the upper terrace were already bending low under an abundance of luscious fruit; while a little later a fine bower of vines supplied an equally welcome complement to my "Chota Hazri." As I sat at work I could see and hear the little cavalcades of cultivators and their women-folk as they gaily rode along the road between the river and the garden, bringing their produce to the city markets. Only beggars seemed to walk on foot, and even they were often provided with donkeys. Breakfast assembled us as the morning wore on, in a stately little arbour, where rows of tall poplars planted in a square, after the fashion of all Turkestan gardens, gave grateful shade at almost all hours. There were luckily no morning papers and daily mails to delay attention to the work of the 'Ustads,' who had in the meantime leisurely settled down to their several tasks. A short stroll taken round the courtyards after breakfast, usually in Mr. Macartney's company, enabled me to control the progress—or otherwise—that their labours of repair or construction were making.

Then my friend retired to his 'Daftar' to write his reports or to go into the cases of his polyglot *clientèle* from across the Indian borders. Punjabi traders, Hindu money-lenders from Shikarpur, Ladaki carriers, Kanjuti settlers in Raskam, and *hoc genus omne*—all had occasion at one time or other to seek the presence of the 'Mulki Sahib' (Political Officer) whom the 'Sirkar's' paternal care had planted far away in the Turkestan capital to protect their persons and interests. I myself, though plentifully provided with writing work, ordinarily managed to give an hour or two about midday to the study of Turki texts with grave Mullah Abdul Kasim, a shining academical light of the chief Madrasah of Kashgar. Muhammadan learning, such as the country knows in these days of infidel rule, is purely theological. I have no doubt that the good Mullah would have preferred a discussion on a knotty passage of some Arabic manual of religious law to our reading of vulgar Turki, even though they concerned the exploits of that royal champion and martyr of Islam, holy Satok Boghra Khan. The hottest hours of the day, in the early afternoon, usually found me in the dark-room I had improvised in the Hospital Assistant's empty quarters, busy with the developing of the many photographs I had taken on the preceding part of the journey. Later on, after tea-time, a walk with my hosts along the shady village lanes, or frequently a ride on my newly-bought Andijani mare would bring welcome recreation. But perhaps the pleasantest hours were those when after dinner we would sit in the mild evening air on the flat roof of my quarters adjoining the main house. From there we could watch the frequent picnic parties of Kashgar families which had gone out early in the day to feast on the profusion of fruit in the orchards owned by almost all respectable citizens in the environs, and which were now gaily returning in long cavalcades of men, women and children. Their songs sounded to me very melodious, often strangely reminding me of airs I had heard long ago on road and river in Hungary.

As if to remind us of the West, which seemed so distant, there reached us at times as we sat in the evenings snatches of Russian airs wafted across by a breeze from the grounds of the Russian Consulate, half a mile away, while the men of the Cossack guard were singing in chorus. Frequently we saw the men on our rides in and about the city, but no opportunity offered for making the acquaintance of their 'Sahibs,' as we should say in India. M. Petrovsky, the Imperial Consul-General of Russia at Kashgar, to whom, in view of his scholarly interest in the ancient history and ethnography of these regions and his activity as a collector of Central-Asian antiquities, I was particularly anxious to pay my respects, was indisposed and could not receive me. It was not until my return from Khotan, nine months later, that I had the satisfaction of making the acquaintance of this accomplished official.

Apart from the small Russian colony gathered at the Consulate, Father Hendricks and a Swedish missionary, Mr. G. Raquette, with his wife, were then the only Europeans at Kashgar, and them we saw often. Father Hendricks, whom Catholic mission labours had brought many years ago from Holland, his native land, to Mongolia and hence to Kashgar, seemed to exemplify in his person the principles of international amity by being an equally frequent and entertaining visitor at Chini-Bagh, the Russian Consulate, the Swedish Mission, and the Chinese Yamens. The visits of the kindly Abbé, always bringing a plentiful budget of news and rumours, impartially gathered from these often conflicting sources of information, might have gone a long way to console any one likely to regret the absence of a local newspaper.

I can only briefly mention the remains of ancient structures which were the object of my first short excursions in the vicinity. Considering that the site of Kashgar in all probability corresponds to that of the capital of the ancient territory of 'Kie-sha,' which Hiuen-Tsiang describes as possessing hundreds of Buddhist monasteries, the remains of the pre-Muhammadan period still traceable above ground are scanty indeed. The most conspicuous is a much-decayed mound of sun-dried brick masonry rising over the deep-cut northern bank of the Tümen-Darya, about a mile and a half to the north-west of Chini-Bagh, which undoubtedly represents the remains of a large Stupa. The present height of the mound is 85 feet, and the diameter of its base from east to west about 160 feet. But notwithstanding the exact survey made I found it impossible to ascertain the original form of the whole Stupa, or even to fix its centre, to such an extent have the masses of soft brick-work fallen or crumbled away. It was for me an instructive observation to find that fully 15 feet of the masonry base now lie below the level of the irrigated fields close by. I had here the first indication of that remarkable rise in the general ground level, mainly through silt deposit, which my subsequent observations on the site of the ancient capital of Khotan clearly demonstrated. Of a similar though smaller Stupa mound, a mile and a half to the south of the city, no details need be given here. Nor is it possible to find space for descriptions of more modern places of interest which I visited in the environs. But I may, perhaps, make an exception in the case of my visit to the "New City," the Chinese cantonment of Kashgar, of which I here give my impressions such as my diary records them.

Mr. Macartney wished to return the call of the Chu-kuan's or City Prefect's chief assistant, and I myself wanted to profit by the occasion to do some "shopping" in things Chinese. The day was gloriously clear and yet comparatively cool. So our ride of some eight miles along the broad, well-shaded road which connects the two cities, was enjoyable even though the sun still stood high. The branch of the Kizil-su, which is crossed about midway, was full of reddish-brown water, a sign that the heavy rain of a few days before had left its mark in the mountains. Close to the north-west corner of the "New City," and not far to the left of the road, rises a stately complex of buildings, the Chinese temple consecrated to the memory of Liu-Kin-tang, the great general who, after Yaqub Beg's death in 1877, reconquered Turkestan. To this we rode first.

The temple stands in the midst of a large and well-kept arbour of poplars, and already its outer court showed, by its clean appearance and the evident care bestowed on repairs, that the means are not wanting to maintain worthily the memory of this modern hero of Chinese power in the "New Dominions." This is fully accounted for by the fact that ever since the reconquest the general's relatives have exercised a preferential claim to all the best appointments in the Province. Through a high gateway decorated with wonderful stucco volutes we entered the second court. Adjoining the gateway and facing towards the innermost court, is a fine wooden stage raised some eight feet above the ground. As we ascended it we noticed with amusement that the walls of what may be called a sort of greenroom, bore cleverly executed drawings in charcoal of Europeans.

The temple itself, approached through a third colonnaded court, is an imposing hall, lavishly decorated outside with boards blazing forth auspicious inscriptions in scarlet and gold. But it is in the inside of the hall that we had occasion to admire the generosity and good sense of those who raised this monument. The whole of the side walls, right and left, are covered with series of large paintings representing in sequence the victorious career as well as the administrative activity and private life of Liu-Kin-tang. There are quaint but graphic pictures of the battles and sieges by which he reduced the rebellious province. The characteristic features of the Andijanis who played the leading part in the revolt, and of the dark-skinned Tartar people of Urumchi and other centres to the east, are reproduced with striking fidelity. We see the general sitting in court, punishing malefactors, and in all the chief functions of a provincial governor. Other pictures show him returning to his ancestral home, his meeting with his aged mother, &c. It is a remarkable cycle of illustrations of a great career, and when properly reproduced, it would be no mean acquisition for an Ethnographic Museum in Europe. The richly gilt altar or central fane contains curiously enough a very Western souvenir of the Chinese general, his portrait in the form of a photograph enlarged to life size.

I could find no representation of any Chinese deity sharing the honours of the place with the departed hero. But on the parts of the main wall not occupied by the altar, two large representations of mythological animals attracted attention. To the right is a remarkably spirited picture of a storm-producing dragon, drawn with a verve and power of imagination which betoken no mean artist. As I looked at the wonderful masses of cloud propelled by the dragon's blast, I thought of old Hiuen-Tsiang's account of the fearful 'Nagas' which guard the Pamir heights with their winds and icy showers. Chinese eyes seem still to see the powers of nature as they saw them then. The royal tiger drawn on the opposite side of the wall is no match for this noble dragon, and bears in his half-human face an expression of such utter dejection that we were unable to withhold our mirth. I wondered whether it was the intention of the artist to show the noble beast in a mood of hopeless resignation at its own wickedness.

The attending priest who greeted "Ma-shao-yieh," as Mr. Macartney is called in Chinese, with unfeigned reverence, seemed a shy and modest specimen of his class. His ways and dress reminded me of a Lama, freshly emerged from some forlorn little monastery. He talked glibly enough of the benefits which the temple enjoys owing to the generosity of the high officials of the province, who look to Liu-Kin-tang as a patron saint watching over their interests. But when it came to being photographed—an operation to which the average Chinaman in these parts submits with relish—he grew hopelessly nervous and looked as if he were preparing himself for the worst. The operation passed off all the same, and a good douceur revived the spirits of this humble devotee.

PRIEST IN LIU-KIN-TANG'S SHRINE.

The little suburb, through which we had to ride on our way to the north gate of the Yangi-Shahr, presented a markedly Chinese appearance. There were groups of Chinese soldiers everywhere with the strangely mixed womenfolk they take unto themselves in these foreign parts. The petty traders are also largely Chinese, and the contents of their booths showed that they cater for Chinese tastes.

I saw, in fact, the Chinese counterpart of the Bazar of an Indian cantonment, only with that easy disregard for order and appearances which the difference of European and Chinese notions justifies. Mutatis mutandis, the soldiers' marketing place outside a Roman Castrum planted somewhere in the East might have offered a spectacle not unlike this.

This suggestion of a Castrum was curiously maintained by the broad street we entered on passing the gate. It contains the main Bazar of the cantonment besides various public buildings, and bisects the whole "New City" from north to south. The Chinese shops are more numerous here than in the "Old City," and owing, perhaps, to the ampler light, looked neater and more inviting. I do not like "shopping" as an

IN THE BAZAR OF THE "NEW CITY, KASHGAR."

occupation. But there was so much of quaint wares in the way of dress, household utensils, &c., to be examined that the time spent in looking for suitable presents to be sent homewards, such as silks, &c., seemed all too short.

It struck me as an intelligent application to modern conditions that among the neatly-docketed files of correspondence which one of the merchants showed us in the pigeon-holes of his snug office, there were letters sent to him by business friends in Ho-nan through Shanghai and the Indian Post Office. The addresses on the envelopes, neatly printed in English, gave the directions as to the route viâ Colombo-Rawalpindi-Gilgit and the numerous "c o's" needed for safe transit with far greater clearness and accuracy than one is accustomed to look for in the case of native Indian correspondents.

Passing on from the shops we paid the intended visit to Mr. Macartney's Chinese friend, Liu-Lai-chin, who owns a modest but clean and well-arranged house close to the City

MY SERVANTS FROM KASHGAR AND YARKAND.

Prefect's Yamen. Our host, apart from his official work, has no mean reputation as an artist, and I had already had occasion to admire the charmingly decorated fan which he had painted as a present for Mrs. Macartney. Sitting in the well-lit and large room which served as office, studio, and drawing-room, it was a pleasure to examine the delicately worked scrolls and paintings with which the artist-official had adorned his walls. Even more, perhaps, I enjoyed watching his eager and animated conversation with Mr. Macartney. It turned in part on antiquarian questions which my references to Hiuen-Tsiang's account of the "New Dominions" had raised. Though only small portions of the discourse could be made intelligible to me through Mr. Macartney's kindness, it was impossible to mistake in his friend's remarks the spirit of true historical interest, that connecting link of Chinese and Western thought. I shall ever retain the pleasantest recollection of the air of culture and refinement which seemed to fill this quiet household.

CARAVAN STARTING FROM KASHGAR.

CHAPTER IX.

KHANUI AND ORDAM-PADSHAH.

On the morning of the 4th of September, I was ready to take the field again. The five weeks of refreshing rest at Kashgar had passed so fast that there seemed at the end scarcely time enough for the completion of the multifarious preparations that my journey eastwards demanded. My start for Khanui, where ancient remains had been reported, was a move of distinct practical utility. It gave me an opportunity for a kind of experimental mobilisation of my caravan. As the site to be examined lay only one long march to the north-east of Kashgar, and as I should have to return to the latter place before proceeding on the journey to Khotan, it was easy to discover and remedy in time any deficiencies which in the hurry of the preparations had been overlooked. On the other hand, it meant a definite start, and duly impressed all 'Ustads' with the necessity of completing their tasks.

My amiable hosts had made light of my announcement that the morning of the 4th of September would see my caravan on the march and their compound clear of the motley accession of servants and followers I had brought there. They had seen several visitors start with a delay of half a day or more, such as illustrates the delightful dilatoriness of Central-Asian travel, and were no doubt prompted in their sceptical predictions also by the wish to extend their kind hospitality yet a little longer. I was, therefore, not a little pleased to find that men, camels, and ponies all fell into their places without much trouble in the early morning. A preliminary weighing of all baggage allowed its quick arrangement and loading. The 'Ustads' had managed to finish their labours late on the preceding evening. No time was taken up with the men's leavetaking—it could be left for the final move—and thus the caravan, to my friends' surprise, was ready to start when I joined them at breakfast.

The camels seemed anxious to emphasise their exemplary punctuality. For loaded as they were, they started off, nobody quite knew by whose order, before breakfast was finished and my hosts prepared to take their intended photograph of my caravan. They had not got far, however, and were promptly brought back to figure in front of my friend's newly arrived camera. The Begs, whom the City Prefect or Hsien-kuan of Kashgar had sent to escort me, were also in attendance, and gave in their Chinese get-up an additional element of picturesqueness to the scene.

When the procession of trimly packed camels with their little escort of mounted Begs and servants had passed on for a couple of miles, I left the hospitable roof of Chini-Bagh, glad at heart that it was not yet a real good-bye to the friends who had treated me with such kindness. My way lay past the Yarbagh Gate of the city and along the foot of its northern walls. Then the river had to be crossed by the bridge of Tarbugaz, with its picturesque little Minars at either end. It was no market day, yet the stream of mounted peasants, droves of loaded donkeys and ponies that passed through the adjoining Bazars, might elsewhere have suggested a great fair. Where the road, flanked by cemeteries, turns off to Hazrat Apak's shrine, the true Via Appia of Kashgar, I overtook the camels, and then rode on between suburban gardens and through shaded

BEGS AND AKSAKAL OF BESHKARIM.

village lanes northwards to Beshkarim. This large collection of hamlets which lies on the caravan route towards the distant Narym and which has since terribly suffered in the great earthquake of 1902, was reached about midday.

In the central village, known as Beshkarim Bazar, a grand

reception awaited me. There was the Beg of the little district, a cheerful Kashgari dressed in orthodox Chinese fashion, ready to welcome me, and on the terrace of his 'Yamen,' under shady elms, a plentiful 'Dastarkhan' of fruit, tea, and sweetmeats. It was a pleasure to sit down in the airy verandah and to partake of the delicious fruit then abounding all over the country. For my companions and servants there was no lack of more substantial refreshments in the form of soups, large plates of mutton, and mountains of flat cakes. The broad market-place in front was filled with men and ponies, each village headman summoned for the occasion having evidently brought a little troop of mounted followers. To walk on foot is an exertion left in these parts only to the poorest.

At Beshkarim Bazar nearly an hour passed, there being no need to hurry on in the heat of the sun before the baggage turned up. Then we mounted and with a following swelled by the local Beg's people and the headmen under him, pursued our eastward way. For some eight miles the road wound through highly cultivated strips, along irrigation canals of varying size, all fringed with rows of poplars and willows. Towards three, we emerged on less fertile ground, and I was expecting to get near the edge of the cultivated area when there rose before me a grove of magnificent old poplars. It was the arbour enclosing the shrine of Bu (Bibi) Mairyam Khanum, the saintly wife of Satok Boghra Khan, the popular hero of Muhammadan local tradition. Entering the courtyard through a small gate in the high mud wall enclosure, I found a delightfully shady quadrangle of old poplars, and in its centre under a grand elm tree a fresh collation. I was not prepared like my better-trained followers to attack large heaps of melons and other fruit after so short an interval. So I strolled away into the inner part of the garden, where there were cool, shady walks between roomy tanks of water, and a fine wood-built prayer-hall. In smaller buildings half-hidden behind the trees and intended for the accommodation of pilgrims, I could hear voices reading chapters of the Koran. But it was no time for popular pilgrimages, and the inmates were only a few itinerant mendicants and 'Talib-ilms' or theological students.

Beyond the garden stretched barren, sun-baked ground, filled with graves and tombs in all stages of decay. In its centre rises the simple but massive cupola which covers the resting-place of the holy Mairyam (Miriam). Yaqub Beg, or Bedaulât as he is popularly known, had raised it with hard-burnt bricks, and the good condition of the building, which has seen no repairs since the death of its founder, speaks well for the solidity of the construction. All around are only crumbling ruins, mud walls slowly mingling with the loess dust from which they were made. The shrine has kept some of the land left to it by former pious benefactors, but it would be against all Eastern notions if any of the proceeds were spent on repairs. The feeding of poor pilgrims and of the ever-present Darwishes is a more urgent task.

At four my hosts and guides had finished their feast of melons and meat with a pious prayer, and we resumed the march. The single canal along which we rode could not supply water for the whole plain. From where we entered the limits of the land of Khan-ui (" the Khan's residence "), stretches of desert ground could be seen both to the north and south. By 5.30 p.m. the last hamlet eastwards was reached. To proceed for camp to the old site which I intended to visit was impossible on account of the want of water. So I gladly assented to the proposal to pitch my camp in a large 'Bostan' or arbour of the hamlet. I found it half-swamped by an excess of irrigation such as this thirsty soil is, no doubt, in periodical need of. But the raised avenues between the cross rows of poplars were above the water and at one point left room enough for my tent. So the pleasure of being among trees and green hedges overcame all sanitary scruples, and when the camels arrived by nightfall I felt quite pleased with my new quarters. The moonlight glittered brilliantly on the water-logged ditches and fields, and around ruled a delightful silence, a foretaste of the desert that lay so near.

On the following morning I started with quite an imposing cavalcade for the ancient site. A mile to the east of my camp all cultivation ceased, and a little further all trace of vegetation disappeared. At a distance of about two miles the low ridges of hard-baked loess were covered with fragments of old pottery, glass, and slag, unmistakable evidence of ancient habitations. But no other indications remain of the buildings ; the walls of mud or sunburnt bricks of which they must have been constructed, have long ago disappeared, mainly, as subsequent experience showed me, through the erosive action of wind and sand. The people know this ruined waste by the name of Hasa-Tam, and suppose it to have once been the capital of a 'Chinese Khakan' until 'Hazrat Sultan,' *i.e.*, Satok Boghra Khan, destroyed it.

In the middle of the pottery-strewn area, where the ground is slightly raised, I found a tent pitched by the Hsien-kuan's order and a fresh Dastarkhan spread. But it was too early to indulge in such comforts, and the hopes of my guides for a continuation of yesterday's picnic series were doomed to disappointment. The view from the rising ground displayed to the south nothing but a desert plain hidden on the horizon by an ominous dust haze. But to the east and north I could make out a few mounds rising high above the low banks of loess and sand. Sop Niaz Baba, the fine-looking old Aksakal of Besh-karim, who knew the neighbourhood well, spoke of these eminences as 'Tims,' the designation current in these parts for mounds formed by ancient structures. So I set off straight to the mound on the eastern horizon, and when I arrived there after a three miles' canter found to my satisfaction that I had got to the remains of a Stupa. The ravages of time had reduced it to a shapeless little hill. But the masonry of sun-dried bricks of which it was formed, displayed itself plainly at several points below the covering crust of earth. Immediately to the S.W. of the mound I could trace in low banks rising above the level of the surrounding country the remains of a great quadrangle, measuring 260 by 170 feet, undoubtedly the monastery once attached to the Stupa.

I had scarcely began a rough survey of the site when a wind of increasing violence rose from the north. The mountains that were at first visible in the distance soon disappeared in the thick haze of dust, and with them too the mounds that had been previously pointed out to me. But my guides knew their position well and set off without hesitation when our work at Topa Tim

(" the Sand Mound ") was finished and I wished to proceed to the 'Tims' northward. The four miles' ride in the face of a sandstorm was not pleasant in itself, but revealed an interesting topographical fact. Unexpectedly I came upon a deep-cut river-bed, now almost completely dry, but showing by its great breadth, of some 500 feet, that it must once have carried a considerable quantity of water. My guides assured me that only after exceptionally heavy rain in the mountains does this ravine now contain any water. It must have been different in earlier times, for it is evident that the water supply of the ancient settlement was derived from it.

There was another interesting discovery awaiting me at the end of the ride. As the mounds I was bound for emerged from the thick yellow haze, I saw to my surprise that one of them was a comparatively well preserved Stupa, closely resembling in its dimensions and proportions the Buddhist monuments of this kind on the Afghan border and in the northern Panjab. It rises on a three-storied square base, with the hemispherical dome above almost intact, to a height of nearly forty feet. The position it occupies, on an isolated tongue of high ground sloping down from the foot of the mountains, makes the structure look still more conspicuous. Behind the Stupa, which still retains on the less exposed southern side portions of the original coating of plaster, I found a great oblong mound of far greater dimensions but much more dilapidated. Traces of niches or cells in a three-fold row preserved on the side least exposed to the winds and the rain suggest that it may be the remains of a monastery attached to the Stupa. On the platform connecting the two structures I could trace low crumbling walls of several small buildings.

The old Aksakal of Beshkarim told me that the people know the site by the name of Mauri Tim, and look upon the 'Gumbaz,' *i.e.*, the Stupa, as the watch-tower of the fabulous " King of Chin and Machin " who resided in the ancient city before Harun Boghra Khan destroyed it. That the Stupa goes back to pre-Muhammadan times is quite certain, and judging from its shape and proportions I should be inclined to date it several centuries previous to the arrival of Islam. It has not escaped

RUINED STUPA OF MAURI TIM

the ravages of man, for on the western side I found a deep cutting, in all probability made long ago by treasure-seekers. It has been carried to the centre of the hemispherical dome and reveals the interesting fact that this Stupa contained, like others examined by me in Swat and Buner, a small square chamber probably intended for the deposit of relics. This chamber was near the top of the dome, and below it a narrow square shaft can still be made out descending into the base.

It must be due to the dryness of the air and the absence of destructive climatic influences that the rows of sticks supporting the plaster mouldings of the circular base immediately below the dome were found still intact. The wood, though certainly over a thousand years old, seemed scarcely to differ in touch and toughness from tamarisk branches dried for a few weeks.

The wind with the blinding dust of sand it carried along was too violent that day to permit the taking of photographs and measurements. But I returned from Khanui on September 6th, and a day's work with the plane-table and photo-theodolite gave me a complete survey of the ruins. I chose for my second day's quarters Eski, a pretty village some eight miles south-west of Mauri Tim, where my tent was pitched among groves of vines and luxuriant fields of Indian corn. On my way back about three miles from Mauri Tim, I examined a curious structure about 22 feet square, open at the top and showing thick walls of clay cast in moulds. The name Kaptar-Khana (" the pigeon house "), by which the people know it, is derived from the rows of little niches, about ten inches square, which line the whole of the inner sides of the walls still rising to a height of sixteen feet. The ground inside was thickly strewn with fragments of human bones, and local tradition asserts that it has always been in this condition. Nothing at or near this desolate structure afforded evidence as to its date, but its shape and apparent purpose curiously recalled a 'Columbarium.' Neither Buddhist nor Muhammadan custom would allow of such a disposal of human remains. Is it possible, then, that this strange ruin is a relic of the times when Kashgar held a considerable population of Nestorian Christians?

On September 7th Ram Singh was sent on survey work to

the south-east while I rode back to Kashgar, greatly pleased with the instructive little tour I had made and the attention shown to me by the local officials. The short excursion to Khanui had been useful in bringing to notice various deficiencies in the outfit of my caravan, chiefly concerning camel gear. Some of the animals showed bruises due to ill-fitting saddles, while the knocks suffered by some of my boxes plainly indicated the necessity of proper packing crates. So the 'Ustads' were set to work again, and by dint of continual pressure managed to complete the desired alterations and additions within two days. On September 10th the camels with the main body of my camp establishment marched off to Khan-arik, where Ram Singh had proceeded direct from Khanui. Thus, when on the morning of September 11th, I set out from Kashgar on the journey that was to take me viâ Yarkand to Khotan and the field of my explorations, there was no imposing caravan to give *éclat* to my departure, but also no final preparations to cause worry or delay. On the preceding evening, a dinner given by the Macartneys allowed me to say a quiet good-bye to those members of the European community with whom I had become acquainted.

On the morning of the 11th I bade farewell to my hosts, whose inexhaustible attention and help had rendered the long halt at Kashgar far more pleasant than I could reasonably have hoped. In the outer courtyard of Chini-Bagh there was quite a little crowd, composed of Mr. Macartney's native staff and others connected with the Agency. Mr. Macartney himself accompanied me round the city walls and through the suburbs to the point where the high road towards the south enters open country.

For my march to Yarkand I had chosen a route east of the ordinary caravan road, so as to traverse the desert tract containing the famous pilgrimage site of Ordam-Padshah. Though visited before by members of Sir Douglas Forsyth's mission and by Dr. Sven Hedin, the exact position of this shrine had never been fixed. The opportunity thus offered for new topographical work and the useful experience of a short desert trip preliminary to longer excursions were an ample set-off for the slight detour. The first few miles of my ride took me along the road leading to the "New City," but when I had once passed the busy Bazar under its bastioned wall with the lounging crowd of Chinese soldiers and those who live on them, I was able to pursue my way free from the bustle and dust of the high road. The village lanes along which I rode, guided by the Beg whom the attention of the Chinese district officials had provided for me, gave welcome shade from poplars and willows. At Yonduma, some twelve miles from Kashgar, I passed over one of the streams into which the Yamanyar, from Tashmalik. divides. Beyond it lay a wide tract of fields of Indian corn and grazing lands, irrigated by a network of shallow canals. At Dangalchi I made a short halt in a shady little garden, and then at a distance of some twenty-eight miles from Kashgar reached Khanarik.

The Bazar into which we rode turned out to be only one of the five market villages which belong to Khanarik, and on inquiry I found that my camp had moved from this, the "Monday Bazar," to the "Sunday (Yak-shamba) Bazar," ten miles further east. The ride had been long and fairly hot, so this announcement was not particularly welcome. But there was nothing for it except to ride on. Towards six in the evening, after passing a strip of barren land which intervenes between these parts of the Khanarik tract, I was met to my surprise by a solemn assembly of well-dressed men.

They turned out to be the Hindus of Khanarik, Khattri moneylenders from Shikarpur, who had ridden ahead to welcome the "Sahib." It was strange to meet in these rural surroundings, so closely resembling those of a European village, the representatives of a class which thrives all through the Punjab. However little sympathy the calling and general character of these men can claim, it is impossible not to feel some satisfaction at the pluck and enterprise which enables them to carry on their operations so far away from their home. The connection of the Shikarpur Banias with Central Asia is undoubtedly an old one. Already in the eighteenth century Forster found them established as far as Samarkand and the Caspian. But the opening up of Eastern Turkestan to Indian trade within the last thirty years seems to have attracted them to these parts in increased numbers.

From the men who greeted me on my approach to Yakshamba Bazar, I learned that Khanarik supports no less than eighteen Shikarpuris. Such an allotment of Hindu usurers to a single village tract, however large, can only imply the progressive indebtedness of the cultivators, and my informants readily admitted that business was brisk. They had all settled down here during the last eight years, and their well-to-do

HINDU MONEYLENDERS.

appearance amply proved that they had employed their short residence to advantage. It would have been unfair to inquire too closely into their profits and rates of interest. But as the latter cannot be less than that currently exacted in India by the village moneylender, it is certain that plenty of gain finds its way through these hardy emissaries into the coffers of Shikarpur bankers. To protect the interests of this class is a task which the representative of the Indian Government cannot afford to neglect, however unenviable it may often be. So I was not surprised to find my welcomers loud in their praises of Mr. Macartney.

The garden of the Beg in which my camp had been pitched was a large and well-secluded place, and consequently I enjoyed a quiet evening after my long ride. The Hindus, true to their native custom, brought a 'Dali' of fruit and sweets, and would not rest satisfied until I accepted some pomegranates and almonds for myself and melons and sugar-balls for my people. The spokesman of the guild was Parmanand, the wealthy banker from Aksu, who had left his distant place of business to look after some debtors in this neighbourhood. He assured me in advance that I should find no difficulty in getting my cheques cashed in Aksu!

On the following day my march lay to Achchik, the last village of Khanarik southwards in the direction of Ordam-Padshah. The distance was only about twelve miles, but a deep-cut river-bed about half-way proved a serious obstacle for the camels. The rickety bridge that spans this branch of the Yamanyar, was scarcely safe even for the ponies; it was certain that camels could not be taken across it. So we had to wait patiently in the scanty shade of some willows until the slowly-moving animals arrived; then to arrange for the unloading of the baggage, which had to be carried over piece by piece. Finally a suitable spot was found nearly a mile higher up, where the banks sloped down less steeply. It was a troublesome affair to drag the shaggy quadrupeds into the water one by one. But once in it they swam better than I had expected, and guided by two villagers swimming in front managed to reach the opposite bank safely. The sum of money invested in them amounted to over seven hundred rupees. So it was with a feeling of relief that I saw, after a delay of nearly three hours, the whole caravan on the march again.

Defective cultivation and patches of barren land on the way to Achchik showed that we were approaching the edge of the desert. But Achchik itself proved a cheerful place. The Yüzbashi, or village headman, had prepared his house for my reception. The rooms looked inviting with their freshly-plastered walls and the plentifully-spread carpets of Khotan felt. But the light and air were rather scanty, and so I preferred to pitch my little tent in a neighbouring field, where the lucerne crop had just been cut. It was a delightful evening, with a distant vista over fields of wheat and Indian corn, hedged with poplars and mulberry trees. Like many a rural view of these parts, it carried me back to the fertile Alföld of Hungary.

At Achchik I heard of a "Kone-shahr," *i.e.*, a ruined site of some sort, that was said to be on the edge of the desert to the south-east. My informants were unable to give any idea of its exact distance, but believed that it could be reached by a detour the same day while my camp moved to Ordam-Padshah. A short visit seemed all that was needed, as no buildings were said to be extant, only scattered heaps of bricks and patches of ground covered with potsherds. So I directed my caravan to start with one guide straight to the desert shrine southwards, while I myself with another guide and the Sub-Surveyor rode off at eight o'clock to take Baikhan, the old site mentioned, on the way. Soon beyond Achchik cultivation ceased, and we entered a wide, scrub-covered plain of sand and loess. Neither beast nor man was seen until we reached Khuruz, a miserable hamlet, about four miles to the south-east. A little watercourse allows the lonely dwellers of the few scattered huts to irrigate some fields. Another four miles' ride over a similar waste brought us to Nurunam, where some shepherds live in a couple of wretched hovels. Every tree forms a distinct landmark on this dreary plain. So we had no difficulty in fixing our position on the plane-table as we moved along. By midday, when the heat grew intense, we reached Bekhtauruk, another collection of huts by the side of a swampy depression fed by a little canal. But of Baikhan nothing was to be seen, and evidence as to its distance was conflicting. The prospect of being benighted over our search, or of having to traverse the sand-dunes towards Ordam-Padshah with no daylight to guide us, was distinctly uninviting. I therefore felt bound to abandon the projected visit and to make for the shrine where I supposed my caravan to have preceded me.

So after securing a shepherd guide, we set off to the south, and gradually approaching the line of white sandhills, after an hour and a half's ride entered the true desert area. All scrub disappeared, and only hardy tufts of grass known as 'Kumush' covered in patches the glittering sand. With the hope of a more extended view we made for a higher sandhill. Far away to the south stretched a sea of sand, curiously resembling the ocean with its long wavelike dunes. Through the dust-haze that lay over the long succession of ridges there appeared to the south-west a darker range of low hills for which the extant maps had in no way prepared me, and nearer to us a series of high posts marking the sacred sites to be visited by the pilgrims. With the help of these far-visible marks it was easy to ascertain the position of Ordam-Padshah, as well as of the subsidiary 'Mazars' of Dost-bulak, Sultanim, and Kizil-jaim.

Following our guide, we struck to the south until we reached the main route of the pilgrims near a lonely rest-house known as Uftu Langar. There we looked in vain for the track of the camels which we expected to have passed long before. After a long and somewhat anxious wait—for it was getting late—we saw at last far away to the north the caravan emerging from behind the sandhill. Assured that I should not have to wait in vain for the baggage, however belated it might be, I rode on in the twilight towards our destination.

The sand-dunes to be crossed steadily increased in height, and the going became more difficult. Even in the failing light it was easy to make out the series of semi-lunes into which the drift-sand forms under the action of wind. In the intervals between these ridges the ground was fairly hard and white with alkaline salts. The ponies' feet sank deep into the loose sand, and each ascent of thirty to forty feet was thus a tiring performance. The lines of sandy ridges ran mostly from south-west to north-east, the steep inner sides of the semi-lunes facing all to the south-east. After a tiresome march of some five miles from where we first entered the moving sand region, we drew near to our goal. A long, open valley appeared between the dunes, and at its entrance from the north we could make out a group of stunted poplars. They grow near a well of brackish water, which is carefully protected by a wooden shed from the advance of the neighbouring sandhills. The water-surface was at the time some six feet below the level of the artificially cleared ground in front of the shed.

It was nearly dark when we reached there. But the water tasted so bad and the neighbouring rest-house looked so dilapidated, that I readily moved on to the main settlement of the desert shrine some half a mile off. There I found a collection of huts and Sarais built for the accommodation of the local custodians or 'Mujawirs' and their pilgrim visitors. One of the rest-houses had been cleared for my party, and there our ponies found grass and water. I myself was glad to discover at some distance a spot where the ground was firm enough for pitching my tent, and where I was safe from the odours that rose from the accumulated refuse-heaps of this strange settlement. It was a long wait till the baggage turned up, towards eight o'clock; but in the pure desert air the evening breeze from the east felt delightfully fresh, and when at last the late dinner appeared and I could retire to rest I had almost forgotten the fatigue and heat of my first day in the long-looked-for desert.

The morning showed me my surroundings in their true colouring; the little plain on which my camp was pitched; the waves of drift-sand in front and behind; the dilapidated mud-built huts and Sarais—all displayed the same monotonous khaki. Even the sun while low down seemed to shed a grey light. I felt pleased to note how well my tent and clothes harmonized with this monochrome picture. A sand-dune some thirty-five feet high, which rises immediately behind the mosque and threatens to bury this modest structure before long, gave a panoramic view convenient for the plane table. From its top we could make out the various 'Langars' (travellers' shelters) and shrines to the north, and thus exactly fix our position. A reference to the available maps showed that Ordam-Padshah had been placed fully half a degree of longitude out of its true position.

The miserable looking Mujawirs of the place had followed me to the dune, and now related the story how the holy Sultan Arslan Boghra had succumbed on this plain to the attack of unbelievers, *i.e.*, the Buddhist antagonists of Islam, and how by a miracle the slain bodies of the faithful were found turned towards Mecca, whereas the sand swallowed up the remains of the infidels. Half a mile to the west there rises a stack of high poplar staffs, marking the supposed resting-place of the sainted king. Like the staffs over all Ziarats in the country, they were covered with little flags and rags of all kinds, ex-votos of pious pilgrims. In a depression about half-way to the proper 'Mazar' is the well used by the attendants of the shrine. They all claim to be descendants of the Sultan. Low mud walls on a flat piece of ground, a little to the west of the line of sandhills now approaching the extant houses, were shown to me as the remains of

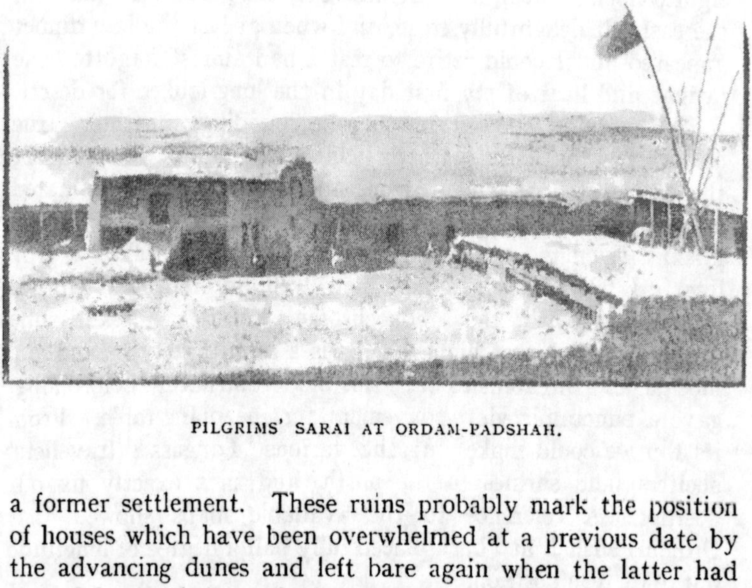

PILGRIMS' SARAI AT ORDAM-PADSHAH.

a former settlement. These ruins probably mark the position of houses which have been overwhelmed at a previous date by the advancing dunes and left bare again when the latter had passed by in their gradual movement to the south-east. The same process may repeat itself in due time with the present houses of Ordam-Padshah.

Notwithstanding the holiness of this curious place of pilgrimage my men were anxious to leave it as soon as possible. So my caravan was already far ahead when I started from Ordam-Padshah. The route to Yarkand lay to the south viâ Hazrat-

Begim, another sacred site on the edge of the desert. The going was heavier even than on the preceding day, for the lines of sandhills were closer together and the direction to be followed made it difficult to utilize the narrow strips of comparatively firm ground that separate the successive waves of sand. My little dog felt so miserable in the basket in which he was to ride on a camel that I had allowed him to follow me on foot. But the sand and the heat told on him before long, and I was glad when, after about four miles, I picked up the camels again and could safely instal 'Yolchi Beg' in his lofty seat. A hole provided in the top of the basket allowed him to look about without giving a chance of escape.

The sand-dunes seemed to grow in height as we slowly approached the previously mentioned ridge to the south-west. But at last the patches of hard loess became larger and larger as the level rose and the ascent became perceptible. The ridge which had looked so high from a distance through the haze proved only about 300 feet above the sandy plain. Its pebble-strewn slopes bore a curiously scarred and withered look, testifying to the force of long-continued erosion by wind and sand. No stone or distinct formation of conglomerate appeared on the slope, swept clean as if with a brush.

On the top of the ridge a number of high staffs serve as a directing mark for the pilgrims. So the place bears appropriately the name of Ulugh-Nishan ("the High Standard"). Arslan Padshah is believed to have addressed from there his last prayer to the holy Beg, his adviser, who lies buried at Hazrat-Begim ("My Beg of holiness"). The latter shrine was visible to the south-west, and as the slope is far steeper on that side and quite clear of drift-sand, we soon reached it. Hazrat-Begim has little to detain the traveller, for around the modest mud-built quadrangle enclosing the saint's tomb there are only a few wretched huts of Mujawirs and a sandy plain strewn with bones and refuse. The camels were, however, tired by the ten miles' march through the deep sand, and Kizil, the next inhabited place, was too far to be reached that day. So my tent was pitched on what I suppose to have been an old burial-ground near the shrine. The water from the well close by tasted extremely brackish, and neither filtering nor the lavish use of "Sparklets" could make it palatable.

On the morning of the 15th of September I resumed my march across the plain, which gradually turned into a scrub-covered Dasht of hard loess. At Saduk-Langar, some four miles off, I hailed with pleasure a little green oasis, created by a small watercourse. It is a Waqf or endowment for the benefit of pilgrims; so we could with a good conscience allow our ponies to graze awhile in the few lucerne fields. By 2 p.m. Kizil was reached, a large village on the main road that connects Kashgar with Yarkand. The sight of its green fields and gardens was truly delightful after the mournful desert behind us. My servants made straight for the Chinese rest-house and seemed surprised when I objected to putting up at that dusty caravanserai, with its courtyards full of carts, donkeys, ponies, and their attendants. Sadak Akhun gravely asserted that the 'Sahibs' coming from Kashgar "always" stopped there. But then I came from Hindustan, and had learned by long experience that the places where "everybody" camps are usually the least attractive. So I set out to search for a camping-ground, and after a while found what I had looked for. A charming little orchard surrounded by open fields gave room and shade for my tent, while the owner hospitably welcomed my followers in his house a short distance off. Grapes and excellent peaches were soon forthcoming, and I feasted on them in honour of my return from a first visit to the desert.

The following day, the 16th of September, was spent on a long march through an arid waste to Kok-robat, the western limit of the great oasis of Yarkand. For a distance of close on twenty-four miles there was neither a tree nor even a shrub to be seen, only the gravel-covered grey 'Dasht' far away to the dusty horizon. As we were now on a post route I found a square, mud-built tower marking each 'Potai,' the Chinese road measure equivalent to ten 'Li.' As the Potai seems to correspond closely to a distance of two English miles it is evident that the value of about one-fifth of a mile still holds good for the Li in Turkestan, as it does by computation, for the road distances recorded in India by Hiuen-Tsiang and other Chinese pilgrims.

I stopped awhile at midday at Ak-robat ("the White Station"), a solitary Sarai in the desolate waste. I found the little rest-house within the enclosure, evidently intended for Chinese officials and better-class travellers, surprisingly clean, and gratefully availed myself of its deep, shady veranda for a short rest while the camels came up. It was nearly five o'clock before my eyes again rested on green fields and trees. Kokrobat ("the Green Station") receives its water, and with it fertility, from a stream coming from the hill range that was dimly visible in the west. I had to ride through the main village, spreading its houses in a single street over a mile long, before I found an arbour suitable for my camp. I could not have desired a shadier or more secluded grove. Curiously enough there was no proper entrance through the wall enclosing it. But sun-dried bricks are a material easily handled and replaced. So when my choice was made the owner without much trouble knocked a hole in the wall and thus established easy communication between the 'Bostan' and his courtyard, where my servants were quartered. The yellow leaves lay thick under the walnut and other fruit-trees, a sad memento of rapidly advancing autumn.

ENTRANCE TO THE YAMEN, YARKAND.

CHAPTER X.

YARKAND AND KARGHALIK.

A MARCH of about eighteen miles brought me on the 17th of September from Kokrobat into Yarkand. The scenery had undergone a welcome change compared with that of the previous day, for along the whole route there was no piece of barren ground to be seen. Sandy as the soil almost everywhere is, ample water is brought to it by canals large and small. Long avenues of poplars and willows give shade along the greater part of the road. Work with the plane-table was not easy in this *terrain coupé*. But when more open ground was reached about half-way, near Toguchak village, and the direction of Yarkand could be clearly made out, we had the satisfaction to note that the distance and bearing of this previously fixed position coincided exactly with that derived from our survey.

For several miles before and after Toguchak the road traverses country that has only within the last few years been brought under cultivation by means of newly opened canals from the Yarkand River. It was a pleasure to see a sandy waste thus reclaimed by dint of skilful labour. The crests of the low sand-dunes still retain their original scrub-covered surface, but everywhere around them spread carefully terraced fields, which were said to have already yielded this year a bountiful crop of wheat. The arrangement of the canals along the road, often crossing each other at different levels, indicated a systematic scheme of irrigation. The result is creditable to the enterprise of Liu-Darin, then Amban of Yarkand, who seems to have carried through a piece of truly productive work with remarkable energy. The labour employed, it is true, is said to have been wholly unpaid, *i.e.*, 'Begar.' Yet are not all great engineering feats of the East due to this agency? The cultivators to whom I talked acknowledged that they had been forced to the work. But now they were glad to occupy the ground they had reclaimed for cultivation, and thus to reap the direct benefit of their labours. The saying of the Kashmir cultivators, "We do not want money, we want the slipper," *i.e.*, compulsion, for any work of general utility, evidently holds true also in Turkestan.

When I had crossed a broad canal from the Yarkand River known as Opa, about three miles from the city, I found the whole colony of Indian traders, with Munshi Bunyad Ali, the "Newswriter" employed by Mr. Macartney, at their head, waiting to give me a formal reception. Most of the traders from the Punjab had already left for Ladak, and the fresh contingent of the year had not yet arrived from across the mountains. All the same it was quite an imposing cavalcade, at the head of which I rode into Yarkand. There were hardy Khattris from various parts of the Punjab, whom I felt tempted to greet as quasi-countrymen; men from Jammu territory, equally familiar to me; and a sprinkling of Muhammadan

Kashmiris, of whom there is quite a settled colony here. They were all in their best dresses, decently mounted, and unmistakably pleased to greet a 'Sahib.' So it was only natural that they wished to make some show of him. Accordingly I was escorted in great style through the whole of the Yangi-Shahr, or "New City," and the Bazars that connect it with the old one. Our clattering cavalcade was undoubtedly a little event for the people that thronged the Bazars. These all seemed broad and fairly clean; in point of picturesqueness far more attractive than those of Kashgar.

Then we turned off to the right and rode round the crenellated walls of the "Old City" into an area of suburban gardens. Here lies the Chini-Bagh which Mr. Macartney had in advance engaged for my residence. It proved quite a summer-palace within a large walled-in garden. Passing through a series of courts, I was surprised to find a great hall of imposing dimensions, with rows of high wooden pillars supporting its roof. Beyond it I entered a series of raised apartments, once the reception-rooms of Niaz Hakim Beg, the original owner of these palatial quarters. There was no mistaking the marks of departed glory. The gilding of the latticework screens separating the rooms had faded, and other signs of neglect were numerous. Yet good carpets covered the floors and the raised platforms; tasteful dados ran along the walls, and over the whole lay an air of solemn dignity and ease. When alone in my temporary mansion I felt the reality of the charms which such an abode offers even more than I had in the old Moghul and Sikh garden-residences, once my favourite haunts in the Campagna of Lahore.

The days which followed my arrival at Yarkand passed with surprising rapidity. I had intended from the first a stay of five or six days, in order to make use of the opportunities which Yarkand offers for the collection of anthropological materials and old art ware; but several circumstances helped in extending it. I had been assured in Kashgar that Yarkand was the place where I could most conveniently arrange for the money needed on my further journey. There I was to find the Indian traders eager to take Government Supply Bills and my cheques and convert them into cash. Unfortunately, those who needed drafts on Indian Treasuries had already started on their way to Ladak, and the remaining Khattris had taken the opportunity to remit with them whatever ready money they had cleared by the sale of their goods. So it was no easy matter to find a market for my drafts, and seeing that only a portion of the money I needed could be raised at a reasonable rate, I was ultimately obliged to despatch a messenger to Kashgar. Until my messenger had returned with the desired cash in silver and gold a start appeared scarcely desirable.

Another discovery made soon after my arrival, and equally annoying, was that two of the camels and two of the ponies had developed sore backs, which needed cure. The fact had before been carefully screened from my knowledge, with the natural result that the evil had got worse than it need have. So nothing less than a week's rest would do to make the transport fit again, and accordingly the camels, after careful examination and dressing of sores, were sent to have an easy time grazing in a wooded tract, a day's march southwards. The experience was not thrown away on me. Thereafter inspections of the animals were held almost daily, and those responsible for their loading learned to understand that the hire of transport in place of animals rendered temporarily unfit would be recovered from their own pay.

It was lucky that my Yarkand quarters were of such delightful spaciousness, for from the first day of my stay there was no want of visitors. Yarkand is the great commercial centre of Chinese Turkestan, and owing to its geographical position at the point where the routes to India, Afghanistan, and to the North meet, has something of a cosmopolitan air about it. The colonies of Kashmiris, Gilgitis, Badakhshanis, and people from other parts of the Indian frontier regions are large, and each of them has members of some position anxious to show attention to a 'Sahib.' So I had to hold regular receptions with the assistance of old Munshi Bunyad Ali, and "the carpet of my presence" was rarely clear of more or less picturesque visitors. If their statements as to the strength

BADAKHSHANI TRADER, YARKAND.

of their respective communities can be trusted, Yarkand must have a strangely mixed population. Immigrants from Wakhan, Shighnan, Badakhshan, and the other Iranian tracts westwards abound; Kashmir and Ladak are strongly represented; even little Baltistan has sent its colony from beyond the ice mountains. So there was no want of materials for anthropometric work, and I did all I could to benefit by it.

The types of my visitors made me feel far nearer again to India and its borderlands. Hearing Kashmiri, Panjabi, and Pushtu spoken at all hours of the day in a place so closely resembling the native country residences of Northern India I might have felt myself on Indian soil. That European fashions have not yet invaded this corner of Asia helped to throw one back in regard to time too. Turki is, of course, the language of general intercourse among the different colonies of immigrants, and as the latter scarcely ever bring wives from their own homes but marry in the country, it is natural that by the second or third generation the knowledge of their father's tongue is already lost. But physical features are not so easily effaced, and a stroll in the Bazars is enough to convince the observer how large an infusion of foreign, particularly Iranian, blood there is in the Yarkand population.

Apart from my visitors, there was for a great part of the day another crowd to fill the outer hall of my temporary palace. Munshi Bunyad Ali had taken care to let it be known that I wished to acquire things of old local art, and in consequence improvised agents of such articles were pouring in every morning. I was specially looking out for specimens of that ornamented brasswork which had once its home at Khotan and which has become well known to lovers of Central-Asian art, though its local connection does not appear to have been realised. Judging from the quantities of beautifully worked 'Aptabas,' 'Chaugans' (tea-pots), 'Chilapchis' (water-basins), jugs, and other metal articles brought to me from houses of once well-to-do families, the supply must still be considerable.

Among the pieces offered for sale I was able to pick out some excellent specimens of open metal work, all showing most clearly the influence of Persian floral design, yet with a distinct individuality of treatment. By the side of these indigenous art products, queer odds and ends of Chinese work turned up—pottery of evident merit and age, and beautiful pieces of embroidery from the Far East. The rich Begs of old days must have looked truly gorgeous in their dresses of state, heavy red or blue silk Chogas emblazoned with artistic designs of pure Chinese style. Fine carpets of Turkoman and Khorasan make indicated that importations from the West had been equally frequent. Thus Yarkand shows also in this respect that it has been a point where, since early Muhammadan times, Chinese influences have mingled with the culture of Iran and Turkestan. It is Khotan, however, which seems to have been the place of origin and the true home for most of the indigenous industries. Curiously enough, almost all the people who brought me these delightfully varied specimens of old art-ware were Kashmiris. The pedlars' instinct, which is so conspicuous in the urban population of the valley, has evidently not been extinguished by emigration across the mountains. So I often felt as if I were besieged again in the camping-grounds of Srinagar by the voluble and irrepressible agents of Kashmirian craftsmen.

Liu-Darin ('Darin' represents the local pronunciation of the Chinese title 'Ta-jen'), the Amban of Yarkand, was absent on tour when I arrived. But he soon returned, and after the due preliminaries had been arranged, I made my call at his Yamen. I found Liu-Darin a very amiable and intelligent old man. Conversation through a not over-intelligent interpreter is not the way to arrive at a true estimate of character. But somehow Liu-Darin's manners and looks impressed me very favourably. On the next day I received the return visit of the old administrator, and found occasion to show him the Si-yu-ki of Hiuen-Tsiang and to explain what my objects were in searching for the sacred sites which the great pilgrim had visited about Khotan, and for the remains of the old settlements overwhelmed by the desert. It was again reassuring for me to find how popular the figure of the pious old traveller still is with educated Chinamen. Though Tang-Seng, "the monk of the Tang Dynasty," is evidently credited with many wonderful relations for which we should look in vain in his "Description of the Western Countries," this scarcely need disturb our conscience.

On the 22nd of September Liu-Darin insisted on entertaining me at a Chinese dinner. Well-meant as the invitation no doubt was, I confess that I faced the entertainment with mixed feelings. My Kashgar experiences had shown me the ordeal which such a feast represents to the average European. However, things passed better than I had ventured to hope. The dinner consisted of *only* sixteen courses, and was duly absorbed within three hours. It would be unfair to discuss the strange mixture of the menu, especially as I felt quite incompetent to analyse most of the dishes, or the arrangements of the table. Having regard to my deficient training in the use of eating-sticks I was provided with a fork (never changed or cleaned) and a little bowl to eat from. As my host insisted on treating me personally to choice bits, a queer collection accumulated on this substitute for a plate. I felt more comfortable when I managed to get it cleared from time to time. For the hot spirit, a kind of arrack it seemed, served in tiny square cups as the only beverage, there was no such convenient depository, and in reply to the challenges of my convives I had to touch it more frequently than I could have wished. Besides my host, two of his chief officials, jovial-looking men, were keeping me company.

It was a little pathetic when, in the course of dinner, Liu-Darin pressingly inquired as to what news I had about the capture of Peking by the allied forces and the flight of the Emperor. I had no direct news from Europe later than the end of July, and thus could not satisfy his curiosity. So I contented myself with describing the relief with which the safety of the legations had been greeted in Europe. The old "Political" would not credit my ignorance, and attributed my reticence to the wish to keep back unpleasant information. Whatever the reliability of the news may have been that reached Chinese Yamens in Turkestan through the wire to Kashgar, it seemed clear that they realised the great danger to the Government they served. There may have been anxiety about the future; but if my Kashgar friends' views were right, it was the doubt about their own individual fortunes, not those of their nation, which secretly troubled the minds of the officials in this land of exile.

It was arranged that after the dinner I should photograph my host and some of his people. So Liu-Darin at the end of the feast duly installed himself on a raised chair of office, with his little daughter and son by his knees, and some implements of western culture, in the shape of sundry clocks, etc., on a small table close by. A crowd of more or less ragged attendants formed the background. The photos were easy to take, as my sitters kept as quiet as if they were sculptured. Then we parted in all friendship. Liu-Darin talked of retiring soon to his native province of Hu-nan. May he return to it in peace and, as my Chinese patron saint, 'Tang-Seng,' did of old, enjoy the rest he was looking for.

The last days in Yarkand were busily spent in completing

the winter outfit of my men and in sorting and packing my purchases. Accounts too had to be settled, and in this respect I was glad to avail myself of the skilled assistance of

LIU-DARIN, AMBAN OF YARKAND.

Lala Gauri Mall, the Ak-sakal (headman, literally "white-beard") of the Hindu traders. Apart from the question of price—no small matter in a country where it would apparently be against all business principles to aṣk less than double the right amount even from local customers—there is enough trouble in the mere payment. The Chinese currency with its 'Sers' or 'Tels,' 'Miskals' and 'Fens,' arranged on a plain decimal system, would be as convenient as can be desired. But its simplicity is of little avail in this outlying province of the empire, which stubbornly clings to its time-honoured reckoning in 'Tangas' and 'Puls.' Each of the little square Chinese coppers known in Turkestan as 'Dachins' is reckoned in Kashgar and Yarkand as equal to two Puls, and twenty-five of them make up a Tanga. The Khotan Tanga is worth twice as much as the Kashgar Tanga.

Coins representing this local unit of value there are none; so all sums have to be converted into Miskals, the smallest available silver coins, at the ratio of eight Tangas to five Miskals, unless one is prepared to handle the dirty rolls of Chinese coppers which the local trader keeps strung up like sausages. But the exchange rate between silver and copper is not stable, and the silver Miskal was just then considerably above the value of forty copper pieces which the ratio just mentioned would indicate. So after successfully converting Tangas into the legal coin, a varying discount has to be calculated before payment can be effected. It only adds to these monetary complications that prices of articles imported from Russia are reckoned in 'Soms' (Roubles), which in the form of gold pieces of five or ten Roubles widely circulate through the markets of Turkestan, while the heavier Chinese silver 'Yambus,' of horse-shoe shape and varying weight, have a discount of their own. During my stay in the country the value of the gold Rouble as against the local currency of Tangas represented by Chinese silver and copper pieces, steadily declined, and with it unluckily fell the Rupee too, the exchange value of which seems in Turkestan to depend mainly on the Rouble rate. For the well-trained arithmetica faculties of the Hindu trader these tangled relations offer no difficulty. But I confess I sadly reflected on the loss of time which they implied for me.

On the 24th of September the weather became cloudy and the temperature distinctly cold. A yellow haze hung all day low over the ground and intensified the effect of the atmospheric change. It felt autumnally chilly in the wide halls of my palace, and I realised how different life in them would be when the winter set in. The haze still continued when early on the morning of the 27th of September my caravan was again set in march. It was market-day, and the endless stream of villagers that passed along the roads with their manifold produce and belongings was a welcome distraction. Women of the cultivating class play a prominent part in all the marketing. I met them in large groups or accompanied by their men and children, but in either case almost invariably mounted. The large caps with peaks of velvet which the women wear looked more comfortable on this chilly morning than when I had first seen them in the heat of early August.

There was little else to occupy my attention after this stream of market visitors ceased with the advance of the morning. The broad and fairly straight road, lined with poplars and mulberries, runs through flat, fertile country. In the fields of maize the harvest was proceeding; for the rice, apparently, the return of warmer days was expected. About five miles from the city I passed the large Bazar of Manglik, a long row of clean mud huts with booths opening on the road, but almost completely deserted, as it was not the local market day. Such Bazars are met at varying distances all along the route to Karghalik, a sure indication of the thick population of the fertile belt of land through which it passes. After a ride of about eight miles we reached the bank of the Zarafshan or Yarkand River. Fed by the streams which drain the whole mountain region between Muztagh-Ata and the Karakorum range, it must carry a mighty mass of water in the height of the summer. Even now it flowed in three arms which had to be crossed by boat. The clumsily built ferry boats could not take the laden animals, so the loads had to be unpacked and refitted again and again. Each of the branches was about forty yards broad, and the depth well up to a camel's girth. It took my caravan three hours to effect the passage, and all through that time the traffic of laden ponies and donkeys was sufficient to fill the two or three ferry boats at each crossing as quick as they could be worked. On the opposite bank of this river-bed, which has the total breadth of a mile, we passed the large Bazar of Painap, and by five o'clock I reached Posgam Bazar, the end of the day's march. Inside the large inner quadrangle of the Sarai I found my tent pitched. In the rooms of the spacious rest-house, which, dating from the time of Yaqub Beg, is kept clean and in a very fair state of repair, I should have been warmer; but I preferred to stick to my little tent and its fresh air as long as possible.

My march on September 28th to Karghalik was a fairly long one, about twenty-four miles, but very enjoyable. A light storm overnight, though accompanied only by dust without a drop of rain, had thoroughly cleared the atmosphere. It was pleasant to walk in the fresh morning air between the carefully cultivated fields and orchards that cover the ground south of Posgam. Irrigation from the Yarkand River provides plenty of water, and the comparative proximity of the villages and Bazars along the route testifies to the prosperity of the tract. About nine miles from Posgam there followed a grassy plain known as Tügülaz, which is intersected by numerous clear streamlets said to be fed by springs further west. The sight of their limpid water, so different from the red, grey, or brown colouring of the larger streams seen since Kashgar, was in welcome harmony with the view of the distant snowy ranges that now showed themselves in the south-west. The mountains which I could see for a great portion of the march belong to the ranges through which the Zarafshan forces its way down from Sarikol. All through my stay at Yarkand the haze had hidden them from view.

Beyond the Tügülaz plain we came to the Tiznaf River, now reduced to a number of narrow channels, but evidently fed with plenty of water when the snow melts in the advanced ranges of the Kuen-luen. The well-constructed bridge which leads over the main river-bed was built, according to the Chinese and Turki inscription at its head, some twenty-five years ago, and measures fully 250 steps. Beyond followed a rich tract with smiling fields of lucerne, Indian corn, and cotton, dotted with comfortable-looking villages. At Ćharvak, the "Tuesday Bazar" of this neighbourhood, I found an animated scene. The Amban of Karghalik was expected to pass through on his way to Yarkand, where he was proceeding to welcome Liu-Darin's successor. He had postponed his journey—as I was told, on account of my approaching visit—but the preparations for his reception were complete. Broad strips of scarlet cloth were stretched across from house to house under the matted awnings that cover the whole long Bazar street; the latter itself was thronged with a crowd apparently making holiday. The local Beg received me in his official Chinese garb, and politely invited me to the large shop that had been fitted up with carpets and felts as a kind of reception-room. So I had to partake of tea that was welcome enough after the dusty ride, and of a fine collation of fruit.

By half-past four I had approached Karghalik through a belt of villages rich in orchards and shrines of all kinds. The pebble-strewn bed of a half-dry stream, which I passed shortly before entering the town, betokened the vicinity of the hills. I soon passed into the tangled net of Bazars that form the centre of Karghalik town, and was struck with their comparative cleanliness and the thriving look of the whole place. It is clear at the first glance that Karghalik derives no small amount of profit from its position at the point where a much-frequented route to the Karakorum Passes joins the great road connecting Khotan with Yarkand. After a long search among the suburban gardens to the south I found a large plot of meadow land with some beautiful old walnut-trees that carried me back in recollection to many a pretty village in Kashmir. It was a delightful camping-ground for myself, and, as my people found quarters in a cottage close by and the ponies excellent grazing, everybody was satisfied.

On the morning of the 29th some Begs sent by the Amban brought a present consisting of a sheep and fodder for my animals. I returned the attention with a collection of Russian sweets, sardine tins, and highly scented soap of German make, bought for such purposes at Kashgar. About noon I went to pay my visit to Chang-Darin, the Amban, at his official residence or Yamen. I was received with all the ceremony due to the occasion, a salute of three popguns included, and soon found myself face to face with my host in his neat little reception-room. Chang-Darin impressed me very favourably with his liveliness and unmistakable intelligence. He had heard from the Tao-tai at Kashgar of my visit and its object. So no lengthy explanations were required as to what I was

YETIMLUKUM MAZAR WITH CEMETERY, NEAR KARGHALIK.

looking for along the route to Khotan, and all needful help about transport and supplies was readily offered.

Chang-Darin insisted on treating me to a light kind of lunch consisting of only a few plates. In addition to these I had to taste a good deal of wine. Fortunately it was not the strong Chinese spirit that appeared on Liu-Darin's table, but a kind of Madeira, possibly from the Caucasus or the Crimean vine-yards. Two little wine-glasses and proper forks by the side of the orthodox eating-sticks also betokened the progressive attitude of my host in matters culinary.

We parted in mutual good feeling, and I utilized the occasion to pay a cursory visit to the Bazars. There were plenty of shops open, though it was not market day, and I was soon able to make the needed purchases in felt materials required for my men's winter outfit. The hills about Kökyar are renowned for the 'Paipaks' or felt socks there produced, and Karghalik is the great market for them. All the Bazars are covered with substantial matting which gives shade for the summer and keeps off the glare. Canals neatly bridged over cross the Bazars at numerous points, and the luxuriant trees that grow by their side give a welcome change of colour. Open kitchens or eating-houses were to be met at numerous spots, and, as a rush of customers was not great on this day, I could conveniently inspect their arrangements. They resemble far more those to be found in similar establishments of the West than anything that could be seen in an Indian town. There were pots and cauldrons kept boiling in regular stoves, plates with breads and cakes, dishes of vegetables, etc. One of these street restaurants struck me particularly by the elaborate floral designs on its whitewashed front walls.

When I returned to my camp much pleased with the stroll I found the Amban already waiting to return my call. He had whiled away the time by a careful inspection of my camp furniture, which evidently met with his approval, as he sent next day a carpenter to take measurements of the neat folding table Messrs. Luscombe & Co., of Allahabad, had made for me. We talked a good deal about old Hiuen-Tsiang and his account of the country. I showed Chang-Darin the Chinese glossaries attached to Julien's translation of the Si-yu-ki, and the plates of Dr. Hoernle's publications on the antiquities of Khotan and Kucha. The ancient Chinese coins and the few fragments of Chinese manuscripts there depicted excited a good deal of curiosity on the part of my visitor. I felt more than ever the disadvantage of my ignorance of Chinese, for it was no easy task to give intelligible answers to the many queries of my visitor through an interpreter so little versed in literary matters as Niaz Akhun. He had, however, been to 'Bajin' (Peking), and this supreme achievement gave him an air of assurance which made him, if not others also, forget the limitations of his intelligence.

On the morning of the next day there arrived the consignment of money, sent by Mr. Macartney from Kashgar in payment for my drafts on Lahore. My halt at Karghalik had been made partly in expectation of it. With the bags of Chinese silver coin and the smaller packet of newly-coined gold Rouble pieces, Mr. Macartney's 'Chaprassi' brought home letters also. He was to return the next day and carry my own mail to Kashgar. So I was kept busy all day with letters and with accounts that were to be despatched to Government. I sometimes wondered how the Babus of the Calcutta office would take to the currency complications reflected in my "Monthly Cash Accounts." The shady grove of walnut-trees in front of my tent made a delightful Daftar. In the evening I strolled up the bank of the stream that flows to the west of the town and got a distant glimpse of the hills towards Kökyar. They produce a great quantity of wool, and by the side of the stream I came upon a place where an enterprising Kashgar trader, who exports to Andijan, has an establishment for washing and cleaning the wool. The people I met there accounted by these exports for the reduced output of felts in the neighbourhood.

The 1st of October was the Karghalik market, and I had decided to wait for it, in the hope that it might bring to the town specimens of the curious hill-people known as Phakhpo, that live in the valley south of Kökyar. Anthropological data regarding them would be most welcome, in view of the doubts that exist as to their ethnic affinity. From the description recorded by members of the Yarkand Mission it appears that the Phakhpo in build and features are eminently "Aryan" lookin Yet they are distinct from the Tajiks of Sarikol, and are believed to speak a Turki dialect. Their small numbers, distant home, and shy habits have so far prevented any close observation. I was no luckier in this respect, as, notwithstanding the watch kept by the Amban's order, no Phakhpos could be discovered among the market crowds. To wait for the arrival of men who might have been fetched from their mountains would have meant the delay of a week, which I could not afford.

Instead of these hill-folk the day brought another interesting acquaintance, a travelling Buddhist monk from the East of China who had begged his way through to Aksu and Khotan and was now again on his way northward. He had somehow heard of the respect I paid to 'Tang-Seng's' memory, and not unnaturally hoped for some help on his onward journey. His was evidently not a pilgrimage in search of sacred sites connected with Buddhism. Yet his simple, jovial way appealed to me, and I was glad to return his gift of a religious tract, nicely painted on red paper, with an offering of silver that sent the humble devotee away quite happy and contented.

BUDDHIST MONK FROM CHINA.

I shall always look back with pleasure to the short stay at Karghalik, or rather Yetimlukum, as the village is called where my camp stood. There was nothing to remind me of the neighbourhood of the desert or the equal barrenness of the outer hills. As far as the eye could reach over the large plots of fields and gardens fertility and plenty reigned. Much reminded me of Kashmir—the variety and luxuriant growth of the trees, the numerous picturesque Ziarats with shady groves near my camp, and in the Bazars the quaintly carved wooden houses.

CHAPTER XI.

ON THE ROAD TO KHOTAN.

On the morning of the 2nd of October my caravan wended its way through the busy little town towards the East gate, from whence the road to Khotan starts. On my way I visited a large Madrasah called after the Ghujak Masjid, opening on one of the principal Bazars. It comprises a large quadrangle with rows of vaulted rooms for about 150 students, and at its west end an open hall of imposing dimensions. The wooden pillars supporting the roof as well as the roof itself are painted in lively colours, chiefly shades of red, suggesting the polychrome splendour of some classical building.

Chang-Darin had sent his principal 'Tungchi' or interpreter to accompany me on my start and bring me his farewell good wishes. Within a mile of the Khotan gate where I parted from the good-looking old man the caravan road emerges on barren desert. A few miles further on this gave way to narrow strips of cultivation forming the little oasis of Besharik, but this was soon traversed, and beyond there received us an unmitigated wilderness of gravelly Dasht. The road is marked all along by wooden posts erected at short intervals—no useless precaution considering how easy it would be for the traveller to lose his way at night or in a sand-storm. At Kosh Langar, where the day's march ended, I was surprised to find in the midst of the barren waste a commodious Sarai built of hard-burned bricks, with vaulted rooms and ample out-houses. This building attests the enterprise of Niaz Hakim Beg, governor of Khotan in the days of Yaqub Beg—the same whose country mansion gave me shelter at Yarkand. A tank is provided into which water flows for one day in the week by a small canal brought down from the outer hills. A ruined mound of sun-dried bricks, some 30 feet high, which rises from the desert plain about a mile and a half northwards, may possibly mark the remains of a Stupa. But its decay was too far advanced to permit any certain conclusion.

On the 3rd of October my march lay entirely through desert ground. To the south the line of outer hills was faintly visible through the haze, but no canal or watercourse of any kind descends from them to the plain. After the chilly nights the heat and glare of the midday hours were very perceptible. The dreary route we were now following along the southern edge of the great sandy desert, the Taklamakan, had for me a special historical interest. It was undoubtedly the ancient line that led from the Oxus region to Khotan and China. Walking and riding along the track marked here and there by the parched carcases and bleached bones of animals that had died on it, I thought of travellers in times gone by who must have marched through this same waterless, uninhabited waste. Hiuen-Tsiang, who travelled here on his way back to China, has well described the route. After him it had seen Marco Polo and many a less-known mediæval traveller to distant Cathay. Practically nothing has changed here in respect of the methods and means of travel, and thus my thoughts could wander back into the past the more readily. It is certain that, with the caravans that once trod this sand, the Buddhist religion and the elements of Indian as well as of classical culture and art travelled to the land of the Sinæ. Shall we ever learn how much they brought back that has influenced the civilization of the ancient world?

Cholak Langar, which I reached in the early afternoon, has a Sarai closely resembling that of the preceding station. It stands on the edge of a broad, sandy ravine, that descends from a gap in the low hill-range south. A large and well-filled tank close below the Sarai was the only redeeming feature in the bleak landscape. The course of the small watercourse that feeds it at times is marked far away northward by a line of low shrubs. In the evening the Chinese clerk in charge of the post station came to call on me. He seemed a quiet, well-educated man, not over-pleased with his desert surroundings. He has nine Dak horses and four postmen under him to carry letters to Guma and Karghalik. The "mails" along the postal routes of the country are ordinarily restricted to the official correspondence of the Chinese authorities. My visitor told me that he had come two years ago from Urumchi with the Karghalik Amban, whose district in the Ho-nan was also his own. That his village was near to the birth-place of 'Tang-Seng,' *i.e.*, Hiuen-Tsiang, was a piece of information, not indifferent to me. So I treated this modest exile to tea and cake, and tried to cheer him with the hope of an early transfer to a more congenial post.

The march from Cholak Langar to Guma was reckoned a long one, nine 'Potais.' So the camels marched off with the heavy baggage by daybreak. My tent and the kitchen things going by ponies could start later. While they were being packed I strolled into the courtyard of the Sarai, the walls of which I found plastered over with official edicts in Chinese and Turki. Conspicuous among them was a long tri-lingual proclamation, in Chinese, Mongolian, and Turki, printed on large sheets of yellow paper. It was an edict in the name of the Emperor, referring to the trade intercourse with the Russian markets, and had been issued some two months before. Niaz Akhun, my interpreter, was eager to know whether it was likely to be the last edict of the Emperor, whose flight from Peking was being reported all through the Bazars.

After a ten miles' march over bare gravel and sand Siligh Langar was reached, a collection of wretched mud-hovels, with a little tank fed by a small watercourse. The tank was full and the water flowed away into the sand. Beyond Siligh Langar scanty scrub and 'Kumush' appeared again and covered the sandy soil up to Hajib Langar, another uninviting wayside station two and a half miles beyond. Then the ground began to show pebble-strewn beds of shallow ravines, and in a long dark line the trees of the oasis of Guma appeared on the horizon. It was a dreary ride of some six miles before we struck the river-bed, then dry, that marks the western edge of the lands of Guma. Beyond it I passed scattered fields and groves half-buried under drifting sand that seems to advance from the west, and at last, after riding up a steep bank, some 30 to 40 feet high, I was once more amidst fertile gardens and fields. Close to a large canal that skirts the Bazar of Guma I discovered a camping-ground just as I wanted it, in a quiet garden enclosed by a hedge of high willows and poplars. While my tent was being pitched I rode off again towards the Bazar, where the weekly market was still in full swing. The large crowds buying and selling cattle, fruit, cotton stuffs, and other local produce were an indication of the extent of the oasis. Over rows of stalls high boots of red leather were hanging, an article evidently in great demand owing to the approach of winter.

The 5th of October was given up to a halt needed for antiquarian inquiries. Among the purchases of Central-Asian antiquities made for the Indian Government by Mr. Macartney and other political officers, paper manuscripts and "block-prints" in "unknown characters" had since 1895 become more and more frequent. These and similar acquisitions which had reached Russian and other public collections in Europe, were all supposed to have been unearthed from sand-buried sites in the Khotan region. Islam Akhun, the Khotan "treasure-seeker" from whom most of these strange texts were acquired, had in statements recorded at Kashgar by Mr. Macartney and subsequently reproduced in Dr. Hoernle's learned report on the Calcutta collection, specified a series of localities from which his finds were alleged to have been obtained. Most of these were described as old sites in the desert north of the caravan route between Guma and Khotan. Information that had reached me at Kashgar helped to emphasise the doubts which had previously arisen as to the genuineness of his "finds." But it was at Guma that I first touched the ground where it was possible to test the "treasure-seeker's" statements by direct local inquiries.

When the local Begs together with the several Yüz-bashis

of the main villages joined me in the morning, I ascertained that there was an extensive debris-covered area known to all as a 'Kone-shahr,' close to the road between Guma and Moji, the next oasis eastwards. But nobody had ever heard of the discovery of "old books" either at this or any other site. Of the string of localities named as find-places in the detailed itinerary which Islam Akhun had given of one of his desert journeys, only two were known to them. As both lay close to the oasis it was easy to arrange for their inspection. Riding to the north-east with a lively following of Begs and their attendants, I soon reached the area of moving sand-dunes 20 to 30 feet high which encircles Guma from the north. Near to the little hamlet of Hasa, passed en route on the edge of this area, the dunes had within the memory of the villagers encroached considerably on the original holdings. A portion of the scattered homesteads was believed also to lie buried under the advancing sands. But as they had been abandoned only within a comparatively recent period, they could never, as my guides sensibly pointed out, have furnished antiquities.

A ride of a little over three miles sufficed to bring me to Karakul Mazar ("the Mazar of the Black Lake") which figured prominently in Islam Akhun's itinerary. By the side of a little lake of saline water, half-covered by reeds, there rises a semicircle of sandhills. On the top of one, the customary erection of poles hung with votive rags, yaks' tails, and skins, indicates the supposed resting place of a saint. Of his life and deeds I could gather nothing except that the holy man came to live here when his beard was black, and died here as an 'Ak-sakal' ("a white-beard"). Of the vast cemetery round this shrine where Islam Akhun alleged that he had made finds of ancient block-prints, I could discover no sign.

The lake is fed by a small rivulet, which flows in a broad, tortuous bed about a quarter of a mile eastwards. It rises from a series of springs and pools about Hasa, and accordingly is known by the name of Kara-su ("black-water"); but during the spring and early summer it is swelled by flood water ('ak-su' or "white water") when the snow melts on the mountains southward. In its bed, which we followed for about three miles to the oasis of Karatagh-aghzi, or Karataghiz, I came for the first time upon the jungle that thrives along the watercourses that penetrate into the desert. Reeds of various kinds, the hardy 'Yulghun' plant with its heather-like small red flowers, and other shrubs filled the dry bed of the Kara-su in picturesque confusion. The autumn had already turned the leaves of many to various tints of yellow. So there was a feast for the eyes, doubly welcome after the dreary monochrome view of the Dasht. At Karatagh-aghzi I found luxuriant groves of poplar-, mulberry-, and other trees scattered among ripe fields of Indian corn. The other produce had already been harvested. The part of the cultivated land which I saw was said to have been reclaimed only some fifteen years ago. The size and luxuriance of the trees that had grown up in this short time was a striking illustration of the capability of the desert soil if once reached by water.

MENDICANT, OR 'DIWANA.'

From Karatagh-aghzi Islam Akhun alleged that he had visited various ruined sites which yielded him "old books" and other strange finds. But the inhabitants, when closely questioned, knew nothing of such sites and still less of such discoveries. So assured of the negative result of my inquiry I turned back to Guma. We took the track across the sand to Töwen-Bazar, one of the more northerly villages which merges imperceptibly into Guma Bazar. It was pleasant to ride in the shady village lanes, with a peep again and again into homely little fruit gardens. The profuse growth of melons and cucumbers was a characteristic feature of all; I passed several open-air paper factories, the pulp, prepared from the bark of the mulberry-tree, drying on little sieve-like screens.

I also met a troop of fantastically clad 'Diwanas,' or beggars, bent apparently on collecting in alms their share of the villagers' harvest. The lanes of the main Bazar through which I returned to camp looked singularly empty after the busy life witnessed on the preceding market-day.

When I left my cheerful Guma camp on the morning of the 6th of October the sky was of radiant clearness, with scarcely a trace of haze. So when I emerged from the shady lanes of the southern part of the Guma oasis on the open Dasht I was not surprised to find parts of the great snowy range distinctly visible. The snows I saw glittering far away over the dark lines of the outer mountains evidently belonged to the main range about the Karakorum Passes. Distances seemed to shrink strangely when I thought that behind those stupendous mountain ramparts lay valleys draining to the Indus. Mist and clouds hung over other parts of the range, and, as the sun rose higher, drew a veil also over the ice-covered ridges first sighted. A couple of miles further, after crossing a broad but now entirely dry river-bed which, lower down, receives the water of the Kara-su, I came upon the first of the old sites which earlier reports had led me to expect on the march from Guma to Moji. All along the right bank of the ravine the ground was thickly strewn with fragments of coarse red pottery. No ornamented pieces could be found, but the exceptional hardness and glaze of these potsherds showed that they belonged to a period far removed from the present. The extent of the area covered by these scattered fragments plainly indicated the site of a large and thickly inhabited settlement. But no other trace now remained of its existence. The innumerable potsherds invariably rested on the bare surface of loess, with never a trace of walls or more substantial remains below.

When to the east of this old site I had crossed the narrow belt of irrigated ground occupied by the hamlets of Mokuila and was passing once more over a barren scrub-covered Dasht, I sighted to the north-east the mound of which my Guma informants had spoken as Topa Tim. 'Tim' is the designation given to all ruined mounds about Kashgar, and as the one now within reach looked through my glasses much like an ancient Stupa, I made haste to reach it. It proved a longer business than I anticipated. For our guide insisted on our first following the road towards Moji and crossing the deep-cut bed of a watercourse, now dry. I accepted his guidance much against my instinct, with the tantalizing result that when wc had got abreast of the mound after a two miles' ride, a cañon-like ravine absolutely cut us off from it. In vain we searched for a place where the perpendicular banks of loess would admit of a descent to the bottom of this fissure, 40 to 50 feet deep. There was nothing for it but to ride back to the road and start afresh on the other side.

The Stupa, when at last reached, was a sight that cheered my archæological heart. In size and proportion it closely resembled the Mauri Tim Stupa near Khanui. Though its exterior had suffered more decay, and an excavation on the top showed that it had not escaped the ravages of the "treasure-seeker," it still rose to a height of nearly 29 feet. Immediately around the Stupa I found the ground strewn with broken bits of ancient pottery, exactly as seen at Mokuila and on the great site subsequently traversed. So the conclusion seems justified that thc habitations which these scanty remains indicate belonged, like the Stupa, to the Buddhist period.

On the first attempt to reach Topa Tim on the other side of the ravine I had passed a débris-strewn area far more extensive than those seen before. Stretching to the north of the caravan route it seemed to cover fully three square miles. My guides called it the 'Tati' of Kakshal. The relics of ancient habitations that lay scattered here in patches of varying extent and thickness comprised, besides pottery fragments of all sorts: pieces of burned brick, slag, broken bits of bone and metal, and similar hard refuse. The conditions in which these remains presented themselves appeared at first very puzzling. But the examination of similar sites which I subsequently traced at many points beyond the limits of the present cultivated area in the Khotan region, and which are all known by the general name of 'Tati,' gradually furnished a convincing explanation. The most striking feature noticed at Kakshal, as well as at all other 'Tatis,' was that the above-named fragments rest on nothing but natural loess, either hard or more or less disintegrated into a sandy condition. It was easy to ascertain that the soil underneath contained neither walls nor other structural remains; for the small banks of loess which rise here and there from the general level of a Tati, sometimes to a height of 10 to 15 feet, and on the top of which the fragments usually lie thickest, invariably displayed on their bare sides the natural soil without any trace of ancient deposits.

In the formation of these banks, as in all other features of such sites, it was impossible to mistake most striking evidence of the erosive action of the winds and sandstorms which sweep the great desert and its outskirts for long periods of the spring and summer. Only the fragments above described could, by the hardness and weight of their material, survive, sinking lower and lower as the ground beneath gets more and more eroded, while everything in the shape of mud walls, timber, etc., as ordinarily used in the construction of Turkestan houses, has long ago decayed and been swept away. Even the potsherds which have withstood destruction bear plain evidence of the slow but continuous onset to which they have been exposed, in their small size and in their peculiarly rough surface, that looks as if it had been subjected to "grounding."

It is evident that such a process of erosion at sites of ancient habitations could not have gone on during the long centuries since their abandonment without also considerably lowering the ground level. But the erosion has not proceeded uniformly over an entire area, as shown by the banks of loess already referred to, which are now seen rising like small plateaus or islands above the more disintegrated parts of a 'Tati.' Whether they derived comparative protection from the greater abundance of hard débris with which they are ordinarily covered, or from some other special feature, it is certain that they are most useful to the archæologist as evidence of the original ground level. Coins, much corroded metal ornaments, stone seals and similar small objects which can withstand the force of the winds, are occasionally picked up from Tatis. A few of the latter situated beyond Guma were found to be named in the list of places where Islam Akhun alleged he had made his discoveries of paper manuscripts or "block-prints." But the examination of the very first sites passed sufficed to show that the physical conditions absolutely precluded the possibility of such relics surviving there.

It was not in the hope of striking finds of this kind that I wandered for a long time over the débris-strewn waste of Kakshal, though it was getting late and Moji, the end of the march, was still far off. There was a weird fascination in the almost complete decay and utter desolation of the scanty remains that marked once thickly inhabited settlements. Occupied in the examination of small pottery pieces with ornamental designs, etc., which my men picked up again and again, I found it difficult to tear myself away even when the last red rays of the sinking sun had strangely illumined the yellow soil and its streaks of reddish-brown pottery. The route to which I rode off at last was difficult to see, for invading waves of low sand dunes had to be crossed for several miles before scrubby ground was reached again near the little village of Chudda. The moon had come up by that time, and as I was riding comfortably along guided by its light I could indulge in reflections regarding the strange places I had seen, without risking loss of the track. It was close on eight o'clock when I arrived at last at Moji, where my tent was ready to receive me.

On the 7th I was induced to make a halt at Moji by the quantity of old coins that were brought to me, almost all of an early Muhammadan ruler who calls himself in the legend Sulaiman Khagan. The site from which they had been obtained, and which I proceeded to examine early in the morning, lies only a mile to the north of the village, and is known as Tögujai. There I found a number of loess banks covered with broken pottery, similar to that seen on the previous day, but less affected by erosion; and the now dry ravines which the flood water of the early summer had cut through them were the place where the old coins had been extracted. A number of men had accompanied me from the village by the local Beg's order, and their search soon furnished me with numerous pieces of pottery showing ornamental designs and often glazed in bright colours. In the bed of the ravine others set to work to seek for coins, and from the burrows they made half a dozen copper pieces were dug out in my presence. There can be no doubt that these coins have been washed out originally from the same débris layers to which the pottery belongs. Thus a clue is gained for the date of the latter, which may help in regard to the chronology of other sites. With the pottery there is found a great deal of broken glass and small bits of j de. Among the former I noticed a number of pieces with that iridescence which is so frequent in the ancient glassware of the West. The production of glass is a long-forgotten art in Turkestan.

From Tögujai I rode to another old site, one and a half miles north-east of Moji, known as Hasa, which had already attracted Dr. Hedin's notice. It is undoubtedly a Muhammadan cemetery, but there is no clear indication as to its date. On a small hillock, from which skulls and skeletons were protruding, I found a number of graves covered with wooden boards. One of them which I opened showed the remains of a child, wrapped in the cotton stuff of the country, and turned towards the Qibla in accordance with orthodox practice. Though the graves are supposed to be those of Shahids, *i.e.*, Musulmans who fell fighting the infidel, the men with me had no scruples whatever in exposing their contents—a proof that fanatical superstition can have no deep hold on them. The sand of the desert has invaded this resting-place, and emphasises its look of desolation. The sky was in full accord with the scene, dust-laden and hazy. Of the mountains no trace could be seen, though Sanju, whence the Karakorum route starts, lies only some twelve miles south of Moji. It seems to me probable that Moji occupies the position indicated by Hiuen-Tsiang for the town of Po-kia-i, where a famous Buddha statue brought from Kashmir was worshipped in the pilgrim's time.

On the 8th of October an easy march of fourteen miles over a gravel-covered Dasht with scanty patches of scrub brought me to Zanguya The bed of the stream, which is crossed immediately before entering the fields of Zanguya, was entirely dry, the water being at this season used up for irrigation. Zanguya is a fairly large oasis, counting over five hundred houses in its several hamlets. I crossed through a long covered Bazar and found beyond it, near the eastern end of the village, a pleasant camping-ground in a field of lucerne. In the evening I visited an old village site, called Kul-Langar, some two miles to the north-west on the edge of the desert. Besides old pottery and the like I here found the remains of two large tanks still clearly traceable.

On the 9th I marched to Pialma, some nineteen miles from Zanguya. The first couple of miles of the road lies through irrigated land; but as the water supply is scant, cultivation shifts every year in turn to one of the four great plots into which the land on this side of the oasis is divided. Were it possible to secure more water by storage or otherwise, no doubt most of the barren Dasht which lies towards Pialma could be brought under cultivation. Light dunes of sand appeared again about the middle of the march, and continued up to the strip of raised ground appropriately known as Bel-kum ("the top sand"). Some miles beyond I sighted the ruined mound of Karakir, which proved to be an ancient Stupa, much decayed but still holding its own among the high dunes of the surrounding drift. The base of the structure when intact must have been about 65 feet square. The size of the bricks agreed closely with that observed in the Stupa of Mauri Tim.

At Pialma, which is quite a small place, counting only about a hundred houses, I reached the last oasis of the Karghalik district eastwards. My camp was pitched in a little fruit garden, the trees of which were still laden with excellent peaches. For my servants the house of the owner offered ample room. Felt carpets and mats are quickly spread over the raised platforms that surround the principal room of these pleasant dwellings, and every time I inspected my servants' quarters along the route I was surprised by their improvised comfort. Not only the average standard of living but also the housing of the agricultural population of Eastern Turkestan, seemed far above the level observed among the corresponding class in any part of India.

CHAPTER XII.

ARRIVAL IN KHOTAN.

A LONG march on the 10th of October was to bring me at last to the very confines of Khotan. Up to Ak-Langar, the regular stage some fourteen miles from Pialma, the route lay over an absolutely barren plain of hard loess and gravel. Two half-decayed pillars on the road a few miles from Pialma mark the boundary between Karghalik and Khotan. At Takhtuwen, about half-way, there is a well sunk to a depth of nearly 200 feet, and at Ak-Langar another, almost equally deep. After the long lonely marches on the flat of the desert, I hailed with delight the appearance of the mountains which from Pialma onwards showed themselves more and more to the south, though the light haze hanging over the landscape never lifted completely. After Ak-Langar sand appeared in low dunes forming the semi-lunes so familiar to me from Ordam-Padshah. By the time I reached the Mazar of Kum-rabat-Padshahim ("My Lord of the Sands Station") we were again in a sea of sand.

Amid these surroundings the lively scene that presented itself at the shrine popularly known as "Pigeons' Sanctuary" (Kaptar-Mazar) was doubly cheerful. Several wooden houses and sheds serve as the residence for thousands of pigeons, which are maintained by the offerings of travellers and the proceeds of pious endowments. They are believed to be the offspring of a pair of doves which miraculously appeared from the heart of Imam Shakir Padshah, who died here in battle with the infidel, *i.e.*, the Buddhists of Khotan. The youthful son of one of the Shaikhs attached to the shrine was alone present to tell me the story. Many thousands had fallen on both sides, and it was impossible to separate the bodies of the faithful 'Shahids' from those of the 'Kafirs.' Then at the prayer of one of the surviving Musulmans the bodies of those who had found martyrdom were miraculously collected on one side, and the doves came forth to mark the remains of the fallen leader. From gratitude, all travellers on the road offer food to the holy birds. I too bought some bags of Indian corn from the store of the shrine, and scattered their contents to the fluttering swarms.

While watching the pretty spectacle I could not help being reminded of what Hiuen-Tsiang tells us of a local cult curiously similar at the western border of Khotan territory. Some thirty miles before reaching the capital, "in the midst of the straight road passing through a great sandy desert," the pilgrim describes "a succession of small hills," which were supposed to be formed by the burrowing of rats. These rats were worshipped with offerings by all the wayfarers, owing to the belief that in ancient times they had saved the land from a great force of Hiung-nu, or Huns, who were ravaging the border. The Khotan king had despaired of defending his country, when in answer to his prayer myriads of rats led by a rat-king destroyed over-night all the leather of the harness and armour of the invading host, which then fell an easy prey to the defenders.

"The rats as big as hedgehogs, their hair of a gold and silver colour," of which Hiuen-Tsiang was told as inhabiting this desert, are no longer to be seen even by the eyes of the pious. But the locality he describes corresponds exactly to the position of the 'Kaptar-Mazar' relative to ancient Khotan, amidst dunes and low conical sandhills covered with tamarisk bushes, while the manner in which the pigeons kept at the shrine are propitiated with food offerings by all modern wayfarers manifestly marks a survival of the Buddhist legend. Just like Hiuen-Tsiang's rats, so now the holy pigeons which have taken their place are supposed to recall the memory of a great victory. It was in fact the first striking instance of that tenacity of local worship which my subsequent researches showed for almost all sacred sites of Buddhist Khotan. In Kashmir and on the Indus it had been no small advantage for me to find the position of old Buddhist or Hindu shrines I was in search of marked invariably by Muhammadan Ziarats. So I might well take it for an auspicious omen that my entry into Khotan territory brought me across a pious local custom which the Muhammadans of this region had derived from their Buddhist ancestors.

Three miles beyond this curious shrine the road emerged from the sandy billows on to a low-lying marshy plain. Here we halted near the solitary hut of Tarbugaz Langar. The news of my coming had preceded me from Pialma. So late in the evening I received the visit of the Beg of Zawa, the next village tract. He was a fine-looking, genial old man, and I appreciated his kindly welcome on this my first night on the soil of Khotan. Camels and baggage ponies had felt the length of the previous day's march. So I decided to divide the remainder of the journey into two short stages. Soon after leaving Tarbugaz cultivated ground was entered, and three miles from it I passed the mud fort which was erected in Yaqub Beg's time, closing the road to Zawa, the first large village of Khotan.

From there onwards there lay an unbroken succession of gardens, hamlets and carefully cultivated fields on both sides. The road itself is flanked by shady avenues of poplars and willows for almost its whole length. Autumn had just turned the leaves yellow and red on most of the trees, and after the monotonous khaki of the desert marches this display of colour was doubly cheerful. On the road the dust lay ankle deep. It was easy to realise the vicinity of a great trade centre from the lively traffic which passed us. I saw strings of donkeys carrying 'Zhubas,' the lambskin coats for the manufacture of which Khotan is famous. Few, indeed, were the passers-by that did not ride on some kind of animal—pony, donkey, or bullock. To proceed to any distance on foot must seem a real hardship even to the poorer classes. No wonder that the people see no reason to object to the ridiculously high heels of their top boots. When riding the inconvenience cannot be felt. But to see the proud possessors of such boots waddle along the road when obliged to use their legs is truly comical.

Some seven miles from Zawa I passed the stony bed of the

Kara-kash ("Black-jade") Darya, the second main river of Khotan. Its bed, fully three-quarters of a mile broad, betokened the great volume of water it carries down in the summer from the glaciers towards the Karakorum. But at this season the river, diminished no doubt by the demands of irrigation, finds room in a single channel, about thirty yards broad and one to two feet deep. I was delighted to come at a distance of about a mile and a half beyond upon a second river-bed, that of a branch of the Kara-kash known as the Yangi-Darya, "the New River." Whatever the age of the designation may be, the position of this bed agrees most accurately with the accounts which Chinese historical records give as to the rivers west of the old capital of Khotan. The site of "Borazan," which I knew to contain in all probability the remains of this ancient capital, lay too far off the road to be visited immediately.

In one of the hamlets of Sipa, east of the "New River," I found a garden that offered a quiet camping-ground. While watching the unloading of my baggage I was not a little surprised by the appearance from a neighbouring house of a man chained by the neck to a heavy iron rod of almost his own length. It was a cultivator who had been sentenced to this punishment some months ago for grievously assaulting a neighbour. Cruel as the weight of the chain looked, I could not help thinking that the mode of punishment had its practical advantages. Instead of being imprisoned the man could remain with his family and follow any occupation not requiring quick movements. At the same time the sight of the inconvenient appendage he has to carry must act as a sufficient deterrent to others, and the guilt of the culprit is constantly brought to notice.

On the morning of the 13th of October I was just about to start from my camp at Yokakun for Khotan when the Beg arrived whom the Amban, on hearing of my approach, had deputed to escort me. The Beg was in his Chinese gala garb and had his own little retinue. So we made quite a cavalcade, even before Badruddin Khan, the head of the Afghan merchants in Khotan and a large trader to Ladak, joined me a few miles from Khotan town with some of his fellow-countrymen. I rode round the bastioned walls of the great square fort that forms the "New City" of the Chinese, and then through the outskirts of the "Old City" to the garden belonging to Tokhta Akhun, a rich merchant, which Badruddin Khan had previously taken up for my residence. The narrow Bazars passed on the way were more than usually squalid. The number of people afflicted with diseases whom I saw in them was also depressing. In the garden which lay close to the southern edge of the suburb

HOUSE OF TOKHTA AKHUN, KHOTAN.

of Gujan I found a large though somewhat gloomy house, but none of the attractions of my Yarkand residence. The maze of little rooms all lit from the roof and badly deficient in ventilation could not be used for my own quarters. Outside in the garden there was a picturesque wilderness of trees and bushes, but little room for a tent and still less of privac So after settling down for the day and despatching my messages and presents for the Amban, I used the few remaining hours of daylight for a reconnaissance that was to show me the immediate environs, and also a more congenial camping-ground.

There is a charm about the ease with which, in these parts, one may invade the house of any one, high or low, sure to find a courteous reception, whether the visit is expected or otherwise. So when after a long ride through suburban lanes and along the far-stretching lines of mud-built fortifications erected after the last revolt against the Chinese, but already crumbling into ruin, I came about half a mile from Tokhta Akhun's upon another residential garden, enclosed by high walls and surrounded by fields, I did not hesitate to have my visit announced to the owner. Through a series of courts I entered a large and airy reception hall, and through it passed into a large open garden that at once took my fancy. Akhun Beg, a fine-looking, portly old gentleman, received me like a guest, and when informed of the object of my search readily offered me the use of his residence. I had disturbed him in the reading of a Turki version of Firdusi's Shahnama. My acquaintance with the original of the great Persian epic seemed to win for me at once the goodwill of my impromptu host, and I hesitated the less about accepting his offer. So when next morning my tent was pitched on the lawn in front of a shady clump of trees, I again enjoyed the peace and seclusion of a country residence.

At noon I paid my first visit to Pan-Darin, the Amban, after the usual preliminaries required by Chinese etiquette. I found him a quiet, elderly man, with features that seemed to betoken thoughtfulness and honesty of purpose. His kindly though somewhat abstracted look and his gentle manners of gesture and speech impressed me from the first as entirely in agreement with the reputation for learning and piety which has followed this Mandarin wherever he was employed in the province. Dressed in his state clothes and surrounded by numerous attendants, Pan-Darin received me with every mark of attention. He had long before been informed from Kashgar of the objects of my visit, and I was curious to see what his attitude would be, both as to explorations in the desert and my proposed survey of the mountains about the sources of the Khotan river.

To my delight there was no trace of obstruction to be discovered in what Pan-Darin had to tell me as to either project. He had no doubt that ancient places amidst the dreaded sands of the 'Gobi,' if they existed at all, were difficult to reach, and that the statements made about them by natives were not to be trusted too readily. In the mountains again the routes were

PAN-DARIN, AMBAN OF KHOTAN, WITH PERSONAL ATTENDANTS.

bad, implying hardships and risks, and beyond the valleys of Karanghu-tagh there lay the unknown uplands of Tibet where Chinese authority ceased, and where, under the strict orders of the Tsung-li-Yamen, no assistance was to be rendered to travellers. But apart from these natural difficulties and political limitations Pan-Darin offered to give me all help that lay in his power. The Amban's simple, earnest ways, his evident comprehension of the scientific objects in view, and the scholarly interest with which he followed my explanations about Hiuen-Tsiang's travels and the old Buddhist culture of Khotan, induced me to put reliance in this promise of help. And subsequent experience showed me how well it was justified. Without his ever ready assistance neither the explorations in the desert nor the survey work in the mountains which preceded it could have been accomplished.

As soon as I had arrived in Khotan I had commenced the local inquiries which were to guide me as to ancient sites particularly deserving exploration and as to the best means for organising a systematic search for antiquities. Apprehensions about possible forgeries had prevented me from sending in advance to Khotan information as to the main object of my journey. I now found that some time would have to be allowed for the collection of specimens of antiquities from the various old sites which "treasure-seekers" were in the habit of visiting. "Treasure-seeking," *i.e.*, the search for chance finds of precious metal within the areas of abandoned settlements, has indeed been a time-honoured occupation in the whole of the Khotan oasis, offering like gold-washing and jade-digging the fascinations of a kind of lottery to those low down in luck and averse to any constant exertion. In recent years, owing to the continued demand of European collectors from Kashgar and elsewhere, the small fraternity of quasi-professional treasure-seekers had learned on their periodical visits to ancient sites to pay attention also to antiquities as secondary proceeds. Nevertheless, all the information that could be elicited about such localities, even from persons who seemed reliable, was exceedingly vague, and I soon realised that if I were to set out without having before me specimens distinctly traceable to specific sites, much valuable time might be lost and labour wasted. In order to secure such specimens, Badruddin Khan, who had previously rendered useful services to Mr. Macartney, offered to organise and send out small "prospecting" parties. Their return, however, could not be expected before a month, and I decided to utilise this interval for the interesting geographical task which I had already marked out for myself in the mountains south of Khotan.

That portion of the Kuen-luen range which contains the headquarters of the Yurung-kash or Khotan River had hitherto remained practically unsurveyed, the scanty information available being restricted to the sketch map of the route by which Mr. Johnson, in 1865, had made his way from Ladak down to Khotan. Colonel Trotter had, in 1875, expressed the belief that the head waters of the Yurung-kash were much further to the east than shown on that map and probably identical with a stream rising on the plateau south of Polu. Captain Deasy, working from the side of Polu in 1898, succeeded in reaching the sources of this stream at an elevation of over 16,000 feet, but was prevented from following it downwards. Thus the true course of the main feeder of the Yurung-kash, together with most of the orography of the surrounding region, still remained to be explored.

The close approach of winter made me anxious to set out for this task with as little delay as possible, while it was necessary to equip properly the men as well as the ponies that were to accompany me, for the cold mountain region to be visited. My camels could be of no use in that direction, and extra ponies were needed for the baggage with which I was to move up, greatly reduced as it was. The animals of the 'Kirakash' or professional caravan men were all away on the Karakorum route, where the autumn months are the busy time for the trade with Ladak. To buy ponies for this comparatively short tour would have been an expensive arrangement. So I felt glad when the Amban, on returning my visit the next day, issued orders to supply me with the transport needed on hire from neighbouring villages.

While Badruddin Khan busied himself with procuring the fur clothing for my men and the felt covers for the ponies, I managed to pay a visit to the village of Yotkan, the site of the old capital of Khotan and a well-known find-place of antiquities of all sorts. It was an interesting day I spent at that locality, where the accumulated débris layers of the old city, embedded deep below the present level, are being regularly washed for gold, and in the course of these operations yield up also ancient pottery, coins, seals, and similar remains. But I need not here detail the impressions of that first hurried visit; for subsequent investigations were to render me far more familiar with this important site.

During the few days of my stay at Khotan much of my time was taken up with the inspection of the coins, terra-cotta figures, and other antiquities that were brought for sale by villagers and "treasure-seekers." Most of the bagfuls contained only the broken pottery and copper coins found so plentifully at Yotkan, and already fairly well known from previously formed collections. But their inspection was a useful training to me, and I thought it advisable to make at first ample purchases so as to stimulate the zest of professional searchers.

I was naturally on the look-out too for those "old books" written or "block-printed" in a variety of unknown characters which, as already mentioned, had during the last five or six years been sold from Khotan in increasing numbers to European collectors at Kashgar. In regard to these acquisitions the suspicion of forgery had before presented itself to competent scholars, but evidence was wanting to substantiate it, and in the meantime these strange texts continued to be edited and analysed in learned publications. Offers in this article were surprisingly scanty at Khotan itself, and curiously enough the very first "old book" that was shown to me supplied unmistakable proof of forgery. Hearing of my presence at the place, a Russian Armenian from Kokand brought me for inspection a manuscript on birch-bark, consisting of some ten ragged leaves covered with an "unknown" script. He had bought it for forty roubles, undoubtedly as a commercial speculation, and now wished to have his treasure properly appraised.

I saw at once that the birch-bark leaves had never received the treatment which ancient Bhurja manuscripts, well known to me from Kashmir, invariably show. Nor had the forger attempted to reproduce the special ink which is needed for writing on birch-bark. So when I applied the "water-test" the touch of a wet finger sufficed to take away the queer "unknown characters" both written and block-printed. It was significant that the "printed matter" of this manifest forgery showed a close resemblance to the formulas of certain "block-prints" contained in the Calcutta collection. In fact, my inquiries indicated a close connection between the person from whom the Armenian had purchased the leaves and Islam Akhun, the treasure-seeker whose alleged places of discovery I had vainly endeavoured to locate about Guma. Local rumour credited Islam Akhun with having worked a small factory for the production of "old books." But at this time he was keeping away from Khotan, and there were reasons to postpone personal investigations about him.

On the day preceding my start for the mountains I was cheered by the opportune arrival of my Dak from Yarkand. The contents of my home mails, despatched viâ India, did not come down later than the 17th of August. But the evening before I had received a letter sent to Kashgar through the Russian post and thence forwarded with the official Chinese Dak, which had been written as recently as the 19th of September. No more convincing proof is needed of the comparative proximity to which the advance of the Russian railway system has brought even this distant corner of Turkestan, described by Sir Henry Yule in 1865 as "the most inaccessible and least known of Asiatic States." The quotation is from the great scholar's "Cathay and the Way Thither," a work which followed me everywhere on my travels, and the reading of which never failed to provide both learned guidance and amusement.

MUZTAGH PEAK, IN KUEN-LUEN RANGE.

CHAPTER XIII.

TO THE HEADWATERS OF THE YURUNG-KASH.

AT midday of the 17th of October I set out for my journey into the mountains, after taking a friendly leave of Akhun Beg, my white-haired host. A five-rouble gold piece, presented in a little steel purse, as a return for the use of his garden, was accepted without much difficulty. I was glad to leave behind in Badruddin's care all stores and other articles not immediately needed. Nevertheless our baggage, including the survey instruments and food supplies for a full month, required ten ponies. The first march was luckily a short and easy one. For about six miles we proceeded south through cultivated land, dotted with hamlets, to the village of Jamada, not far from the left bank of the Yurung-kash. Beyond it the bare Dasht rises gently towards the foot of the mountains, which now stood clear of the haze that had veiled them at Khotan.

On the sandy plain south of Jamada I found a 'Tati' with relics of ancient settlement. Fragments of pottery are strewn over the site, and some villagers brought me old coins, beads, and a few small seals, one showing the figure of a Cupid. We then rode for four miles over the high banks of stone and gravel which the river has brought down from its course in the mountains, and at last crossed to the right bank. The bed of the Yurung-kash is over a mile broad at this point, but the water flowed only in a few narrow channels. The rest is diverted into the canals that feed the villages of the eastern part of the Khotan oasis. Our night's quarters were at Bizil, a small village close to the river-bed, where many burrows and pebble heaps showed the working of jade-seekers. The stone, which has from ancient times been so highly prized in China, and to which the river owes its name, "White-jade," is still an important product. As I crossed the river-bed I thought of the distant lands to which it has carried the name of Khotan.

Beyond Bizil, to the south, low, undulating slopes of much-decayed conglomerate ascend towards the mountains. Over these we travelled on the morning of the 18th of October. Several ridges, fairly steep on the north side, but joined by almost level terraces on the south, form natural steps in the ascent. Gravel and coarse sand, with scarcely a trace of vegetation, covers the ground; and the landscape, save for the distant view of the Khotan oasis below, was one of complete desolation. When the last of the steps was crossed by the Tashlik-Boyan Pass, I found myself in full view of the outer ranges through which the Yurung-kash flows in a tortuous gorge, and greeted with relief some snowy peaks that raised their heads above them, far away to the south. A long descent over a sandy slope brought us to the Kissel Stream, along which our onward route lay. Half smothered by the dust that the ponies raised as they scrambled down, we reached the bottom of the valley at the little hamlet of Kumat. A narrow strip of level ground by the side of the Kissel and irrigated from it, supports some fifteen families. It was soon dark in the deep and narrow glen, and the four miles we had to march to Yangi-Langar, our night quarters, seemed very long. The night air was still and warmer than in the plain of Khotan, the thermometer showing 48° F. at 8 p.m.

On the 19th of October a march of some eighteen miles up the winding gorge of the Kissel brought us to Tarim-Kishlak;

On the whole way there was no habitation, nor indeed room for one. The rough path crossed innumerable times the stream that flows between high and precipitous spurs of conglomerate and what looked to me like sandstone. In more than one place there was a difficulty in getting the laden ponies over the rocks that fill the narrow bottom of the gorge. As this jumbled mountain mass has never been surveyed, it was tantalising to wind along between the rocky walls without a chance of an open view. But there was no time to be lost with climbs to points that might give one. Tarim-Kishlak ("cultivated holding") consists of a single miserable mud dwelling amid a few fields of oats. Apart from the small patch of sloping ground that is irrigated from the stream, there is nothing around but decayed rock and ravines filled with gravel. Compared to the absolute barrenness of these hill-sides, the vegetation of the Hunza or Sarikol glens would look quite luxuriant.

On the morning of the 20th of October I found the little stream, by the side of which my tent was pitched, half covered with ice. The boiling-point thermometer indicated an elevation of close on 9,000 feet, and the air at 7 a.m. was just at freezing point. The gorge we ascended continued for another eight miles in a south-easterly direction. Then the path leaves the stream which comes from a high mountain capped with snow, and strikes up a dry side gorge to the south. Here all trace of rock disappeared from the surface of the hill-sides. Loose earth and detritus were alone to be seen, with scanty patches of hardy scrub. Before we reached the pass, a strong wind sprung up that overcast the sky with clouds and shrouded us in dust. So when at last by 2 p.m. we stood on the Ulugh-Dawan ("High Pass"), the distant view to the south was seen through a haze. All the same, when I had climbed with the Sub-Surveyor a ridge rising about 500 feet above the pass, we were rewarded by the sight of a grand glacier-girt mountain rising in solitary splendour to the south-east. It was impossible to mistake the "Kuen-luen Peak, No. 5," which the tables of the Indian Trigonometrical Survey showed with a height of 23,890 feet. Right and left of it stretched a chain of ice mountains, but their crests were hidden in clouds, and our endeavour to recognize among them other peaks fixed from the southern side was in vain. The wind on the pass was cutting and the temperature close to freezing-point. By boiling-point thermometer we found the height to be over 12,000 feet.

I was glad to leave by 4 p.m. the cheerless ridge. The descent into the Buya Valley, which runs from east to west draining by an inaccessible gorge into the Yurung-kash, was very steep and trying. The bleak mountain-side is fissured by narrow ravines, and the path follows the ridges between them: The landscape looked wild and lifeless in the extreme. It was quite dark before we had extricated ourselves from the rocky ledges that project from the decomposed slopes and lead ladder-like down to the valley. With some difficulty our guide found the way to the main group of huts of Buya, but the straggling baggage animals were much belated, and I had to sit till midnight in a smoke mud hovel before my tent was pitched and my dinner ready.

Next morning when I rose I found to my delight that the sky had completely cleared. In order not to lose the good chance for survey work, I decided to push on to Pisha, though men as well as animals seemed in need of a day's rest. The valley of Buya, about a mile broad at the principal hamlet, supports from its scanty fields of oats a population of thirty odd holdings. The level of our camp was close on 8,000 feet. To the south of the valley rises a series of plateaus showing on the surface only detritus and gravel, with conical hills crowning them at intervals. When we had climbed the crest of the nearest plateau the whole of the great snowy range towards Ladak and the westernmost border of Tibet lay spread out before us. Over the whole chain towered the great Kuen-luen Peak already referred to, with its glaciers now clearly visible. The Un-bashi ("head of Ten") of Buya, an uncouth looking hillman or 'Taghlik,' knew the peak only by the name of 'Muz-tagh' ("the Ice-mountain"). Apart from the glittering walls of snow and ice in the far south, there was nothing to be seen before us but the yellowish slopes of the plateaus that mark where transverse ridges must once have risen. The extremes of temperature, and possibly the excessive dryness of the climate, with the consequent absence of vegetation, may partly account for the extraordinary disintegration of the soil. In colour and outlines the near view reminded me of the hill ranges that are seen when passing along the Egyptian coast of the Gulf of Suez. The plateaus are separated by broad depressions in which tiny streams of saltish water try to make their way towards the Yurung-kash. Except when the snow melts on the distant mountains eastwards, there is no moisture to fill these ravines.

Thus we marched for about ten miles to the south-west, glad that the ground offered no difficulty to the tired ponies. From a high ridge that crowns the last plateau southwards, I sighted the broad and partly cultivated valley of Pisha, and on its other side the ridge that still separated us from Karanghutagh, the last inhabited valley at the northern foot of the Kuen-luen, our immediate goal. At 5 p.m. I arrived at Kuldöbe, the main hamlet of the Pisha Valley, where two dozen or so of Taghliks were assembled to welcome me. There seemed little in their speech or manners to distinguish them from the people of Khotan. But their sheepskin coats and hard weather-beaten faces indicated the difference of the climatic conditions. Many among them had never seen the plains. Harsh and bare of all graces are their surroundings. I wondered whether they ever see flowers such as carpet the Pamir grazing-grounds.

The 22nd of October was needed as a day of rest for men and beasts, and I was glad to grant it in a locality where there was at least plenty of shelter. The sky was heavy with clouds, and cold blasts swept up the valley from time to time, enveloping it in a haze of dust. After a morning spent over notes and letters I went for a walk along the stream through cheerless fields and with nothing in view but the bare grey spurs that line the valley. On my return I found the whole grown-up male population of Pisha assembled in the courtyard of the mud dwelling where my men had established themselves. It seemed that for many years past Pisha had known no such time of excitement and novel interest. In Hakim Shah, the oldest man of the valley and father of the local Yüzbashi, I found an intelligent interlocutor. He claimed an age of fully a hundred years, and his wrinkled face and snowy hair seemed to support his assertion. Though bent by the burden of his years, the old man was still active enough in mind, and he talked glibly of the days of early Chinese rule before the Muhammadan revolt. He had once in his life been to Khotan, and was evidently in the eyes of his people a man well-up in the affairs of the world.

My men had been told that a difficult and long march lay before us. So on the morning of the 23rd they were quicker than usual about the start. When I got outside my tent a little after six o'clock I saw to my delight a gloriously clear sky. The cold was also a surprise. Even at 7 a.m. the thermometer showed 23° F.; the little watercourse near my tent was hard frozen. As soon as we had climbed the edge of the plateau some 500 feet above Pisha, a grand view opened out upon the whole ice-crowned range. Kuen-luen Peak No. 5 now lay in full view to the south-east, and its glacier-crowned head appeared quite close in the absolutely clear atmosphere. For about eight miles we rode over a broad, barren plateau that rose with an easy gradient towards the south. Then I turned off the track and climbed a high ridge eastwards that from a distance promised a good surveying station.

Its height, 13,950 feet above the sea, commanded a panorama more impressive than any I had enjoyed since I stood on the slope of Muztagh-Ata. To the east there rose the great Kuen-luen Peak with its fantastic ridges separated by glittering glaciers and its foot rising from a belt of strangely eroded bare ridges, as shown by the photograph at the head of this chapter. By its side the gorge of the main branch of the Yurung-kash could clearly be made out as it cuts through the series of stupendous spurs that trend northwards from the main snowy range of the Kuen-luen. From the latter the great peak was thus entirely separated—an interesting observation fully in accord with the orography of the Karakorum and Hindukush. There it has long ago been remarked that the points of greatest elevation are not to be found on the actual watershed, but on secondary spurs detached from it.

The deep-cut valleys and serrated ridges descending from the main range presented a most striking contrast to the flat, worn-down features of the plateaus behind us. To the west the course of the Yurung-kash was lost in a jumble of rocky walls that gradually sank away towards the plain. In the north there showed itself as one unbroken mass the gaunt conglomerate range which we had crossed on the way to Buya, culminating in a broad, snow-covered peak, the Tikelik-tagh, some distance to the east of the Ulugh-Dawan. Nature could not have created a better survey-station than the ridge on which I stood. With the enjoyment of the grand panoramic view there mingled the satisfaction of seeing so large and interesting a tract hitherto unsurveyed suddenly spread out before me as if it were a map. While Ram Singh worked away at his plane-table I was busily engaged in taking a complete circle of views with the photo-theodolite. Notwithstanding the perfectly blue sky it was bitterly cold on that height, as my fingers soon felt in handling the delicate instrument.

It was nearly three o'clock before our work was done, and I was able to hurry down hill. I had noticed how distant the valley of Karanghu-tagh was where we were to finish the day's march, and the guides from Pisha had, with unwonted animation, dwelt on the badness of the track leading to it. After a comparatively easy descent of two miles we reached the line where the high plateau so far followed falls off towards the Yurung-kash Valley in a series of precipitous ravines. The one which the track follows at first looked exactly like the gorges I had seen in Astor leading down to the Indus. High rock-faces lined its sides, and the withering effects of atmospheric influences seemed here less marked than on the ranges passed northwards. At an elevation of about 11,000 feet the path crossed a rocky neck eastwards, and then led down precipitously to the river flowing more than 3,000 feet below.

It was just getting dark as we began this trying part of the descent, but even if it had been broad daylight it would have been impossible to ride. The angle at which the path zigzags down the precipitous cliff was so steep that the ponies could be dragged forward only with difficulty. The loose stones that cover the path increased the trouble, while the deep dust in which they are imbedded at times almost smothered us. Never had I marched in such a dust-cloud as that which enveloped us until, after an hour and a half's scramble, the bottom of the valley was reached at the point where the Yurung-kash is joined by the Kash stream flowing out from the side valley of Karanghu-tagh.

It was perfectly dark when we crossed to the left bank of the Yurung-kash by a rickety bridge consisting of three badly joined beams laid over a chasm some 70 feet wide. The foam of the river tossing deep down in the narrow bed of rocks could be made out even in the darkness. In daylight, and in a less tired condition, the crossing might have affected one's nerves more. As it was, I felt heartily glad when I saw the ponies safely on the other side. Karanghu-tagh means "Mountain of blinding darkness," and at the time of our approach the appropriateness of the name could not have been doubted. For about an hour we and our tired beasts groped our way between the boulder-strewn bank of the Kash stream and the foot of steep hill-slopes before we reached at last the village that bears that cheerful name. The baggage had arrived safely, but also with great delay, and thus it was late in the night before I could retire to rest.

The 24th of October was spent at Karanghu-tagh, where arrangements had to be made for men and yaks to take us further into the mountains. The survey of the previous day had shown me that the only way by which the source of the main branch of the Khotan River might possibly be approached would lie in the gorge of the river itself. The Yüzbashi and the old men of the little village, whom I summoned in the morning, at first denied stoutly that the valley of the Yurung-kash was accessible beyond the point where we had crossed it. By-and-bye, however, I elicited the fact that there were summer grazing-grounds in some of the nullahs descending from Muztagh, and then the fact of their being reached by a track up the Yurung-kash had to be acknowledged. Of a route across the main range south, by which Mr. Johnson appears to have come on his rapid descent from Leh to Khotan in 1865, I could get absolutely no information. It was evident that the hill-men feared the trouble and exposure of a tour in those high regions. At the same time the serious and very puzzling discrepancies I discovered between the sketch-map of Mr. Johnson's route and the actual orography of the mountains south of Pisha convinced me that I could not dispense with local guidance. My interest, however, lay eastwards where the course of the Yurung-kash was to be traced. After a time Islam Beg, a young and energetic attendant of the Khotan Yamen, whom Pan-Darin had despatched with me, succeeded in making it clear to the surly Taghliks that the Amban's order for assistance to me must be obeyed. So those who rule Karanghu-tagh set about to collect the yaks which were to take on my baggage and the men who were to accompany me.

It was no difficult task, for Karanghu-tagh, though hidden away amid a wilderness of barren mountains, is a place of some resources. When I inspected it in the morning I was surprised to find a regular village of some forty closely packed houses. The scanty fields of oats below and above could scarcely support this population. But Karanghu-tagh is also the winter station for the herdsmen who graze flocks of yaks and sheep in the valleys of the Upper Yurung-kash. These herds belong mostly to Khotan 'Bais,' or merchants, and the visits of the latter seem the only tie that connects this strangely forlorn community with the outer world. From time to time, however, Karanghu-tagh receives a permanent addition to its population in the persons of select malefactors from Khotan, who are sent here for banishment.

It would indeed be difficult to find a bleaker place of exile. A narrow valley shut in between absolutely bare and precipitous ranges, without even a view of the snowy peaks, must appear like a prison to those who come from outside. It was strange to hear the hill-men, who during the summer lead a solitary life in the distant glens, speak of Karanghu-tagh as their 'Shahr' or "town." For these hardy sons of the mountains this cluster of mud-hovels, with its few willows and poplars, represents, no doubt, an enviable residence. To me the strange penal settlement somehow appeared far more lonely and depressing than the absolute solitude of the mountains.

I was glad to start soon on a climb to one of the steep

TAGHLIKS AND EXILED CRIMINALS AT KARANGHU TAGH.

ridges north-east of the village, which offered a convenient station for further survey work. But the day was far less clear than the preceding one, and the views too were less inspiriting. On my return I passed the cemetery of Karanghu-tagh. The number of tombs it contains may, in view of the very scanty population (barely amounting to 200 souls), be taken as a sign of long-continued occupation. There were plenty of decayed little domes of mud and wooden enclosures marking graves. Over them rose high staffs, invariably hung with a yak's tail. I counted also two mosques in the place, and half-a-dozen simple Mazars, where a bundle of sticks bedecked with rags and yaks' tails marks the reputed resting-place of some holy man. I could well believe that the dreariness of their earthly surroundings might turn the minds of the dwellers in this gloomy vale to a happier world beyond.

The information extracted with no little trouble from the Yüzbashi of Karanghu-tagh and his people about a route up the main valley of the Yurung-kash was by no means encouraging. They acknowledged that a little settlement existed in the Omsha Jilga, one march up the main valley, and that a path accessible to yaks led beyond to a point where a hot spring flows into the river. But after this no possible track could be found through the mountains. Whether this was true or not could be made certain only by personal inspection. Yaks were to carry the indispensable baggage and to serve as riding animals for myself and my men. The ponies which had been severely tried by the preceding marches were to remain at Karanghu-tagh in charge of Niaz Akhun, the Chinese interpreter. He had complained of the hardships previously experienced. It was easier for me to part with him than with 'Yolchi Beg,' my little terrier. He had bravely kept up so far, but the long marches had evidently told on him, and a rest would give him fresh strength for the fatigues still before us.

By 10 a.m. on the 25th of October the yaks were packed and the caravan was ready to start. With each animal I took a hill-man to guide it. Yaks are as sluggish as they are sure-footed, and without a man to drag each animal by the rope which is passed through its muzzle the rate of progress would be amazingly slow. I arranged that each man should be provided with food for ten days, and secured extra yaks to carry these rations. Karanghu-tagh has perhaps never seen so grand a procession as when my caravan set out on the march. The whole village turned out to witness the spectacle.

After passing down the Kash valley for about two miles we struck to the east, and, crossing the spur I had before ascended, moved into the side-valley of Busat. Not far from the point where it bifurcates into two narrow gorges leading up to the mountain wall southwards, the path ascended a high cross-spur. From its top, at an elevation of close on 12,000 feet, the glaciers of the great Muztagh, and all the gorges leading down to the main stream, were visible in great clearness. So the photo-theodolite was brought to work again, though the weather was not as favourable as on the day when I marched to Karanghu-tagh. Early in the afternoon for several days past I had noticed the same atmospheric change, a strong north wind rising and bringing clouds and a dust-haze that soon covered the sky.

From the Boinak spur an easy path led down for some three miles to where the mouth of the Omsha Valley descending from the west face of Muztagh opens into the Yurung-kash gorge. The river, which we here crossed to the right bank, was about 50 yards broad, and nowhere deeper than 3 feet. Its water had a delightful bluish-green tint, and reminded me by its limpidity of the mountain streams of Kashmir and the Alps. I wondered how to account for this clearness of the water, seeing that the Yurung-kash must be fed very largely by the glacier water of the Muztagh and other peaks. Of the large volume of water which it carries down during the summer months, the broad strips of boulder-strewn ground were a plain indication.

On the 26th of October I woke again to a gloriously clear morning, and soon forgot in the rays of the rising sun that it had been 24° F. at 7 a.m. From Terek-aghzi, where I had camped by the river-bank, a steep path led up to a long grassy spur known as Zilan, jutting out from the mountain side northward. On reaching its top, after a climb of two and a half hours, I was rewarded by a splendid view of the glacier-girt Muztagh and the rugged snowy range southwards. Some four miles to the south-east the Yurung-kash gorge completely disappeared between the series of stupendous spurs of rock which descend from the great peak on its left and the main range opposite. Looking up towards the mighty southern buttresses of "K.5," and the frowning ice-peaks showing their heads above them, it required almost an effort of imagination to believe that behind lay those Pamir-like uplands in which, as I knew from Captain Deasy's explorations, the Yurung-kash takes its rise. That there was no practicable route over the rock-walls through which the river has cut its way past Muztagh, was absolutely clear from the view before us. But there remained the chance of the river-bed itself offering the desired passage. This hope occupied my mind as I

VIEW UP THE YURUNG-KASH GORGE, WITH SPURS OF PEAK K.5 ON LEFT.

descended by a difficult track just practicable for yaks to the left bank of the river, at the point known as Issik-bulak, "the hot spring." On the sheer cliffs opposite my camping-ground, and at a height of about 300 feet above the level of the river-bed, I could see a hot spring issuing in considerable volume. The hill people are said to bathe in its water when the winter makes the river easily fordable. The half-a-dozen herdsmen of Omsha, who had joined me on the way, unanimously declared that they had never passed beyond this spot, and that the gorge further up was inaccessible for human feet. Whether their assertion was true, or whether the formidable ravine ahead would not yield us an opening, was a question that only the morrow's exploration could answer.

On the 27th of October a day's hard climbing among the rocks, shingle, and boulders of the Yurung-kash gorge verified the Taghliks' prediction. As soon as the sun had fairly risen over the great mountain walls to the east I started with Ram Singh, Tila Bai, the most active of my people, and three hill-men from Omsha. Foreseeing that we should have to cross the river in the course of our reconnaissance, I had three of the biggest yaks taken along. At first we followed the steep hill-side above the right bank where our camp was pitched, as its height promised a better view of the ground ahead. We had made our way for about a mile and a half onwards when all further progress was barred by a ravine descending from a great height and flanked by wholly unscaleable rocks. The view I had before me was wild in the extreme. I could now clearly make out the walls of frowning cliffs which, broken only by almost equally precipitous shoots of rock and shingle, lined the foot of the great spurs falling off to the river. The passage left for the river seemed nowhere more than 200 feet wide, and at places considerably less. The volume of water reduced by the autumn now filled only one-half to three-fourths of this space. But the beds of huge boulders seen along the actual channel were not continuous, but alternately on the left and right bank. Where the river flowed with light green colour over boulders and ledges, we might hope to effect a crossing. But where it whirled round the foot of sheer cliffs the water showed a colour of intense blue, and was manifestly far deeper. Yet it was clear that our only hope lay in being able to follow up the river-bed.

To descend to it was no easy matter from where we stood. But after marching back for half a mile we found a practicable slope and managed to scramble down to the edge of the water. When the yaks had been dragged down too, with much trouble, we began to make our way up the ravine. A wall of impassable rock, with a stretch of deep water at its foot, forced us soon to search for a ford to the opposite side. This we found, and thanks to the yaks, which waded splendidly in the ice-cold water undismayed by the rapid current, we managed to get safely across. The yak is a difficult animal to guide, even on the best ground; when in the water any attempt to control its movements would be useless. So it was with a feeling of relief that I noticed the instinctive care with which our yaks made their way from one convenient boulder to the other. The limpid water made it possible for them to see their way as much as to feel it.

On the left bank we had scarcely advanced a few hundred yards over jumbled masses of rock that had been swept down from the slopes above, when we were stopped again by a precipitous rock-face washed at its foot by the ominous blue water. To cross over to the opposite bank, where a stretch of boulder-strewn ground might have allowed an advance, was quite impossible. The yak we drove into the water to test its depth was soon obliged to swim, and had we attempted the passage we should have had to follow its example. In order to effect a crossing here with the needful baggage a raft or boat was manifestly indispensable. But how could we secure it in this forlorn region, where wood was practically unobtainable, and where the people had never even heard of that most useful implement, the 'Massak,' or inflated skin?

The only chance of progress left was to take to the crags above us, and to trust that further on a descent might be found again to a practicable portion of the river-bed. After a difficult climb of some 500 feet I managed to bring myself and my men safely to a narrow flat ledge, but the yaks had to be left below. We followed the ledge for some hundreds of yards until it ended at the flank of a ravine that would have defied any cragsman. A careful search for a point where we might descend again to the river was in vain. The steep shingly slope terminated everywhere in cliffs that offered no foothold. Baffled in these endeavours, I climbed up the precipitous hillside above the ledge that had brought us so far, in the hope of turning the ravine. But after an ascent of about 1,000 feet I convinced myself that the ground beyond was one over which I could never hope to move either yaks or men with loads.

While I was resting on a little projecting ridge the noise of falling stones drew my attention to a herd of wild goats (Kiyik) that were evidently about to descend from the cliffs opposite. The tracks of these animals I had already noticed on the hill-side. They alone are likely ever to have penetrated into the wild gorge that lay before me. The point where a large stream from the glaciers of Muztagh falls into the Yurung-kash seemed temptingly near. Once beyond this junction there would be less difficulty in crossing the river, and consequently in ascending its bed. Yet there was no hope of reaching this point until perhaps the river was completely frozen, an eventuality for which it was impossible to wait. Even then I doubt whether a practicable passage could be found, considering the climatic conditions and the masses of fallen rock likely to be encountered.

All day an icy wind had been blowing down the valley, giving a foretaste of the cold that might be encountered at this season on the elevated plateau where, in view of our survey results, the source of the river can now be definitely located. I did not envy the yaks the bath they got in crossing back to the right bank, and was heartily glad to reach the shelter of my tent at the hour of dusk. The night was cloudy and still, and on the following morning snow was falling on the mountains down tc about 3,000 feet above our camp, the elevation of which by aneroid was close to 9,000 feet. Down in the river gorge the temperature at 7 a.m. was a little higher than on previous days (34° F.), but as soon as we ascended by the path we had come before it became bitterly cold, and the wind was piercing. Winter had already set in for these regions.

For the return to Karanghu-tagh I chose the route through the Omsha Valley, into which we crossed without much difficulty over the ridge of Soghak-Öghil, at an elevation of about 11,500 feet. At the central hamlet of Omsha I found two low mud-built houses among a few fields of oats and some troglodyte shepherds' dwellings. The weather cleared in the afternoon, and I felt grateful for the warming rays of the sun before he set behind the mountains. The valley of Omsha, though scarcely a quarter of a mile broad, looked quite spacious and inviting after the awful gorge of the main river. Notwith-

YAKS CARRYING BAGGAGE IN YURUNG-KASH GORGE, NEAR KARANGHU-TAGH.

standing the elevation of about 10,000 feet, oats are said to grow well in years when a sufficient snowfall on the mountains around assures irrigation.

The elevation of Omsha, together with the change in the weather, made itself felt by a truly cold night. On the morning of the 29th of October the thermometer at 7 a.m. showed only 17° F. But the sky was of dazzling clearness, and in the crisp mountain air the cold had an almost exhilarating effect. After a pleasant march of two hours we reached the right bank of the Yurung-kash, close to Terek-aghzi. Instead of the previous route, I now followed the path by the riverside. It crosses the Yurung-kash about two miles below the above junction, and then winds along the precipitous cliffs of the left bank for another three miles. The ups and downs over slopes of loose conglomerate were very fatiguing, but the picturesque views of the wild river-gorge amply made up for this. At one point the river has cut its way through walls of solid rock, scarcely 50 feet apart, for a distance of several hundred yards. Elsewhere the vehemence of floods has excavated yawning caverns from the huge alluvial fans. Not far from the point where the Kash Valley from Karanghu-tagh joins this gorge, the path led over a succession of rocky ledges of remarkable steepness. The ascent indeed looked like a huge flight of stairs built by nature along the brink of a precipice more than 500 feet high. The yaks climbed it with astonishing surefootedness, but it was uncomfortable to look down on the track over which they had carried us.

CHAPTER XIV.

OVER THE KARA-KASH RANGES.

OUR previous survey, including the expedition up the Yurung kash gorge, had cleared up the important question as to the true origin and course of the main feeder of the Khotan River. The next and equally interesting task was to map the head waters of the streams which drain the portion of the Kuen-luen range south and south-west of Karanghu-tagh, and are manifestly the principal tributaries. In the course of my inquiries from the Omsha herdsmen about dominant points that would enable me to sight again the series of magnificent glaciers which feed the Kash River, I had ascertained that there was a difficult path just practicable for laden yaks crossing the transverse range north-west to Karanghu-tagh. It was said to lead to the Nissa Valley, whence a track could be found to the mountains on the upper Kara-kash River. I was delighted at this intelligence. For it showed not only, what the Karanghu-tagh people had carefully hidden from me, that there was a connection with the outer world besides the route viâ Pisha, but also that this connection would take me into a region which had so far remained an absolute terra incognita.

The start for Nissa, on which I accordingly decided for the morning of October 30th, was attended with some difficulty. The Yüzbashi of Karanghu-tagh, who had before proved obstructive, evidently did not cherish the idea of helping us to follow a route the knowledge of which he seemed anxious to keep for his own people. So, notwithstanding the previous orders, no yaks turned up in the morning. When the man saw that I was in earnest and that further delay was likely to involve him in more serious consequences than the voluminous objurgations to which Islam Beg and Niaz, the Chinese interpreter, had treated him already, the yaks were dragged out from the neighbouring glens. But we had lost two hours—a long time at that season when night falls so early in the narrow valleys.

At 10 a.m. we started up the Kash stream, and after about two miles turned into a narrow glen known as Gez Jilga. When after a toilsome climb of close on three hours we had reached the Pom-tagh Pass, about 12,400 feet above the sea, a grand view opened to the east and south. It comprised the whole glacier-crested range from 'Muztagh' on the extreme left to the hoary peaks which showed their heads above the glaciers closing the Karanghu-tagh Valley. No visible point in the glittering crest-line which filled about one-third of the horizon could be much under 20,000 feet, while quite a number of the peaks, as subsequent triangulation showed, reached 22,000 to 23,000 feet. Nearer to the south-west and west there rose a perfect maze of steep serrated ridges and steeple-like peaks. Embedded among them, but quite invisible lay the narrow valleys forming the grazing grounds of Nissa. I climbed a knoll on the water-shed ridge some 400 feet above the pass, where work with the plane-table and photo-theodolite kept us busy for a couple of hours. It was an ideal day for survey work; scarcely a cloud lay on the horizon, and the air, with 50° F. in the shade, felt deliciously warm.

An extremely steep track, by which our ponies were led with difficulty, took us first along a bare rocky ridge and then down, at least 3,000 feet, by a narrow ravine to the Karagaz gorge. When we had reached its bottom by half-past four it was getting quite dusk between the high and precipitous rock-walls. As we descended for about two miles in this narrow defile to where it joins the gorge of the Nissa stream, the reddish glow of the evening sun that had set for us long before lit up some towering pinnacles in front. It was like a magic illumination, this display of red light on the yellowish crags devoid of all trace of vegetation. Only in the Tyrol Dolomites, and on a smaller scale in the defiles where the Indus breaks through the Salt Range, had I seen the like.

The Nissa gorge which we had next to ascend was equally confined, and the darkness which now completely overtook us made the long ride, with our ponies slowly groping their way between the boulders of the river-bed or along the narrow ledges, most wearisome. Here and there in bends of the defile we passed scanty patches of cultivated ground, with low mud huts inhabited only during the summer months. The wicked Yüzbashi who by his delay had caused this trying night march, and who was now accompanying the baggage, came in for some blows from my men as we passed the belated yaks, a long way yet from the end of our march.

When at last we arrived at Nissa, I was glad of the temporary shelter which the hut of the 'Bai' of the little settlement offered. My host owed this proud title to the possession of some yaks and a flock of sheep, and his habitation was but a mud-built hovel. All the same, it was a cheerful change from the raw night air to the warmth and light of his fire-place.

The 31st of October we halted at Nissa. The men needed rest and Ram Singh time for astronomical observations. I used the day to collect information regarding the mountain routes that lead to the Kara-kash Valley westwards and towards Khotan, but found it no easy task; for the apprehension of the trouble that my tours might cause made the hillmen more than usually reticent. Nissa counts some twenty houses, but most of the men who inhabit it during the winter were still away with the sheep and yaks on the higher grazing-grounds. Apart from a few willows and a bold snowy peak visible at the head of the valley, there was nothing to break the monotony of the dusty grey of the rocks and the little plain between them. But the sky showed the purest blue and the sun shone warmly. So the day passed pleasantly even in these surroundings.

It is lucky for historical geography that the name Nissa is not that of a locality further West. Else it could scarcely have escaped identification, at the hands of amateur antiquaries, with Nysa, the mythic residence of Dionysus in the Indian Caucasus, which Alexander too is supposed to have visited. It amused me to think of the flights of imagination that would be required in order to clothe these most barren of rocks with the vines sacred to the god whom the great conqueror flattered himself by imitating in his Indian conquest.

On the morning of November 1st I set out for the Brinjak Pass, which connects the Nissa Valley with the mountain defiles northward. As I was anxious to utilise the extensive view likely to be obtained from its height for a final survey of the head-waters of the Yurung-kash, I decided to camp as near as possible to the pass in order to secure plenty of time for the morrow's work. It was not easy to carry out this plan, as the steep rocky ravine in which the ascent lay was exceptionally narrow. But at last a point was reached about 12,800 feet high by aneroid, where the narrow bottom just left room for a couple of tents. So giving order to pitch the camp here, I climbed the steep ridge south of the ravine. My reconnaissance showed that a splendid survey station could be secured by ascending a high arête north-east of the pass. The piercing cold wind soon drove me down to my tent, which seen from above in the narrow gorge looked curiously like a stretched-out bat, the outer flaps touching the rocky slopes on either side. The interior did not give ease, for the steep slope allowed the use of neither table nor chair, and the camp-bed, too, could not be placed at an angle of less than 25° Whether it was through the unaccustomed position or the continual slipping away of the rugs that were to keep off the bitter cold, I got little sleep that night.

At 7 a.m. the temperature was only 21° F., and the little stream close by was frozen solid. An hour's stiff climb brought me up to the Brinjak pass, for which the aneroid showed a height of about 14,000 feet. To ascend the steep ridge previously singled out for survey work was no easy task, as the whole of it proved to be covered with confused masses of boulders and flaked rock, showing the force with which decomposing agencies are at work at this altitude. After a few hundred feet the yaks carrying the instruments could be got no further. The theodolite could not be exposed to the risk of this scramble from rock to rock, but the Taghlik to whom I entrusted the photo-theodolite managed to follow though with great difficulty. The ridge gradually narrowed to a precipitous grat. After an hour and a half's climbing I had reached its highest knoll, where hard frozen snow filled the interstices of the rocks.

To the north-east, but separated from us by a great dip in the ridge, rose a steeple-like peak, the Mudache-tagh, we had already sighted from the Pom-tagh Pass. To climb it would have been a stiff piece of mountaineering, even if time had sufficed. This

KUEN-LUEN RANGE, WITH GLACIERS OF NISSA VALLEY, SEEN FROM BRINJAK.

peak, 17,220 feet high, shut off the view of the second triangulated peak above Buya, upon which we should have had to rely for theodolite work. But otherwise the view was as grand and clear as could be desired. 'Muztagh' showed itself in full majesty, and beyond it to the south-east there now appeared several distant snowy ridges previously invisible that guard the approach to the main Yurung-kash source. How should we have fared between them if the passage above Issik-bulak could have been negotiated? Further to the south the line of the horizon for a distance of close on one hundred miles was crowned by an unbroken succession of snowy peaks and glaciers.

The nearest to us were those at the head of the Nissa Valley below a prominent cone, for which subsequent triangulation showed a height of 23,070 feet. But bigger still looked the ice-streams that descend in a huge amphitheatre above the valley of Karanghu-tagh. Further to the south-west and west the steep crags of the Chankul and other neighbouring peaks shut off a distant view. They were all glittering with fresh snow, probably from that fall which we had witnessed at Issik-bulak; but the beds of snow filling the ravines of the Iskuram valley enclosed by these peaks looked old, more like incipient glaciers.

The sky was the brightest azure, and its colour only heightened the effect of the dazzling glacier panorama southwards. Though it was midday and the actinic power of the sun's rays considerable, the temperature in the shade kept about 25° F. Fortunately there was little wind, so I managed to do the photo-theodolite work without much trouble. But I was glad when, after an hour and a half's exposure, I could again warm my benumbed fingers. The aneroids showed a height of 15,300 feet.

By half-past one our work was finished; Ram Singh had been able to verify by good intersections the plane-table work of the last ten days. Once back on the pass our yaks could be used again for the descent northwards into the valley which drains the Iskuram peaks. But an unexpected difficulty retarded the descent. About half a mile from the pass where the track enters a narrow ravine we suddenly came on hard ice below a crust of detritus dust. It was the recent snow that had melted in the few hours of sunshine, and had subsequently got frozen. Even the yaks slid uncomfortably on this treacherous ground, and the slopes below the path were sufficiently steep to make a slip dangerous. The leather mocassins ('Charuk') of my companions here gave safer foothold than my boots with Alpine nails worn flat by previous marches. So I gladly availed myself of their assistance at the worst bits.

Ice and dust—the combination appealed to me as characteristic of this strange and forbidding mountain-land of Khotan. But I felt grateful when, after about an hour's cautious progress, we had got clear of this trying ground. Lower down the ravine somewhat widened, and just as it was getting dark we arrived at the little grazing-ground of Chash, which gives its name to the valley. My tent was pitched on a small plot of withered grass; behind it under the shelter of a projecting rock-wall my men established themselves. Close by, huddled under the side of some rock cavities, I found a couple of small felt huts inhabited by Taghlik families who live here summer and winter. They owned only a few sheep, and were said to subsist mainly upon charitable gifts from the shepherds of the Borazan canton who drive their flocks up here during the summer months. The ample scrub growing in the valley enabled these poor people to withstand the rigours of the winter which, at an elevation of about 10,100 feet, must be considerable.

In the course of the evening four Taghliks arrived from Mitaz, the nearest hamlet northwards, in response to the summons sent by my Beg. They assured us that fodder had been sent ahead to an intermediate halting-place. This was welcome news, as our supply from Nissa was running out; but the hoped-for information as to a route across the mountains to the Kara-kash Valley was not to be got out of the distrustful hillmen. Every question about localities was met with a stereotyped 'bilmaidim' ("I do not know"), until even the stolid herdsmen from Nissa laughed at this pretended ignorance. It was evident that the arrival of strangers, such as they had never before beheld or perhaps even heard of, filled these good people with all kinds of apprehensions.

After the hard work of the previous day I was glad that on the 3rd of November my men could start late when the air had warmed up a little in the bright sunshine. For about three miles we descended the Chash Valley, until it turns eastwards to flow through an impassable rock defile towards the Yurung-kash. Our way continued to the north up a narrow side valley flanked by sheer cliffs of conglomerate. At its entrance we watered the ponies; for the glen higher up is absolutely waterless, except for a salt spring unfit for drinking. After another eight miles we arrived at the foot of the Yagan-Dawan, and pitched camp at the highest point where there was still room for a tent in the steep ravine leading up to the pass. Three bags of ice had been brought from Chash to provide us with water.

The night, thanks to the sheltered position, was passed in comparative comfort, and next morning the bright sunshine induced me and Ram Singh to clamber up the pass long before the baggage was ready to start. Some of the Nissa men had bolted overnight, and this caused trouble, for the yak is an obstinate animal and each wants one man quite to himself when carrying baggage. That day one man had to suffice for three or four of them, and the poor fellows left behind were manifestly in for a bad time. The Yagan-Dawan proved a very narrow saddle flanked by steep ridges on the east and west. In order to get a full view we climbed the western ridge, and reached its top at an elevation of about 12,000 feet. It was a splendid survey station, completely commanding the confused network of rocky ridges and deep-cut ravines which extends between the middle courses of the Yurung-kash and Kara-kash. We now stood on the watershed between the two rivers. But the high serrated range we had crossed from Nissa shut off the view of the great snowy mountains south, and even of the dominating Muztagh we could only sight the glacier-covered northern buttresses. So the hope of triangulation was once more doomed to disappointment.

I shall never forget the view that opened westwards and in the direction of the distant plains. There were lines upon lines of absolutely bare rocky spurs, closely packed together and running mostly from south to north; between them, shut in by unscalable rock slopes, was a maze of arid gorges, of which the bottom could not be seen. It was like a choppy sea, with its waves petrified in wild confusion. Far away on the horizon this rocky waste was disappearing in a yellow haze, the familiar indication of another region which knows no life —the distant sea of sand.

The impressions gathered in front of this panorama were heightened when, after three hours' busy work, we descended into the ravine leading down from the pass to the north-west.

About 1,500 feet below the saddle the bottom was reached, and then began a passage of fantastic rock defiles, the like of which I had never seen. For nearly three hours I marched between walls of conglomerate and apparently chalky rock rising thousands of feet above the narrow fissure at the bottom. As it appeared to me in my total want of geological training, only the erosive action of water, aided by extreme disintegra-

ERODED RANGES TO NORTH-WEST, SEEN FROM ABOVE YAGAN-DAWAN.

tion of the rocks under peculiar climatic conditions, could have produced these extraordinary formations. But of water there was no trace, only ankle-deep dust overlying the detritus. For the first four or five miles there was scarcely even scrub growing in these terribly barren gorges; animal life seemed completely absent. The want of water did not physically distress me, as it did our ponies and yaks, which had tasted no drop for more than twenty-four hours. Yet my attention was ever turned to it in contrast, by the sight of the huge, overhanging cliffs, the cavities, and isolated pinnacles, which all looked as if water had worked them.

Above my head the sky was still blue, and the higher cliffs reflected bright sunlight; yet the gloom of these ravines and their desolation were depressing. I also knew that my baggage was painfully straggling, the yaks proving unmanageable with so few men, and knocking off their loads whenever they found a conveniently projecting rock. So I was doubly pleased when after a march of about eight miles from the pass I emerged into the fairly open valley of Mitaz. There I found still warm sunshine and a lively stream from which my pony drank in long, long draughts. I enjoyed the splash and sound of the water after those silent dead ravines, and sat cheerfully by its side until my baggage appeared at dusk. It was pleasant to read in the tiny seventeenth-century edition of Horace, which always travels in my saddlebag, of the springs that gave charm for the poet to another mountain region far away in the West. And then the question touched my mind: What is this vast mountain world in human interest compared to the Sabine Hills? It has no past history as far as man is concerned, and what can be its future?—unless destiny has reserved the prospects of another Klondyke for the auriferous rivers of Khotan.

On the 5th of November our start was late; for the men from Nissa had to be paid off, and it took time before those of Mitaz had got their animals ready and loaded. Mitaz is a very small hamlet, and its eight or nine holdings lie scattered higher up the valley. The latter after our previous route, looked comparatively open, but in reality the only available track lay close along, or in, the river-bed. The water, beautifully clear, was nowhere more than two feet deep. So our continual crossings, necessitated by projecting rock spurs, caused no great trouble except to 'Yolchi Beg,' who had to be caught each time and carried across on horseback—a procedure to which the little fellow never submitted in good grace.

We marched this day some sixteen miles down the stream to the north, but saw no human being, except the children of a shepherd family living in a little cave close to where the Sukosai Valley runs down from the west. The eldest of four children was a blind boy of seven. Smallpox had deprived him of his eyesight, but he knew his way about the valley, and I had less trouble than usual in getting from him the local names of the immediate neighbourhood. The only reward I had at hand was a silver piece, which he promised to give to his mother. We camped at the point where an alternative route to the plains, by the Kunat Pass, leaves the Mitaz valley eastwards. It was said to be impassable for horses, and its entrance, a narrow rockbound gorge, looked sufficiently forbidding.

At Kunat-aghzi, where the hypsometer showed a height of only 6,890 feet, and where the temperature at 7 a.m. was just at freezing-point, I had the feeling of nearing the plains. But the Ulughat Pass that was still to be crossed had a surprise in store. On the 7th of November we marched for about eight miles down the Mitaz stream, when the view to the right showed us a broad, sandy slope leading up to a high ridge. In striking contrast to the serrated cliffs of the ranges around, no rock protruded from this uniform slope. Hence it looked far lower than in reality it was. I knew the optical deception which made Ram Singh estimate the height before us at only about 1,000 feet; yet I was not prepared for the climb that awaited us. For two and a half hours our ponies toiled upwards in zigzags along a slope of which the angle seemed nowhere less than 25 degrees. The soil was gravel and loose earth, the last remains of rock formations that had withered away during unknown ages. The longer the climb lasted the higher rose my almost abandoned hope of getting a panorama of the whole range that would give us at last a simultaneous view of several peaks already triangulated from the Ladak side. On this depended the chance of fixing our position with absolute certainty and ultimately connecting Khotan itself with the Indian Trigonometrical Survey. The great Muztagh, which had again and again during our previous climbs appeared before us in unmistakable majesty, could alone not suffice for this purpose; and other triangulated peaks on the main watershed we had been unable to recognise with any certainty as long as we were comparatively near to the unbroken screen of icy ridges.

It was thus with a feeling of eager expectation that I pushed upwards. The long-stretched back of the mountain forming the Ulughat-Dawan had become visible when the slope changed into a series of less steep shoulders. But a projecting spur shut off the view to the south and kept me in suspense. An hour ahead of my people and followed only by Ram Singh, I gained at last a small saddle in the main ridge. By ascending a broad knoll to the south I should soon learn whether my hope was to be fulfilled. So we left the ponies and hurried up. It was a moment of intense joy when, arrived at the top, I beheld the grand panorama that suddenly revealed itself. The whole of the mountain-world traversed during the last three weeks lay before me, and beyond it a semicircle of great snowy peaks which had been hidden hitherto by nearer ranges. Far beyond Muztagh we could see glittering ranges in the direction of the main Yurung-kash source. The glaciers we had passed at the head of the valleys between Issik-bulak and Nissa were now seen to be surmounted by ice-peaks of the most varied shapes, domes, pyramids, and bold steeple-like cones. To the west there rose a grand chain of snowy mountains encircling the head waters of the Kara-kash River. No European eye had ever seen them from the south. Towards the north only a narrow belt of eroded rocky ridges separated us from the great desert plain and its fringe, the Khotan oasis.

The sky was brilliantly clear all around, but over the plains there hung the ever-present haze of dust. It covered and effaced with its tinge of brownish-yellow alike the sand of the desert, the river courses, and the belt of cultivated land. Where it touched the horizon, far away in the Taklamakan, the skyline showed a brilliant light green. Yet in height this cover of dusty atmosphere could scarcely exceed 1,000 ft. For we could clearly see the foot of the outer range rising above the bed of the Kara-kash where the latter winds through the low glacis-like plateaus stretching away northwards.

It was three in the afternoon when I arrived on this commanding height. It was manifest that no time remained for theodolite work, for which nature herself seemed to have destined the position, and that we should have to remain there for the night. The saddle on the main spur offered a convenient spot on which to place the camp, but the want of water was a difficulty. Fortunately I had foreseen this chance and sent Islam Beg ahead to Pujia, a village on the Kara-kash. He had orders to meet us on the pass with fresh ponies and a supply of water. So when my baggage arrived a little before sunset, the tents were pitched close below our survey station. Before this the plane-table had come up, and we eagerly searched the horizon southwards for points previously triangulated and shown on our section sheet.

This time my hopes were not to be disappointed. Having once determined our position on the plane-table, it was easy to recognise in a great ice-pyramid towering above the Kash valley glaciers the Kuen-luen Peak No. 1 of the Indian Survey, 21,750 feet high. Its position coincided most accurately with the direction indicated by our map. In the east the identity of another high landmark, the "Tartary Peak No. 2," was equally assured, and in order to dispel any lingering doubt, there appeared in a gap of the Iskuram range the glittering snowy top of a far more distant peak, exactly where the Survey tables place the "Kara-kash Peak No. 2," also reaching close to 22,000 feet. This rapid survey made it certain that it was possible to triangulate the surrounding region down to Khotan itself with assurance. The direct connection of Khotan with the system of the Indian Surveys, on which the determination of its exact longitude depends, had long been sought for in vain. Yet here a position within a few days' march from Khotan, to which luck and, perhaps, a little topographical instinct had guided us, gave the desired opportunity. It only remained to pray for a clear sky on the morrow.

The sunset on the grand chain of the south was a sight of incomparable beauty. Long after the serrated crests of the intervening ranges had sunk into blueish shadows, the icy peaks beyond the glaciers which feed the western tributaries of the Yurung-kash continued in brilliant sunlight. Then one after the other shone in rosy tints until the glow became a deeper and deeper red, to pass away into purple and darkness. At last, only the grand dome of 'Muztagh,' with its highest pinnacle shaped like a Phrygian cap, and our newly discovered Kuen-luen Peak No. 1 reflected the light of the sun that had long before set for us.

The changes of colour in the tints of yellowish haze over the plains were delightful to watch. But the increasing cold and the wind that sprung up from the east soon drove me down to the tent. There a cup of tea boiled from the water I had brought up in my water-bottle was for hours the only refreshment my establishment could offer. There was no trace of Islam Beg and his water supply. But I cheerfully put up with the prospect of not eating my dinner until next morning, in view of the result which to-day's work promised. The glorious sight of the full moon rising below us soon drew me outside the tent. Her light was as clear at our altitude as I had ever seen it in India, and showed up every crag and recess in the withered conglomerate ridges eastwards. She looked as if rising from the sea when first emerging from the haze of dust that hid the plains, and her light shimmered on its surface. But when she climbed high up in the sky it was no longer a meek reflection that lit up the plain below. It seemed as if I were looking at the lights of a vast city lying below me in the endless plains. Could it really be that terrible desert where there was no life and no hope of human existence? I knew that I should never see it again in this alluring splendour. Its appearance haunted me as I sat shivering in my tent, busy with a long-delayed mail that was to carry to distant friends my Christmas greetings. At last, about ten o'clock, a cheerful commotion in the camp announced the arrival of Islam Beg and the water-filled gourds he had managed to get brought up. The supply was small, and scarcely sufficed for a cup of tea for each man. Nevertheless, Sadak Akhun succeeded in cooking my modest dinner, and after a last look at the magic city below I could retire to rest close upon midnight.

Next day when I rose a little before 7 a.m. the sun was just rising above a lower ridge to the east. He shone brightly into the tent, but light fleecy clouds were floating in the sky. Fortunately the horizon to the south above the mountains was clear, and I lost no time in beginning the work of triangulation on our "hill-station" close by. It was no easy task to select in this vast panorama the peaks that were the best landmarks of the numerous ranges within view and also likely to be recognised again from other positions. But after five hours' steady work twenty-six prominent points were safely triangulated. The light clouds that gathered as the day advanced luckily kept clear of the mountains; but coupled with a breeze from the north-east they made it cold on the exposed height, for which the triangulation results have indicated an elevation of 9,890 feet.

I took a round of photo-theodolite views, and then we set about building a mark to enable us to identify our position with accuracy from the next triangulation station. No stone could be found anywhere. So the men from Pujia had to collect the low withered scrub and heap it up mixed with loose earth. When I descended to the tent I was glad of a cup of tea. But even more delightful it was to get enough water for washing hands and face. A fresh supply had been sent up from Popuna, the next village north on the bank of the Kara-kash. So even my men ceased grumbling at the halt on this inhospitable Dawan, and were cheered by the prospect of our early descent to the plains.

On the morning of the 8th of November we left Ulughat-Dawan under a sky of speckless blue. Notwithstanding the elevation the temperature was a little above freezing-point at 7.30 a.m., an indication of the atmospheric influence of the neighbouring plains. For an hour and a half the path led down steeply over disintegrated slopes of earth and sand which completely covered the rock structure of the mountain. Only when close to the head of a narrow gorge did I see rocks showing strata of mica exposed. Down the bottom of this gorge, scarcely two or three yards broad, a little stream of water wound its way. It was so saline that the ponies would not drink from it. After a mile or two its water was lost in the ground. For fully three hours the route led between high cliffs of conglomerate and slate, until a turn round a projecting screen of rock suddenly brought us out into the open valley of the Kara-kash, just below Popuna. It was pleasant to see a stretch of level ground again and rows of trees in their vivid autumn tints. The valley of the Kara-kash, about half a mile broad, was bounded to the north by a bank of gravel some 200 feet high, sloping like a natural glacis gently away towards the plains. Twice we crossed the Kara-kash, now a stream of beautifully clear greenish water, some forty yards broad and two to three feet deep, before Langhru was reached three miles below Popuna. The village, though counting only about sixty houses, looked quite a large place to me after my wanderings amidst the solitary mountains. I could let my men enjoy its comforts only for a single night. For I knew that a wind raising the haze would effectually stop further survey work. So I felt anxious soon to reach another high ridge called Kauruk-kuz, which had appeared from the Ulughat-Dawan, the only point in the neighbourhood sufficiently elevated for a second triangulation station, and at the same time accessible with instruments.

In order to reach it I started on the morning of the 9th of November back into the arid range southwards by the valley which leads towards the Kunat Pass. Against all expectation this valley proved fairly open for a distance of about nine miles. Then it contracted to a narrow gorge at a point known as Kuchkach-bulaki, where a little stream of brackish water trickled down between the rocks, covering the bottom with a saline deposit that looked like ice. The cliffs on either side grew higher and wilder as we advanced up the ravine, and I began to doubt whether after all a practicable way would offer out of this maze of contorted rocks to the high ridge I had sighted from Ulughat. It was getting dark by 4 p.m. when the highest point was reached to which ponies could advance.

But to my relief there rose on the left a steep slope of detritus, much like that leading to Ulughat, and evidently the hoped-for route to the Kauruk-kuz ridge. Camp was pitched in the narrow ravine, at an elevation of about 8,000 feet by aneroid. I took it as a lucky omen that just there I came upon a little party from Nissa, who had crossed the Kunat Pass with four yaks and were now waiting for the flour that was to be brought up to them from Khotan. The yaks had tasted no water for the last two days, but were all the same fit to help us.

The next day's climb proved a stiff one. The ridge which I had singled out for our station was close on 3,000 feet above our camp, and the slope was exceptionally steep. But the yaks carried us safely over the most trying part of the ascent, and when after three hours the top was reached, Ram Singh as well as myself was ready to set to work at once. The view was in some directions more extensive even than that from Ulughat. But the sky was less clear, and from the first I noticed an ominous haze that made me hurry on the observations. It was not long before my apprehensions were verified. A strong wind, passing from the plains southward, carried the haze further and further into the mountains; there was no mistaking the dust of the desert that was threatening to overtake our work. Luckily the identification of the peaks to which previously angles had been measured by us, caused no delay, and though it seemed like a race with the veil of dust that was steadily rising, the round of theodolite observations could be carried through with all needful accuracy. The peaks in the outer range of hills nearest to Khotan, by which the longitude of the town itself might be determined thereafter, were first in danger of being wiped from our horizon. But we were still in time; and when the haze, two hours later, had also obscured the view of the distant high ranges above the Kara-kash Valley, all but three out of the twenty-six peaks requiring triangulation had been safely observed. It was with a feeling of relief that I saw this task completed; for I knew how persistent an obstacle the foglike haze of this region can prove to survey operations. Had I delayed but for a single day—and, I confess, there had been strong temptation—the chance of this triangulation might have been lost to us completely. The triangulated height of the ridge was 10,820 feet.

An hour's scramble down the steep slopes brought me again into the ravine, where the ponies were waiting. As there was no water at the camp beyond that which had been brought up from Langhru on donkeys, I had sent word to my people earlier in the day to move back to the village. The ponies which had been left behind for us seemed eager too to get at water, and hurried down the valley at a good pace. But it soon got dark and our progress slackened. In the end our guide missed the track, and in order to make sure of nothing worse happening, took to the boulder-strewn bed of the dry stream. It was terribly bad ground for the ponies, and we all felt thoroughly tired by the time when a big camp-fire guided us late at night to camp in a field near Langhru.

CHAPTER XV.

ANTIQUARIAN PREPARATIONS AT KHOTAN.

On the 11th of November the short march to the village of Ujat, some eight miles lower down on the left bank of the Kara-kash, was made in an atmosphere so thick and grey that I had the sensation of a foggy autumn day somewhere near London. All view of the mountains, near as they were, was effaced as if with a brush, and from where my tent was pitched even the bluff spur just across the river at scarcely a mile's distance loomed only in faint lines through the dust-laden air. It was this spur, known as Kohmari, the last offshoot of the Ulughat range towards the plains, which made me place my camp at Ujat.

Topographical indications that need not be detailed here had convinced me that M. Grenard, the companion of M. Dutreuil de Rhins, was right in identifying Kohmari with the holy Mount Gosringa which Hiuen-Tsiang describes as a famous pilgrimage place of Buddhist Khotan. A Vihara, or monastery, raised on it marked the spot where Sakyamuni was believed to have preached a "digest of the Law" to the Devas. A cave in its side was venerated as the approach to "a great rock dwelling" where popular legend supposed an Arhat to reside "plunged in ecstasy and awaiting the coming of Maitreya Buddha." The Muhammadan Mazar, worshipped as the resting-place of the saintly "Maheb Khwoja," which now occupies the crest of the conglomerate cliff rising almost perpendicularly above the right river-bank, has inherited the religious merit of the old Buddhist shrine. It forms a favourite place of pilgrimage for the faithful of Khotan, who believe that the intercession of the saint is most efficacious when the low state of the rivers makes the cultivators fear a failure of their crops. On this account official recognition, in the form of a liberal offering from Amban Pan-Darin, was said to have recently been accorded to the shrine.

The cave which the Chinese pilgrims saw still exists in the side of the cliff some fifty feet below the crest. It is approached along a ledge of rock which contains the semi-troglodyte dwelling of the Sheikhs attending the Mazar. The cave itself, which is about 40 feet deep and from 8 to 10 feet high, is believed to have been the refuge of the saint whom the infidels killed here with smoke. Thus the legend accounts for the black soot that covers the rock walls. Pious pilgrims are wont to sit and pray in the cave, and the fires they light to keep themselves warm in winter time have naturally left their traces on the rock. A small upper chamber, approached from below by a ladder, shows above a narrow fissure running into the rock. The legend heard by the Chinese pilgrim represented this fissure as a passage which had been miraculously blocked by fallen rocks to hide the Arhat.

Apart from its association with Hiuen-Tsiang's visit, the Kohmari cave possessed for me a special interest. From it the fragmentary birch-bark leaves of the ancient Indian manuscript in Kharoshthi characters, now known as the Dutreuil de Rhins MS., were alleged to have been obtained. M. Grenard's account shows that the leaves were delivered to him and his companion on two successive visits to Kohmari by natives who professed to have found them with other remains inside the grotto. But it is equally clear that neither of them was present on the occasion or was shown the exact spot of discovery. The men who sold those precious leaves to the French travellers seem to have prevented them from a personal inspection of the cave by alleging religious objections.

No difficulty whatever was raised in my case. I found the Mullahs, jovial, well-fed fellows, curiously resembling in their ways my old Purohita friends at Indian 'Tirthas,' ready enough for a consideration to show me the cave, including its mysterious recesses. The close examination I was thus able to effect gave me strong reason to doubt the possibility of the manuscript having been really found there. Though the visit of the French explorers was well remembered by the Sheikhs, nothing was known to them or the villagers of the alleged discovery in the cave. Taking into account that other fragments of the same manuscript had been sold separately into Russian hands at Kashgar, it appears probable that the native "treasure-seekers" concerned made the statement connecting their find with the cave simply in order to disguise the true place of discovery.

In the course of my inspection of this sacred cave I had occasion to appreciate the easy-going ways of Khotan local worship. Nobody, however good a Musulman he may be, thinks of taking off his boots on approaching a sacred spot. Those who wear a kind of over-shoes with their top-boots leave them outside, it is true. But the common people not possessed of such refined footgear freely retain their high leather 'Charuks' (mocassins) or the sandals fastened with long cloth bandages. The winter is cold in this region, and I wonder how frequent the occasions are when the Khotanese really do remove their footgear during the winter months. I have always managed to make friends with the priestly attendants of Indian shrines, be they Hindu or Muhammadan, and have almost invariably escaped the necessity of taking off my boots—a kind of déshabillé which for a European is gruous and inconvenient, without in reality marking in any way religious conciliation. But in Khotan there seemed no need even for the little diplomacy which elsewhere is usually required to save oneself this chance of catching cold.

Ujat is a large village, its straggling dwellings surrounded by grape-gardens, for which it is famous. The dried grapes and currants of the place are said to find their way as far as the markets of Aksu, Kashgar, and Turfan. The vines are trained, as throughout Chinese Turkestan, along low fences, ranged in parallel lines. The work of covering up the stems with earth for the winter was just proceeding. The people of

Ujat seem to have retained for a long time after the acceptance of Islam the reputation of being weak in the faith and addicted to heretical ways. I wonder whether the extensive cultivation of the vine has something to do with this.

My local enquiries and the arrival of a long-expected mail from Kashgar, which brought me home and Indian letters of a whole month and required early disposal, helped to detain me at Ujat. But on the 15th of November I marched back to Khotan by the shortest route, crossing the bleak pebble 'Sai' that stretches from the Kohmari ridge to the southern edge of the cultivated area near the village of Kosa. I was surprised to find how rapidly the fertile tract towards the city had assumed its winter aspect. The long alleys of poplars and willows stood leafless; the same storm that put a stop to our survey work on the mountains had brushed away the bright autumn colours which greeted me on my first descent to the Kara-kash.

At Khotan it became necessary to make a short halt in order to give to my men and ponies the rest they required after the month of fatiguing marches. I also wanted time for the examination of the antiques which had found their way from various localities into the hands of the agents sent out on my behalf after my first visit. The small parties despatched to ancient sites in the desert also turned up with their spoil during my week's stay. The party which had gone out under the guidance of Turdi, an old, and as experience showed, reliable "treasure-seeker" from a village of the Yurung-kash canton, had visited the most distant of the locally known sites, called by them Dandan-Uiliq ("the houses with ivory"). Among the specimens brought back by them I found to my great satisfaction several pieces of fresco inscribed with Indian Brahmi characters, fragments of stucco relievos representing objects of Buddhist worship, and also a small but undoubtedly genuine piece of a paper document in cursive Central-Asian Brahmi.

It turned out, on further examination of the "treasure-seekers," that the ruins from which they had unearthed these remains, and which they described as reached after nine

TURDI, "TREASURE SEEKER."

to ten marches north-eastwards through the desert, were apparently identical with the site which Dr. Hedin had seen on his memorable march to the Keriya Darya, and which is spoken of in the narrative of his travels as the "ancient city Taklamakan." He had reached it by another route from Tawakkel on the northern edge of the oasis. So Pan-Darin, whom I informed of the results of this reconnaissance, sent word to the Beg of Tawakkel to produce the two hunters who had guided Dr. Hedin on his journey. On November 20 Ahmad Merghen and Kasim Akhun, the men I wished to examine, were duly produced by the Beg himself, who had brought them to Khotan in person. Their examination in the presence of Turdi, the leader of my pioneer party, left no doubt as to the identity of Dandan-Uiliq. I was thus able to arrange definitely the programme of my tour for the exploration of this site, which in view of the specimens secured by Turdi seemed the best place for commencing systematic excavations.

Immediately after my return I visited my kind friend the Amban, and thanked him for the thorough-going help by which he had made my survey in the mountains possible. On that occasion I invoked again the evidence of the great 'Tang-Seng,' in order to explain to Pan-Darin the object of my desert journey. When after two days he returned the visit I was able to show him the finds brought in by Turdi. So Pan-Darin by ocular inspection became convinced that I had a good guide in the famous old pilgrim, and promised to do all he could to further my explorations. I thought that I could not more fittingly express my gratitude than by wishing that the blessed spirit of Hiuen-Tsiang himself might reward the Amban for the assistance he was rendering me. Niaz, the interpreter, managed to reproduce this pious compliment better than I had expected; for the Amban answered it by asking quite seriously whether I believed in the continued existence of 'Tang-Seng's' soul! It seemed indeed that in the memory of Chinese Buddhists Hiuen-Tsiang lives like a glorified Arhat or Bodhisattva. If so, Indian archæologists would be still better justified in proclaiming him as their own patron saint.

I had pitched my tent again in the garden of dear old Akhun Beg, my former host. But though the place gave the desired privacy it offered no protection whatever against the increasing cold. Tokhta Akhun's house seemed too gloomy and close after the long journey in the free mountain air. So I preferred to put up for the time with the cold and to stick to my little tent outside. Many repairs of outfit, saddlery, etc., required my attention too; for the terribly rough tracks of the "Mountains of Darkness" and the wily ways of the yaks had caused damage of all kinds. So the saddler, blacksmith, and tailor were kept busy under my eyes. Vendors of antiques, bringing seals, coins, old pottery, and similar small objects, mostly from Yotkan, frequently presented themselves. But of the "old books" none were offered. It seemed as if the particular "treasure-seeker" to whom I had reason to trace them, credited me with a more inquisitorial turn of mind than was convenient for him—and his factory.

But my days at Khotan were taken up not only with these avocations. There had been since I returned an increasing rush of people seeking benefit from my medicine case. Patients from among the local Begs and the Chinese officials could not be denied, and though my "Tabloids" could scarcely effect the wonderful cures expected by these visitors, they evidently spread my fame as a "Hakim" throughout the district. From what I saw and heard Khotan seems to be a hotbed of diseases of all kinds. Numerous "cases" of a sickening type were daily brought to me, though rarely was I able to administer remedies from which I could expect any real good. A medical man would find here a splendid field of work, but I doubt whether his fees would suffice even to balance the charities expected by a large portion of those seeking relief. Chinese mendicants and loafers were frequent among my patients, and their condition

KHOTANESE WAITING FOR MEDICINES.

fully justified the requests for a present which were invariably made after I had attended to their ailments. I wondered whether the Chinese officials realized how detrimental to their régime must be the presence of large numbers of these destitute compatriots, living on charity and, no doubt, occasional loot.

It was manifest that my desert campaign would necessitate a prolonged absence from the oasis. Accordingly I decided to make, previous to my start, a thorough examination of old localities within the oasis itself, with a view to settling its ancient topography. At the same time I decided to send out Ram Singh independently for a survey of the high range east of the Kuen-luen Peak No. 5, by which the gap could be filled that was left between our recent survey and the tract explored by Capt. Deasy about Polu. On completing this task within about a month Ram Singh was to march to Keriya and then join me eventually at Dandan-Uiliq.

On the 23rd of November we both left Khotan. Our way was in common as far as Jamada, the village on the Yurung-kash which I had passed before when marching to Karanghu-tagh. I halted here for the night and received a cheerful welcome from Wang-Daloi, a Chinese acquaintance of my previous visit. For the last ten years the little Chinaman had lived there, trading in jade, which is washed from the Yurung-kash bed in the neighbourhood. He seemed to have ventured occasionally on speculative jade mining too, but fortune had never shown him favour; for my interpreter told me that he was still a long way from the sum that might take him back to Peking, apparently the life ambition of this exile. I found in Wang-Daloi an intelligent guide to the old sites which extend from Jamada to the south along the left river-bank, and also genial company, as he talked a little Turki. Next morning I passed over the eroded old site known simply by the general designation of 'Tati,' forming an area of about a square mile covered with fragments of pottery. Chinese coins up to the time of the Tang dynasty are also found, but of structural remains there was no trace.

Some six miles beyond we entered the region of the jade-diggings. On the flat plain, from half a mile to one mile broad, which extends between the left bank of the river and a gently sloping ridge of gravel westwards, the precious stone is found among the beds of rubble deposited by the river at earlier periods. Jade is the produce that has made Khotan famous all over the east since ancient times. In China it has ever been valued more than anywhere else, and most of the information which the Annals of the Celestial Empire give about old Khotan, we owe mainly to the interest attaching to its jade.

It was therefore with a good deal of interest that I examined the burrows crossing the barren plain in all directions. For the first mile or two they seemed to have been deserted long ago, as sand had partly filled the great hollows. But higher up we came upon diggings of more recent date not far from the old site known as Chalmakazan. A vast quantity of pottery fragments, mixed here and there with bits of broken glass and slag, strews the plain for about a mile and a half, from the river to the foot of the ridge. In the middle of this area a low mound, covered with large stones from the river bed, attracted my notice. Its round shape suggested a Stupa, and a closer examination proved this to be true. Unfortunately, others before me had guessed the nature of the structure, and a large trench run down into the very centre of the mound showed that "treasure-seekers" had been at work. The mound in its present condition has a diameter of about ninety-eight feet, and rises about fifteen feet above the ground. From the excavation made, it could be seen that it was constructed of closely packed layers of rough stones as a base, with a circular wall of similar material above it. A kind of well in the centre filled with loose earth probably contained the relic deposit.

There can be little doubt that the old settlement indicated by these remains was connected with the jade mining of the immediate neighbourhood. On the southern edge of the site the jade pits are still worked. For a mile and a half we had to thread our way between them before reaching the little miners' camp of Sirik-Toghrak, where I pitched my tent. The pits vary greatly in size and shape. Usually, a square or oblong cutting is made through the layer of gravel and river sand. At a depth from ten feet downwards strata of rubble are reached, and in these search is made for the pieces of jade that the river once washed down. Finds of great value occur very rarely; but there is always the chance of sudden wealth, and this suffices to attract at all times 'Bais,' *i.e.*, small capitalists from Khotan and other Turkestan towns. They engage parties of labourers, ten to thirty strong, from among the poorest of the agricultural class, and set them to work on a digging of proportionate size. The men receive food, clothing, and six Khotan Tangas (say two Rupees) as monthly pay. They have no share in the jade finds, but get extra rewards in case of special profits. According to Wang-Daloi's testimony, many never see any return for the money they have sunk in these mining ventures. Yet from time to time great hits are made. A Kashgar

JADE PIT WITH DIGGERS, NEAR DEBOUCHURE OF YURUNG-KASH.

Bai, whom I found at one of the diggings superintending his twenty men, acknowledged that during the last three years he had cleared a hundred Yambus of silver (say Rs. 13,000) worth of jade at an expense of some thirty Yambus.

Though the Chinese administration exercises no control whatsoever over the jade mining, "claims" once opened are scrupulously respected by other prospectors. I saw diggings which had been left partially unexploited for many years; yet I was assured that the right of the original workers would never be disputed. None of the diggings went to a greater depth than twenty feet from the surface; lower down, I assume, the water from the river would probably percolate and stop the work. The flat deposits along the river banks for a day's journey up the valley, up to the point where the latter becomes a narrow gorge, are visited by jade-diggers. But the work is carried on only intermittently and by small parties at the various points which bear the general designation of 'Kumat.' Now in the winter months only about two hundred men were engaged in mining, and even in the summer, when the privations of life in this barren region are less, the number probably is not more than doubled.

Quite distinct from this jade-mining, the ancient industry of "fishing" for jade in the river bed after the summer floods still continues all along the valley above Jamada, just as described in the old Chinese chronicles. No capital is wanted for this kind of search; so annually for a short period it attracts a large number of the poorer agriculturists of the oasis, who look to it as a kind of lottery. Very few find their labours rewarded, but the hope of turning up a valuable piece of jade among the rubble is as strong now among the poor of Khotan as it has been for many centuries.

The Annals of the old Chinese dynasties, from the Han period downwards, contain many curious data and anecdotes about the jade ('yü') which made the little kingdom of Yü-t'ien or Khotan famous in the Celestial Empire. Abel Rémusat, the Sinologist, collected and translated many of these notices in his *Histoire de la ville de Khotan* (Paris: 1820), and it was a satisfaction to me to read this earliest contribution to the European literature on Khotan near the very pits which furnish the precious stone so learnedly discussed in it.

CHAPTER XVI.

YOTKAN, THE SITE OF THE ANCIENT CAPITAL.

MY march on the 25th of November to Yotkan, the site of the old Khotan capital, took me over ground that I had partly seen before, but the day did not close without a novel, though somewhat annoying, experience. Coming from the south, I had, within a couple of miles from my destination, passed two deep ravines, or 'Yars' as they are called, cut into the loess beds by the action of flood water. Though the banks were steep, the ponies found no difficulty in crossing, and I did not give a thought to the question how the camels with the baggage would fare at these obstacles. I reached Yotkan, to which I had already paid a preliminary visit in October, about sunset, and selected a suitable ground for my tent close to the Yüzbashi's house, overlooking the area where the excavations of treasure-seekers have laid bare the soil of the ancient capital. The best room of the well-to-do villager was quite a cosy place, with its carpets and coloured Khotan felts, and with a cheerful log fire burning in the little fire-place. So the time of waiting for the arrival of the baggage passed quickly at first. The Yüzbashi's little red-cheeked son kept me company and amused 'Yolchi Beg,' my faithful follower.

At last, long after it had got pitch-dark outside, one of the camel men arrived—not with the eagerly expected animals, but with the news that they had stuck fast at the bottom of the first ravine and could not be got to move further. So a rescue party was despatched under the orders of the village headman. I have reason to suspect that easy-going young man did not move far beyond the neighbours' houses, but left the task to some myrmidons of his who managed to mistake the place and never came to help the belated party. When another hour had passed, Islam Beg and Tila Bai were sent out into the night. But it was not until about 10 p.m. that the unfortunate camels turned up at last. An attempt had been made to send on one of the animals that carried my tent and bedding, with the result that it slipped in crossing a canal and gave a thorough ducking to its load. When dragged out of its bath, this camel with the rest had to be taken by a great detour round the heads of the two ravines. The late arrival of the party was thus accounted for; but the explanation did not exactly console me for a half-wet tent, and bedding that had first to be dried. It was nearly midnight when dinner appeared, and some of the rugs had been made fit for use.

The ravines which proved such an obstacle to my clumsy camels had little claim to my regard. And yet my archæological conscience felt grateful to them; for without the formation of one of them, known as the 'Yotkan Yar,' that has cut through the fields of the village of Yotkan, the remains of the old Khotan capital might have been left buried for ages to come. From the statements of the old villagers which I tested with care in the course of my stay, I ascertained that no finds of any kind indicating that an ancient site was buried here below the ground had been made, until the time of Niaz Hakim Beg, the first governor under Yaqub Beg. Two or three years after his appointment, which took place about 1866, the small canal conveying water from the Kara-kash River for the irrigation of the Yotkan fields began to cut for itself a deeper bed in the soft loess, that is, to turn into a 'Yar.' This is the origin of the ravine which begins about one and a half miles to the west of Yotkan at the village of Chalbash, and joins the Yars of Kashe about a mile to the east of the site presently to be noticed. A small marshy depression ('kul') formed a little to the east of Khalche, as that portion of Yotkan is called which lies to the north of the excavated area, and there the villagers accidentally came across little bits of gold amidst old pottery and other petty débris. The latter objects possessed, of course, no interest for them; but the gold naturally excited the cupidity of the villagers, many of whom had, like the rest of the poorer agricultural population, tried their luck "prospecting" for jade and gold in the river beds. So they set to wash the soil near the incipient Yar, and the proceeds were so rich that they came to the governor's knowledge.

Niaz Hakim Beg was an administrator of considerable enter-

NORTH-WEST CORNER OF EXCAVATED AREA AT YOTKAN, WITH ENTRANCE TO 'YAR.'

prise. He sent to Yotkan large parties of diggers from Karakash town whom he employed like the men working in the jade pits. The owners of the fields which were gradually cut away by these "washings," received compensation. Subsequently the excavations were continued by private enterprise, the usual arrangement being that the owners of the soil and the diggers share the proceeds equally. The earth excavated from the banks has to be washed, just like the river deposit. The larger supply of water needed for this purpose caused the Yotkan canal to cut its bed deeper and deeper and to form the extant Yar, the bottom of which is from twenty to thirty feet below the ground level. Finally the canal had to be diverted to a higher level, but springs came to the surface at the bottom of the ravine, and these account for the swampy condition of the excavated area. In the recollection of old villagers the land of Yotkan was everywhere a level flat; there were no springs or swampy ground—nor any knowledge or tradition of the "old city" below.

Former travellers, who paid to Yotkan only a flying visit, have spoken of "the frightful ravages in the soil" and attributed them to some extraordinary flood catastrophes of which, it is true, they were unable to trace any recollection. But in reality the great extent of the excavated area which forms, as my careful survey showed, an irregular oblong of more than half a square mile, is almost exclusively due to systematic digging and washing for gold, as it still continues to this day on the north and west sides. The banks there are yielding a small but "paying" quantity of gold, and in recent years antiques, such as ornamented fragments of pottery, engraved stones, and coins have come to be counted as a kind of secondary product. The gold is usually found in tiny flakes of leaf-gold, of which I was able to secure samples. It is easily distinguished by the villagers from the gold-dust ('kepek-altün') washed from the river-beds. No gold coins or solid ornaments of gold and silver are admitted to have been found. But I have my doubts on this point, as the villagers or miners would have reason to be reticent about such finds. In any case it is acknowledged that during the first years and near the original spot the workings yielded rich quantities of gold. I myself subsequently purchased at Yotkan a tiny figure of solid gold of excellent workmanship, representing a monkey, that had been found during the year's washings. Larger articles of this kind are doubtless melted down speedily after discovery.

It seems at first difficult to account for the prevalence of gold in the form described and over sc large an area. But the use of leaf-gold on an extensive scale in the decoration of statues and buildings offers a probable explanation. From the detailed description which the earlier Chinese pilgrim Fa-hien gives of the splendid Buddhist temples and monasteries he saw on his

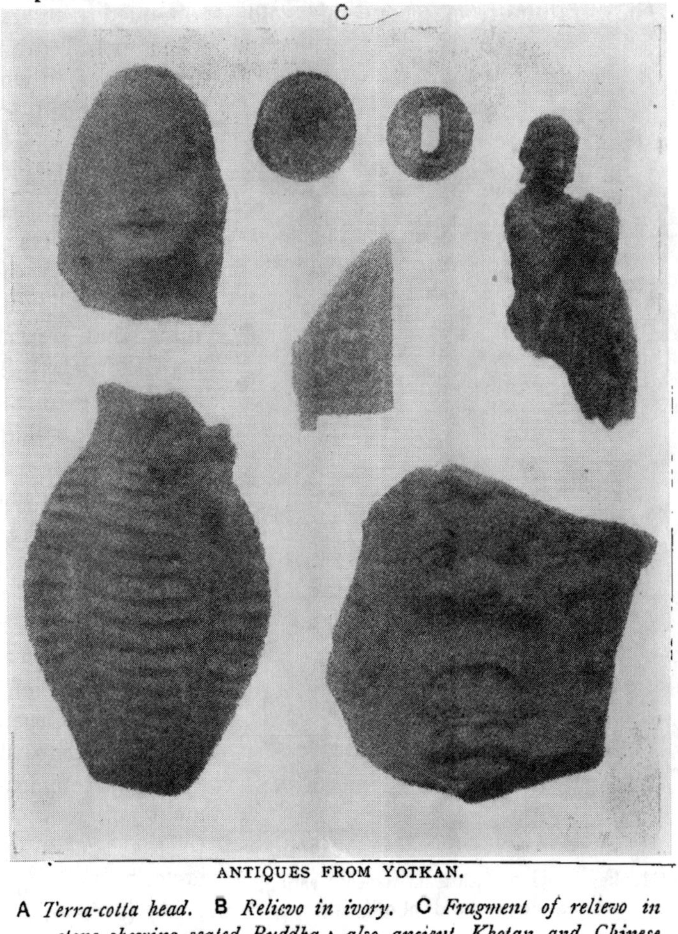

ANTIQUES FROM YOTKAN.

A *Terra-cotta head.* B *Relievo in ivory.* C *Fragment of relievo in stone showing seated Buddha; also ancient Khotan and Chinese coins.* D *Terra-cotta vase with monkey-shaped handle.* E *Piece of decorated vase.* (Scale one-half of originals.)

visit to Khotan (circ. 400 A.D.), it is certain that not only images but many parts of sacred buildings were richly overlaid with leaf-gold. Much of this must have fallen off and mingled with the dust when these structures crumbled away, not to be recovered until the soil could be washed by the method now followed.

The stratum from which this gold is obtained consists of decomposed rubbish and humus, in which are embedded fragments of ancient pottery, plain or ornamented, bones of animals, pieces of much decayed wood, and ashes, all indications that we have here the débris that accumulates on a site occupied by buildings for centuries. The copper coins, which are found plentifully, range from the bilingual pieces of the indigenous rulers, showing Chinese characters as well as early Indian legends in Kharoshthi, struck about the commencement of our era, to the square-holed issues of the Tang dynasty (618–907 A.D.). The stratum which represents the deposits of these and possibly also of earlier centuries, shows a uniform brownish colour, but varies in thickness. On the south and west it is on the average from five to eight feet deep. But on the north of the excavated area, the banks worked immediately below the houses of Khalche, where the proceeds

TERRA-COTTA FIGURINES FROM YOTKAN.

(Monkeys playing musical instruments, eating, &c. Scale two-thirds of original.)

in antiques, such as terra-cotta figurines, seals, etc., are richest, show a "culture-stratum" thirteen to fourteen feet thick. It is evident that this varying depth is due to the different length of the periods during which particular localities were occupied, and to the different character of the uses to which they had been put. The frequency of pottery fragments and of bones also varies at different points.

But in one respect all portions of the "culture-strata" exposed show a regrettable uniformity; nowhere did I come upon traces of remains of buildings, nor could I hear of such having been found during previous excavations. This is easily accounted for by the fact that, owing to the total absence of suitable stone, sun-dried bricks and clay supplemented by timber must have been in old days, just as now, the only obtainable materials for the construction of houses in the Khotan region. Whatever of the mud walls of buildings had not crumbled into dust, was bound to decay completely in the course of the centuries during which the site was taken up for cultivation and the soil kept constantly moist by the percolation of irrigation water. The same fate overtook whatever of the wood once contained in the buildings had not been extracted and utilised by successive occupiers of the soil. It might have been different if the old town had been overwhelmed by some sudden catastrophe and its site left deserted. Then we should expect to find under the ruins the original materials preserved in a recognisable form. But there is nothing to support the assumption of such a catastrophe.

The strata containing the old remains are everywhere covered by a considerable layer of alluvium from nine to twenty feet thick at various points. This layer, which by its light colour is easily distinguished from the "culture-strata" below and is absolutely free from remains indicating subsequent occupation of the site, interested me greatly. Some of the earlier European visitors to Yotkan have hazarded the assumption that the thick cover of earth under which the relics of the old town are hidden was due to a great flood, and they accordingly attributed its destruction to this supposed catastrophe. But a few hours' careful examination of the excavated banks sufficed to dispel such a notion once for all. Nowhere did I find the slightest trace of that stratification in the soil which such a flood or series of floods would necessarily have left behind. At every point the earth immediately above the "culture-strata" proved exactly the same in substance and colour as that which is to-day turned up by the plough of the Yotkan cultivator.

What, then, is the explanation of this deep cover under which the remains of this old town have rested? I think it is not far to seek. Cultivation in Khotan, as everywhere else in Turkestan, demands constant and ample irrigation; and as the river from which the water for the Yotkan fields is drawn in the spring and summer carries down enormous quantities of disintegrated soil from the mountains, the accumulation of silt over the fields on which the earth thus suspended is ultimately deposited, must be comparatively rapid. Thus the level of the cultivated portions of the oasis is bound to rise steadily; and considering how near these lands are to the region where the river collects most of this silt on its passage through the outer ranges, the thickness of the deposit left during a thousand years can by no means surprise us.

Observations I had occasion to make again and again after my first visit to Yotkan fully supported this explanation. Everywhere in the oasis I noticed that the main roads were sunk considerably below the surrounding level where they pass through cultivated land, while elsewhere, on waste or within the village areas, they kept flush with the adjoining ground. This low position of the roads is so uniformly observable and so marked that it is impossible not to seek for a natural cause. And none I could think of seemed more probable than that the level of the fields is constantly rising by irrigation, while that of the roads cannot undergo any marked variation. This observation led me to notice an equally characteristic fact—the low position of all the old cemeteries that are surrounded by fields. Cemeteries of any age are easily distinguished by their extending around some Mazar or shrine, and in their case I invariably found a ground-level considerably below that of the neighbouring fields. This curious fact becomes easily intelligible if we remember that the fields are continually receiving a deposit of silt from irrigation, while the cemeteries are naturally kept clear of water and consequently of this accretion.

The Yar which passes through Yotkan from west to east, and the excavations of the gold washers to the south of it, enable us to form some idea as to the position and extent of the old town. The banks of the Yar cease to yield any remains about 200 yards below the houses of Khalche. Accordingly, digging has stopped there. In the south the diggings near the portion of Yotkan known as Allama have been discontinued, as the ground did not yield the coveted gold in paying quantities. It is on the banks to the west and north-west that the work of washing the soil still continues vigorously, and it is under the fields lying in that direction that the remaining parts of the old town are likely to have been situated. The Yars which intersect the ground to the south and east of Yotkan nowhere cut through layers containing old remains. The negative evidence thus furnished excludes the idea of the town having ever extended in those directions.

There can be no doubt that the site discovered under the fields of Yotkan is that of the old capital of Khotan, as already suggested by M. Grenard. The proof, however, does not lie in an alleged tradition of the villagers (this could only be a very modern growth if it really existed), but in the exact agreement of the site with the topographical indications furnished by the early Chinese Annals, and in the ease with which I was able to identify from this starting-point the positions assigned by Hiuen-Tsiang's narrative to the most prominent Buddhist shrines he visited in the vicinity of the capital.

On the morning of the 28th of November I started on a survey of the villages to the west of Yotkan, in order to trace, if possible, the positions of these sacred places. Nearest among them was the Stupa and convent of 'Sa-mo-joh' which the pilgrim visited at a distance of five or six li (a little over a mile) to the west of the city[1]. It was founded in honour of an Arhat who had by various miracles won the special worship of one of the first Buddhist kings of the country. Under its Stupa, which was a hundred feet high, a great collection of sacred relics from Buddha's body had been deposited. Fa-hien also, two and a half centuries earlier, had seen this monastery, and describes "the magnificent and very beautiful hall of Buddha" that rose behind its Stupa. Judging from what previous experience has taught me of the fate which has overtaken all ancient structures within the cultivated area of the oasis, I did not expect to find remains of what was undoubtedly only a pile of sun-dried bricks doomed to rapid decay. All the more delighted was I when among the villages westwards I heard the name of Somiya mentioned. Other phonetic analogies prove that this represents the direct derivative of the ancient local name which is intended by the Chinese transcription of 'Sà-mo-joh,' and to the evidence of the name there was soon added topographical confirmation.

Leaving the excavated area of the ancient city at its north-west corner, I reached first the hamlet of Eskente half a mile to the west. There I was told of a 'Döbe' or mound that exists near the cemetery of Somiya. The latter place I found to be situated only three-fourths of a mile further west, and to consist of some thirty scattered dwellings. I went at once to the local Mazar, which is surrounded by an extensive cemetery, and on asking for the 'Döbe' was taken to a field adjoining its north-eastern corner. A little low mound, rising scarcely five feet above the surrounding ground, is respected by the villagers with a kind of superstitious fear, though it shares in no orthodox way the sacred character of the neighbouring Mazar and cemetery. I soon had the oldest men of the village summoned to the spot, and in what they told me of the mound we may, I think, yet trace the last lingering recollection of the ancient shrine that has left its name to Somiya. Shami Sope, a withered old man of about ninety, had heard from his father and grandfather, who had both died at a great age, that the little mound had ever been respected by the folk of Somiya as a hallowed spot not to be touched by the plough-share. Some unknown saint is supposed to have sat at the spot, and evil would befall those who should touch the ground. The name of the saint is forgotten, and the villagers would not assert whether he rests under the mound or not. But the people of Somiya never pass without saying a prayer, and according to the testimony of Shami Sope and his forbears, they have clung to this custom for the last two centuries.

I take it as a sign of the antiquity of the tradition that no name is assigned to the saint whose memory lingers about the 'Döbe,' whereas the names of the three Mullahs who are supposed to sanctify the Mazar of the village are currently known to young and old. Nobody seemed to know of any other spot similarly surrounded with superstitious awe in the neighbour-

OLD VILLAGERS OF SOMIYA.

hood. Considering the concordant evidence of the name and position of Somiya, I think it highly probable that the worship of this nameless mound is the last trace left of the 'Sa-mo-joh' Stupa of Buddhist days. And if this assumption be correct, we have here another proof of the tenacity of local worship which in Khotan, as elsewhere in the East, has survived all changes of creed.

The day's search enabled me to identify in all probability yet another sacred site mentioned by the Chinese pilgrims. Hiuen-Tsiang saw at a distance of ten li (two miles) to the south-west of the capital the monastery of 'Ti-kia-po-fo-na,' which was distinguished by the possession of a miraculous statue of Buddha. The name in this case can no longer be traced, but exactly in the direction and at the distance indicated there lies the popular Ziarat of 'Bowa-Kambar' visited by people from all parts of the Khotan district. I found it to consist of a large square cemetery enclosing the high mud tomb of the saint, who is supposed to have acquired holiness as the groom of 'Ali Padshah.' The level of the cemetery lies some twelve feet below the surrounding fields—a certain indication of its antiquity according to my previously detailed observations. A grove of fine old trees faces the eastern entrance, and a row of booths testifies to the popularity of the fairs which take place here at the time of pilgrimages.

It was dark when I returned from Bowa-Kambar, else I should have paid another visit to the still more popular shrine of Imam Musa Kasim at Kosa, which I had already passed on my way from Ujat. Its position due south of Yotkan makes me suspect that it has taken the place of the Virochana-Sangharama which was famous in the days of Hiuen-Tsiang as one of the earliest sanctuaries of Buddhism in Khotan. Its distance, a little over three miles from Yotkan, is somewhat in excess of the ten li south of the capital which the pilgrim indicates as its position. But then we do not exactly know the extent of the old city, and in any case there is no shrine of any note due south of Yotkan that comes nearer to the distance indicated.

On the 29th of November I left Yotkan to return to Khotan town, where the preparations for my desert journey were now urgently calling me. It was a misty cold morning as I bade good-bye to my host the Yüzbashi and rode along the Yotkan Yar eastwards. About two miles from the village I crossed by a bridge the fairly deep stream formed by the united waters of the Yars of Yotkan and Kashe, and on the other bank of the ravine reached the lands of Halalbagh, a collection of large hamlets which I was anxious to see once more, as a local tradition connects the site with the pre-Muhammadan rulers of the country. Close to the central hamlet there stretches a marsh, known as Aiding-kul, covering about a square mile. It is overgrown with reeds and fed by copious springs which form quite a little stream at the northern end where the marsh drains towards the Yurung-kash.

Islam Beg secured me here a very intelligent guide in the person of Ibrahim Mullah, a man well known for his learning and piety. Though eighty-six years old at the time of my visit, he was still quite active. His comfortable embonpoint and his showy silk dress well-lined with fur showed plainly that, despite Koran and pilgrimages, he had not neglected the good things of this world. Ibrahim Mullah owns Turki 'Taskiras' of the varous Imams who are worshipped at the most popular of Khotan Mazars, and soon showed me in them chapter and verse for his assertion that it was at Halalbagh that there once stood the city of the 'Khalkhal-i Chin-u-Machin,' the legendary heathen ruler of Khotan. According to the popular tradition recorded in these texts, the four Imams whose blessed bodies now rest in a famous Mazar at Hasha, killed this opponent of Islam, and his city became a waste. The shrine of Kum-i-Shahidan, about half a mile to the west of the marsh, is supposed to mark the spot where three hundred and sixty faithful followers of the Imams found martyrdom in the final struggle.

According to Ibrahim Mullah, Mirza Abu-Bakr, the ruler of Kashgar and Khotan in the early part of the sixteenth century, had the old site excavated for the sake of its hidden treasures. He brought river-water to the place to enable his workmen to wash the soil—just as is now done at Yotkan—and in the hollow left by his diggings there formed the marsh of Halalbagh. No old remains of any kind are now found, and it is thus difficult to judge whether there is any historical foundation for the story. Mirza Abu-Bakr, about whose doings we are well informed by the Tarikh-i-Rashidi, the interesting chronicle of Mirza Haidar, his nephew, certainly carried on treasure-seeking operations on a great scale at various old sites in his dominions. But whether Halalbagh was really among the places he exploited, or whether his reputation alone induced the local literati to connect with his name the supposed origin of the Aiding-kul marsh, can scarcely be decided without tracing old remains at the site or earlier evidence of the tradition. The mound called 'Nagara-khana' ("the hall of kettle-drums') which rises to a height of about twenty-seven feet close to the southern edge of the marsh, is popularly supposed to represent a remnant of the ancient city wall. But on close examination it proved to be a natural bank of loess, without a trace of brickwork or other mark of artificial construction.

The rigour of winter was now setting in rapidly. So I was glad to avail myself during the short halt at Khotan, which the final preparations for the desert journey demanded, of the shelter offered by Tokhta Akhun's suburban residence. In its dimly lighted but tolerably warm rooms I was hard at work writing up accounts of my geographical and antiquarian observations for despatch to Europe, and carefully sorting and re-packing the baggage. In order to keep the camels, on which we should have to depend entirely for the difficult marches through the sands, as lightly laden as possible, I decided to leave behind in charge of Badruddin, the Afghan Aksakal, a depôt of all stores and materials not immediately needed. The elimination was no easy matter. On the one hand it was impossible to estimate the length of time during which my explorations would keep me away from Khotan · on the other it was clear that in the inhospitable regions in which we were to pass the winter, any deficiency in the necessary supplies and equipment might have a very serious effect on our health and thus hamper my movements. It was largely through the care bestowed on transport and supplies, that I was subsequently able to carry my operations so much farther from the Khotan base than originally anticipated.

CAMELS STARTING FOR DANDAN-UILIQ.

CHAPTER XVII.

TO THE RUINS OF DANDAN-UILIQ.

THE morning of the 7th December, a misty and bitterly cold day, saw our start for the winter campaign in the desert. My goal was Dandan-Uiliq, the ancient site I had decided upon for my first explorations. To reach it I chose the route viâ Tawakkel; for though longer than the track leading straight into the desert north-east of Khotan which Turdi, my "treasure-seeking" guide, was in the habit of following, it somewhat reduced the extent of actual desert-marching with its inseparable privations for men and animals. The first day brought me, at Yangi-arik, to the edge of the cultivated area north of Khotan town. The next two days were passed in dreary marches along the barren left bank of the Yurung-kash, where there was nothing to be seen but sand-dunes to the west and reed-covered strips near the winding course of the river.

It was getting dark when we crossed on the evening of the third day to the right bank and approached the southern end of the Tawakkel oasis. It was formed some sixty years ago by the construction of an irrigation channel, which takes off the river waters a few miles further south. It has since developed into a prosperous settlement estimated at some thousand households. Its Beg, instructed in advance from Pan-Darin's

Yamen, had awaited me at the crossing, and now escorted me with an imposing array of followers to the southernmost hamlet. The big bonfires which lit up our way, and the prevalence of wood in the construction of the houses indicated the proximity of the forest belt which accompanies the Khotan River on its course through the desert and furnishes a plentiful supply of wood to this outlying colony.

On the following day I moved my camp to the Beg's house at Atbashi, some six miles further north, where the arrangements were to be completed for the party of labourers I wished to take along as well as for our supplies. In view of the observations already detailed as to the rise of the ground level in the old cultivated area of Khotan, I was interested to note that in this comparatively recent oasis the roads and waste spaces lay nowhere more than about one foot below the level of the neighbouring fields. It was evident that the period of irrigation and consequent silt deposit had been too short here to permit of any appreciable rise in the level of the fields. Still less was I surprised to hear that the area of the colony might be greatly extended towards the desert by the construction of additional irrigation channels. The abundant supply of water which the river carries down during the spring and summer months might bring fertility to large tracts now covered by low dunes. But here, as elsewhere along the southern edge of the great Turkestan desert, there is no surplus of population available for such extended cultivation, nor an administration capable of undertaking fresh irrigation works on a large scale.

Thanks to the stringent instructions issued by Pan-Darin, I was able to collect at Atbashi a party of thirty labourers for my intended excavations, together with four weeks' food supply. Owing to superstitious fears and in view of the expected rigours of the winter, the cultivators were naturally reluctant to venture so far into the desert, though they appreciated the pay offered, 1½ Miskals per diem, which was more than twice the average wages for unskilled labour. Fortunately, the Amban's authority was not to be denied; and there were also the two Tawakkel hunters, Ahmad Merghen and Kasim Akhun, to inspire confidence.

I had already from Khotan secured their services as guides, and soon found them most useful in looking after the labourers. They were indeed splendid men, inured to all hardships by their roving life in the desert and river jungle, and by their experience intelligent far beyond the horizon of the villagers. They did their best to convince the more fainthearted that this season, when neither sand-storms nor thirst need be apprehended, was in reality the safest for the work I had in view; that travelling in so great a party they had nothing to fear from the 'Jinns' or demons of the desert; and that plenty of dead wood would be forthcoming to keep them from getting frozen to death.

AHMAD MERGHEN AND KASIM AKHUN, OF TAWAKKEL.

I on my part took care to select the physically fittest from among the men brought before me, and made the respective village headmen responsible for their being supplied with all needful warm clothing and food sufficient to last for four weeks. The liberal cash advance I paid myself into the hands of each of my "Levies" facilitated these domestic preparations. In order to provide for professional help far away in the desert, I arranged to include among the labourers a young cultivator who had been to a Mosque school and had acquired the art of writing Turki, not according to any high standard of orthography, it is true, but still legibly. Another was used to practise tailoring in his spare hours, while a third was proficient in leather work and could look after the men's boots. Each man had to bring his 'Ketman,' the hoe in common use throughout Turkestan, which proved an excellent implement for excavation work in the sand. Steel shovels of German make I had brought along from Kashgar; but I soon found that, except where there was a risk of causing damage to buried remains, the 'Ketman' to which the men were accustomed yielded much better results.

For the carriage of the men's food, supplies, and other impedimenta the few camels I could spare were not sufficient. So a dozen donkeys were engaged which offered the advantage of needing a minimum of fodder. For the camels only a quantity of oil made of rape seed could be taken along. Half a pound daily of this evil-smelling liquid for each animal proved wonderfully effective in keeping up their stamina during the trying desert marches, when they had to go without grazing or fodder of any kind and sometimes for a number of days without water. Our ponies, for which the desert to be crossed offered neither sufficient water nor fodder, were sent back to Khotan in charge of Niaz, the interpreter. The dejected faces of my servants, when it was made clear to them that they would have to trudge through the sands on foot like myself, were truly amusing.

A severe cold brought on by exposure made me glad for the day's halt at Tawakkel which these various preparations demanded, and which was the last I could pass in comparative comfort. My attempt to utilise it also for getting rid of a troublesome tooth through the local barber's help proved a painful failure. This worthy first vainly tortured me with a forceps of the most primitive description, then grew nervous, and finally prayed hard to be spared further efforts. Perhaps he had lost confidence in his hands and instrument, since I had insisted on seeing them thoroughly cleaned with soap and hot water previous to the intended operation.

When at last on the forenoon of the 12th December the camels were ready with the freshly packed loads and my troop of labourers duly collected, half the population of Tawakkel seemed to be assembled to witness our departure. Those who had come to wish luck and a safe return to relatives among my party followed us to the northernmost hamlet. Then beyond, where cultivated land gave way to scrub-covered low dunes by the river bank, the Beg of Tawakkel, who escorted me with two picturesque attendants carrying falcons as a sign

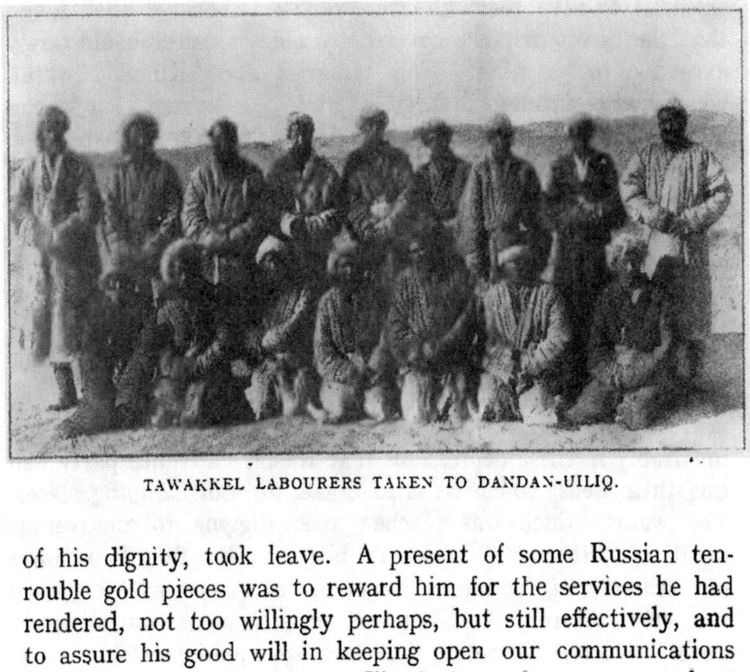

TAWAKKEL LABOURERS TAKEN TO DANDAN-UILIQ.

of his dignity, took leave. A present of some Russian ten-rouble gold pieces was to reward him for the services he had rendered, not too willingly perhaps, but still effectively, and to assure his good will in keeping open our communications while we were in the desert. The first march was a very short one, to a deserted shepherd station ('satma') by the side of the river; for following the advice of the guides, I wished to let all our animals have a plentiful drink in the evening before entering the sands eastward. On the following morning we struck to the east, and soon found the track marked by the footprints of the small advance party which I had sent ahead two days previously under the guidance of Kasim. He had orders to dig wells at all places suitable for camps, and after reaching the ruins of Dandan-Uiliq to push on to the Keriya Darya, whence Ram Singh was to join me.

Marching in the drift sand was slow work, though the dunes were low, rising only to 6 to 10 feet in the area crossed during the first two days. The feet of men and animals sank deep at every step into the fine sand, and the progress of the heavily laden camels was reduced to about 1¼ miles per hour. In view of the want of sufficient fodder and water, it was essential to save them all over-exertion; hence I soon found that the direct distance covered by a day's march could rarely exceed 9 to 10 miles. The tamarisk and 'Kumush' scrub which was plentiful at first, grew rare in the course of our second march, while the wild poplars or 'Toghraks' disappeared altogether as living trees. Luckily amidst the bare dunes there rose at intervals small conical hillocks thickly covered with tamarisk scrub, the decayed roots of which supplied excellent fuel. Close to these hillocks there were usually to be found hollows scooped out of the loess soil, evidently by the erosive action of wind. These hollows, which reach down to at least 10 to 15 feet below the level of the little valleys separating the neighbouring sand dunes, offer of course the nearest approach to the sub-soil water. It was accordingly invariably in these depressions that Kasim's advance party had dug their wells, which we also chose for our camping places. The water, which was reached after digging to an average depth of 5 to 7 feet, was very bitter at the first two camps and scarcely fit for human consumption. But as we moved further away from the Khotan River it became comparatively sweet. I have no doubt that geology would furnish a satisfactory explanation for this observation, which was well known to my guides as generally applicable to these parts of the Taklamakan and has been noticed already by Dr. Hedin. The supply of water furnished by these wells was decidedly scanty for so large a party as mine; and as it was stopped altogether by the damp soil getting frozen overnight, men had in the evening to be detailed gradually to collect spare water in two of my iron tanks where it could be stored as ice for use on the next day.

The winter of the desert had now set in with full vigour. In daytime while on the march there was little to complain of; for though the temperature in the shade never rose above freezing point, yet there was no wind, and I could enjoy without discomfort the delightfully pure air of the desert and its repose which nothing living disturbs. But at night, when the thermometer would go down to minimum temperatures from 0° to 10° Fahr. below zero, my little Kabul tent, notwithstanding its extra serge lining, was a terribly cold abode. The "Stormont-Murphy Arctic Stove" which was fed with small compressed fuel cakes (from London!) steeped in paraffin proved very useful; yet its warmth was not sufficient to permit my discarding the heavy winter garb, including fur-lined overcoat and boots, which protected me in the open. The costume I wore would, together with the beard I was obliged to allow to grow, have made me unrecognisable even to my best friends in Europe. When the temperature had gone down in the tent to about 6° Fahr. below freezing-point, reading or writing became impossible, and I had to retire among the heavy blankets and rugs of my bed. There 'Yolchi Beg' had usually long before sought a refuge, though he too was in possession of a comfortable fur coat of Kashmirian make, from which he scarcely ever emerged between December and March.

To protect one's head at night from the intense cold while retaining free respiration, was one of the small domestic problems which had to be faced from the start of this winter campaign in the desert. To the knitted Shetland cap which covered the head but left the face bare, I had soon to add the fur-lined cap of Balaclava shape made in Kashmir, which with its flaps and peak pulled down gave additional protection for everything except nose and cheeks. Still it was uncomfortable to wake up with one's moustache hard frozen with the respiration that had passed over it. Ultimately I had to adopt the device of pulling the end of my fur-coat over my head and breathing through its sleeve! Also in another way these first campings in the wintry desert brought some trying experiences.

17

The tooth I had vainly endeavoured to get rid of at Tawakkel continued to cause trouble, and the neuralgic pains it gave me were never more exquisite than at night. The only remedy I had within reach to secure some rest was chlorodyne, and to take its drops I had need of water. But for this it was first necessary to melt the solid lump of ice contained in my aluminium tumbler, and the minutes which passed until I had secured over my candle the little quantity of liquid, were enough to benumb hands and fingers.

On the evening of the fourth day after entering the desert, as we were pitching camp amidst desolate sand dunes covering dead tamarisk scrub, two of the men sent ahead returned to report that Kasim's party had failed to trace the ruined site we were in search of. It was now the turn of old Turdi, my "treasure-seeking" guide and factotum, to prove his knowledge of this dreary region. He had only once in his life approached Dandan-Uiliq from this side, and had apparently, from a feeling of professional etiquette or pride, refrained from pressing his advice against the guidance of the two Tawakkel hunters. But he had more than once on the march told me that he thought our route was leading too far north, and now, on the plain avowal of their inability to discover our goal, I could see a gleam of satisfaction pass over his wrinkled face. A short conversation with the returned men sufficed for him to locate the point which Kasim's party had reached, and early next morning they were sent ahead again with full instructions that were to guide Kasim back into the right direction. We ourselves set out later, now under the guidance of old Turdi, who, with an instinct bred by the roamings of some thirty years and perhaps also inherited—his father had followed the fortunes of a treasure-seeker's life before him—found his bearings even where the dead uniformity of the sand dunes seemed to offer no possible landmark.

Skirting the foot of several higher ridges of sand or 'Dawans' running as usual from N.W. to S.E., we crossed in the evening a belt of ground where dead trees were seen emerging from heavy sand. Shrivelled and bleached as they appeared, Turdi and the men could recognise among them trunks of the 'Terek' or poplar, the willow and other planted trees, unmistakable proofs that we had reached the area of ancient cultivation. About one and a half miles further to the S.E. we came upon stretches of bare loess with an extensive line of hollows, curiously resembling a dry river course, yet undoubtedly only a result of wind erosion. In one of these steep-banked hollows we succeeded in digging a well, and thus saved ourselves a search in the dark for the spot which alone, according to Turdi's knowledge, offered water in the immediate vicinity of the ruins. On the following morning, the 18th of December, after turning a great Dawan, Turdi guided us to this spot, and a couple of miles further south I found myself amidst the ruined houses which mark the site of Dandan-Uiliq.

Scattered in small isolated groups over an area which my subsequent survey showed to extend for about one and a half miles from north to south with a width of three-quarters of a mile, there rose from among the low dunes the remains of buildings modest in size, but of manifest antiquity. Where the sand had blown away, the walls constructed throughout of a timber framework with thick layers of plaster were exposed to view, broken down to within a few feet from the ground. Elsewhere in places covered by low dunes the walls could still be made out by the rows of wooden posts rising from the sand. All structural remains left exposed showed signs of having been "explored" by treasure-seekers, and the marks of the damage done by their operations were only too evident. Yet even thus the ruins, on a first hurried inspection, furnished unmistakable proofs of their character and approximate date. In the remains of frescoes which had once adorned the much-injured walls in some of the larger rooms, I could easily recognise representations of Buddhas and Bodhisattvas. These plainly indicated that I was standing in the ruins of Buddhist places of worship. Peculiarities in the style of the frescoes seemed to mark the last centuries preceding the introduction of Islam as the probable date when these shrines and the settlement to which they belonged had been deserted. And this conclusion received curious support on the first day by Chinese copper coins bearing the date of the Kai-yuen period (A.D. 713–741), which were picked up under my eyes from the débris-strewn ground near the buildings.

Old Turdi felt quite at home among these desolate surroundings, which he had visited so frequently since his boyhood. It was the fascinating vision of hidden treasure which had drawn him and his kinsfolk there again and again, however scanty the tangible reward had been of their trying wanderings. Yet the familiarity thus acquired with the silent relics of the past had developed in him an instinctive interest in all traces of the life that once reigned there. As he guided me among these ghostly wrecks of houses and answered the many questions I put to him about his own observations, I could see the shy man grow more and more animated. It was evident from his communications that the conditions of the dunes were changing very slowly at this site. Consequently Turdi had no difficulty in recognising the places where he and his companions had been at work during previous visits. Luckily their scanty resources had never allowed them to overcome the difficulty experienced in carrying to this distant site supplies sufficient for a prolonged stay or to bring working parties of more than a few men.

Hence the structures more deeply buried in the sand had escaped unopened. It was important to select these in the first place for my excavations, and I felt grateful for Turdi's excellent memory and topographical instinct which enabled him readily to indicate their positions. Guided by this first rapid survey, I chose for my camp a spot from which the main ruins to be explored were all within easy reach. There were practical considerations which compelled me to make my choice carefully. For in order to keep my men at work as long as possible every day, it was necessary to spare them tiring tramps through the drift sand. It was still more essential that we should keep to a spot at which fuel could be readily obtained in the ample quantities I foresaw would be needed for our long stay. The dead trees of ancient orchards could alone supply it, and their occurrence in various parts of the ruined site was very unequal. As soon as the baggage had been unloaded at the point which appeared best to answer these conditions, I hastened to despatch the camels under Ahmad Merghen's guidance on their three days' journey eastwards to the Keriya Darya. There in the jungle lining the river's course they were to find the fodder they so badly needed, and to gather fresh strength for subsequent desert marches. The donkeys, too, which had carried the men's food supplies, with the meagrest rations for themselves, were sent back to Tawakkel under the care of two of the villagers.

CAMP IN THE DESERT, DANDAN-UILIQ.

CHAPTER XVIII.

EXCAVATION OF BUDDHIST SHRINES.

On the morning of the 19th of December I commenced my excavations by clearing the remains of a small square building immediately to the south of my camp. Turdi knew it as a 'But-khana' or "temple of idols," and well remembered once having searched it in his own fashion. But the sand, though lying only two to three feet high, had not been removed, and by laying bare the foundations and floor I could expect to gain useful preliminary knowledge as to the general construction and arrangement of such shrines. In this I was not disappointed. A careful examination of the remains of walls which were brought to light on the north and west sides showed that there had been an inner square cella enclosed by equi-distant outer walls twenty feet long, forming a kind of corridor or passage on each side. Both inner and outer walls consisted of hard plaster laid on a framework of wood and reed matting, which itself was held in position by massive square posts fixed at regular intervals.

Of the manner in which the upper portions of the inner cella walls, long ago decayed, had once been decorated, I could not remain in doubt when fragments of flat stucco relievos, which must have originally belonged to plaques of regular patterns, turned up in dozens from the sand covering the interior. Mixed with frequently repeated architectural ornaments there were numerous reproductions in low relievo of the figure of Buddha, in the orthodox attitudes of teaching with hand raised or seated in meditation. Other small relievos showed attendant figures in adoration, such as the graceful garland-holding woman rising from a lotus and probably meant for a Gandharvi, which has been reproduced on the cover of this book. Conventional as all these representations are and evidently casts from a series of moulds, they at once arrested my interest by their unmistakable affinity to that style of Buddhist sculpture in India which developed under classical influences. Nor was I less gratified to observe how well many of these small relievos retained the bright colours with which they had been painted. Equally reassuring proof of the preserving power of the desert sand was furnished by the remarkable freshness in which elaborately painted figures of Buddhist saints appeared on pieces of wooden posts and beams that evidently once belonged to the ceiling.

The clearing of this single small shrine not only yielded some one hundred and fifty pieces of stucco relievo fit for transport to Europe, but supplied me with the indications I needed in order to direct the systematic excavation of structures more deeply buried in the sand. So when on the next day I proceeded to a group of small buildings buried below six to eight feet of sand by the slope of a fairly high dune, just half a mile south of my camp, I was able correctly to gauge their construction and character, though only the broken and bleached ends of posts were visible above the sand. They are seen in the accompanying photograph, which shows the place before excavation. The posts soon proved to belong to the walls of two temple cellas (marked as D. II.), once richly decorated with frescoes and stucco images.

As their constructive features and adornment are typical of those observed in other shrines subsequently excavated at this site I shall describe them here briefly. The larger cella forms a square of ten feet inside, with a door opening from the north. The walls, which here again were constructed of a wooden frame-

RUINS OF BUDDHIST SHRINE D. II., AT DANDAN-UILIQ, BEFORE EXCAVATION.

work with layers of hard plaster on either side, showed a uniform thickness of six and a half inches. The cella was enclosed by a quadrangular passage about four and a half feet wide, with outer walls of the same materials. This passage, which almost certainly served for the purposes of the circumambulation ('pradakshina') common to all traditional forms of Indian worship, also had its entrance in the centre of the north wall. The interior of the cella was once occupied by a colossal statue made of stucco and painted, which most probably represented a Buddha. But of this only the feet remained, about thirteen inches long, raised on an elaborately moulded oblong base about three feet high. The other parts of the statue had crumbled away long ago, and the fragments comprising parts of the legs and of the lower drapery which were found in the sand above the base broke at the slightest touch. Of the wooden framework, too, which once supported the heavy image, only the lowest part was still intact, fixed within the left foot. Each of the four corners of the cella was occupied by a draped stucco figure standing on a lotus-shaped pedestal. But of these statues only the one in the north-west corner was found intact up to the waist. A photograph of this cella, taken after the excavation, is reproduced on p. 266.

The walls of the cella, which, judging from the size of the statue, must have been of considerable height, were decorated inside with frescoes showing figures of Buddhas or Bodhisattvas enveloped in large halos. As these too were over life-size, only the feet with the broad painted frieze below them showing lotuses and small figures of worshippers, could be seen on the walls still standing. The colours looked faded and worn, as if the frescoes had been exposed for a considerable time before the protecting sand invaded the building. But the outlines, drawn mostly in a kind of terra-cotta colour on the fine-grained, well-prepared plaster surface, were still sharp and clear. The decoration of the outside of the cella walls consisted mainly of fresco bands containing small representations of seated Buddhist saints in the attitude of meditation, only the colours of the robes and halos varying. But amidst these conventional designs there was found a picture which, though much effaced,

CELLA OF BUDDHIST SHRINE, D. II., AT DANDAN-UILIQ, AFTER EXCAVATION.

at once attracted my interest as representing some sacred legend, perhaps of a local character. It shows rows of youths riding on horses or camels each holding a cup in his outstretched right hand, while above one of the riders a bird, perhaps meant for a falcon, is swooping down on this offering. The popularity of the subject was subsequently attested by my discovery of a well-preserved painted tablet in another temple ruin on which a similar scene is figured.

Frescoes of Buddhist saints over-lifesize, similar to those found in the cella, once adorned the inside of the walls enclosing the passage. Below them there ran a decorative frieze in which lotuses floating in the water and small human figures, perhaps meant for Nagas or deities of springs, supporting the feet of the sacred personages above, could still be made out. From the south wall of the passage I succeeded in removing the piece of painted plaster which is seen on p. 268, and which is now safely deposited in the British Museum. It shows the figure of a seated Buddha or Bodhisattva, occupying the triangular space left between the lower portions of two larger frescoes. The inscription painted beneath in black colour is in a cursive variety of the Brahmi script; its language, however, like that of some other short inscriptions found on the frescoed walls of the Dandan-Uiliq ruins, is not Indian, but probably the same as appears in the Non-Sanskritic Brahmi documents I discovered at this site.

The excavations, when extended on the 21st of December to the remains immediately adjoining the west wall of the shrine just described, brought to light another Buddhist temple cella which, notwithstanding its smaller dimensions, proved particularly rich in interesting art relics. This little chapel, as it might be called, measured only 12 ft. 8 in. from north to south with a width of 8 ft. 8 in., and had no enclosing square passage. Its walls, built of the usual wooden framework and plaster, were only four inches in thickness and had in consequence crumbled away to within a foot or two from the ground, except on the east side, where the closely adjoining outer wall of the larger cella gave support, and on the south where a long platform, surmounted by a massive base for the principal image, had been built against the wall. Of the stucco statue which once occupied this base only the scantiest fragments could be found ; for with a pedestal raised close on four feet above the ground it must have long remained without the protecting cover of drift sand, as testified by the extremely friable condition of the few recovered fragments of coloured stucco that belonged to this image. The

FRESCO FROM OUTER WALL OF SHRINE, D. II., DANDAN-ULIQ.

(Scale one-eighth of original.)

front of the base, which was nearly three feet broad, proved to be flanked on either side by the half-detached figure of a lion, and was thus manifestly meant to represent the 'Simhasana,' or 'lion's throne,' on which ancient Indian tradition seated both heavenly and earthly rulers. The heads of the lions had decayed long ago, but the curls indicating the manes falling over the fore part of the bodies were still clearly recognisable.

In the top layer of the sand which covered the south-eastern corner of the cella (shown by the photograph reproduced on p. 270), were found numerous small relievos in stucco, from 5 to 8 in. high, representing Buddhas or Bodhisattvas with the right hand raised in the attitude of teaching. The robes of these figures are painted reddish brown, the orthodox colour for the garb of Indian monks, while their heads are surrounded by halos in a light green shade. Some specimens were still attached to portions of a hard stucco ground, decorated in relievo with elaborate wreaths and rosettes and gaily coloured. It was evident that all these pieces once belonged to plaques which, perhaps in the form of large halos, had adorned the uppermost part of the walls in this corner. The fact of these fragments being found in loose sand, several feet above the platform already referred to, is a clear indication that the interior of the little shrine had been invaded by the drift-sand while its walls were still intact to a considerable height.

Comparatively well protected as this south-eastern portion of the cella was, the stucco image which once occupied the corner had decayed, just as in the case of the other three corners, down to the feet. These, however, as well as the elegantly moulded lotus-pedestal of circular shape, can still be made out in the photograph. Luckily this corner had afforded better protection for some other adornments of the shrine. On clearing the platform between the corner pedestal and the base of the principal statue, I found a small detached statue in stucco about 1⅓ ft. high and well preserved but for the head and arms. The photograph shows it placed subsequently on the main base. The seated figure represented in it must, by evidence of the carefully indicated dress, have been intended for a Buddha or Bodhisattva. The colour of the robe, a reddish brown, has survived very well. The small wooden board on which the image had been set up, evidently for the purpose of convenient transport, was still intact, and as the stucco too had kept comparatively hard I was able to risk its removal. Carefully packed away in one of my mule-trunks, amidst cotton wool and plenty of soft country paper I had provided myself with at Khotan, the little statue accomplished its long journey to London far better than I had expected.

SMALLER CELLA OF BUDDHIST SHRINE, D. II., AT DANDAN-UILIQ, AFTER EXCAVATION.

At the foot of the principal base and leaning against it were found five painted panels of wood, all oblong, but of varying sizes. The largest measures 11 in. in length, with a height of 5½ in., and has a thickness of about a quarter of an inch. Owing to their position near the ground the wood of these panels and also the thin layer of water-colour with which they are painted has suffered much, evidently through damp. For the same reason the removal of the crust of sand and siliceous matter which adheres to the surface proved a very delicate task. But even the imperfect cleaning I could attempt at the time sufficed to show that these little paintings represent personages of Buddhist mythology or scenes bearing on Buddhist worship and legends. On one of them two figures evidently meant for Bodhisattvas, can be seen seated on lotus-flowers, with coloured vesica and halo behind them. In another I could, notwithstanding the much-faded outlines, recognise the quaint features of that popular figure of the Indian pantheon, the elephant-headed god of learning, Ganesha. A third panel exhibits the figure of a dancing-woman, drawn in full movement and with remarkable freedom. From the head, which is thrown back, there flows downwards a quantity of black tresses, while the left hand holds the loop of a sash or veil poised in graceful curve over the head.

These painted tablets, like all the others subsequently discovered at the bases of sacred images in ruined temples of Dandan-Uiliq, were undoubtedly still in the same position in which they had originally been deposited as the votive offerings of pious worshippers. And curiously enough, as if to show the care which must have been taken by the last attendants of the little shrine to keep the sacred objects clear of the invading dust and sand, I discovered several ancient brooms both near the principal base and in other parts of the cella (reproduced p. 358). They were about 16 in. long and constructed in a very ingenious way from stalks of some hardy grass. At their bottom these stalks were plaited into a continuous strip subsequently rolled up tightly and bound round with twisted grass, while their feathery ends, being thus brought into a bunch, form a convenient birch-like broom. The sand against which these humble implements were once used to wage war had been the means of preserving them in almost perfect condition; and the same was the case with another curious relic, a little cloth bag filled with fragments of bones and human teeth, which turned up in the south-eastern corner close to the small seated image already described. Had they been brought here by some visitor as reputed relics of the body of a saintly personage, or were they ex-votos deposited with some superstitious object?

As the work of clearing proceeded along the east wall of the cella it revealed a series of very interesting frescoes, together with a relievo statue in stucco of a peculiar character. As seen in the photograph it is a male figure, complete but for the head and left arm, standing close to the platform already mentioned and over the body of a prostrate foe. The figure, which measured a little over three feet from the heel to below the arm-pit, is clad in a coat of mail reaching below the knees and elaborately decorated. The gay colours of the successive rows of small plates which form the mail, alternately red-blue and red-green, were remarkably well preserved, and not less so all the details of the ornaments which are shown along the front and lower edge of the coat and on the girdle around the waist. Even the arrangement of the rivets which join the plates of mail, and the folds of the garment protruding below the armour, are indicated with great accuracy. There can be no doubt that the artist has carefully reproduced here details of armour and dress with which he was familiar from his own times. The feet, which seem to be clad in wide top-boots of leather, just like the 'Charuks' still worn throughout Eastern Turkestan, are placed over the contorted body manifestly of a vanquished demon. The features of the latter's head, which alone is raised somewhat from the ground, with the eyes wide open and the teeth displayed, express terror. The representation of the thick hair by elaborately worked spiral tufts strongly reminded me of the treatment of the hair in many a sculpture of Græco-Buddhist type familiar to me from the Lahore Museum. The body appears to have been painted dark blue, but owing to the low position of this relievo the stucco retained little of the original coating of colour. The standing figure probably represents one of the Yakshas, or divine "guardians of the gate" popular in Buddhist mythology.

The cella wall immediately adjoining this relievo group revealed a series of small fresco paintings which, by their unconventional subjects and their spirited drawing, at once attracted my attention. The one to the left of the mail-clad statue shows a woman bathing in a square tank of water, enclosed by a tesselated pavement and filled with floating lotuses. The figure is nude, except for a large red headdress resembling an Indian Pagri and profuse ornaments round the neck, arms and wrists, and is drawn with remarkable *verve* in simple yet graceful outlines. The right hand with its shapely fingers rests against the breasts, while the left arm is curved down towards the middle of the waist. Fourfold strings of small bells are shown hanging around the hips, just as seen in representations of dancing-girls in early Hindu sculpture; while, curiously enough, an elaborate vine-leaf appears where post-classical convention would place its fig-leaf. The face of the bather is turned to her proper right, down towards a small male figure, apparently a boy, who is shown as if trying to rise from the water by holding to her side.

The delineation of the lotus-flowers which rise from the tank in a variety of forms, closed or half-open, as well as their colours, ranging from dark blue to deep purple, seemed remarkably true to nature, and distinctly suggested that these sacred flowers were familiar to the painter from personal observation. I remembered the splendid tank of lotuses I had seen at the Tao-tai's Yamen in Kashgar which had been grown from seed imported from China. In view of this pictorial representation I feel convinced that already ancient Khotan had known the graceful plant dear to the gods of India. Considering the close historical connection between Kashmir and Khotan which the local traditions recorded by Hiuen-Tsiang indicate, it needs no effort of imagination to believe that the lotuses that once adorned the gardens of settlements now buried by the desert sand were originally derived from the great Himalayan Valley, on the lakes of which I had so often admired them.

The appearance of a riderless horse in front of the tank and some other features of the fresco suggest that its subject may perhaps be identical with the curious legend which Hiuen-Tsiang relates of a Naga lady residing in a stream east of Khotan and of her strange wooing by a pious mortal. But the point is too uncertain to permit more than an allusion here.

Of the adjoining frescoes, however, it is impossible to mistake the significance. A well-drawn though now much effaced male figure of youthful appearance, seen seated in cross-legged fashion and dressed in a dark-blue cloak that leaves the right shoulder bare, is manifestly that of a Buddhist scholar. His right hand holds the oblong leaves of a 'Pothi,' or manuscript book arranged in the traditional Indian fashion, on which the eyes are fixed in intent study. By the side of this figure and likewise turned to the proper right, an old man is depicted in the act of teaching. His robe, which seems to be made up of patches of varying shades of brown, curiously suggests the orthodox garb of mendicant monks of all Indian sects, termed 'chiravastra' in Sanskrit. While the right hand, with the second and third fingers stretched out, is raised in the gesture of teaching, the palm of the left supports a closed 'Pothi.' The two boards of thin wood between which the leaves are placed after a fashion still commonly observed in the case of Sanskrit manuscripts, are quite distinctly marked. The cleverly drawn features of the old man's face seem to express complacent assurance in his teaching and full abstraction in its subject. In front of him, too, a tank is shown with open lotuses floating on the surface. Two birds, looking like wild geese, disport themselves in the water, and with necks marked dark-blue and green, raise their heads towards the old teacher.

To remove any portion of these interesting frescoes proved quite impracticable, owing to the friable condition of the plaster on which they were painted. Nor can it, in view of the faded state of the colours, be surprising that the photographs which I secured of them do not permit of satisfactory reproduction by any mechanical process. But drawings have been made from these as well as other photographs of Dandan-Uiliq frescoes by the hand of my artist friend, Mr. F. H. Andrews. These, when published in my Detailed Report, will, I hope, render it easier to judge of the remarkable resemblance which, in style of composition and the drawing of figures, exists between these frescoes and the later of the Indian paintings in the cave temples of Ajanta.

Little, indeed, of early Indian painting has survived in India itself. Hence all the more interest must attach to the specimens which the frescoes and painted tablets of Dandan-Uiliq shrines have preserved for us of that selfsame Indian art as transplanted to the Buddhist region of Khotan.

ROOM OF MONASTIC DWELLING, D. III., DANDAN-UILIQ, FIND-PLACE OF ANCIENT MANUSCRIPTS.

CHAPTER XIX.

FIRST FINDS OF ANCIENT MANUSCRIPTS.

It had not needed the discovery of the pictorial representation of 'Pothis' to make me eagerly look out for finds of ancient manuscripts. None had turned up during the excavations of the first three days. But as if to revive my drooping hopes, a painted tablet, badly defaced by decay and accretion of siliceous matter, which was found in the last cleared cella, displayed a narrow strip of paper with three lines of Indian Brahmi characters sticking to the top edge and running transversely across the panel. The paper, which, as it covers part of the painting, is plainly proved to be a subsequent addition, had decayed even more than the tablet itself. While on the latter two female figures, each holding a swathed infant, could just be made out, it was impossible to read more than a few detached characters in each line of the rotten paper. But these letters were in a bold literary hand, very different from the cursive writing seen below a few of the frescoes, and clearly suggested a Sanskrit text.

The little temples so far excavated had shown me something of the cult and art which this sand-buried settlement possessed before its abandonment. But for indications of the conditions of everyday life and for other documentary evidence it was manifest that I should have to turn to remains of a different character. So, on the 22nd of December, I directed my men to the excavation of a structure close by, which by its position and ground-plan as deducible from the arrangement of the wooden posts that were seen sticking out above the sand, appeared to suggest an ancient dwelling-place. It lay about twenty yards to the north-west of the temple-cella last described, just at the northern end of a sand-dune which, with its crest, rose to a height of fully 16 ft. above the original ground level. The bleached trunks of dead fruit-trees, which were visible around where the sand was less high, indicated that this building, together with the cellas already excavated, had stood in the midst of an orchard or garden. The digging started on the west side soon brought to light the top part of massive and fairly-well-preserved walls in wood and plaster, belonging to what was evidently the lowest storey of a dwelling-house. The apartment formed by them had been an oblong of 23 by 20 ft., and about 10 ft. high. The photograph at the head of this chapter shows a part of it after excavation.

By noon, at a depth of 2 ft. from the surface, a small scrap of paper showing a few Brahmi characters was found in the loose sand which filled the building. I greeted it with no small satisfaction as a promise of richer finds. In order to stimulate the efforts of my labourers, who, with the sand continually falling in from the side of the adjoining dune, had no easy task in effecting a clearance, I offered a small reward in silver to the man who should be lucky enough to hit upon the first real manuscript. Barely an hour later a cheerful shout from one of the men working at the bottom of the small area so far excavated on the north-west side of the apartment announced the discovery of a 'Khat,' or writing.

Carefully extracted with my own hand and cleared of the adhering sand, it proved a perfectly preserved oblong leaf of paper, 13 inches long and 4 inches high, that had undoubtedly formed part of a larger manuscript arranged in the shape of an Indian 'Pothi.' The circular hole intended for the string that was passed through the separate leaves in order to keep them together and preserve their order is placed on the left side of the leaf, as in most of the ancient manuscripts that have previously been acquired from Chinese Turkestan. The six lines of beautifully clear writing which cover each side of the leaf show Brahmi characters of the so-called Gupta type, but a non-Indian language. The photograph reproduced on p. 279 shows one side of this leaf.

While the men gathered around to watch me cleaning the precious find, I heard more than one humorous remark about the chance which had placed this first 'Khat,' as well as the cash reward for it, in the hands of the youth who alone of the party could read and write, and whom, as already related, I had brought along from Tawakkel just on account of these acquirements. Niaz, our 'Mullah,' to give him his proud title (he is seen kneeling on the extreme left in the group reproduced in my photograph, p. 255), was himself beaming with boyish delight at his good luck, and subsequently did his best to prove worthy of it by additional care in digging and in penning my Turki "despatches."

The interesting find just described was made at a depth of about 5 feet from the surface and close to the rough wooden post seen upright on the left side of the apartment as photographed after excavation p. 276. It was quickly followed by a series of other manuscript finds, either in loose leaves, more or less complete, or in little sets of fragments. They all showed Brahmi writing, of an early type and had, as their conformity in paper, size and handwriting showed, originally belonged to at least three distinct 'Pothis,' or books. Their contents were soon recognised by me as Sanskrit texts treating of Buddhist canonical matter. The position in which all these manuscript pieces were found, embedded in loose sand several feet above the original flooring, proved beyond all doubt that

LEAF OF BRAHMI MANUSCRIPT, D. III. 7, IN NON-INDIAN LANGUAGE, FROM MONASTIC DWELLING, D. III
(*Scale two-fifths of original.*)

OBVERSE OF PORTION OF LEAF, D. III. 15A, OF BUDDHIST TEXT IN SANSKRIT (VAJRACCHEDIKA), FROM D. III.
(*Scale two-thirds of original.*)

they could have got there only by accident. Their distribution in varying depths and places suggests that they had fallen in from an upper storey, while the basement was gradually filling up with drift-sand. This assumption was fully borne out by the small pieces of felt, leather, oilcakes ('kunjara'), and similar refuse which turned up in the same layers. The pagination numerals which I could make out on the margin of some leaves, and which in one instance go up to 132, plainly showed that the pieces thus rescued were mere fragments of larger texts which had probably perished with the destruction of the upper floor.

The earlier these fragments had reached the safe resting-place offered by the sand-covered basement, the more extensive they might reasonably be expected to be. So I watched with growing eagerness the progress my men made on the 23rd of December in clearing the sand nearer down to the original floor. It was no easy task, for the drift-sand from the slope of the dune to the south was ever slipping to fill the space laboriously cleared, and as the wall on that side had apparently decayed long ago, additional exertions were needed. As the work proceeded towards the centre of the room a massive beam of poplar wood, nearly a foot in thickness, was laid bare. Its length, close on 19 feet, and its position showed that it had once stretched right across the room, undoubtedly supporting its roof. Two well-carved octagonal posts with bell-shaped capitals surmounted by a circular band, in which I easily recognised the Amalaka ornament of Indian architecture, had turned up before; they had undoubtedly served to support this central beam.

A little beyond the latter, towards the east, the men clearing the sand just above the floor came upon a closely packed bundle of manuscript leaves, evidently still retaining the order they had occupied in the original 'Pothi.' A little later two more packets of leaves belonging to the identical manuscript were brought to light, practically intact, though the action of moisture to which these leaves must have once been subjected, owing to their position not far above the ground, had stuck them closely together and made them so very brittle that their successful separation could only be accomplished in London through the expert help of the Manuscript Department of the British Museum. The ends of the leaves had been bent over near the usual string-hole already referred to, and had often got detached through this folding of centuries; but they could be fitted again without difficulty to their proper places.

The leaves in their complete state measure 14 inches in length and show on each side six lines of bold Brahmi writing of the so-called Gupta type. The text, which is Sanskrit, deals with some subject of Buddhist 'Dharma,' or canonical law. In view of the extent of the well-preserved portions it will in all probability permit of an exact identification by Dr. A. F. Rudolf Hoernle, the distinguished Indologist, who has undertaken the decipherment and publication of all manuscript materials in Brahmi characters discovered by me. [While these pages are passing through the press, Dr. Hoernle informs me that he has recognised in this manuscript almost the whole of the Vajracchedika, a famous Sutra text of the Mahayana School of Buddhism.] Certain palæographic features of the writing, which need not be set forth here in detail, make it difficult to assign to this and the other Sanskrit manuscripts recovered from this ruin a date later than the seventh century A.D. But as far as other observed criteria go, some of them might well have been written a century or two earlier.

The religious character of their contents makes it appear highly probable that these manuscripts formed part of the library of a Buddhist monastic establishment, or 'Vihara,' that had once occupied the structure and no doubt supplied the attendant priests for the adjoining small temples. That the basement room I was actually excavating had offered only accidental shelter to these fragmentary relics of Buddhist literature, and had originally served the more prosaic purposes of a cook-room for the little monastery, became abundantly clear as the work of clearing proceeded towards the east wall. Built against the latter we found a big fireplace, constructed of hard plaster with an elaborately moulded chimney that reached to a height of over 6 feet from the floor.

By the side of it a broad wooden bench filled a kind of recess.

Judging from a similar arrangement still observed in Turkestan houses, and from the broken pottery discovered below it, this bench probably served for the handy storing of cooking utensils. In front of it, and not far from the fireplace, there stood a rough wooden tripod, such as is still used throughout the country to support large water-jars required for kitchen purposes, while a short post with branching head, which I found fixed in the ground close to where the first manuscript leaf was discovered, certainly served to hang a kettle from. Remains of animal bones, oilcakes, and small layers of charcoal found scattered over the floor in various places fully bore out the conclusion indicated.

My attention was still fixed on the manuscript remains that were successively emerging from the depth of this sand-buried dwelling, when at noon on the 23rd of December the sound of a distant gun-shot was heard over the silent dunes eastwards. Old Turdi, who with me was keenly watching the excavation work, at once interpreted the faint sound as a signal that Ram Singh was approaching from the direction of the Keriya Darya. An hour later the Sub-Surveyor was by my side, together with faithful Jasvant Singh, his Rajput cook and companion, both manifestly as pleased as I was at our successfully effected junction. Considering the distances covered and the various incidents for which it was impossible to make proper allowance in our respective programmes, the rendezvous I had arranged for had been kept most punctually.

I was greatly relieved to find from Ram Singh's report that he had fully carried out the topographical task I had assigned to him, and had experienced no difficulties from either the Chinese or the native local authorities. Marching back by our former route to above the Pisha Valley, he had effected a supplementary triangulation of the great peaks above the headwaters of the Yurung-kash. He had then made his way north of the massive of Peak K. 5, or 'Muztagh,' to the slopes of the great glacier-crowned range which sends its numerous streams down to the small oases fringing the desert west of Keriya. By plane-table work and triangulation carried across the elevated spurs which descend from this range, he had succeeded in connecting our surveys eastwards with the work done by Captain Deasy around Polu. In accordance with my instructions he then proceeded to Keriya, and thence a fresh 'Darogha,' supplied as a guide and escort by the local Amban, had taken him through the jungle belt flanking the Keriya River down to the point where he fell in with the party I had sent ahead under Kasim, the hunter.

Ram Singh, reticent at all times, had little to relate either that day or thereafter of the mountain tracts he had passed through, apart from topographical details which appealed to his professional training, and which had already been duly recorded in his plane-table "sections." That his little party had undergone considerable hardships both on account of the cold and the want of all local supplies, I could readily believe from my own experience. But what had evidently impressed him more than anything else, and what prompted him to a short outburst of quite unusual communicativeness, was the weird desolation of the desert, the total absence of life of any kind among the high waves of sand he had crossed since leaving the banks of the frozen river. I could see that the curiosity excited by the manifestly Indian character of the sculptures and paintings I had unearthed was by no means sufficient to counter-balance the uncanny feelings which these strange surroundings, pregnant with death and solitude, had roused in my otherwise hardy Hindu followers. I did my best to cheer them by sending as a welcome gift when their camp was pitched such little luxuries as I had—packets of my own compressed tea, some frozen eggs, raisins and almonds, etc.

In the evening when the dusk had put a stop to excavation and I could tramp back through the sand to the shelter of my little tent, I lost no time in sending for Ram Singh to examine his plane-table work. A comparison of the position indicated in it for Dandan-Uiliq with my own fixing of the site would be a decisive test for the accuracy of our respective surveys. Considering the very deceptive nature of the desert ground over which we had carried so much of our route traverses, I could not help feeling uneasy about the result. All the greater was my delight when I ascertained that the difference between the positions which our wholly independent surveys showed for our actual camp, amounted only to about half a mile in longitude and less than a mile in latitude. If it is taken into account that, since leaving our common camping place in Khotan, Ram Singh had brought his survey over approximately 500 miles of route (on which for the last 130 miles or so no intersections could be obtained owing to the absence of all prominent landmarks), while my own marches extended over about 120 miles, and lay almost wholly through desert, this slight difference represents in reality a very striking agreement. It could not fail to assure me as to the accuracy of our survey work even far away in the desert sands where the frequent dust-haze, if not the great distances from any elevated point, practically exclude all hope of exact checks by means of triangulation.

Neither Ram Singh nor Jasvant Singh took at first kindly to life in the wintry desert. They both complained bitterly of the badness of the water which our single brackish well yielded. With the true Indian belief in the omnipotence of 'pine-ka pani,' they were eager to ascribe to this sole factor the unpleasant symptoms for which the combination of trying climatic conditions and previous fatigues and exposure were mainly responsible. Jasvant Singh, probably in consequence of the total want of fresh vegetables, showed signs of an incipient scorbutic affection, which, however, I was soon able to stop by the administration of lime juice I had brought with me from Gilgit. That it had first to be melted did not reduce the effectiveness of this remedy.

For Ram Singh, who anticipated a return of the rheumatic complaint which he had originally contracted while employed on Captain Deasy's explorations, the work requiring plentiful movement which I could assign to him in the preparation of a general survey of the ruins and of detailed plans of the structures excavated, proved perhaps the best antidote. He subsequently stood the undoubted hardships which our winter campaign in the desert entailed far better than I had ventured to hope. He also bravely held out against the pains inflicted by his old enemy, when at last in the spring it seriously attacked him. Nor did my servants from Kashgar and Yarkand, though better prepared for the rigours of the desert winter, escape without suffering from the inevitable exposure. One after the other in the course of this and the next two months was attacked by painful swellings on the legs or arms, resulting in large boils, which for the time being incapacitated the victim from any useful service.

Old Turdi, whom many former 'treasure-seeking' expeditions had inured to heat and cold alike and to all sorts of privations, was not likely to come on the sick list. Yet the quaint pleasure he took in showing me over what I used jokingly to call his own village and temples, and the honest pride that lit up his wrinkled face whenever I had occasion to appeal to his quasi-antiquarian instinct and his experience of desert conditions, were soon overcast by a cloud. Its real significance I failed to comprehend during my first few days at these ruins. While I felt overjoyed by the interesting discoveries which the first excavations had yielded, poor Turdi Khwojam ('my pious Sir Turdi'), "the Aksakal of the Taklamakan," as we soon got to call him, was contemplating with sad apprehension the imminent failure of a commercial venture quite serious for his modest resources. The spirit of speculation, perhaps natural in a 'treasure-seeker,' had induced him to invest the greatest part, if not the whole, of the advance of pay I had given him before leaving Khotan in the purchase of an old pony. The intention was that it should carry Turdi's provisions and slender outfit to Dandan-Uiliq and should then be killed there to provide meat for sale to my labourers.

Turdi would, no doubt, have reaped due benefit from this ingenious combination of "transport and supplies" if the men I brought from Tawakkel had not been mean enough to seize upon the idea for their own advantage. They took along an old cow as a joint-stock affair and duly slaughtered her near their camping-ground soon after our arrival at the ruined site. Both these time-honoured animals had been carefully kept out of my sight by their respective owners while on the march, probably from a correct surmise that I should have insisted upon the carriage of adequate fodder for them to prevent downright starving. Nor did I learn the facts until several days after our arrival, when Turdi had at last to resort to a strange and desperate expedient in the vain hope of saving his pony. He had failed to come to terms with the Tawakkel labourers for the sale of the animal, and had also let the opportunity go by of sending it either back to their oasis or on to the Keriya River. So he tried to keep it alive by sending it with a young fellow of his own fraternity, who accompanied him as a kind of acolyte, for a considerable distance to the south, where it might get some grazing on dry tamarisk leaves and Kumush.

Just when the poor creature had no more strength left for the daily journey in search of this miserable diet, Turdi made a curious discovery, which to his confiding soul appeared at first a quasi-miraculous saving. Scraping the sand-covered bank of a small depression that had formed through wind erosion by the side of a ruined dwelling house, the remains of which were visible about a hundred yards to the south of my tent and which he had searched years before, he laid bare a closely-compressed mass of straw. It had evidently been once deposited in a corner of the fenced court-yard of that house and had, like the fence itself, remained in a remarkably well-preserved condition, though darkened and, of course, completely dried by the long centuries that had passed since the sand covered it.

Turdi was exultant over his discovery, and at once brought his starving pony, the existence of which could no longer be hidden from me, to feed on this providentially preserved antique fodder store! I had, of course, from the first strong doubts as to the nourishing capacity of this perhaps the most "desiccated" fodder stuff that was ever offered to a horse. But the poor famished creature swallowed it ravenously at the beginning and seemed to justify old Turdi's hopeful expectations. However, a day's experience sufficed to prove that Turdi had badly over-estimated the feeding value of his ancient straw, or rather, as I ought perhaps to put it from consideration for my honest "treasure-seeking" guide, that he was less of an authority on the keeping of live animals than on most matters dead and buried beneath the desert sands. So when, a day later, Ram

Singh arrived with some of my camels that carried his baggage from the Keriya Darya, I had as much as possible of the little store of dry Kumush they had brought along given to the poor famished pony.

Turdi, still finding no purchasers, was now anxious to have it returned to Tawakkel, and, as the return of Kasim's small party made it easier now to spare men from the work, I arranged at once to have it sent back there in charge of two labourers, who were also to take my mail-bag for transmission to Khotan. I had, of course, great doubts as to whether the victim of Turdi's ill-fated experiment would be able to cover the sixty miles or so of desert marching to the river bank. Hence it was no surprise to me when the first arrivals from that side—two men who brought me news from the kindly Amban of Khotan—reported that the pony had succumbed to its sufferings two marches from Dandan-Uiliq.

The last I heard of the ill-fated animal was a request which Turdi addressed to me, before I finally left the ruined site, and which showed how curiously the rules of the local administration would affect the quondam owner even far away in the desert. Turdi wanted to have at least the pony's skin carried back to Tawakkel by his companion and sold there. In order to save the tax which would otherwise have to be paid to the local Beg on account of this sale, I was obliged to endorse in due form the quaintly-worded and still more queerly penned Turki application setting forth all the sad circumstances of the case which Turdi got written out by the hand of Niaz, our 'Mullah.' I thought at the time how puzzling a document it would be for an archæologist who might have the good fortune to light upon it in the desert sand some two thousand years hence!

CHAPTER XX.

DISCOVERY OF DATED DOCUMENTS.

CHRISTMAS DAY was spent in clearing a group of ruined structures situated about half a mile to the north-east of my camp, in which I could without difficulty recognise the remains of a square temple cella and of an adjoining dwelling-place, probably a monastic habitation. These ruins had suffered badly from erosion, which, in the unprotected soil immediately to the north and east of them, had produced broad depressions to a depth of about twenty feet below the original ground level. The ruins, owing to this lowering of the surrounding ground, seemed now to occupy a raised tongue of land quite clear of dunes, and nowhere retained more than two or three feet of covering sand. Above this there rose the splintered short stumps of posts that once formed the framework of wattle and plaster walls, their rows clearly marking the original division of the rooms. The exposed condition of these ruins had, of course, attracted the visits of "treasure-seeking" parties, including some Turdi had personally conducted in former years, and the débris of plaster, timber, ancient pottery, etc., scattered about on the surface plainly told of their burrowings.

Notwithstanding the damage thus caused, there remained some very curious relics to reward my careful clearing. In the western part of the quadrangular passage that enclosed the cella we found two painted panels of wood, showing on both sides representations of sacred personages and undoubtedly the votive offerings of some pious worshipper. On the larger and better preserved of these panels, which measures 18 by 4 inches, there appears seated between two attendants a half-length human figure with the head of a rat, and wearing a diadem. It was only long afterwards, when the little painting had been cleaned of its adhering layer of sand in the British Museum, and examined by the trained eye of my friend, Mr. F. H. Andrews, that I realised the peculiar shape of the figure and its true significance. It is manifestly meant to represent the king of those holy rats which, according to the local legend related by Hiuen-Tsiang and already referred to, in connection with the Kaptar-Mazar (p. 180), were worshipped at the western border of the Khotan oasis for having saved the kingdom from a barbarian invasion. The sacred character of the rat-headed figure is sufficiently marked by the semi-elliptical vesica or halo which encloses it, and by the worshipping attitude of the attendant figure on the left, which carries in one hand a long-stemmed, leaf-shaped fan or punkah.

In a corner of the temple-cella, close to the floor, there turned up two scraps of thin water-lined paper, showing writing on one side only, and that in characters which I could at once recognise as belonging to that peculiar cursive form of Brahmi already known to us from certain ancient documents in a non-Sanskritic language that had reached Dr. Hoernle's collection through purchase from Khotan. On clearing the largest of the rooms in the ruined dwelling-house adjoining the shrine, I found several small sheets of the same coarse paper and with similar writing, either crumpled up or folded into narrow rolls, just like the Chinese documents I subsequently unearthed at this site. It was no easy task to open out these flimsy papers with fingers half-benumbed with cold, and the more delicate part of such work was accomplished only in the British Museum. But the cursory examination that was possible on the spot showed that these more or less fragmentary sheets could not have belonged to manuscript books or 'Pothis,' but evidently contained detached records of some kind.

The impression I had gained from the outward appearance of these and similar documents in cursive Brahmi found in other ruins of Dandan-Uiliq, has been fully borne out by the result of Dr. Hoernle's painstaking researches, as since published in the second part of his "Report on the British Collection of Antiquities from Central Asia" (1902). The materials upon which that eminent scholar worked comprised a considerable number of well-preserved documents of this type which had been purchased in the years 1895–97 by Mr. Macartney and Captain Godfrey from Badruddin, the Afghan Aksakal of Khotan. Internal evidence, as well as the information secured by me, makes it highly probable that these documents represent chance finds made by Turdi during his earlier visits to Dandan-Uiliq. Their minute analysis has enabled Dr. Hoernle to establish a series of philological facts which are of great interest, and possess considerable importance also from a historical point of view. He has succeeded in determining a number of words, either names, or terms, or numerals, which "seem to prove clearly that the language of the documents is an Indo-Iranian dialect, having affinities both with Persian and the Indian vernaculars, in addition to peculiarities of its own," pointing towards a connection with the so-called Ghalchah dialects of the Pamir region. He has also ascertained the interesting fact that the majority of the complete documents are fully dated, though the key to the chronology has yet to be discovered.

A number of ingenious observations, such as the discovery of lists of names at the end of certain documents, accompanied by what manifestly are the marks of witnesses, support Dr. Hoernle's conclusion that we have in them records of official or private transactions similar in character to the deeds of loan, requisition orders, etc., which are contained in the Chinese documents from Dandan-Uiliq to be described below. The detailed examination of my finds of this kind which Dr. Hoernle has very kindly undertaken has not proceeded sufficiently far to throw further light on the interesting questions thus raised. But the certainty which exists as to all circumstances attending the discovery of the documents contained in my collection has already helped us to settle definitely the period to which these records in cursive Brahmi belong.

Dr. Hoernle, judging from palæographic evidence, had suggested the eighth century of our era as their probable date. The correctness of this approximate dating is now fully proved by the fact that I found some of these documents mixed up in the same place and conditions with the Chinese records to be mentioned below which bear definite dates ranging from 781 to 787 A.D. If we are right in supposing for these documents in cursive Brahmi such practical contents as above indicated, it follows with great probability that their language was that actually spoken by the inhabitants of the ruined settlement immediately before it was abandoned. It still remains to be ascertained whether this language is identical with the unknown tongue already mentioned above which appears in some fragmentary manuscript books or Pothis from Dandan-Uiliq written with Brahmi characters. Judging from certain Sanskrit terms found interspersed in the latter texts, it seems probable that they treat, like the Sanskrit Pothis with which they were found, of Buddhist religious matters. They may possibly prove to be translations of Sanskrit treatises from the Buddhist Canon into a Central-Asian language that had obtained literary use in the Buddhist Church of these regions.

The room which had yielded those paper documents in cursive Brahmi held nowhere more than three feet of sand. Yet, even this scanty layer had sufficed to protect a variety of interesting remains, found mainly at the foot of the walls adjoining the south-west corner. Two small oblong tablets of thin wood, rounded off on the right end and provided with a string-hole, proved to contain several lines of the same cursive Brahmi script already discussed. Another and somewhat larger tablet, about fourteen inches long and three inches broad, at once attracted my interest by showing in its shape and handle the closest resemblance to the 'Takhta,' that traditional wooden board which in all native schools of Northern India fills the place of our slate. This tablet was found blank, but the marks of plentiful scraping plainly show that it had once been used for writing. In the light of subsequent discoveries we must look upon these few tablets, just like the Indian 'Takhta' itself, as quasi-archaic survivals. But at the time of their discovery

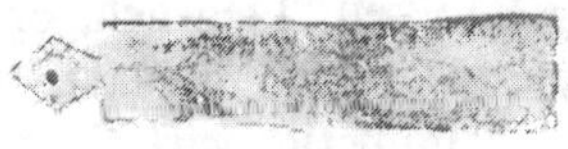

ANCIENT 'TAKHTA' FOR WRITING.

I little suspected what much more extensive finds of the same ancient writing material were awaiting me elsewhere.

The elaborate floral decoration on a portion of a lacquered and painted wood bowl which I found in the same corner clearly betokened Chinese work. And very soon after, as if to confirm a conjecture as to the dwellers in this room, the first finds of Chinese documents rewarded my search. One consisted of a stick of tamarisk wood, about fourteen inches long and one inch wide, partly flattened on two sides, on each of which there appear in vertical lines about a dozen Chinese symbols. The ink of most has badly faded, and no certain interpretation of the few clear characters has as yet been obtained, though it seems probable that the stick had once been used as a kind of tally, making mention of a certain load. More important from a historical point of view is the second document, a sheet of thin water-lined paper, originally folded up into a narrow roll and recovered almost complete.

According to the provisional translation which Mr. Macartney kindly supplied to me at Kashgar, and which has been confirmed in all essentials by Professor Chavannes, of the Collège de France, the main purport of this paper is a petition for the recovery of a donkey which had been let on hire to two individuals, who after a lapse of ten months had failed to come back or to return the animal. It is precisely dated on the sixth day of the second month of the sixteenth year of the Ta-li period, which corresponds to 781 A.D. The locality from which the petition originates is referred to by a name which, owing to certain doubts as to the phonetic value of the two characters composing it, may be variously read as Li-sieh, Lieh-sieh, or Li-tsa. Now this find is of special value, not merely because it supplies an exact date but also because, in conjunction with three Chinese documents which Mr. Macartney had obtained in 1898 through Badruddin, and which have been published in Dr. Hoernle's Second Report already quoted, it makes it possible to fix with great probability the name of the settlement represented by the ruins of Dandan-Uiliq, as well as the Chinese administrative division to which it belonged.

The three documents I refer to in general appearance and style of writing closely resemble those excavated by me at Dandan-Uiliq, and are, like the latter, official records of a public or private character. The translations with which Mr. Macartney kindly supplied me at Kashgar show that the first of them, dated in the third year of the Ta-li period, corresponding to A.D. 768, contains the draft of a report from the officer in charge of Li-sieh (Li-tsa) on a petition from the people of that locality. The report recommends a postponement of the collection of miscellaneous taxes in view of the distress caused by the depredations of robbers. Another document, dated only by month and day, is a military requisition sent from the Li-sieh camp to a civil authority for a skin to re-cover a drum and for feathers to re-fit arrows. The third, dated in the seventh year of the Chien-Chung period, corresponding to A.D. 786, records the issue of a loan of 15,000 cash on the security of a house in a village (name not deciphered) belonging to Li-sieh

In view of the close agreement shown by the dates and contents of these documents with those of the Chinese papers which I discovered in various ruined buildings at Dandan-Uiliq, it appears to me practically certain that they represent some of the finds of Chinese manuscripts which Turdi well remembered to have made on a visit to the site some years previously, and which with other "old things" he had sold to Badruddin, his usual employer at Khotan. It is possible that these particular documents came from one of those rooms in the ruined house D.V. which I found already thoroughly searched, or from some other ruins that had similarly been "explored" before by Turdi's parties. In any case their comparison with the first Chinese document I unearthed at the site, the petition (D.V. 6) already referred to, leaves no reasonable doubt as to Li-sieh (Li-tsa) being the name of the settlement or small tract to which the ruined shrines and dwellings of Dandan-Uiliq belonged.

It makes it further clear that the administrative division in which this settlement was included bore a Chinese designation meaning "Six Cities" (Liu-Cheng); for this identical term is used in the title of the "Inspecting Superintendent of the Six Cities" to which the report preserved in Mr. Macartney's first document was addressed, and it also occurs in my first find immediately after the name of Li-sieh. According to the information supplied by Sun, Mr. Macartney's Chinese literatus, and verified also from other sources, the term "Six Cities" is still well known by Chinese administrators in the "New Dominions" as an old designation of the Khotan District. It is supposed to be derived from the six towns (Ilchi or Khotan, Yurung-kash, Kara-kash, Chira, Keriya, and a sixth of doubtful identity) which were reckoned to belong to it previous to the modern division of the Ambanships of Khotan and Keriya.

Those few interesting finds, together with hours of bright sunshine that gave relief after the bitter cold of the night, had helped me to pass Christmas Day in good heart. In the evening on leaving the buildings excavated, I had occasion to learn by experience how easy it was to lose one's way amidst the monotonous sand-waves. The discovery of a well-preserved Chinese coin bearing the mark of the Kai-yuen period (A.D. 713–741), which I picked up at the foot of a dune close to the south of the ruin, and the search for more relics made me tarry behind the men who were hurrying back. Remembering how near the camp was, I did not think it necessary to retain any one with myself. When after a while I set about to return in the twilight I mistook the track, and then after tramping through the low dunes for about a mile vainly attempted to locate my camp. There was no sound nor any other indication to guide me. Realising the risk of completely losing my bearings as it was getting dark (my magnetic pocket compass had unfortunately been left in the tent that day), I was just about to retrace my footprints while I could still distinguish them, when I suddenly recognised sticking out from the sand some remains of walls which days before I had noticed at a considerable distance to the south-east of my camping-ground.

Trusting to my recollection of their relative position, I turned off to my right and, keeping along the crest-line of the dunes which I knew to be running mainly from north-west to south-east, made my way slowly onwards until I heard my shouts answered by some of my men. Old Turdi and Islam Beg, my faithful Darogha, had grown uneasy at my absence, and had sent the men out in couples to search for me. The shelter of my tent and the hot tea that awaited me were doubly welcome after this little incident. There was nobody to share my Christmas dinner but 'Yolchi Beg,' my sociable little terrier, who was ever ready to let his own dinner outside the tent get frozen hard while sitting up amidst the rugs of the bed for choice bits from my table. I sometimes doubt whether even the friends whose kind thoughts turned towards me that evening from the distant South and West could realise how cheerful is the recollection of the Christmas spent in the solitude and cold of the desert.

The ruined structures which had helped to direct me that evening were the next to be excavated. Curiously enough, the finds made in them formed the best complement of the results of the previous day's work. A small Buddhist temple, constructed in the usual style of these ruins, with square cella and enclosing passage, was first brought to light, and furnished a number of interesting frescoes, as well as some painted panels and manuscript fragments in cursive Brahmi characters. When subsequently the ground floor rooms of a small dwelling-house (D. VII.) close to the north of the shrine were cleared from the deep sand that filled them, we came on the floor of the central room, measuring about 18 by 13 feet, upon quite a small collection of Chinese documents on paper. They were all folded into narrow rolls, just as the one found in the ruin D.V., and lay scattered about on the ground near the well-preserved fireplace, either separate or sticking together in little packets. The leaves, of which the rolls had been made up, proved on the average eleven inches high.

Owing to the damp that must have once reached them through the mud floor some of these rolls had decayed in parts. But others were recovered more or less complete, and though the translations of four of these, which I obtained through the kindness of Professors Chavannes and Douglas, are only provisional, they amply suffice to settle all doubts as to the date and character of the records. Two of them, dated in the third year of the Chien-Chung period, corresponding to A.D. 782, are bonds for small loans specified in copper cash or grain issued on interest to different borrowers by one Chien-ying, who is designated as a priest of the Hu-kuo monastery. As security for these loans the

CHINESE DOCUMENT (D. VII. 2), CONTAINING BOND, FROM DANDAN-UILIQ, DATED A.D. 782 (1/3).

CHINESE WOODEN TABLET, N. XV. 315 (2/3).

borrowers, whose names and ages are appended together with those of certain relatives as sureties (mother and sister, wife and daughter), pledge the whole of their household goods and cattle irrespective of any valuation. A third document, dated in the year equivalent to A.D. 787, records an agreement of similar purport, without clearly showing the name of the lender. That this unknown capitalist was also in some way connected with the Hū-kuo monastery becomes very probable from the contents of the fourth paper (reproduced already in my "Preliminary Report"). This, undated, conveys instructions from the three priests superintending the Hu-kuo convent to the monk or caretaker in charge of some outlying landed property of theirs. He is therein directed how to carry out certain urgent field-labours, employing all available men in cutting grass for three days after receipt of the order, while one labourer is to be retained to irrigate the fields, etc.

From the nature of these petty records it can safely be concluded that the ruined dwelling-house in which they were found, together with the adjoining shrine, represents either the Hu-kuo convent, or a monastic residence directly attached to it. The Chinese designation of the convent (Hu-kuo, literally "country-protecting") and the Chinese names of the superintending priests, which are recorded in the last-named document, leave little doubt as to the nationality of the monkish establishment. But that the population which supported it was not Chinese is plainly indicated by the transcribed names of the borrowers and their sureties, as well as by the short inscriptions in cursive Brahmi found beneath some of the frescoes of the temple. The more learned of the monks may be supposed to have been versed also in Sanskrit, the sacred language of the Buddhist Church throughout the North; a small fragment of a Sanskrit 'Pothi' was, in fact, among the manuscript finds of this ruin.

The very pettiness of the affairs recorded in the Chinese papers of this small convent increases to no small extent their value from a chronological point of view. Unimportant in character and insignificant in size and material, it is highly improbable that these documents should date back to a period preceding by any great length of time the final abandonment of the building. Now it deserves to be noted that all the papers from this ruin which can be dated with accuracy, belong to the years 782–787 A.D. Taking into account that the first-described Chinese document, found in the ruined building D.V. under exactly similar conditions, also bears the date of A.D. 781, we are almost by necessity led to the conclusion that the settlement to which these shrines and dwelling-houses belonged was deserted about the close of the eighth century of our era. In each case the papers were discovered closely adhering to the original floor, which proves that the sand must have entered the rooms very soon after these petty records had been scattered about there. For light and flimsy as they are, the little paper-rolls could not have resisted very long the force of the storms that pass over the country each successive spring and summer.

It is a particularly fortunate circumstance that such unmistakable chronological evidence has been obtained in the very same structure which has furnished us with the best preserved, and perhaps the most interesting specimens of contemporary painting from this site. The three painted panels of wood I refer to were found lying in the loose sand a few inches above the flooring, and not far from the east wall of the central room. From this position, and from the dowels still clearly marked on the back of two of them, it is evident that these pictures had once been fixed high up on the wall, from which they dropped only when the little monastic building was gradually being filled with sand. This accounts for the remarkable preservation of the colours and the wood underlying them. No verbal description can take the place of adequate reproductions in colour which it has been impossible to provide for the present publication. But until such will be made accessible in my Detailed Report, now under preparation, I may at least draw attention to one of these pictures which by its subject presents unusual interest, and which can already be seen on a reduced scale in one of the coloured collotype plates illustrating my "Preliminary Report."

This panel, which has a rectangular shape, with pointed arched top, is fifteen inches high and seven inches broad. It shows two figures, both mounted and manifestly of high rank, one above the other. The upper figure is seen riding on a high-stepping horse, the colour of which, white with large spots of black, curiously recalls the appearance of the piebald 'Yarkandi' horse, which, until very recent times, was so much fancied by natives of Northern India. The rider, whose handsome, youthful face shows an interesting combination of Indian and Chinese features, wears his long black hair tied in a loose knot at the crown, while a yellow band passes round the head holding in front a large elliptical jewel. The long pink tunic, and the narrow light scarf that descends from the back of the head, with its two ends floating behind the arms to indicate rapid movement, are drawn with the same care and freedom of outline as the rest of the details. The feet are cased in high black boots with felt soles, very much like those still worn by men of means in Chinese Turkestan, and are placed in stirrups. While the left hand holds the rein, the right raises a patera, towards which a bird is shown swooping down in full flight. From the girdle hangs a long sword, nearly straight, and of a pattern that appears early in Persia and other Muhammadan countries of the East.

The horse, which is remarkably well drawn even to its legs and hoofs, carries a deep and narrow saddle over a large 'Numdah or felt-cloth, and shows elaborate trappings. These include a single bridle, a surcingle, breastplate and crupper, as well as a large ornamental plate that covers the forehead and nose. Two curious horns project from this plate, the one at the forehead carrying what might be the Trisula, or Indian trident, while the other above the noseband is surmounted by what looks like a mango-shaped tassel in red silk, represented also on other parts of the trappings. We could not have wished for a more accurate picture of that "horse millinery" which in the eighth century evidently flourished throughout Turkestan as much as it does nowadays. No less interesting is the representation of the second figure below, riding on a two-humped camel, shown in full movement and with striking fidelity to nature.

The rider, whose face is partly deleted, wears over his short curly hair a curious sugar-loaf hat, with its broad brim turned up into 'Vandyke' points. Marks on the hat indicate some spotted fur as its material. The long and loose-fitting green garment worn by the rider is gathered below the knee into the wide tops of red boots, or mocassins without soles, closely resembling the 'Charuks' still used through the whole of Eastern Turkestan, particularly during the winter months. While the left hand is guiding the camel by a nose-cord, the right, in the same pose as that of the rider above, raises a shell-shaped cup. The elaborate fittings of the saddle and the stirrups show that the animal bestridden by this personage is meant for a riding camel, a mount rarely used nowadays in these regions. Some freely drawn contour-lines visible behind the camel indicate a hilly country, or else high ridges of sand. The nimbus painted round the head of each of the mounted figures shows plainly their holy character, and the identity of their attitude leaves no doubt as to their connection in what evidently was a sacred legend. But as to the nature of this legend, which, as already stated, appears also elsewhere in the decoration of Dandan-Uiliq shrines, no clue has as yet been traced.

It is impossible to give here either reproductions or detailed accounts of the other panels, one of them painted on both sides, recovered from what we may briefly call the refectory of the 'Hu-kuo' monastery. The paintings of Buddhas or Bodhisattvas which they contain must prove of exceptional interest for the study of the history of Buddhist art in Central Asia. For, apart from the high opinion which their good drawing, graceful composition, and free execution must give us of the merits of the Indian art transplanted to Khotan, these paintings also strikingly illustrate the early development of the elaborate conventional details in emblems, poses, etc., which are so characteristic for all representations of the Buddhist Pantheon in Tibetan art. As the latter is so far known to us only from comparatively late specimens, and as scarcely any remains exist of early Indian paintings illustrating Buddhist worship of the Northern or so-called Mahayana type, the value can scarcely be over-rated of such well-preserved and approximately dateable pictures treating subjects thoroughly familiar to that system of worship.

But to me perhaps even more curious, because certainly less expected, are the traces of the influence of Persian art which appear unmistakably in the treatment of face and dress on some of these and subsequently discovered paintings. The evidence of this remarkable fact will be duly furnished by means of proper illustrations in my scientific publication. In the meantime, however, I may point out that this connection with later Iranian art finds its exact parallel in the still more remarkable influence of classical art imported from the Far West, of which my subsequent discoveries have revealed such tangible proofs for a much earlier period.

The description so far given of the structures I excavated during the first part of my stay at Dandan-Uiliq will suffice to indicate the general character and contents of the ruins of this site. The survey and excavation of other detached shrines and dwelling-places scattered amidst the dunes kept me for another week busy from morning till evening. It brought the number of buildings that were thoroughly cleared and examined up to a total of fourteen. But though the results of these excavations helped to confirm and supplement my former observations, they did not bring to light novel features requiring detailed mention here. In regard to materials and mode of construction all the buildings resembled each other closely, showing plainly that they had been built and probably also deserted in approximately the same period. But their state of preservation greatly differed, according to the measure in which they had been exposed to the erosive action of the winds and the equally destructive diggings of "treasure-seekers." In some instances I came upon unmistakable evidence of their operations even in structures that had since been covered up again by deep sand.

Thus in a small temple-cella the well-moulded octagonal base of the principal image had been dug into from behind in search of supposed treasure. Yet the votive tablets that had been leaning against its foot in front were left untouched, and equally so a fairly thick packet of manuscript leaves comprising probably more than one 'Pothi.' But, alas! the damp rising from the floor when water still reached this neighbourhood had here done its work of destruction far more effectively than the "treasure-seekers" ever could. The leaves of paper had decayed completely into compact layers, which could not be detached from the hardened crust of what once was dust enveloping them. Ultimately these lumps of earth had to be cut off as a whole from the ground to which they adhered; but even with the utmost care in slicing, the flakes of paper since laid bare reveal only fragmentary groups of Brahmi characters. The upper board of wood which once covered one of these books, and which I was able to remove in a half-rotten condition, figures now as an instructive relic in my collection of ancient manuscripts and writing implements.

But opportunities for interesting antiquarian observations were by no means restricted to the finds which the excavation of extant ruins yielded. A careful survey of their surroundings also taught much that helps us to reconstruct the general aspects and conditions of the life which once flourished here. I have already referred to those strange witnesses of ancient orchards and avenues, the gaunt, splintered trunks of poplars and various fruit trees, which could still be seen, half-buried in the sand, near most of the buildings. On some patches of the original ground left uncovered between the moving dunes the traces of old irrigation channels, running between small banks of earth, and evidently constructed after the fashion that still prevails in the country, were easily recognisable. But owing to the dunes or else the effects of erosion it was impossible to follow them for any distance.

In many places between the scattered ruins, the ground was thickly strewn with fragments of coarse pottery, small corroded pieces of metal, and similar débris. These remains, found in places where at present no traces of old structures survive, probably mark the positions occupied by less pretentious dwellings which, like the houses of common Khotan cultivators of the present day, were built wholly of sun-dried bricks or stamped clay. These were likely to crumble away far more quickly than buildings with a timber frame-work covered by hard plaster. The latter mode of construction also is still used in the towns and villages of Khotan, but being far more expensive, owing to the distance from which wood has to be brought, it is restricted to the houses of the well-to-do and to Mosques, Sarais, and similar buildings. This observation helps to explain, at least partly, why, at sites like Dandan-Uiliq which must for various reasons be supposed to have been occupied by comparatively large settlements, the extant structural remains are limited in number and so widely scattered.

But the striking preponderance of religious buildings among the Dandan-Uiliq remains also suggests the possibility that these local shrines and their small monastic establishments continued to be kept up and visited, perhaps as pilgrimage places, for some time after the rest of the settlement had been abandoned. The conditions in which Muhammadan Ziarats are now often found beyond the present cultivated area of oases, would furnish an exact parallel. In this case the complete decay of the deserted village structures was likely to have been accelerated by the demands that the attendants of the shrines, as well as the pilgrims, would necessarily make upon them for whatever in the way of wood and other useful materials had remained in them.

However this may be, it must be considered as certain that the abandonment of the settlement was a gradual one, and in no way connected with any sudden physical catastrophe such as some European travellers have been only too ready to assume, on account of popular legends they had heard about the so-called "ancient cities" of the Taklamakan. The Sodom and Gomorrah legends related all over Eastern Turkestan about "old towns" suddenly submerged under the sand-dunes, are more ancient than the ruins of Dandan-Uiliq themselves. Hiuen-Tsiang had already heard them more or less in the same form in which they are now current, as is seen from the story of the town of 'Ho-lo-lo-kia,' which we shall have occasion to refer to in connection with the site of Pi-mo. These legends undoubtedly are interesting as folk-lore. But where we have such plain archæological evidence to the contrary as the examination of the Dandan-Uiliq ruins, and in fact of every other ancient site in this region, has supplied to me, scientific inquiry need have no concern with them.

My detailed survey of Dandan-Uiliq, together with other observations of a semi-topographical, semi-antiquarian nature which gradually accumulated during my explorations at this and other sites, make it very probable that the lands of Dandan-

Uiliq were irrigated from an extension of the canals which, down to a much later date, brought the water of the streams of Chira, Domoko and Gulakhma to the desert area due south of the ruins. The débris-covered site of Uzun-Tati, which I discovered there amidst the sand-dunes, is identical with the 'Pi-mo' of Hiuen-Tsiang, Marco Polo's 'Pein,' and can be proved by unquestionable evidence to have been occupied for at least five centuries longer than Dandan-Uiliq. A number of historical as well as topographical considerations, for a detailed discussion of which I must refer to my scientific publication, point to the conclusion that the successive abandonment of both Dandan-Uiliq and 'Pi-mo' was due to the same cause, the difficulty of maintaining effective irrigation for these out-lying settlements.

I cannot attempt here to investigate the question to what extent this receding of the cultivated area may be attributed to neglect of irrigation works, caused probably by political troubles and consequent depopulation, or to a change in the physical conditions attending the supply of water from those streams. I may, however, with advantage call attention here to my subsequent observations at certain villages of the Gulakhma and Domoko oases, the cultivated area of which has, owing to the difficulty of carrying the irrigation water sufficiently far, been shifted, within the memory of living men, as much as six to eight miles further to the south. The crumbling ruins of the deserted village homesteads which I saw there, stripped of all materials that could be of use, and the miles of once cultivated ground which the desert sand is now slowly over-running, but on which the lines of empty canals, irrigation embankments etc., can still be made out, were the best illustration of the process by which the lands of Dandan-Uiliq became finally merged in the desert.

In this connection I may note that our survey furnished no evidence in support of the assumption put forth by Dr. Sven Hedin, that the Keriya Darya in historical times flowed close to Dandan-Uiliq, and that the abandonment of the site was connected with the subsequent shifting of the river to its present bed, some twenty-eight miles in a direct line further to the east. Probably, the distinguished explorer would have hesitated to make this suggestion had he known the indisputable antiquarian evidence which shows that the ruins to which, mainly on the basis of conjectural calculations as to the movement of the sand-dunes, he was prepared to assign an age of about two thousand years, were in reality abandoned only about the close of the eighth century of our era.

CHAPTER XXI.

THROUGH THE DESERT TO KERIYA.

On the 3rd of January, 1901, the explorations at Dandan-Uiliq were completed. The previous evening my long-expected mail had arrived from Kashgar, a heavy bag this time with the postal accumulations of some six weeks. The latest of the letters and papers sent from Europe viâ India dated from the beginning of October. One of the most welcome letters was a communication from the Indian Foreign Office, which informed me that the request I had made some nine months before from Calcutta, to be allowed eventually to return through Russian Turkestan, had received the sanction of the Russian authorities. The safe packing of my fragile antiquarian finds, and the making up of my own mail kept me busy all day and as long as work was possible in the tent. The camels had, in accordance with previous instructions, duly arrived from the river, where they had managed to gather fresh strength even on the scanty fare offered by the wintry jungle. From the unusual animation with which the preparations for the start were proceeding, it was easy to see how much all my men, from Ram Singh downwards, enjoyed the prospect of saying good-bye to this trying camping-ground. So there was some disappointment when they learned that before altogether leaving the desolate neighbourhood I intended to visit some ruins of which Turdi had spoken as situated to the north and known to treasure-seekers by the name of Rawak ("High Mansion").

On the morning of the 4th of January I paid off and dismissed to Tawakkel a portion of my little force of labourers who had worked so valiantly. With the rest I set out to the north, and after a march of about seven miles across gradually rising sand-ridges reached again ground where broken pottery between the dunes indicated the former existence of habitations. We halted at a spot between deeply eroded banks of loess, where Kasim's party eighteen days before had camped and found water. But the well would yield no water now, as the ground was frozen quite hard, and when at last water was reached by fresh digging it proved even more brackish than that we had to drink at Dandan-Uiliq.

Though Turdi had not visited the place for nine years he guided me on the next day without hesitation to where behind a long-stretching ridge of sand, some 60 feet high, the ruins were situated. They proved to consist mainly of two much-decayed mounds, lying quite close together, composed of fairly hard sun-dried bricks, probably the remains of small Stupas. They had evidently been dug into repeatedly and had suffered badly; but in the case of the larger one it was still possible to make out what looked like a circular base about 32 feet in diameter. From among the small débris of ancient pottery, broken glass, etc., strewn over the ground near the mounds I picked up a fragment of remarkably hard stucco on which the practised eye of Turdi at once discovered traces of a thin gold-layer. Judging from its shape this stucco piece is likely to have belonged to a statue that had once been fully gilded.

Old Chinese coins without legend, as issued under the Han dynasty, also turned up at various places among the pottery débris which covered the low ground between the dunes. As the latter rise here to heights over 25 feet and are proportionately large, it was scarcely surprising that we could trace the ruins of only one house built with timber. Its walls had decayed by erosion to within a few feet of the ground, and the high dune rising immediately above it made it impossible to clear more than a single room. Within it and close to the floor we found two small wooden tablets of oblong shape, inscribed on one side with cursive Brahmi characters. The socket which appeared on the back of one of them was proved by subsequent discoveries elsewhere to have once held a clay seal.

The fact that only Han coins were found here, as well as other indications, make it appear probable that Rawak was deserted a considerable time before Dandan-Uiliq. But until the peculiar physical conditions of the various parts of the Taklamakan, and particularly those concerning the movement of the sand-dunes, have been systematically studied for a prolonged period, it would be hazardous to draw conclusions as to the rate of progress in the general advance of the desert southwards. And even when such observations are available—and I for one shall respect the devotion of those who may hereafter charge themselves with their collection on this forbidding ground—it is very doubtful whether their results could be relied upon to give a true view of the conditions prevailing at earlier periods.

The examination of the scanty remains at Rawak completed the task for which I had set out just a month previously from Khotan. So on the morning of the 6th of January I began the march to the Keriya River after paying off Merghen Ahmad with the last batch of the Tawakkel labourers. They parted from me in good spirits, well satisfied with the reward their work had earned them, and evidently none the worse for their long camping in the desert. Islam Beg, too, who had managed these people so well, now left me for Khotan, glad to regain once more the comforts of a warm homestead. He was to carry to the Khotan Amban my news and thanks for his help which had rendered the exploration of Dandan-Uiliq possible; also my mail-bag was entrusted to him to commence its long journey westwards.

It was with mixed feelings that I said farewell to the silent sand-dunes amidst which I had worked for the last three weeks. They had yielded up enough to answer most of the questions which arise about the strange ruins they have helped to preserve, and on my many walks across these swelling waves of sand I had grown almost fond of their simple scenery. Dandan-Uiliq was to lapse once more into that solitude which for a thousand years had probably never been disturbed so long as during my visit. For me the recollection of this fascinating site will ever suggest the bracing air and the unsullied peace and purity of the wintry desert.

The day was cloudy and as my caravan slowly moved off about 11 a.m. a steady breeze met us from the north-east. About two miles from Rawak camp we passed a broad strip of ground where broken pottery, glass fragments, etc., cropped up again on the hard loess banks between the dunes. Beyond, all traces of ancient habitation ceased, and soon I saw also the last of the shrivelled dead trees standing in little clumps, the sight of which had become so familiar to me during these weeks. As the day wore on the breeze increased sufficiently to treat us to the spectacle of a gentle dust-storm. The air became filled with a gray fog, and the dust carried by the wind threatened to efface the track marked by the footprints of Kasim and Turdi, who marched ahead as guides. So I had to keep our party, which now looked much reduced, close together. The sand-hills rose gradually as we advanced to the east, and I realised that the apprehensions of old Turdi about the difficulty of finding water north of the line which the camels had previously followed to and from the river, were not without foundation. At the foot of a great ridge of piled-up dunes we had to halt for the night, though there was no chance of getting water there. Some withered roots of tamarisk supplied scanty fuel, but there was no living scrub to show where we might dig a well. Fortunately a small supply of water, or rather ice, was kept available for this emergency in the tanks which had already rendered good service at Dandan-Uiliq for storage.

I had at first intended to steer due east for Gharib-Chakma, which the Sub-Surveyor's map showed as the nearest point on the river. But the thought that in doing so we were likely to get beyond the line up to which water could be got by digging, induced me on the next day to change our course to the south-east, with a view of reaching the track by which Kasim had previously brought the camels to and from the river. The wind had subsided during the night, and the haze slowly dissolved in the course of the day. The individual sand-dunes we passed were all between 30 and 50 feet high, but the line of march ed also across three great Dawans' running from south to north. Their height above the little valleys between the ordinary dunes on either side seemed over 150 feet. It was with a feeling of relief that after having covered about eleven miles in a straight line and reached the ridge of the third Dawan we noticed on the easier ground beyond a few sand cones covered with live tamarisks. Kasim at once declared that water might be found at their foot. His prediction proved correct. After digging to a depth of 6 feet through ground which for about 2 feet from the surface was frozen, the men got at water. It was very salt but none the less most welcome. I in particular was glad of the wash which I had to deny myself at the previous camp for the sake of economising the water supply in the tanks. The camels, too, were glad to get a drink again; for heavily laden as they necessarily were now, they had felt the long march over these formidable sand-ranges.

After a cold night, when the thermometer fell to 5° Fahr. below zero, we started early. Everybody was eager to pass out of the region of sand and reach the river. After about two miles' marching Kasim's sharp eyes discovered faint traces of the track which the camels had left in the sand when returning to fetch us from Dandan-Uiliq, and by following this track we soon came upon the well previously dug by Kasim's party. Four Dawans had then to be crossed in succession, each piled up of terrace-like dunes and apparently between 120 and 150 feet in height. The dunes in the broad valleys between them sank now to about 20–30 feet; yet there was no other indication that we were approaching the river, until at last from the top of the last huge ridge of sand the dark line of trees fringing the Keriya Darya came into view.

Four miles more we tramped on over dunes that showed broad backs and gradually diminished in height, until a belt was reached where tamarisks and 'Kumush' grass was growing freely. When passing a last low bank of sand, I suddenly saw the glittering ice of the river before me. While I was glad to sit down on its bank after the tiring walk of some fourteen miles, Kasim went to search for the ponies which had brought the Sub-Surveyor's party from Keriya and were to await us here. Half an hour later they turned up under the escort of

Ibrahim, the 'Darogha' whom the Amban of Keriya had sent to look after my camp. A cheerful fire was then lit under the poplars that line the river-bank, and by its side I sat contentedly until the camels turned up in the darkness. It was pleasant to view in the dusk the high trees still bearing partly their red autumn foliage, the thick shrubs and the wide ice-belt of the river, after those weeks when one's eyes had rested only on yellow sand and the wavy lines of its expanse.

On the following morning Kasim with a single companion left us to start on the march back to the Khotan Darya, while I was grateful to get into my saddle once more for the rest of our march to Keriya. The river along which the route led was now almost everywhere completely frozen over. It flows in a deep and extremely tortuous bed about 50–60 yards across at the narrowest points, but widens at occasional great bends to fully three times as much. The ground on the left bank, along which the day's march took us, is covered for a breadth of about a mile with patches of forest and a belt of reed-jungle. Beyond stretch the sand-dunes westwards. On the right bank a high and well-defined ridge of sand, known as Kizil-kum (" the Red Sands "), which seems to rise 300 feet or so, could be seen following the river-course. The growth of willows and poplars seemed equally luxuriant on either side.

I passed a number of shepherds' huts ('Satmas') built of a rude framework of wood with walls of rushes closely packed, but met no human being until after a ride of about sixteen miles I reached the shrine which was to offer me shelter for the night. The tomb of Saiyid Burhanuddin Padshahim (" my Lord S. B.") seems a very popular place of pilgrimage for the people of the Keriya and Khotan districts, and the comfortable quarters and appearance of the five Sheikhs in attendance on the saint's resting-place attest the veneration enjoyed by the latter. The Sheikhs were unable to tell me any particulars of the holy man's story, except that he was connected in some way with the still holier Imam Jafar Sadik, worshipped at a famous desert shrine where the Niya River ends:

The Sheikhs, who receive so many hundreds of pilgrims every year, know how to prepare for the comfort of "paying guests." So I found a neat little room with felt carpets and a blazing fire ready to receive me by the side of the saint's tomb. While waiting for my baggage, which did not arrive till late in the evening, I had plenty of time to think of the curious inroad made by civilization, as represented by this sacred establishment, into the solitude of the desert. The shepherds who frequent the lonely grazing-grounds of the Keriya River, cannot fail to benefit largely as regards their knowledge of the outer world by the stream of pilgrims that passes in the autumn and spring to the local saint's tomb. Is it possible that the Buddhist shrines I unearthed at Dandan-Uiliq had also been once the object of similar pilgrimages?

Three fairly long marches brought me from the 'Mazar' into Keriya. They led along the side of the Keriya River and through scenery very much like that passed on the first day after we had struck its bank. Every day we saw some reed-huts of shepherds, but their occupants seemed to have moved away from the river. The belt of vegetation grew broader as we progressed further south, but the thickets of trees gradually became rarer and most of the ground was covered only with tamarisk scrub and Kumush. These alone will grow in the loose sand which the fertilising water is unable to reach. The spots where we camped for the night, Bulak and Chogalma, showed as little sign of human habitation as the rest of the jungle we had been traversing. But our guide the 'Darogha' knew the camping-places of the shepherds and always managed to produce some of this folk to help in collecting fuel. The days were hazy, and the murky atmosphere made me regret the clear, bracing air of the desert.

On January 12th, about noon, I arrived at Bostan Langar, a tiny hamlet in the midst of a wide, marshy plain where the river gathers the outflow of numerous springs. Now all the water-logged ground was hard-frozen, and there was no need to follow the turns and bends by which the road avoids quagmires. At Bostan Langar I was met by Abdullah Khan, an Afghan merchant from Pishin, who had been settled in Keriya for some fifteen years. He was a fine-looking old man and evidently anxious to make himself useful to the 'Sahibs,' towards whom he, like his fellow-countrymen all over Turkestan, pretends to cherish a feeling of allegiance. Unfortunately disease seems to have played havoc with his constitution, and his utility was further impaired by a strange confusion of tongues. Persian had long ago passed from Abdullah Khan's knowledge; Turki he did not appear to have fully learned; and Hindustani he heard so rarely nowadays that conversation in it also presented difficulties. My knowledge of Pushtu was too scant to permit my judging how much he remembered of his mother-tongue. However, the message sent to him in advance had been duly grasped, and he had accordingly arranged for quarters during my stay at Keriya.

Soon after meeting this claimant of the "Sirkar's protection" I was welcomed in the Amban's name by a cavalcade of local Begs and their followers. The Begs were fat and jovial, and when they had convinced themselves that I could really talk their own tongue we kept up quite a lively chat while riding on towards the town. Etiquette evidently required that they should meet me in their quasi-Chinese official garb. The fur-lined little cape of 'Khitai' fashion was easily worn over their warm, homely 'Chappans' or long coats. But the black silk cap with the red button of office is a poor head-covering for a good Turki Muhammadan, accustomed to shelter his shaven head under a substantial fur cap when the temperature is so low as it was just then. So my Begs soon compromised comfort and appearances by making one of their attendants wear the cap imposed by their Cathay masters, while they themselves kept their heads warm with mighty furs.

About four miles from Bostan Langar we reached the edge of the cultivated area of the oasis. I was once more among the hamlets with their canals and poplar avenues, so uniform in appearances all over Turkestan. After a month's life in the solitude of the desert the bustle of these homesteads was a welcome sight. 'Yolchi Beg,' my little terrier, also felt this stirring effect of seeing fellow-creatures once more, and we had no little trouble in protecting him from the large village dogs which he persisted in provoking by his self-assertive behaviour. Keriya town presents no very striking appearance even for the wanderer from the wilderness, and I was far advanced amidst the low mud-houses of its outskirts before I realised that I had entered the headquarters of a territory that extends over some five degrees of longitude.

I was glad to find that the quarters Abdullah Khan had

STREET IN SUBURB OF KERIYA.

arranged for me were in a kind of suburban villa, far removed from the Bazar. The house, which belonged to a relative of his, a well-known Mullah, proved large and airy. Passing, however, a series of half-open courts and halls I arrived at a couple of little rooms dimly lighted by a hole in the roof, but more comfortable at this season. In one of these I found felts spread and a fire blazing, and here I took up my abode. Long before my baggage arrived the Amban's chief interpreter and factotum presented himself to deliver his master's greetings and presents of welcome. They were all of a thoroughly practical nature, including firewood, fodder for my ponies, sheep and fowls for myself, and on so lavish a scale as to render a worthy return a little difficult. However, the Amban's kind intentions were amply testified, and, I felt sure, would not suffer from any

HUANG-DALOI, AMBAN OF KERIYA.

inadequacy of a traveller's counter-gifts. Etiquette permits the feeing of the bringer of such presents, and I did not fail to impress the interpreter with a due sense of my satisfaction. My state visit to the Yamen was duly notified for the morrow.

My interview with Huang-Daloi, the Amban, passed off most satisfactorily. At 1 p.m. I rode to his Yamen through the modest Bazar of the 'Yangi Shahr.' The tortuous lanes of the equally humble "Old Town" I avoided by riding outside along the foot of the high loess-bank on which it is built. The Yamen of Keriya closely resembles the similar structures I saw at Yarkand, Karghalik and Khotan. Architectural etiquette evidently prescribes all details as to the direction of the gates, the arrangement of the courtyards, nay, even the position of the table and seats in the reception room. The salute of three pop-guns solemnly fired at my entry through the outer gate showed that the Amban wanted to be polite, and the reception he himself accorded to me at the inner gate was distinctly hearty.

Huang-Daloi seemed a man of about forty-five, well built and with a ruddy face which bore a look of good-nature and humour. He was dressed in elegant Chinese silks; the brocaded yellow petticoat and the fine embroidered centre-piece of his state jacket particularly attracted my attention. I found the little table on the raised daïs, between the two seats which host and guest must always occupy, decked with sweets which looked clean and wholesome, and the customary cups of tea replaced by little wineglasses of European make. A kind of Madeira had to serve in place of the orthodox Cathay beverage; whether from a wish to please supposed European taste or from the Amban's own predilection I did not know.

Though my interpreter, Niaz Akhun, the humorous Tungani, had not arrived from Khotan with the ponies I had left behind on entering the desert, our conversation went on with some ease. The Amban's intelligence made up for the imperfect comprehension his 'Tungchi' showed for my Turki. I had to relate to him at length how I fared at Dandan-Uiliq, and, of course, took occasion to tell him how all I saw and found there agreed with the account old 'Tang-Seng,' *i.e.*, Hiuen-Tsiang, has given us of Buddhism in these regions, I only wished that I knew how to talk about Buddhist things through the ordinary Chinese interpreter, invariably a Muhammadan with very hazy notions on the religious systems *en vogue* among his infidel masters. When I told the Amban of my wish to visit an ancient site which had been reported to me north of Niya, the Ni-jang of Hiuen-Tsiang, he readily promised the issue of all needful orders for help. My thanks and little compliments were always requited by a smile so cordial and amiable, that the best diplomatic actor might have envied its expressiveness. When I left, escorted according to etiquette by the Amban to the side of my pony, I found the whole of his retinue, down to the scarlet-dressed executioners, drawn up on the way through the inner gate. The dresses of the men looked clean and new, and altogether there was an air of neatness and order about the place which seemed a reflex of the Amban's personal habits.

I had scarcely left the Yamen when information reached me that the Amban was starting immediately to return my visit. So I rode back in haste and just arranged to get tea ready in time and the little inner room of my airy villa tidied up. A cover for my camp table was difficult to improvise. White is the colour of mourning in China, and hence no ordinary table-cloth would do. If I visit Chinese territory again I shall bring a table-cloth of auspicious red. This time a light rug from my bed had to do instead. I thought I was playing at European court etiquette when I had to receive as my guest the host of a few minutes ago. But it was easy enough to continue a conversation so recently broken off, and volumes from my little travelling book-case, among them Stanislas Julien's edition of Hiuen-Tsiang, helped to entertain. I showed Huang-Daloi some of the manuscripts found at Dandan-Uiliq and let him read the legends of the Chinese coins of by-gone dynasties in my collection. He was too polite to show whether they interested him as much as my camp table, chair, and bed, which he also closely examined.

I had originally planned a halt of three days at Keriya, but the non-arrival of the ponies expected from Khotan caused an extension of two more days. To tell the truth, all of us were not particularly sorry for the delay. My men, Ram Singh included, were glad to have a little respite after the roughing and exposure in the desert. I myself, the interviews with the Amban once over, found so much to do in the way of notes to be written up, accounts to be prepared, etc., that I could scarcely spare an hour for a daily walk in the dusk. Dandan-Uiliq was no place for clerical work, and it was only now that I was able to write a short account of my work there for the Royal Asiatic Society's Journal. The last four days at Keriya were cold and gloomy. On the 14th and 15th of January there were light falls of snow, scarcely more than an inch deep each day, yet sufficient to give a thoroughly wintry aspect to the bare fields along the river. It was cheerful to have a fire by which to spend the days of busy work. But I missed in my little den the light and 'plein air' of my camp life. As usual in all houses of Khotan and the regions around, light is admitted to the inner rooms inhabited during the winter only by a small square opening in the roof. It is naturally scanty and ill-distributed.

My inquiries for antiquities made through Abdullah Khan and others brought me little that was of interest. Keriya is not itself an old place and the "treasure-seeking" profession does not flourish as in Khotan. But on the first day after my arrival I received information about ancient remains in the desert north of Niya which decided me to extend my tour in that direction. Abdullah, a respectable cultivator of Keriya, told me of having seen about ten years earlier houses evidently of the same type as at Dandan-Uiliq, half buried in the sand, some marches beyond the famous Mazar of Imam Jafar Sadik. Others too had heard stories of this "old town." The eagerly expected ponies for some unaccountable reason had failed as yet to arrive. But in a country where there is neither telegraph nor a real post-office, one learns to take such little delays calmly, and the Amban's help amply provided for all needful transport.

CHAPTER XXII.

TO NIYA AND IMAM JAFAR SADIK.

On the morning of the 18th ot January I started in glorious sunshine, doubly enjoyable after the confinement of the last few days. As usual after a halt of some days, my caravan took a good deal of time to set out again. So there was sufficient delay to allow half the boys and idlers of 'Old Keriya' to gather in the road and on the roofs of surrounding houses to watch the exciting spectacle. The jovial fat Begs of Keriya and Niya (the latter away from his charge for the time) duly saw me off. After crossing the river-bed, about a quarter of a mile broad, but now all dry but for a modest streak of water, we passed the little villages of Besh-toghrak and Ghadghang. Scarcely two miles beyond the town we were again in barren sands, the outskirts of the great desert northwards. On the right an absolutely bare plain of coarse sand and pebbles leads up gradually like an enormous glacis to the foot of the mountain-wall rising to the south. It was the outer range of the Kuen-luen, east of Polu, usually hidden by the haze from the eyes of the traveller who follows this ancient route to the Lop-nor region and the confines of true Cathay. One or two peaks, which Ram Singh had triangulated on his trip east of Pisha, were clearly recognisable again and offered safe points for further survey work. The outer range was completely covered with recent snow and thus looked more imposing than it probably does at other times. The high peaks about Polu and behind, which reach up to 21,000 ft. and more, glittered dimly in the distance.

Ui-toghrak, reached after an easy march of about fourteen miles, is a small oasis of some two hundred houses, scattered about in hamlets. Under the trees and elsewhere in the shade a good deal of snow still lay on the ground. The wind all day was biting cold, and I gladly availed myself of the shelter prepared for my party in the roomy house of a local 'Bai.' Clean mud walls and gaily-coloured Khotan felts ('Kirghiz') make even a bare little room look cheerful and homely on a winter evening.

Clouds had come up in the evening and stopped the astronomical observations for latitude. On the morning of January 19th it was snowing hard when I got up, and the white trees of the orchard behind the house looked delightfully European. The temperature at 8 a.m. was 9° Fahr. The snow stopped by the time I got my caravan to move off, but all day the clouds hung low and the mountains were hidden. The ground traversed was a pebbly 'Sai' very much like the soil on most of the marches to Khotan. High ridges of sand were visible on the left, stretching away to the north. After a ride of about sixteen miles we passed the broad and shallow bed of a stream now completely dry, and a little beyond arrived at the tiny oasis of Yesyulghun. It consists of about a dozen mud-hovels, which serve as wayside quarters for travellers to Niya and the goldfields of Surghak. The few fields irrigated in the summer would not suffice for the keep of the inhabitants, who derive their maintenance from providing quarters and supplies. The water of the place is obtained from a well, said to be 40 'Gulach' (fathoms) deep, and it was curious to observe how this form of water supply has affected the topography of the hamlet. Whereas in Turkestan villages the houses are usually scattered about among fields and gardens, the dwellings of Yesyulghun range themselves neatly round the open space with the well in the centre just as if it were a market-place. Some fine old poplars growing in a group near by on the edge of a storage tank give a picturesque look to the spot.

The clouds cleared overnight, and the minimum thermometer showed −1° Fahr. The mountains immediately south again became visible and I could recognise the valley at the entrance of which the Surghak gold mines lie. The march was over a stony steppe and almost too short, only about eleven miles. But our 'Darogha' thought, probably rightly, that the camels could not cover the whole distance to Niya in one day, and as there is neither water nor shelter to be found on the remaining twenty-four miles, I had to acquiesce. Ovraz Langar consists of a solitary mud-house, tenanted by a 'Langarchi.' Supplies and ice had been sent on from Ui-toghrak, so we were fairly comfortable. The room I occupied was low, and the fireplace smoked badly; but even thus it was preferable to a tent in the sharp wind that blew from the east.

The start for Niya next morning was made cheerful by the arrival of Niaz Akhun, who, with the ponies and my mail from Khotan, overtook me before I had left Ovraz Langar. He brought me letters from home which had travelled by the Farghana route to Kashgar and thence by Chinese post. The latest of them had left my brother's hand on the 7th of December, and seemed quite recent, considering that the mail from Europe that reached me viâ Gilgit bore dates in the second week of October. It was impossible to ignore the postal advantages which the Trans-Caspian railway has secured for the European in Central Asia, though for safety I preferred to rely on the Indian post-office and its Dak viâ Hunza.

The whole of the twenty-four miles' march from Ovraz Langar lay over a pebble-strewn 'Sai,' the detritus washed down from the great southern range. Here and there sand-dunes advancing from the desert stretched their last offshoots across the hard 'Sai.' There was no trace of vegetation until we got within about six miles of the Niya oasis, when tamarisks and some hardy brushwood appeared in small patches. The oasis of Niya is formed by a series of hamlets and villages extending along the river that leaves the mountains near Surghak. In its upper course it is known as the 'Darya' of the Ulugh-Sai Valley. After 3 p.m. I had reached the western edge of the cultivated area at the hamlet of Kang-sarigh, and a further two miles brought me into the central village containing the Bazar of Niya. I was received in due form by the local Beg's deputy, and found decent quarters prepared in a Bai's house close to the entrance of the Bazar. It was the weekly market day of Niya, and though it was getting dark in the narrow street overhung by awnings, there was still busy life in front of the booths that line its sides for about a furlong. There were plenty of dried fruits, plums, raisins from Khotan, with tea and various condiments of Chinese origin. Excellent walnuts and fair red grapes were local produce. People seemed busy buying such little luxuries on account of the Id festival, marking the close of the Ramzan fast.

My people had as travellers taken dispensation from the observance of Ramzan, yet they were anxious to celebrate the day in due fashion as good Muslims, and hence asked for a halt on January 22nd. I could not well refuse the request, particularly as arrangements had to be made for the labourers and the supplies which were to be taken to the desert site I was bound for. All Niya was in holiday attire, and the prayers from the mosque sounded sonorously into my room. I was busy with making up my mails for India and home, but used the bright midday hours to take photographs of local people. There were plenty of fine-looking greybeards to choose from, and no want of nicely-dressed children. Shy at first, the little ones were readily enticed before my camera by the present of a few coppers for sweets. 'Diwanas,' too, or wandering mendicants, in fantastic rags showing patches in all colours of the rainbow did not object to giving a sitting in return for my alms. The rural population here, as at Khotan, shows on the whole remarkably good features—of course, Caucasian as the popular term has it. Noticing the thoroughly European appearance of physiognomies in the great mass of this Turki population, I feel inclined to wonder at all the efforts that have been made to account for the same fact in the Western Turks and their kindred in Europe.

Niya is an ancient place. Hiuen-Tsiang, travelling towards Lop-nor and China, duly notices the town of Ni-jang, *i.e.*, Niya, which "the king of Khotan makes the guard of his eastern frontier." Niya remained, indeed, the easternmost of the smaller oases included in the Khotan district until the construction in recent times of Keriya as a separate administrative unit.

The pilgrim's description shows that the desert pressed then, as now, close round the small oasis. A huge jar of ancient pottery, nearly 3 feet in diameter, which had been found years ago at the old site to be visited, was at first the only antiquity that Niya could show me. But in the afternoon I received unexpected proof of the great age of the ruined site I was to visit. Hassan Akhun, my inquisitive young camel-man, had acci-

VILLAGE BOYS AT NIYA.

dentally come across a villager possessing two inscribed wooden tablets brought away from that site. When these objects were produced before me, I discovered to my joyful surprise that they contained writing in that ancient script of the extreme North-West of India known as Kharoshthi, and of a type which closely agreed with that prevailing during the period of Kushana rule in the first centuries of our era.

The man who brought me the tablets had picked them up

on the road to Imam Jafar's Mazar. But I soon ascertained the original finder in the person of Ibrahim, an enterprising young villager who had dug them out from a "house of the old town" in the desert beyond. He had gone there a year before in search of treasure, but had found only a number of these, to him, useless tablets. He brought away six, only to throw some away on the road and to give the rest to his children to play with. The latter specimens were soon destroyed, and Ibrahim now greatly regretted their loss, when he saw how well I rewarded the more sensible man who had picked up what he had cast aside. I tried to hide my delight as well as I could, but did not fail to secure Ibrahim as a guide for my party, and to assure him of a good reward if he could show me the ruined structure where he made his find. Kharoshthi writing had before been found in Central Asia only on the earliest Khotan coins approximately assigned to the first and second centuries of our era, and in those remarkable fragments of a birch-bark codex which M. Dutreuil de Rhins, the ill-starred French traveller, acquired in Khotan in 1892. It was a happy evening when I examined these most promising finds. The very cursive form of the writing and the faded appearance of the ink prevented any attempt at immediate decipherment. Certain linguistic features seemed to prove that the tablets I held in my hands contained documents with an early Indian text, and the writing alone sufficed to assure me of the antiquity of the ruins that had furnished them. But full of expectation as I was, I little anticipated at the time what a rich harvest was awaiting me there.

A three days' march from Niya brought me to Imam Jafar Sadik's shrine, the starting-point of my fresh expedition into the desert. Scenery as well as the weather helped to make these days pleasant. I left Niya on a delightfully sunny morning, and the sky kept clear all the way, but the cold was still severe, the temperature at night falling to somewhere about 8° Fahr. below zero, and in daytime never rising much above 22° Fahr.

The route lay, of course, all along the Niya River, as the "old town" of my present quest had to be reached from where the river dies away in the sand. Its course proved almost as winding as that of the Keriya Darya, but its volume far smaller. Just like the river of Keriya, the Niya stream gathers water from springs and marshes a short distance below the town. This is, of course, the water that has been absorbed higher up by irrigation channels, and comes again to the surface lower down. Very soon after losing sight of the cultivated area we were in a broad belt of jungle land covered with luxuriant Kumush and forest vegetation. The sands receded to more than two miles from the left river-bank, and nearly as much from the right. The route, owing to the large number of pilgrims who annually frequent Imam Jafar's Mazar in the autumn, had the well-trodden look of a high-road. On the first day it touched again and again the bank of the stream, now a glittering sheet of ice. Its breadth was there usually 30–35 yards, its depth as far as I could ascertain from holes that had been cut into the thick ice, nowhere more than about 3 feet. As the banks were only about 2–3 feet above the surface of the ice, it is probable that during the time of the melting snows a good deal of overflow must occur. This may account for the luxuriance of the jungle growth that distinguishes the riverine belt. The grazing-grounds of the Niya shepherds begin, therefore, close below the little oasis, and evidently maintain a considerable number of flocks. They are said to be divided among ten shepherd stations, and all belong to 'Bais' of Niya.

The thought that all this fertile stretch of ground might well be brought under cultivation had occupied me as I rode along. It was, therefore, a pleasant sight to me when a little below Nagara-khana, the shepherd's hut where my first night's camp had been pitched, I came upon the head of a canal begun only two years previously under the Amban's orders. From this point, which is about nineteen miles distant from Niya Bazar, the fertile belt of soil widened considerabl' and the ridges of the desert sand disappeared from view. The river winds away on the eastern side, while the route led through the central part of what looked like a smal tract of jungle. Close to the route runs the new canal, a modest worl so far, only 6–8 feet broad, yet likely to bring life and wealth to this lonely woodland. The soil is a fertile loess, and the level of the ground so uniform that its irrigation will be easy when the jungle is once cleared away.

For over eight miles we followed the canal, and I pictured to my mind the changes it is likely to bring soon to this silent scene. No doubt in ancient times irrigation was carried all along the streams which cut into the desert area, and by a careful storage of their waters probably much ground beyond, that now seems irretrievably lost to the moving sands, was secured for cultivation. A strong and capable administration, whether on European or Eastern lines, might any day take up again the old struggle with the desert and successfully push forward the borders of human habitation, just as it has in the Turkoman steppes and the Doabs of the Punjab, by nature scarcely less arid. But whence is that impulse to come?

Wherever the forest left sufficient open ground I could see the distant snowy range rising far away to the south of Niya. The atmosphere kept so clear that even up to Otra Langar, where a few reed huts form a half-way rest-house for the pilgrims, our position on the plane-table could always be fixed by intersections from the prominent points in the great mountain range. Truly a remarkable testimony in favour of the winter atmosphere of the desert, considering that at Otra Langar we were close on seventy miles away from the nearest of those peaks.

But these distant vistas ceased when the thickets of poplars and tamarisks were entered a little beyond that station. Here the woodland seemed to expand considerably over ground that bears ample evidence of having once been occupied by the shifting bed of the river. According to our shepherd guides the width of the jungle tract is here 8–10 miles, and the bearings obtained from certain elevated points on the day's march seemed to confirm this estimate. Under the trees and in all depressions of the ground there remained a thin layer of snow, evidently of the previous week's fall. With the bare trees and their thick undergrowth it made up a landscape that reminded me more of a winter scene in Northern Europe than anything I had seen for long years.

For over twelve miles we rode through the forest without getting a glimpse of the river or of a shepherd's hut that might have indicated its vicinity. At last a little before sunset we reached the deserted reed-huts of Döbe-Bostan, the second camping-ground. Here the sand-hills of the desert-edge reappeared westwards, while the river came again within reach about a mile off to the east. The camels with the baggage did not arrive until 7 p.m. My men kept up splendid bonfires with the fallen trees close at hand, and thus I was able to enjoy the delightfully clear night sky without feeling the cold too acutely. But when my tent was ready at last the temperature in it was 10° Fahr.

My march on the 26th of January was considerably shorter, only about thirteen miles, and brought us to the famous Mazar that was to be our point of departure for the desert. The river, when we met it again in the morning, appeared as a narrow band of ice scarcely over 20 feet in width, and yet constantly sending off little branches. It looked as if the much-reduced stream were trying where it could bury itself quickest. Yet just here, so near its end, the fertilising power of its water visibly reasserted itself. The trees increased in size and the shrubs in height as we came nearer to the shrine, and the scenery around the latter looked quite pretty even in the bareness of its winter dress. Scattered at various points amidst groves of large poplars are huts intended for the shelter of pilgrims. On the ridge of what looked like a huge sand-dune to the west there appeared a tangled mass of staffs and flags of all kinds, marking the resting-place of the martyr prince whose memory renders the place sacred. At last we were in front of the collection of mosques, Madrasahs and houses of the hereditary attendants which make up the 'Mazar.' It looked imposing enough to eyes that had seen besides the desert only the mud huts of Keriya and Niya for the last two months. A group of little lakes, formed apparently by the river between the group of buildings and the hill which the tomb crowns, greatly added to the picturesqueness of the scene.

After a rapid inspection of the buildings, among which only a large quadrangular Madrasah built by Niaz Hakim Beg with burnt bricks can claim some merit, I proceeded across the ice of the northernmost lake to the hill opposite. Its foot is occupied by groves of fine old trees, amidst which pious donors have erected praying platforms and various little Sarais for pilgrims and the scholars who attend the school of the shrine.

TREES WITH EX-VOTOS, ON PATH TO IMAM JAFAR SADIK'S TOMB.

All the trees were decked with little flags, yak tails or simple rags, the votive offerings of visitors. The path to the hilltop ascends through a large number of rough wooden arches, all bearing the same marks of pilgrims' devotion. At the first of these arches there is to be seen the motliest collection imaginable of rags. All colours and materials are represented, from fine Indian muslin to Birmingham cotton prints, Chinese silks, Russian chintzes, and the coarse 'Kham' of the country

The custom which prompts pilgrims to leave behind these tokens of their devotion prevails equally at Muhammadan and Hindu pilgrimage places throughout India. I thought at the time how curious an archæological find this exhibition of textile samples would make if it were safely buried beneath the sands and laid bare again after centuries.

The pilgrims' path to the tomb winds round the hill, and on its inner side are everywhere little heaps of earth arranged like graves. They are intended to symbolise the resting-places of the 'Shahids,' the faithful Muslims who fell here with Imam Jafar Sadik, their holy leader, fighting the infidels of 'Chin and Machin,' *i.e.*, Khotan, as related in the Taskirah or legendary of the shrine. More curious to me, however, was the observation that the hill, which rises about 170 feet above the lake, does not consist of sand but of stony detritus overlying reefs of salt. The latter crops out at several points and is of greyish-white colour. The presence of rock-salt, and of the gravel which covers it, is remarkable enough in this locality. Both to the west and east of the riverine belt there is nothing but sand. If the sanctity of the hill goes back to pre-Muhammadan times, as is likely enough in view of what has been observed of other pilgrimage places in this region, this natural peculiarity would suffice to explain it.

From the hilltop we enjoyed an extensive view over the desert northward. The forest, which marks the extent of the river's fertilising influence, seemed to die away some six or seven miles beyond the Mazar. The stream, before losing itself in the sand, takes a turn to the north-west, and that direction, too, my guides indicated for the ancient site.

It took a long time to get my caravan into marching order on the morning of January 26th. The men went in turns to pay their respects to the saint's tomb on the hilltop, and later on the filling and securing of the water-tanks that were to supply us at "the old town" caused further delay. No water is to be got by digging at the site I was about to visit, and accordingly I knew that we should have to depend for a lengthy stay on the tanks. Those two, which had come all the way from Calcutta, being constructed of strong galvanised iron, had already during their use at Dandan-Uiliq proved equal to the strain caused by the freezing of their contents. In hot Calcutta, I confess, neither the makers (Messrs. Thomson) nor I myself had thought of nights like the last one, when the minimum thermometer showed 12° F. below zero, our lowest temperature yet recorded. The other tanks, notwithstanding the precautions taken, proved to have sprung leaks owing to expansion, when the ice into which their contents had turned was again melted. Luckily the great cold prevailing permitted the transport of additional ice in improvised sacks and nets—a most useful expedient which materially facilitated the regular supply of the indispensable minimum of water while my camp, counting from forty to fifty people, was pitched far out in the desert.

The day was brilliantly clear and the sunshine and the gay colours of the landscape made the march quite enjoyable through the forest land where the river finally loses itself in the sand. About three miles below the Mazar the tiny river-course spreads out in some shallow marshes and then finally disappears, at least in winter-time. During summer the flood water, as shown by the deep-cut 'Yars' or ravines we passed several miles lower down, is carried for some distance further. Near the marsh known as Tulkuch-kol lie the huts and the sheep-pens of Nurullah, the guardian of the flocks which belong to the shrine. These were said to number over four thousand sheep; and Nurullah, who acted as our guide up to the end of the grazing-grounds, plainly showed by his get-up and manners that he was more than a common 'Koichi,' or shepherd. He cultivates close to his huts a plot of land which produces wheat and maize sufficient to maintain his family. At this little farm the ponies were to remain during our stay in the desert.

The trees grew so thickly in this amply-watered tract that the camels had often to halt until a path could be cleared for them. Everywhere the traces of deer, hares and other game were to be seen. Gradually the jungle area became more and more invaded by drift-sand; clumps of trees which had withered and died showed themselves more frequently; and at last, some eight miles below the Mazar, the forest changed to a wide expanse of low sand-cones thickly overgrown with tamarisks and a hardy shrub known as Ak-tiken. Groups of dead poplars and other trees rose between, their large stems now gaunt and twisted by age, bearing evidence of a time when the river carried life further into the desert. From a high sand-hill close to my camp I could see how the scrubby jungle spread out between the great ridges of sand that mark on the east and west the commencement of the true desert. The breadth of this area was here fully four miles, and at various points it formed bays that indent still further into the true desert. The old course of the river must have extended towards the north-west; for in that direction the jungle-scrub could be seen for a considerable distance, spreading over ground nowhere broken by high ridges of sand.

The surmise I formed, that the ancient site would be reached by following these traces of the former river-course, was confirmed by the next day's march. This also showed, for the first time in my experience of the desert, that the distance given by the local guides was exaggerated. I had been told that the ruins to be visited would be reached in three marches from Imam Jafar's shrine. In reality we reached the southern edge of the area containing them by a second march of about fourteen miles on the 27th of January. It lay all along in the direction—more exactly N.N.W.—in which on the previous evening I had sighted the continuation of the old river-bed. For the first five miles or so the patches of dead forest were so thick that we had often to pick with care a way for the camels. Tamarisk brushwood still grew vigorously amidst the dead trees, chiefly Toghrak. The time when the latter flourished equally cannot have been very remote. For many of the lifeless trees still retained their branches, unlike the shrivelled skeletons of trunks seen elsewhere. A dry channel, about 4 feet deep, could be traced for some distance, winding along the eastern edge of the old jungle. The men promptly called it the 'Ustang' (canal) of the "old town." But I was unable to find any proof of its artificial origin.

Further down we had to pass through a belt of steep, conical sand-knolls from 15 to 30 feet high, rising close together and all covered on their tops with tangled masses of living and dead tamarisks. On the northern slopes the snow that had fallen a week before still lay plentifully to the depth of an inch. In the midst of this belt, extending for a distance of about three miles from south to north, I came upon broken pottery remains and an enclosure made of thickly-packed rushes. Inside it the men recognised trunks of fruit-trees and planted poplars, or 'Terek.' We had evidently passed the site of some ancient farm. Beyond, the sand-hills were lower, but also bare. Living tamarisk bushes could be seen only on isolated sand-cones rising here and there over the low dunes. Pottery fragments strewn over the sand, with bits of slag and similar hard refuse, assured my guides that we were near the goal.

Soon I sighted the first two "houses," standing on what looked at first sight like small elevated plateaus, but which subsequent observation proved to be merely portions of the original loess soil that had escaped the erosion proceeding all round. The wooden posts of these buildings rose far higher above the sand than in the case of the dwellings at Dandan-Uiliq. A rapid inspection sufficed to show that their mode of construction was materially the same; but the dimensions here were larger and the timber framework was far more elaborate and solid. That these remains were of far greater antiquity became evident almost immediately when, in a room of one of the houses, I came upon some finely carved pieces of wood lying practically on the surface, which displayed ornaments of a type common to early Gandhara sculptures. Marching about two miles further north across fairly high dunes, I arrived at a ruined structure of sun-dried bricks, which Abdullah had already mentioned to me at Keriya as a 'Potai.' It proved, as I had expected, to be the remains of a small Stupa, buried for the most part by the slope of a high conical sand-hill, and hence comparatively well preserved.

Close to it I pitched my camp, in a position conveniently central for the exploration of the scattered ruins. The ground in the immediate vicinity seemed greatly eroded, and where not actually covered by dunes, displayed in profusion large pieces of broken pottery, withered trunks of poplars and garden trees, as well as much decayed remains of ancient timber that splintered and broke almost as soon as lifted. Even more than this débris, the fragments of stone that covered the bare loess, evidently the remains of larger pieces that must have been brought here from the river-bed near the foot of the mountains for use in the houses, attested the destructive force of the desert winds and of the extremes of climate. As I retired to my first night's rest among these silent witnesses of ancient habitations, I wondered with some apprehension whether Ibrahim's story would prove true, and how much of the other precious documents on wood which he declared to have left behind at the time of his "prospecting" visit were still waiting to be recovered by me.

RUINS OF ANCIENT DWELLING-HOUSE (N. III.), WITH GARDEN.

CHAPTER XXIII.

FIRST EXCAVATION OF KHAROSHTHI TABLETS.

My first business on the morning of the 28th of January was to despatch Ram Singh with Ibrahim Akhun, our plucky little Darogha, on a reconnoitring expedition westwards. They were to observe how far fuel and ground easy enough for laden camels could be found in that direction. My object was to make sure whether, on the conclusion of my work at this site, an attempt could safely be made to move my caravan straight across the desert to the ruins of Aktiken or Karadong, which were to be visited on the lower Keriya Darya. In the event of no objective offering for exploration further to the east, this march of some fifty miles through the desert might save us the great detour viâ Niya and Keriya.

As soon as I had seen the little party safely off with camels to ride and a sufficient store of ice and food, I hastened to set out to the ruined building, where Ibrahim had a year previously picked up his ancient tablets inscribed with Kharoshthi characters. At Niya he had declared that plenty more of them were left *in situ*. It had been impossible to hide from him the value which I attached to these tablets, and as he subsequently seemed to regret not having himself made a haul of them, I had him watched *en route*, and after our arrival, to prevent his escape or any possible interference with the spot. The mingled feelings of expectation and distrust with which I now approached it soon changed to joyful assurance. About a mile to the east of the camp I sighted the ruin towards which Ibrahim was guiding us, on what looked like a little terrace rising high above the depressions of the ground caused by the erosive action of the wind. On ascending the slope I picked up at once three inscribed tablets lying amidst the débris of massive timber that marked wholly eroded parts of the ruined structure; and on reaching the top, I found to my delight many more scattered about within one of the rooms, still clearly traceable by remains of their walls.

Only a year had passed since Ibrahim had thrown them down there, and the layer of drift-sand was so thin as scarcely to protect the topmost ones from the snow that still lay on the ground. Ibrahim at once showed me the spot where he had unearthed the relics he had treated in such utter ignorance of their value. It proved to be the south-west corner of a small room, which was situated between other apartments in the northern wing of the building, and is seen on the left in the photograph showing this ruin (N. I.) after excavation. There in a little recess, about four feet wide, between the large brick-built fireplace, well recognisable above the sand and the west wall of the room, he had come upon a heap of tablets by scooping out the sand with his hands. The "treasure" he looked for was not there, and the ancient documents which he found, apparently still lying in horizontal rows with some sort of arrangement, were thrown away into the next room. I blessed the good luck which had brought me to the site so soon after this discovery. For, fully exposed to wind and sun, these thin wooden boards could not long have retained their writing in such wonderful freshness as they had during their safe interment of many centuries beneath the drift of sand. As it was, the sun of one year and perhaps the recent snow (patches of it are seen on the ground in the photograph on the next page) had bleached and partly effaced the fully exposed writing of the topmost tablets.

RUINED BUILDING (N. I.), FIRST FIND-PLACE OF INSCRIBED TABLETS, AFTER EXCAVATION.

My first task was to put a guard over the place where Ibrahim had scattered these precious finds, so as to prevent further injury or abstraction. Then the men were set to work to clear the room where he had first come upon them. It was an easy matter, as the room measured only 14 by 16 feet, and the sand which covered its floor was not deep. On the north side, near the eroded slope, it only lay to a depth of about two feet, which increased to about four feet towards the south wall. While this clearing proceeded, I had time to examine more carefully the character of the whole structure. It was essentially one based on the use of timber, which the forest land along the river and the plantations of 'Terek' or white poplar subsequently traced at many points of the ancient site must have supplied in abundance. Massive wooden beams, which surprised my workmen by their thickness and perfect finish, formed a kind of foundation. On this were set wooden posts about four inches square, which supported the roof and at the same time served as a frame for the walls. These and smaller intermediary posts, fixed at regular intervals of about a foot, were joined by light cross-beams, of which some were still found in position. To this framework was fixed a strong kind of matting of tamarisk branches woven diagonally, which again was covered on each side with layers of hard, white plaster of varying thickness. The walls had completely decayed where not actually covered by sand, but most of the posts originally holding them, now bleached and splintered, still rose high above the surface.

As the room was gradually cleared, about two dozen inscribed tablets were found at various points of the original floor and on the raised platform that flanked the fireplace on the west. There was nothing to indicate whether they had been separated from the main deposit of documents which Ibrahim had lighted upon in the recess at the south-west corner of the room. The careful search which I then made myself for the scattered remains of his find, resulted in the recovery of no less than eighty-five tablets, and as the clearing of the remaining rooms of the north wing still further added to their number, I found myself before the day's work was done in possession of materials far more abundant than I could reasonably have hoped for.

The remarkable state of preservation in which a considerable portion of the wooden tablets was found made it easy for me, even during a first cursory examination on the spot, to acquaint myself with the main features of their use and outward arrangement. With the exception of a few oblong pieces, all tablets found that day were wedge-shaped, from 7 to 15 inches long, and showed evidence of having been originally arranged in pairs. These pairs had been held together by a string which passed round the square ends of the wedges, usually from 2¼ to 1½ inches broad, and also through a hole drilled into both tablets where their left end tapered to a point. In the case of many such double tablets, even where the two pieces had got detached, portions of the ancient string were still intact, and on some also the clay sealing which had been inserted over the string in a specially prepared square socket. But it was only by the subsequent discovery of practically perfect specimens that I was able to ascertain all details of the ingenious method of fastening adopted for these ancient documents on wood. I therefore leave their full description, as well as that of other technicalities connected with their use, for a later chapter.

The text, invariably written in Kharoshthi characters, and running from right to left parallel to the longer side, occupied the inner surfaces of the tablets, *i.e.*, those originally turned towards each other when the tablets were still fastened in pairs. On the outside surface which bore the clay seal, and soon proved to have served the purposes of a kind of envelope, there usually appeared brief entries in the same script, forming a single line. Their very position and form at once suggested that they were intended either as records of the contents or else to convey the names of the sender or addressee. It was naturally with intense curiosity that I examined the writing of each tablet as it was extracted from the sand. Where double tablets had remained together and thus protected each other, the black ink of the Kharoshthi lines written on the inner surface looked as fresh as if penned yesterday. On others it was necessary to apply the brush to clear away an adherent crust of sand, but only on comparatively few had the writing faded so far as to become illegible.

Wedge-shaped double tablet (N. xv. 137), with attached seal. (Scale one-third.)

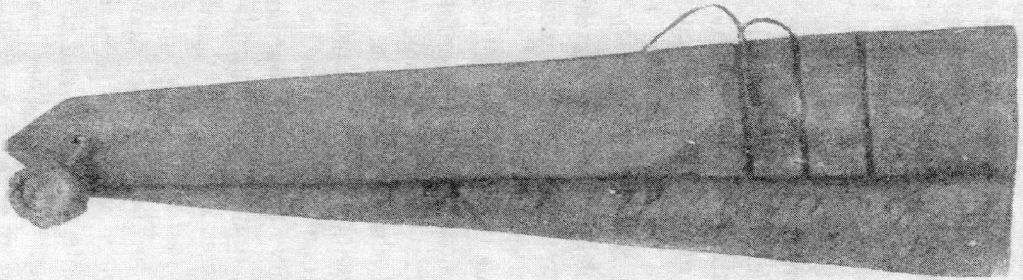

Oblong tablet with hole (N. iv. 29), showing columnar writing. (Scale two-thirds.)

Takhta-shaped tablet (N. xvi. 2), containing "file" record. (Scale one-third.)

KHAROSHTHI DOCUMENTS ON WOODEN TABLETS.

22*

It was easy to recognise that the tablets, though written by many different hands, showed throughout the characteristic peculiarities of that type of Kharoshthi writing which in India is invariably exhibited by the inscriptions of the so-called Kushana or Indo-Scythian kings. The period during which these kings ruled over the Punjab and the regions to the west of the Indus falls within the first three centuries of our era. The earliest coins of Khotan and the fragmentary birch-bark leaves of the Dutreuil de Rhins Manuscript, which were the only relics of Kharoshthi writing so far known in Central Asia, have with good reason been assigned to the same period. Thus even while still engaged in gathering the remarkable documents that were coming to light here in such surprising numbers, and long before any careful examination became possible, I felt absolutely assured as to their high antiquity and exceptional value.

And yet during that day's animating labours and as I marched back to camp in the failing light of the evening, there remained a thought that prevented my archæological conscience from becoming over-triumphant. It was true that the collected text of the hundred odd tablets, which I was carrying away carefully packed and labelled as the result of my first day's work, could not fall much short of, if it did not exceed, the aggregate of all the materials previously available for the study of Kharoshthi, whether in or outside India. But was it not possible that these strange records, with the striking similarity of their outward form and almost all, as I had noticed, showing when complete an identical short formula at their commencement, might prove to be mere replicas of the same text, perhaps a prayer or an extract from sacred Buddhist writings? The care taken about the sealing of most of the tablets seemed indeed to point to contents of a more practical nature—letters, perhaps, and contracts or documents of some official character. I knew well that the historical and antiquarian interest of the finds, if they were really to furnish such records, would be increased beyond all proportion. Yet the supposition seemed almost too good to be readily indulged in.

Once in the comparative shelter of my tent, as soon as the detailed account of the first excavations had been written up, I began with impatience to compare and study the best preserved of those remarkable tablets. I knew from the experience furnished by the Dutreuil de Rhins fragments and more than one Kharoshthi stone inscription from the Punjab, how serious a task the proper decipherment of these documents would necessarily prove even to the epigraphist working in his study. I was thus prepared for the exceptional difficulties likely to be presented by the cursive character of the writing and all the uncertainties as to the language and contents. Yet sitting up that evening wrapped in my furs until the increasing cold drove me to seek refuge in bed—the thermometer showed next morning a minimum of 9° F. below zero—I gained assurance on two important points.

A series of philological observations bearing on the phonetic value of the characters, single or compound, that could be read with certainty, and on the recurrence of particular inflectional endings, etc., convinced me that the language was an early Indian Prakrit, probably of a type closely akin to the dialect found in the legends of the oldest Khotan coins and in the Dutreuil de Rhins fragments. It became equally certain from a cursory comparison of the tablets that their text varied greatly both in extent and in matter, notwithstanding the brief initial formula with which most of them opened. It was only some days later that I succeeded in definitely deciphering the latter, when its wording—*mahanuava maharaya lihati*, "His Highness the Maharaja writes [thus]:"—plainly established that these particular documents conveyed official orders. In the meantime, however, the previous observations together with others, such as the occurrence of numerical figures in the body of various tablets, sufficed to relieve me of the doubt that this unexpected wealth of epigraphical finds might after all resolve itself into numerous repetitions of identical religious texts so much in favour with the pious among all Buddhist communities.

Though I could not feel sure as yet in regard to the real nature of the contents, there was enough in the day's discoveries to justify the conclusion that, with the Kharoshthi script transplanted from the extreme North-West of India, an early form of Indian speech had also been brought into popular use within the territories of ancient Khotan, probably from the same region. Such a fact could be accounted for only by historical events of far-reaching importance, which hitherto seemed wholly lost to our field of vision. The fascinating prospect of bringing them again to light made me look out with intense interest for such additional finds as the site might have in store.

That my hopes in this direction had indeed been well founded was proved on the following morning, when I began the clearing of the southern wing of the ruined building. This adjoined at right angles the eastern end of the row of apartments excavated on the preceding day, and communicated with them by a door leading at first into a small room, only 10 ft. broad, which might have served as a kind of ante-chamber. A broad platform, built of plaster some 3 ft. above the floor, and extending along most of the length of the room, looked as if intended to accommodate attendants, an exactly similar arrangement being observed in modern Turkestan houses. A well-preserved oblong tablet, which was the sole find made here, shows a handle at one end and thus closely resembles the Indian 'Takhta' or wooden writing board to which I have already referred in connection with a discovery at Dandan-Uiliq. It also attracted my attention by exhibiting on both sides narrow vertical columns of writing which suggested either a metrical text or else lists.

There was little time to bestow on individual finds when the clearing of the large apartment (N. iv.) immediately adjoining on the south had begun; for from the shallow sand which covered it inscribed tablets of all forms and sizes soon began to crop up in unexpected numbers. It was a room 26 ft. square, with a raised platform of plaster running round three of its sides, while the remains of eight posts arranged in a square indicated a central area which probably had a raised roof to admit light and air, after the fashion still observed in the halls of large Turkestan houses. As the protecting layer of sand was here only 2 ft. deep, little more was left of the walls than rows of broken posts. The first inscribed tablets, too, which turned up in the sand close to the surface, had suffered greatly, their warped and split wood showing plainly the effect of the terrible summer heat to which they must have been exposed since the winds had carried away most of the sand that originally protected them.

All the more delighted was I when I found that even the light remaining layer of sand had sufficed to preserve in a more or less legible condition the threescore of tablets that were found covering the platform along the southern side of the room. In some places, particularly near the centre of the wall, they were rising in small closely packed heaps above the plaster flooring, evidently just as left by the last occupants. But a considerable number of other inscribed tablets showed plainly by their position that they had been disturbed at some early period, apparently not long after the building had been deserted. For, in addition to some twenty tablets which were found scattered about in the loose sand covering the floor just in front of the south and east platforms, I unearthed over two dozen more from the southern part of the central area of the room marked by the posts already referred to.

As the layer of these tablets was being removed, it was seen that they had rested on a square piece of strong matting which, supported by some light rafters also recovered, must have once formed a roof over the central area. The matting was found lying about a foot above the floor, thus showing the depth to which the invading sand had accumulated before the roof fell. The tablets found above the matting could only have got there subsequently. They may well have been thrown there when the abandoned dwelling was visited by some one anxious to search its remaining contents after the fashion of the modern "treasure-seekers." The ancient records left behind by the last occupiers as so much "waste-paper" (to use an anachronism) were not likely to have been treated by him with more respect than Ibrahim had shown for the collection of tablets he so luckily unearthed in another part of the building.

Below the matting I discovered some more tablets which owed their excellent state of preservation evidently to this safe covering, and then I came upon a small oval-shaped platform of plaster which, judging from the raised rim enclosing it, must have served as an open fireplace. But more interesting and more puzzling too than these structural details were the epigraphical finds. Their variety in respect of shape and size was truly remarkable. The wedge-shaped tablets familiar from the first day's work reappeared again; but in numbers they were far surpassed by inscribed boards of wood, to which, notwithstanding great variations in detail and proportions, the designation of oblong appears generally applicable. The use of those which were provided with a handle, usually rounded or pentagonal, and exhibited Kharoshthi writing on both sides, could readily be accounted for by their resemblance to the Indian Takhta (for a specimen, see p. 339).

Other tablets attaining considerable dimensions in length, up to 30 in., but comparatively narrow, curiously reminded me, by their appearance and the hole regularly found near one end, of the palm leaves which we know to have been used from the earliest times for manuscripts in India. Useful as this hole must have been for handling and storing these tablets of wood, it was nevertheless evident that it could not have been intended, as in the case of palm-leaf manuscripts, for a string to unite a series of them into a sort of 'Pothi.' For not only were such tablets of entirely different sizes, but their great majority (close on thirty pieces) showed plainly by the irregular arrangement of their writing, in small columns and often running in different directions and concluding with numerical figures, by the appearance of various handwritings, erasures, bracketings, and similar indications, that they did not contain texts, or even connected communications, but in all probability memoranda, tabular statements, accounts and other casual records.

Two series of oblong tablets largely represented among the finds of N. iv. (as this particular room was designated by me) showed far greater regularity and care in writing as well as workmanship, without being the less puzzling at the time of their discovery. These were tablets of rectangular shape, varying in length from 4 to 16 inches, which soon attracted my attention by the raised rim resembling a margin they invariably exhibited at the narrower sides of their single inscribed surface. The writing extending between these rims in five to thirteen lines always parallel to the longer side, ordinarily bore at the commencement a Kharoshthi numerical figure preceded by a word which I read before long as *samvatsare,* meaning in Sanskrit or Prakrit "in the year." In the text immediately following there appeared with equal regularity figures preceded by the words *mase* and *divase,* "in the . . . month" and "on the . . . day." There could be no doubt that I held in my hands dated documents or records of some kind. Yet there was nothing in this to enlighten me as to the peculiar form of these tablets or the manner in which they might have been used.

Busily occupied as I was in directing the excavation and clearing and numbering each find, I failed to realise at the time the close relation that existed between these tablets and another class of which the same ruined apartment furnished numerous specimens. They consisted of rectangular pieces of wood not exceeding eight inches in length and five in width, and often much smaller, which on their flat reverse rarely had any writing, while the obverse in its raised centre invariably showed a square or oblong socket, manifestly intended for the insertion of a seal, together with a transversely written line or two of Kharoshthi characters. It was only later, when the remarkable rubbish-heap to be described below had yielded up its antiquarian treasures, that an explanation, as definite as it was simple, revealed itself of these curious seal-bearing tablets, and of the rims appearing on the wooden documents to which they had once been fitted as envelopes (for illustrations, see pp. 346, 374, 375).

The structure which had so richly rewarded my first two days' labours was too far decayed to permit of any certain conclusion as to its real character. The records which had escaped destruction, buried low on its floors, would, no doubt, furnish the clue, though I foresaw that their complete elucidation might be a labour of years. Whether, however, the building I had excavated had once served as the residence of some local official or perhaps as a monastic dwelling, it was clear that the writings found in it could only be the remains of a collection that had gradually accumulated and been left behind by chance when the place was abandoned.

It was hence a fact of archæological significance that among all this wealth of written documents not a single scrap of actual paper was found. Nor could I discover a trace of paper among

KHAROSHTHI DOCUMENT ON WOOD, UNDER-TABLET (N. IV. 139).
(Scale one-half.)

ANCIENT WOODEN PEN, WITH BONE KNOB (FROM N. XV.).
(Scale nine-tenths.)

the miscellaneous rubbish which was brought to light in other rooms of the building. It was evident, therefore, that the use of this writing material, so much more convenient than wood, however old it may have been in China, had not spread in Eastern Turkestan at that early date which palæographic considerations indicated for my discoveries. Wooden tablets for writing purposes are indeed mentioned in very early Indian texts, particularly Buddhist ones; and it is easy to realise that their use recommended itself in a country like Turkestan which produces neither palm-leaves nor birch-bark, the other ancient writing materials known in India. None the less was it a delightful surprise when, far away at this sand-buried site on the eastern limits of ancient Khotan territory, I found myself in possession of the first specimens ever discovered of Indian records on wood.

All that day a breeze was blowing from the north-east, light yet sufficiently piercing in the prevailing cold and strong enough to drive before it a light spray of sand. As this passed over the ancient tablets laid out in rows as they were being recovered, it ever threatened to efface the pencil figures which I wrote with half-benumbed fingers on the often soft wood of their surface to mark the succession of the finds. I scarcely needed to be thus gently reminded of the erosive power of the desert winds. With the view of the ruined building before me as reproduced in the photograph taken from a sand-hill close by (p. 336), it was impossible to ignore the extent to which this and other structures of the site have suffered by erosion. The small plateau which the ruin is seen now to occupy, raised some twelve to fifteen feet above the immediately surrounding ground, is unmistakably due to the erosion which proceeded around the building. While the strip of ground actually covered by the débris of the structure retains the original level, the open surface near by, consisting of mere loess, has been lowered more and more by the action of the wind. The drift-sand carried along over this portion of the area, which was once watered from the Niya River, is not sufficient at present to fill the depressions thus created or to protect the ruins. Broad ravines, from fifteen to thirty feet deep, were to be seen in many places where the excavating force of the winds could freely assert itself in the bare loess soil. That part of the ground, too, still occupied by ancient buildings, is being slowly cut into and undermined, just as if it were exposed to the erosive action of running water. The result finally produced by this slow process of destruction is aptly illustrated by the photograph just referred to; for the heavy timber débris there seen on the slope of the foreground marks a part of the original building which has completely fallen, owing to the soil beneath having been eroded. Thus at more than one spot near my camp I found scattered fragments of beams and posts as the sole remains of ancient structures. Ultimately the wood, rendered brittle by long exposure, breaks up into splinters which the winds are able to carry away with ease, and only potsherds and small fragments of stone or metal remain to indicate the place of ancient habitations.

SPECIMENS OF ARCHITECTURAL WOOD CARVING, FROM RUINED DWELLING-HOUSE (N. VIII.).

CHAPTER XXIV.

EXCAVATION OF ANCIENT RESIDENCES.

THE danger to ruins involved in erosion was strikingly demonstrated by the condition of a large group of ancient dwellings which I found about half a mile to the north-west of the building first excavated, and which I next proceeded to examine. Here an area roughly measuring 500 square feet proved to be closely occupied by the timber débris of ancient houses. But as the dunes were only a few feet high, and the ground everywhere was greatly eroded, very little remained of the walls, and still less of the contents of the rooms. Even thus careful search led to interesting finds of inscribed tablets in a detached room immediately to the south of the best preserved of these houses, which is seen in the foreground of the photograph reproduced on p. 351.

The sand covering the floor of the detached room (N. V.) lay only half a foot to one foot deep. Being thus poorly protected against atmospheric influences, the majority of the fifty odd tablets of wood we here picked up had withered and bleached until all trace of writing was lost. Others, though much warped and often perished on the surface, still show Kharoshthi writing. Oblong tablets of considerable length and irregular shape are particularly frequent among these finds, and, so far as legible, usually exhibit matter in narrow, closely-written columns. The list of names and items of accounts which seem to be contained in them, again point to records kept in some office. The extent of the clerical labour once carried on here could be measured by the size of these tablets, one piece, unfortunately entirely bleached, attaining the inconvenient dimensions of 7 feet 6 inches in length, with a width of 4½ inches.

The slight depth of the sand covering this area permitted me to clear in the course of two days a considerable number of small ruined houses. They served to acquaint me with the typical arrangement of the rooms, cattle-sheds, etc., composing these homesteads, though, owing to the far-advanced decay, finds of interest were scarce. Among these I may mention an ancient ice-pit in the outhouse of a modest dwelling-place on the western edge of the area. Here in a small room my labourers came upon two unhewn trunks of Toghrak, lying close together and parallel. Abdullah, my guide from Keriya, at once suggested that we had found a 'Muz-khana,' or ice store-room, trunks being used now in exactly the same way to keep the ice from touching the ground. The thick bed of ancient poplar leaves, which were soon brought to light in the space of about two feet between the trunks, proved the correctness of Abdullah's conjecture, heaps of such leaves being still the usual covering for the ice which well-to-do villagers store for use in the summer season.

On the 30th of January my Darogha returned safely from his reconnaissance into the desert. For about three marches westwards he had found the sands practicable, and the supply of fuel yielded by occasional patches of tamarisk and Kumush growth sufficient. This showed that the short route to the Keriya River could eventually be taken by us, even if the snow which Ibrahim Akhun reported to be about a span deep there,

REMAINS OF ANCIENT HOUSES, AT GROUP OF RUINS N. II.

should have completely melted. There were already signs that the rigour of the desert winter could not be depended upon to help us for many weeks longer. The minimum temperature on the 30th of January was still –4° Fahr., but at midday the thermometer rose to 42° Fahr. in the shade. I had now got so accustomed to the cold as to find 26° Fahr. quite a comfortable temperature for writing, and while walking that day to some ruins yet to be explored, I felt it almost too warm. The thought of what life in the desert would be like after March had once passed was in itself a sufficient inducement to hurry on work.

The object of my next excavations was the remains of two large dwelling-houses which I had passed on my first arrival, about two miles to the south of the Stupa. Their position on isolated terrace-like banks of loess, due to erosion of the neighbouring soil, and the rows of fallen poplars of great size marking ancient gardens and avenues close by, made these ruins particularly prominent. The one to the east, N. III. (see photograph, p. 334), which, judging from the size and number of the apartments, must have been the residence of a man of position, was far deeper in the sand than any of the buildings previously examined, and consequently proved much better preserved. Its excavation occupied my band of labourers for fully four days, though their numbers had by this time been strengthened by every able-bodied man from Imam Jafar Sadik, a reinforcement which I summoned in haste as soon as the first inspection had shown me the great extent and importance of the site.

The most striking feature of this building was the large central apartment, which measured 40 by 26 feet, and probably served as a kind of reception-hall. Four massive beams of poplar wood, full 40 feet long, once supported the roof. The corbel, which was fixed beneath the two central beams, was also a fine piece of wood, nearly 8 feet long and 10 inches in thickness, showing bold mouldings. The post, which once carried this corbel, had fallen long ago; yet when the excavation began the beams were still in place, resting on the deep sand that had meanwhile filled the hall. As the work of clearing proceeded, the stuccoed walls revealed remains of a carefully executed decoration in fresco. This proved to consist of horizontal bands, painted in dark red and black, on a plaster ground of creamy white. The broad upper band contained a scroll ornament of large lotus flowers; below it extended a narrow band in black with leaves like those of a fern painted in white, and from this again descended elegant festoons of budding lotuses.

To prop up the walls and prevent their falling in during

PORTION OF ANCIENT DWELLING-HOUSE (N. III), BEFORE EXCAVATION.

excavation was no easy task. The photograph on p. 355 shows part of the north wall with a side door leading from the hall into a sort of ante-room. On the extreme left of the photograph is seen the top of the single wooden leaf which once closed another small door connecting the ante-room with an apartment westwards. This leaf was found in perfect preservation and still on its hinges, leaning against the wall, just as when it had been last opened.

Another curious memento of life long departed were the

remains of embers I found on the small raised platform of plaster occupying the floor in the centre of the hall, and evidently once serving for the reception of an open fire.

The hall had been completely cleared by the last dwellers or visitors of any articles it may have contained. But the smaller rooms adjoining it to the north furnished a very interesting series of relics, illustrating the manufactures and arts of the period. The specimens of textile industry were particularly numerous. Besides pieces of felt and coloured cotton cloth, not unlike the modern 'Kham' of the country, there turned up portions of a delicately worked rug, resembling in make an Indian 'Durrie,' and showing elaborate geometrical patterns and harmoniously blended colours which only wanted a little brushing to reappear in their original brilliancy. The coloured reproduction of part of this rug, given in a plate of my "Preliminary Report," will show the interest which these finds possess for the history of Central-Asian handicrafts. Small pieces of carved ivory, including an ivory-tipped bâton, attested the skill of the ancient turner.

A number of small wooden tablets with Kharoshthi writing, wedge-shaped, or else having the appearance of labels, turned up in the refuse that covered the floor of an outer apartment, and what seems to have been once the kitchen. In the kitchen there was, just as in modern Turkestan houses, a mud platform to hold the water-jars and other stores, also a large wooden trough. More curious were the finds in a small closet-like apartment, which evidently served as a storage room. There I found a bow of tamarisk wood, still crisp and capable of use; carefully turned shafts of light poplar wood, broken, yet still over six feet long, which must have once served for spears; a section of a shield of wood (willow) about 3 feet 6 inches high; spindles and other small household implements, all of wood, including a stout walking-stick of apple-wood that I found to come in very handy for use.

Among the articles of ornamental wood-carving found in the building none can compare in point of artistic interest with the ancient chair reproduced on p. 356. Its pieces, though disjointed, lay close together on the floor of one of the outer rooms and

NORTH WALL OF CENTRAL HALL OF ANCIENT DWELLING-HOUSE (N. III.), DURING EXCAVATION.

23*

could easily be fitted together. The excellent preservation of the elaborate carvings was all the more surprising as progressive erosions had left scarcely any of the sand which no doubt previously covered and protected them. The decorative motives shown in these carvings are familiar to us from relievo sculpture

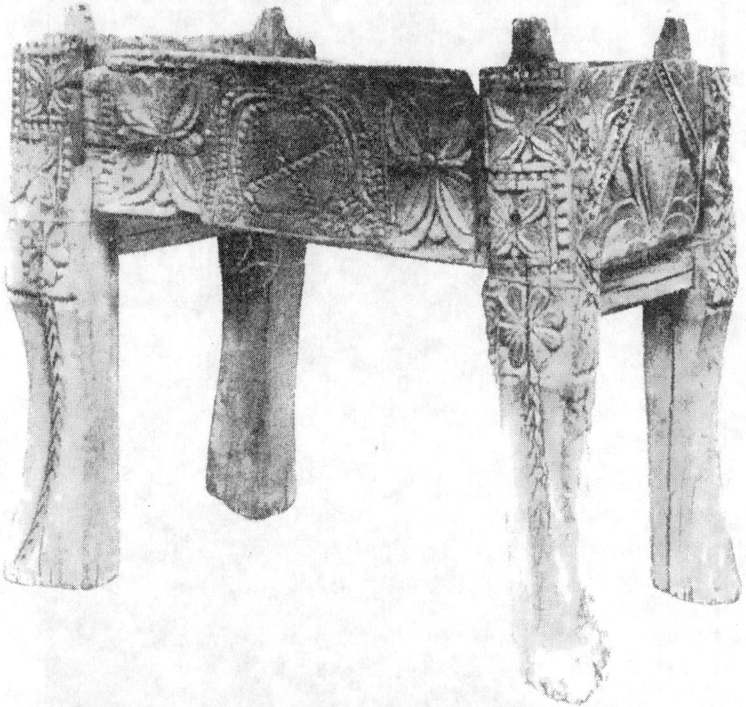

ANCIENT WOODEN CHAIR FROM RUINED DWELLING-HOUSE (N. III.).
(Scale one-eighth.)

that once adorned the Buddhist monasteries of Yusufzai and Swat, the ancient Gandhara. I was glad to note at the time how closely the date thus indicated agreed with the chronological evidence deducible from the Kharoshthi writing of the tablets. My men were duly impressed by the fine appearance of this ancient piece of art furniture when it was set up before their wondering eyes.

The large size of the house, which covered an area nearly 100 feet long by 80 in width, also helped to suggest that this was the residence of a man of means, and possibly in authority. So my labourers promptly christened the place as the 'Yamen.' It is true they did not find in it the hoped-for horseshoes of silver, but several Chinese copper coins were picked up from the sand in its immediate vicinity. The fact that these coins, as well as all subsequent numismatic finds on the site, belonged to issues of the second Han dynasty, greatly strengthened my reliance on the palæographic evidence of the tablets.

Equally curious results rewarded the clearing of another large dwelling-house, N. IV., some three hundred yards to the south-west, which occupied us during the 4th and 5th of February. The plan of this house and of the garden adjoining it, reproduced on p. 360, will help to illustrate the internal arrangement of these ancient residences. It strangely recalled the disposition of rooms, etc., I had observed in modern Khotan dwelling places of some pretensions. In a room, which seems to have served as an office, there were found, besides a number of inscribed tablets of varying shape, apparently orders and memoranda, several tablets that had never been used, blank stationery left behind by the last occupants; also writing pens of tamarisk wood; eating-sticks of wood like those still used by the Chinese; and a large sleeping-mat or hammock made of tamarisk rushes. In the long, narrow passage that traverses this house I came upon the well-preserved upper part of a guitar, resembling the 'Rabab still in popular use throughout Turkestan, and retaining bits of the ancient string, as well as upon more samples of carpet materials.

But even more interesting were the remains of an elaborately decorated wooden arm-chair which were also successively recovered there. The legs represent standing lions, in evident imitation of the Indian 'Simhasana' ("lion-seat"), and retain in part their original colouring in red and black. The arm-rests are formed by a pair of well-carved monsters, male and female. The heads and busts are shown as human, the parts from the waist downwards apparently birdlike, while the legs are those of a horse with strongly-marked hoofs. The terra-

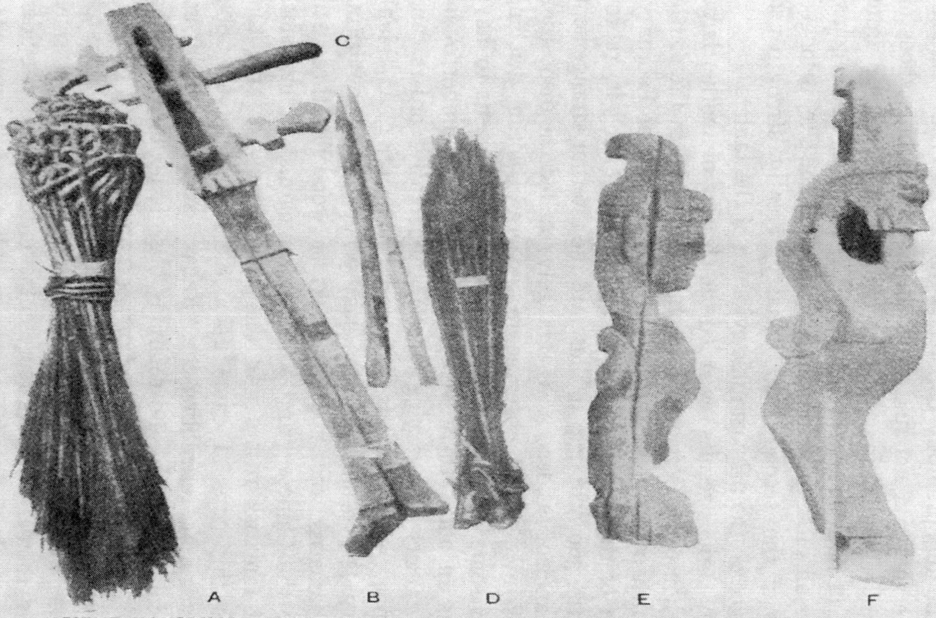

ANCIENT HOUSEHOLD IMPLEMENTS, ETC., MAINLY FROM RUINED DWELLING N. IV.

A *Ancient broom (from Dandan-Uiliq shrine).* B *Rabab or guitar.* C *Writing-pens of tamarisk wood.* D *Broom.* E *Arm-rest, and* F *leg of ancient arm-chair.*

(Scale of A, B, C, D, one-fourth; of E, F, one-sixth.)

cotta ground colour is well preserved, and over it appear traces of black and dark blue paint marking the plumage and hoofs. Have we to recognise in these strange creatures a reminiscence of the Kimnaras of Indian mythology, or of a still more distant hybrid, the Centaurs of Greece?

A very curious feature of this ruin was the clearness with which the arrangement of the adjoining garden could be traced. The trunks of the poplars, which still rise 8 to 10 feet from the original surface, and are thus clearly visible above the drift-sand, are grouped in the same little squares and enclosing rectangular avenues which can be seen in every well-kept 'Bostan' from Kashgar to Keriya. The trees were planted at regular distances, which are marked on my plan. The hedgerow or rush fence enclosing the garden was also mostly intact, though covered in parts by the sand. It was with a strange feeling, obliterating almost the sense of time, that I walked between two parallel fences of rushes that still form a little country lane just as over 1,600 years ago. The wind had swept the ground between them clear at various places, thus displaying the pottery fragments, bits of charcoal, and decayed foliage on which the last inhabitants must have trodden. Searching at the bottom of the fences my antique walking-stick disclosed the rustling dead leaves of poplar and fruit trees, perhaps the same that still raised their shrivelled trunks in scattered groups near by. Among these withered relics of ancient orchards, which I observed here as at some other points of the site, my diggers had no difficulty in distinguishing various fruit-trees, such as the peach, plum, apricot, mulberry, the wood of which they knew from their own homes.

There might have been during those days a temptation for me to forget altogether my living surroundings through the antiquarian fascination of the dead past. It was, perhaps, in order to provide against any such eventuality that my faithful myrmidons from Kashgar took the opportunity to attract my attention to their several human failings and consequent mutual bickerings. The incidents which arose thereby have their humorous interest when looked back upon; but at the time, I must own, I should have gladly done without them.

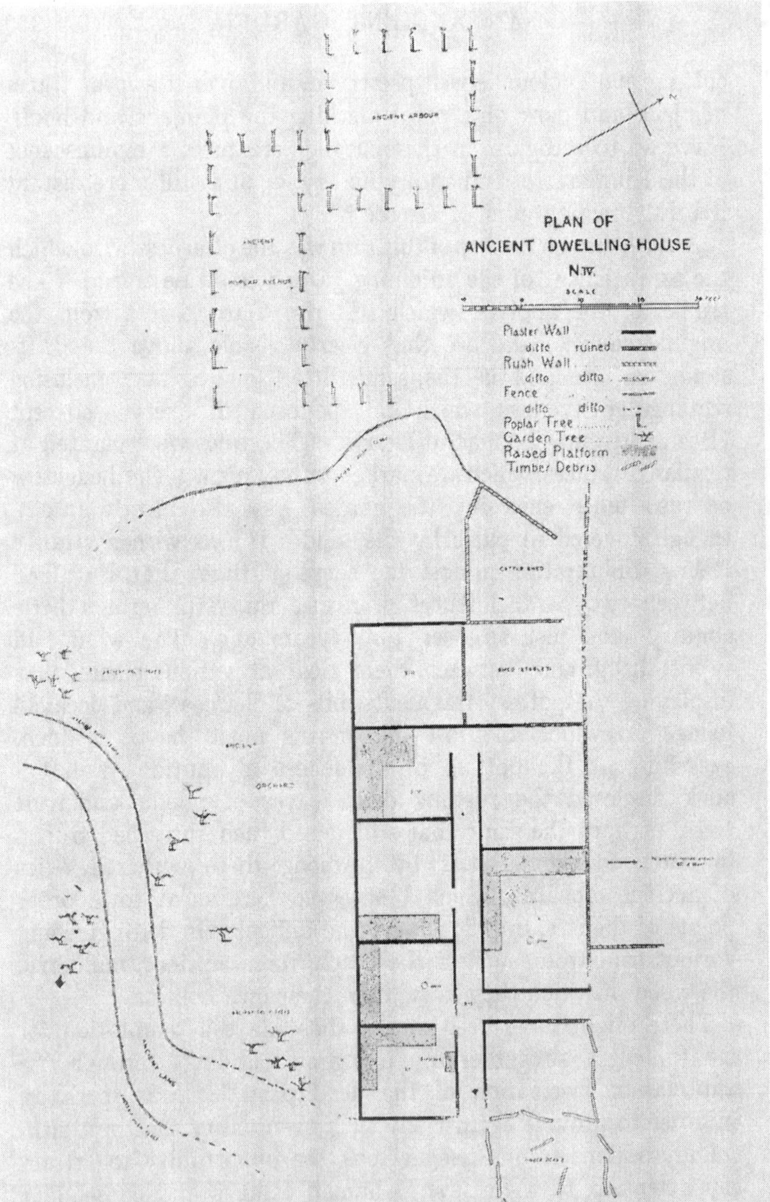
PLAN OF
ANCIENT DWELLING HOUSE
N.IV.
SCALE
Plaster Wall
ditto ruined
Rush Wall
ditto ditto
Fence
ditto ditto
Poplar Tree
Garden Tree
Raised Platform
Timber Debris
ANCIENT ARBOUR
ANCIENT
POPLAR AVENUE
CATTLE SHED
ANCIENT
ORCHARD
ANCIENT LANE
M.A.STEIN. FECIT.
F.H.ANDREWS. DEL.

It was with Niaz Akhun, my Chinese interpreter, that these troubles began. Knowing how little disposed he was to make himself useful during work in the desert, or to bear patiently with its inherent hardships, I had left him behind in charge of the ponies which were to await our return at Nurullah's, the shepherd's, huts beyond Imam Jafar Sadik. There were no Chinese there to gamble with, and, in fact, scarcely any people to fight or to bully. So I thought my troublesome follower fairly out of the reach of mischief. Reports, however, which began to arrive with the convoys bringing ice, and with the men ordered up from the shrine as reinforcements, soon convinced me that I had underrated Niaz Akhun's truculent propensities.

That he was supplementing the ample rations left for him by requisitions of whatever the resources of the Sheikhs of the shrine could supply in the way of eatables would scarcely have brought matters to a crisis. But his amorous demands on the attentions of the women-folk living at the Mazar grew in excess of what even the hospitality and easy morals of these parts would tolerate. The result was the despatch to me in the desert of a pitiful petition praying for the holy settlement to be speedily relieved of the infliction represented by my semi-Chinese attendant. There was only too good reason to believe in the substantial truth of the complaints, and as the only safe course was to keep Niaz Akhun under my own eye, I sent peremptory orders for him to give over charge of the animals to another of my men, and to join camp at once. It was a truly comic sight when the sinner arrived, weary with the two days' tramp through the sand to which he was little accustomed, yet in his genuine dejection acting with consummate skill the part of injured innocence. According to his own story, he was the victim of a wicked conspiracy between some of his enemies among my own men and the shameless mendicants at the shrine, etc. In order to make his appeal for justice still more impressive he had donned over his comfortable coat white rags to indicate mourning. He pretended to have just received news of the death of his mother, far away at Aksu, but he failed to explain how the sad intelligence could have arrived so opportunely. At first he offered to commit suicide in order to clear his reputation, and to rid me of further trouble on his account. Gradually, however, he settled down to a more resigned behaviour, and I began to hope that he would submit with good grace to the privations of desert life, the worst punishment I could inflict, when on the next day the storm broke.

It pleased Niaz Akhun to attribute his ignominious recall from the fleshpots of the Mazar to the enmity of Hassan Akhun, one of my young camel-men. So he promptly denounced the latter to me as having secreted an antique gold ring which he had picked up near one of the ruined houses, against my standing order that all chance finds were to be reported, thus giving me an opportunity to acquire them for an adequate compensation. When Hassan Akhun arrived with the next ice-transport, he readily delivered the ring, which proved to be of brass, and took the reward I offered for it. But the incident stirred up still more the spite felt by my Muhammadan followers against Niaz Akhun, so that on returning to camp in the evening he was attacked in open fight by the pugnacious little camel-man. The encounter might have been as amusing to watch as that other heroic fight described by Horace in his journey to Brundisium, could I only have trusted the temper and balance of mind of my Chinese interpreter. Half-maddened by his disgrace and the taunts of the other men, he seemed quite prepared to give a tragic turn to the affair by the use of his knife, when I managed to separate the combatants not without vigorous application of the antique walking-stick I happened to have in hand. Just as I had succeeded in this, with the help of Ram Singh, Sadak Akhun, the cook, came rushing up in wild excitement, brandishing the sword which he prided himself upon carrying about as an old 'Dakchi' of the British Agency at Kashgar. I thought at the time that he might have run "amuck"; for Sadak Akhun's conduct had grown very queer for weeks past under the baneful influence of the 'Charas' drug to which he was addicted, and of which he took increasing quantities as the hardships of our winter campaign continued. Luckily his brain had not given way, as his frantic behaviour might have made one believe. So while violently protesting his wish to avenge his misery as well as Islam (!) on the renegade Niaz, he at last allowed himself to be disarmed and led away. The interval during which my attention had been diverted by Sadak Akhun's appearance on the scene, was promptly utilised by Niaz for a dramatic attempt at suicide. With astonishing rapidity he had loosened his waistband, and drawing it tightly round and round his neck, was doing his best to strangle himself in a fit of frenzied energy. His face was getting to bear a strange look by the time we succeeded in loosening the convulsive grip of his hands, and the utter exhaustion which then overcame him convinced me that it was not a mere exhibition of mimic power to which he had treated us.

It was evident that, to prevent fresh affrays with possibly more serious results, Niaz had to be kept away from the rest of my Muhammadans. So I was glad that my two Hindu followers, Ram Singh and Jasvant Singh, were ready to share their camp-fire with him and in a general way to keep an eye on him. Hassan Akhun, for his unwarranted attack, was sentenced to a number of stripes, which Ibrahim, my excellent Darogha from Keriya, administered next morning with an arm practised in such functions and which had a very salutary effect upon the young offender. There remained only Sadak Akhun to worry me by mad fits of despondency and sneaking attempts at insubordination. To his repeated demands for discharge I could not possibly consent; for like the rest of my men he had been expressly engaged for the whole of the journey, and I was not prepared, if I could help it, to go without European food which he alone in camp knew how to cook. To the rest of my men he would wildly talk of running away at night; but the fear of losing his way and still more the knowledge that I could easily get him stopped at Keriya or Khotan and detained in the Amban's Yamen until my return, sufficed to prevent the execution of such foolish plans. All the same I thought I had reason to compliment myself on successful management when I brought Sadak Akhun in the end safely back to Kashgar. Restored to the pleasures of Bazar life, with substantial accumulations of pay to spend upon his elegant person, he was then wont to attribute the troubles he had caused, not to his own innate fickleness and the effects of the 'Charas' habit, but to the 'Jinns' or evil spirits of the sand-buried sites who had gained possession of his mind during the long nights in the desert. May he keep clear of them thereafter!

CLAY IMPRESSIONS OF CLASSICAL SEALS, FROM KHAROSHTHI TABLETS.

CHAPTER XXV.

DISCOVERIES IN AN ANTIQUE RUBBISH HEAP.

THE excavations previously described plainly showed me that the ancient houses of this site had been cleared by their last inhabitants, or soon after their departure, of everything possessing intrinsic value. It was evident that I must base my hopes for further archæological finds mainly on any rubbish remains which might have been left behind. These hopes received gratifying confirmation in the course of a reconnaissance to ruins reported north of my camp. I sighted on that occasion over half-a-dozen groups of old structures scattered over an area of about three and a half miles from south to north and more than two miles across. In one ruin, greatly decayed and in no way attracting special attention, I had come upon a number of bleached tablets lying exposed, and a little digging had within half-an-hour brought to light nearly thirty inscribed pieces. Among them there were two novelties which, though small in size, could not fail to arouse my utmost interest. One was a fragment of a narrow piece of wood showing Chinese characters; the other a small strip of well-prepared leather, also fragmentary, with a line of Kharoshthi characters recording a date. These finds clearly betokened a rich deposit, and as the ruin in question lay nearly two miles to the north, I decided to move my camp there.

While my men were busy on the morning of February 6th effecting the shift, I found time to make a close examination of the little Stupa below which my camp had stood. At first sight it appeared that the small hemispherical dome about seven feet high rose on a single base 13 feet 6 inches square and 6 feet

RUINED STUPA, AT ANCIENT SITE BEYOND IMAM JAFAR SADIK.

6 inches high. But observations as to the original ground level made me suspect that the structure now visible above the sand on the southern slope of a large tamarisk-covered sand-cone did not represent the whole of the Stupa. And in fact, on clearing the sand heaped up on the east face by the prevailing winds, I came upon a second base below. It was also square, projecting on each side 3 feet beyond the upper base and 6 feet high. The whole of the Stupa thus rose to a height of about 20 feet. I

was much interested to note how closely the arrangement and proportions of the dome and its bases agreed with that observed in the ruined Stupas of Khanui, Moji, and Pialma. The size of the bricks too (circ. 22 by 17 by 4 inches) proved nearly the same as in those structures. Nor was the shaft wanting in the centre of the Stupa dome. It was only one foot square and had been laid open from the west by a cutting into the brickwork. That treasure-seekers had been at work was shown also by two large holes excavated in the upper base. What relic deposit there once was in this modest "memorial tower," as Hiuen-Tsiang would have called it, must have been abstracted long ago.

Promising as the finds were which my previous "prospecting" had yielded, I little anticipated how extraordinarily rich a mine of ancient records I had struck in the ruin I proceeded to excavate. On the surface there was nothing to suggest the wealth of relics contained within the half-broken walls of the room, 23 by 18 feet large, which once formed the western end of a modest dwelling-place. But when systematic excavation, begun at the north-western corner of the room, revealed layer upon layer of wooden tablets mixed up with refuse of all sorts, the truth soon dawned upon me. I had struck an ancient rubbish heap formed by the accumulations of many years, and containing also what, with an anachronism, we may fitly call the "waste-paper" deposits of that early time.

It was not sand from which I extracted tablet after tablet, but a consolidated mass of refuse lying fully four feet above the original floor, as seen in the photograph reproduced p. 369. All the documents on wood, of which I recovered in the end more than two hundred, were found scattered among layers of broken pottery, straw, rags of felt and various woven fabrics, pieces of leather, and other rubbish. It was evident that the consistency which these varied remains had acquired in the course of centuries had more than anything else helped to protect them against the erosive action of the winds, from which the other parts of this ruin had suffered considerably. Thus it is mainly to the unsavoury associations of the dustbin that we must ascribe the remarkable state of preservation shown by the great mass of these precious records.

I had ample occasion to console myself with this thought while engaged in the laborious task of clearing this room (N. xv.). As soon as I had realised the peculiar character of its deposits it became a matter of importance to keep accurate record of the relative position in which each object turned up. This would thereafter help to ascertain the chronological order, and possibly the internal connection of the various documents. Accordingly,

RUINED DWELLING-PLACE, CONTAINING ANCIENT RUBBISH HEAP (N. XV.), SEEN FROM SOUTH-EAST.

every inscribed piece had to be carefully tabulated before it was removed and cleaned, no easy task with fingers half benumbed by cold and in the dust which a fresh north-east breeze raised from the dug-up refuse heap. For three long working days I had to inhale its odours, still pungent after so many centuries, and to swallow in liberal doses antique microbes luckily now dead. But in the full enjoyment of my great antiquarian haul I did not think of these little discomforts.

The diversity in form and material of the documents which

ANCIENT RUBBISH HEAP (N. XV.), IN COURSE OF EXCAVATION.

came to light from amidst all this ancient litter and dirt, was not less remarkable than their good preservation. The first few hours' work was rewarded by the discovery of complete Kharoshthi documents on leather. The oblong sheets of carefully prepared smooth sheepskin, of which altogether two dozen came to light here, showed different sizes, up to fifteen inches in

A

B

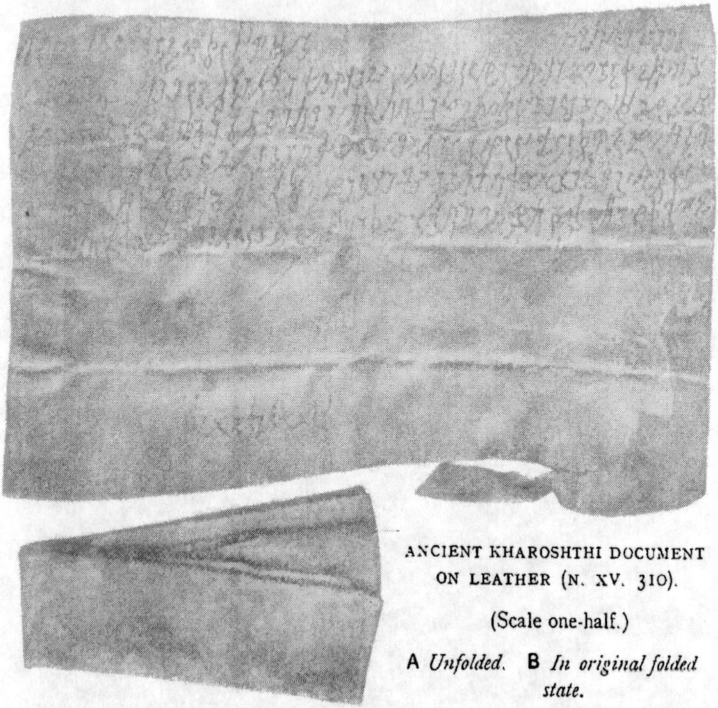

ANCIENT KHAROSHTHI DOCUMENT ON LEATHER (N. XV. 310).

(Scale one-half.)

A *Unfolded.* B *In original folded state.*

length. They were invariably found folded up into neat little rolls, but could be opened out in most cases without serious difficulty. The Kharoshthi text, which covers the inner surface, is usually written in a neat clerical hand, and its black ink has retained a remarkable freshness. At the head of each document I was now able to read with certainty the introductory formula previously seen less clearly on many of the wedge-shaped tablets: *Mahanuava maharaya lihati*, "His Highness the

Mahārāja orders in writing." There could be no further doubt that these were official documents. Most of them, I could see, were dated, but only by month and day, while the single lines on the otherwise blank reverses were manifestly addresses. In them I thought I could recognise two personal names or titles appearing again and again. But who were the recipients of these and so many other documents, the administrative officers or simply the clerks of this ancient settlement?

Quite apart from their contents, these documents have a special interest as the first specimens as yet discovered of leather used for writing purposes among a population of Indian language and culture. Whatever the religious objections may have been, it is evident that in practice they had no more weight with the pious Buddhists of this region than with the orthodox Brahmans of Kashmir, who for centuries back have used leather bindings for their cherished Sanskrit codices. The finish given to the leather of those ancient documents indicates extensive practice in the preparation of the material. Small pieces of blank leather of this kind, unmistakably shreds left after the cutting of full-sized sheets and subsequently swept out of the office room, turned up plentifully among the rubbish. The discovery of an ancient pen made of tamarisk wood (see p. 346), in the same refuse heap, helps us still better to realise the conditions of clerical work in that period. The bone knob of the pen had probably served as a burnisher.

But interesting as these details were, they could not compare in importance with the information yielded by the far more numerous kinds of Kharoshthi tablets. Many of those unearthed from N. xv. were in excellent preservation and retained intact the original clay seals and strings with which they were fastened. There could be no doubt as to wood having been the general writing material, and it was hence particularly fortunate that I was thus enabled definitely to ascertain all technicalities connected with its use. The wedge-shaped tablets, which seem to have been in favour for short communications, invariably consisted of pairs of pieces fitted exactly to match each other in size, as seen in the specimen reproduced on p. 372. One end of the double tablet thus formed was cut off square; the other runs out

24*

into a point, near which a string-hole is drilled through both pieces. The text occupies the smooth obverse of the under-tablet and is protected by the upper or covering tablet, which rests on it and serves as a kind of envelope. If the length of the communication required it, the writing was continued on

KHAROSHTHI DOCUMENT ON DOUBLE WOODEN TABLET (N. XV. 137).
(Scale one-third.)

A *Obverse of covering tablet with seal.* B *Reverse of under-tablet.* C *Obverse of under-tablet.*

the reverse of the covering tablet. The wood of the latter shows greater thickness towards the square end, and in this raised portion of the outside surface a square socket was neatly cut, intended for the reception of a clay seal. A string of hemp was passed in a cleverly devised fashion through the string-hole and then drawn tightly over both tablets near the square or right end. Grooves communicating with the seal socket held the string in regular cross-folds. The socket was then filled with clay, covering these folds of the string. When once the seal of the sender had been impressed into the clay, it became impossible to separate the pair of tablets without either breaking the seal impression or cutting the string.

The ingenious arrangement here briefly described, which the accompanying diagrams of Mr. F. H. Andrews' drawing will help

Diagram of wedge-shaped double tablet, showing obverse of covering tablet, with string-hole (A) *and string fastened in seal socket* (B).

Diagram of wedge-shaped double tablet, showing reverse of under-tablet, with string-hole (A) *and folds of string held by grooves* (B).

to illustrate, rendered the communication written on the inner sides of the two tablets absolutely safe against unauthorised inspection. If the recipient desired to preserve the sealing and also retain a convenient fastening for the two tablets after having acquainted himself with the contents—an obvious advantage when such letters had to be kept for record—he had only to cut the string near the string-hole. The under-tablet could then easily be slid out from the folds of string running beneath the seal, and after being read be passed back again into its original position, just as we can do this now, after so many centuries, in the case of the double tablet reproduced on p. 372. Usually to the right of the seal on the obverse of the covering tablet there appears the name of the addressee, while entries in a different hand, traceable in some instances on the reverse of the under-tablet, may possibly represent "docket" notes by the official who received the communication.

Scarcely less ingenious is the method of fastening which the

A

Covering tablet of oblong Kharoshthi document (N. xv. 167), showing double seal.

(Scale one-half.)

B

Detached seal-socket (N. xv. 133.)

(Scale one-half.)

C

Covering tablet of Kharoshthi document (N. xv. 330) showing seal with Eros.

(Scale one-half.)

finds of N. xv. prove to have been used for the oblong tablets. From a number of double tablets of that shape which I recovered here practically intact, it became clear that the under-tablet was in this case provided with a raised rim on either of the shorter sides. Between these rims fitted exactly a covering tablet, the obverse of which, in its raised centre, had a square or oblong socket for the reception of a clay seal. Here, too, a string passed transversely over both tablets and secured below the seal, effectually prevented any unauthorised opening and reading of

A

B

C

KHAROSHTHI DOCUMENT ON DOUBLE OBLONG TABLET (N. XV. 166).

(Scale two-thirds.)

A *Double tablet unopened.* B *Reverse of covering tablet.* C *Obverse of under-tablet.*

the document written on the inner sides of the two tablets. The accompanying plate (p. 375) shows such a double tablet which was found with the string broken but otherwise intact, both before and after its opening. "Envelopes" of oblong double tablets, the corresponding under-tablets of which have not been found or identified, are seen on p. 374. There also a wooden seal-socket found detached, with its clay seal-impression still intact, has been reproduced.

I cannot attempt, from want of space and of adequate illustrations, even briefly to indicate here all the curious discoveries made in connection with this ancient stationery in wood. But some notice must be accorded to that remarkable series of clay

SEAL-IMPRESSIONS IN CLAY FROM KHAROSHTHI TABLETS.

seal-impressions which were found still intact on a number of tablets and some of which can be presented here from well-executed drawings of my friend Mr. F. H. Andrews (see above and p. 365). From an historical point of view they claim exceptional interest, for they have furnished convincing evidence of the way in which the influence of classical Western art asserted itself even in distant Khotan. It was a delightful surprise when, on cleaning the first intact seal impression that turned, up I recognised in it the figure of Pallas Athene, with ægis and thunder-bolt, treated in an archaic fashion. This particular seal (seen, though not so distinctly as elsewhere, on the covering tablet reproduced on p. 365) was found thereafter to recur frequently, and probably belonged to an official who was directly connected with the administration of the ancient settlement.

Another and larger seal (seen in the reproduction of the covering tablet C, p. 374, also in the headpiece of this chapter) shows a well-modelled naked figure of pure classical outline, perhaps a seated Eros. Another Athene, a standing Eros, and probably Heracles, are also to be found among the Greek deities represented. On other seals, again, there appear portrait heads of men and women showing classical modelling, though barbarian features, etc.

Just as in the case of the engraved stones of similar make found in the débris layers of Yotkan, it is impossible to make sure which of these seals were actually engraved in Khotan territory and which were imported from the West or other parts of Asia reached by classical art. But though we have yet to learn the exact functions or place of residence of those who once used the seals, there can be no reasonable doubt that the documents bearing their impressions originated in the vicinity of the ancient site or at least within the borders of the Khotan kingdom. As the date, too, of the documents can, as we shall see, be fixed with fair accuracy, these seal-impressions are to us far more valuable than if chance had preserved the original seals. The vista thus opened out to us is one of far-reaching historical interest. We already knew that classical art had established itself in Bactria and on the north-west frontier of India. But there was little to prepare us for such tangible proofs of the fact that it had penetrated so much further to the east, half-way between Western Europe and Peking. As if to symbolise this strange mixture of influences from the Far West and the Far East, the covering tablet reproduced in Fig. A, p. 374, presents to us a seal with Chinese lapidary characters in juxtaposition with one showing a portrait head unmistakably cut after Western models.

REMAINS OF ANCIENT TREES NEAR SAND-BURIED DWELLING-PLACE (N. VIII.).

CHAPTER XXVI.

DECIPHERMENT OF ANCIENT DOCUMENTS ON WOOD AND LEATHER.

THE historical importance attaching to the records themselves was ever vividly before my mind, and in each fresh Kharoshthi document which this precious refuse-heap continued to yield up I had reason to welcome additional help towards the study of both script and contents. But from the first I recognised that the decipherment of this wealth of materials would require much time and patient labour. The many exacting tasks which have claimed my attention since my return have left me no leisure to supplement the cursory examination I was able to make at the time of discovery and in the rare moments of rest on my subsequent travels. Fortunately, however, my friend Mr. E. J. Rapson, of the British Museum, to whose care I had for a time to entrust the whole of my antiquarian collections, readily agreed to charge himself with the study of all epigraphical finds in Kharoshthi. The painstaking researches concerning them which he has carried on for the past year with scholarly zeal and acumen are not likely to be concluded for a long time. But they have advanced sufficiently to make it possible for me, with his permission, to indicate in broad outlines certain main results and some of the more curious details.

It is a source of gratification to me that the conclusions I first arrived at regarding the language and general character of these documents have been fully confirmed by Mr. Rapson's labours. From his exact analysis of a considerable number of Kharoshthi documents on wood and leather, it can now be asserted with certainty that the language is an early Indian Prakrit, possessing a large admixture of Sanskrit terms. The latter are particularly prevalent in the introductory and other formal parts of the letters and reports, that is, exactly where the epistolary custom of modern Indian vernaculars has large recourse to phrases of the classical language. As regards the great mass of the documents there can be no doubt that they contain, as surmised by me from the first, official correspondence of various kinds. Reports and orders to local officials on matters of administration and police, complaints, summonses, safe-conducts, and similar communications seem to constitute the bulk of the documents. Others, again, may prove to be records of payments or requisitions, agreements, bonds, and the like. Accounts, lists of labourers. etc., are probably the contents of the mass of miscellaneous "papers" written on single tablets of irregular shapes and usually in columns ending with numerical signs.

Exceptionally great as are the difficulties with which the work of detailed decipherment has to contend, on account of the very cursive character of the Kharoshthi script and the puzzling phonetic peculiarities of the Prakrit dialect employed, we already obtain many interesting glimpses from the passages which can be definitely interpreted. The titles given to the ruler in whose name orders are issued, and with reference to whose reign the more elaborate documents are dated ('Maharaja,' 'devaputra,' *i.e.*, "son of the gods," etc.), are purely Indian. They agree strikingly with the official nomenclature observed under the Kushana or Indo-Scythian princes who ruled the extreme North-West of India and Afghanistan during the first centuries of our era. The majority of the persons to or by whom documents are despatched bear purely Indian names, among them appearing a Kushana-sena, as if to emphasise some connection with Indo-Scythian dominion far away to the South-West.

In strange contrast to the names, some of the titles borne by these officials are distinctly non-Indian (Chodbo, Shodhoga, Kala, etc.). But we meet also with official designations familiar from ancient Indian usage ('rajadvara-purasthita,' "president of the royal court of justice;" 'dibira,' "clerk," etc.). Letter-carriers, 'lekhaharaka,' are frequently referred to by their Sanskrit designation. The often recurring introductory formulas, with their stereotyped greetings, honorific addresses ('priyadarshana;' 'devamanushya - sampujita,' 'priyadeva-manushya,' "dear to gods and men," etc.), and polite enquiries after the health and spiritual welfare of the addressees, possess a distinct flavour of that quaint phraseology to which the Sanskrit correspondence of my Kashmirian Pandit friends has accustomed me. But in other documents we find a style far less ornate, in fact quite peremptory, as, *e.g.*, in some office "memos" ordering the submission of affidavits ('savatha') according to a specified list; the production of certain witnesses; arrests of individuals, etc.

The particular interest attaching to some petty records is well illustrated by an oblong tablet, dated in the ninth year of King Jitroghavarshman, which relates a transaction by a certain Buddhagosha, slave of the Sramana or Buddhist monk Anandasena, concerning some household goods, pawned perhaps or taken over on mortgage. The articles are enumerated in detail and their value indicated in a currency that we may yet succeed in determining. It is curious to find that this list, besides sheep, vessels, wool-weaving appliances and some other implements, enumerates also 'Namadis.' We may well recognise here the earliest mention of the felt-rugs or 'Numdahs' so familiar to Anglo-Indian use, which to this day form a special product of Khotan home industry and of which large consign-

ANCIENT KHAROSHTHI DOCUMENT ON LEATHER (N. XV. 305).

(Scale two-thirds.)

ments are annually exported to Ladak and Kashmir. In another document we read that all the 'Shodhogas' and 'Drangadharas,' evidently local officials, of the district are complaining of the want of water; and many of the tablets seem to have reference to disputes about water used for irrigation.

The frequent references in the tablets to 'Khotāna' and its officials shows us not only how ancient the name of Khotan is in its present phonetic form, but also that the district containing this settlement was part of the kingdom of Khotan. It is of interest that, alternating with that old popular name, we also find the duplicate form Kustana[ka] known to us from Hiuen-Tsiang's records. It represents, in all probability, a learned adaptation of the local name made for the sake of a Sanskrit etymology, which the pilgrim duly relates to us together with its attendant pious legend (' ku-stana ' meaning in Sanskrit " the breast of the Earth "). As if to remind us of the position which the ruined settlement must have occupied on the outskirts of the cultivated territory, we meet with frequent mention of " frontier-watch stations," designated by the Sanskrit term 'Dranga,' the true significance of which I first demonstrated years ago in Kashmir. That the faith of Buddha must have been widely spread among the people can be proved by a number of passages. Thus the Buddhas, Arhats and other sacred categories of the Buddhist Pantheon are distinctly enumerated in one tablet, while in another the addressee is with polite unction designated as a " Bodhisattva incarnate."

Not the least curious among the facts revealed by the work of decipherment is the discovery that there existed a recognised official terminology for the various classes of stationery represented. With unchanging regularity the wedge-shaped tablets are designated in their context as 'kila-mudra,' literally, " sealed wedges "; the 'Takhtas' with handles, apparently used for files, as 'stovana'; the oblong tablets with envelopes as 'lihitaka,' or " letter "; the documents on leather as 'anadilekha,' or " rescript," etc. It is evident that the clerks of those ancient offices had quite as keen a sense for bureaucratic distinctions of this kind as the Babu of modern

India, who would never make a mistake about supplying himself with "octavo note" for his D.O.'s, foolscap for his "fair dockets," or slips for his "office memos."

The necessarily brief notes here presented will suffice to show that these Kharoshthi documents are bound to bring back to light many aspects of life and culture in an early period of Central-Asian history which seemed almost entirely lost from our field of vision. The very nature of the contents and the complete absence of similar records of ancient date in India itself will render their full elucidation a slow and laborious task. But whatever revelations of interesting detail may be in store for us, one important historical fact already stands out clearly. The use of an Indian language in the vast majority of the documents, when considered together with their secular character, strikingly confirms the old local tradition recorded by Hiuen-Tsiang and also in old Tibetan texts, but hitherto scarcely credited, that the territory of Khotan was conquered and colonised about two centuries before our era by Indian immigrants from Takshasila, the Taxila of the Greeks, in the extreme North-West of the Punjab. It is certainly a significant fact that within India the Kharoshthi script used in our tablets was peculiar to the region of which Taxila was the historical centre. Neither the language nor the script presented by our documents can satisfactorily be accounted for by the spread of Buddhism alone, seeing that the latter, so far as our available evidence goes, brought to Central Asia only the use of Sanskrit as the ecclesiastical language, and the writing in Brahmi characters.

It seemed strange that these ruins far away in the barbarian North, overrun by what Hindu legends vaguely knew as the "great sand ocean," should have preserved for us in an Indian language records of everyday life older than any written documents (as distinguished from inscriptions) that have as yet come to light in India proper. But from the first there was ample evidence pointing to this chronological conclusion. The Kharoshthi writing of the tablets and leather documents, as already stated, showed close agreement in its palæographic features with the Kharoshthi inscriptions of the Kushana kings, whose rule in North-Western India undoubtedly falls mainly within the first two centuries of our era. This testimony was fully supported by the fortunate discovery in another ruin, N. VIII., of a unique tablet showing by the side of Kharoshthi some lines of Brahmi characters which clearly display the peculiarities of Brahmi writing of the Kushana period. The evidence of the coins was equally eloquent, since the numerous finds made during my stay included only Chinese copper pieces of the Later Han Dynasty, whose reign came to a close in A.D. 220. Finally there was in the use of wood as the only writing material, apart from leather, another proof of considerable antiquity. Though the use of paper is attested in Chinese Turkestan from at least the fourth century A.D. onwards, yet I failed to discover even the smallest scrap of paper among all the ruined houses and ancient rubbish heaps.

But with all these indications at hand, I felt particularly gratified when a recent discovery revealed the incontrovertible chronological evidence for which I had always longed. It came from one of the small pieces of wood inscribed with single lines of Chinese characters, of which the excavation of N. XV. ultimately yielded up over twoscore (for an illustration, see p. 296). Their preliminary examination at Kashgar and in the British Museum seemed to show that they contained brief orders, chiefly concerning the movements of specified individuals who were to be arrested or allowed to pass certain posts, etc. References to ancient localities such as Kucha, Shen-shen, Su-le or Kashgar, and the description of two persons as 'Ta-Yue-chi,' *i.e.*, Indo-Scythians, were points possessed of considerable historical interest. But it was only when Dr. S. W. Bushell, the distinguished Sinologist, had occasion to examine these Chinese tablets that one of them was discovered to be fully and precisely dated. The initial characters, as since verified also by my friend Professor Chavannes, plainly and unmistakably indicated the fifth year of the Tai-shih period of the Emperor Wu-ti, corresponding to 269 A.D.

Thus an exact date has at last been found which fixes the period when this remarkable collection of documents accumulated. A careful comparison of the years recorded in the

Kharoshthi tablets with the relative depths of the layers of rubbish in which they were found, may yet enable us to determine a number of important chronological details. A discussion of these would be out of place here, but I may call attention to a point of more general historical interest. We know from the Chinese Annals that the sovereignty of the Imperial Government over Eastern Turkestan, which during the Later Han Dynasty (24–220 A.D.) had vigorously asserted itself, was rudely shaken and for long periods practically effaced under the far less powerful dynasties which followed until the advent of the Tangs (A.D. 618). Of Wu-ti, however, the first Emperor of the Western Tsin Dynasty (A.D. 265–290), it is distinctly recorded that he succeeded in re-establishing Chinese authority in the westernmost provinces during his reign. The discoveries just described fully confirm this, as they show that Chinese posts then existed at this ancient settlement and probably also in other parts of Khotan territory. It is difficult to believe that the buildings of the ruined site continued to be inhabited for many years after Wu-ti's time. We are thus tempted to connect its abandonment with the great political and economic changes which undoubtedly accompanied the withdrawal of Chinese authority from these parts.

But, whatever the historical events may have been, there was ample evidence in this refuse-heap for the closeness of commercial relations with China. The pieces of remarkably well-finished lacquered ware and the bits of delicately woven silk fabrics, which lay embedded here with other litter, could only have come from the far eastern parts of the Empire. Whether the fragments of cut green and yellow glass, showing great transparency, and very different from the coarse material found at other sites, were also of foreign origin, has not as yet been definitely decided. But the discovery of a seal made of a piece of ancient Chinese porcelain plainly points to such imports.

Far more numerous, of course, were the objects for which local manufacture may be assumed. Mixed up with pottery fragments of all kinds there were rags of cotton and woollen materials, some showing delicate patterns and colours; eating-sticks and spindles of wood; remains of leather shoes and women's slippers coloured red just like the 'Charuks' still in favourite use; thick wooden horse-combs; spoons made of bone; and other articles of domestic use. The large number of sheep's knuckle-bones, often painted red or yellow, shows that gambling with this simple form of dice must have had its votaries in the household. Besides these there were found also an ivory die, of the peculiar elongated shape still popular in India, and marked with round punches on its four sides.

When the rubbish had all been cleared out, I found that one corner of the room was occupied by a circular mud-platform, about 5 feet in diameter and 3 feet high, with its centre hollowed out to a depth of 10 inches. The men from Niya at once expressed the belief that it was a trough, such as is used to this day in the houses of better-class people for keeping flowers fresh under water or wetted leaves. If the contrivance really served this object, it must have continued in use during all the time the rubbish around it was accumulating. For the hollow on the top was found filled only with drift-sand.

The other rooms of the house had evidently been cleared long ago. Yet even here the search was not entirely fruitless. In the sheltered corner of the apartment next adjoining N. xv. I came upon a heap of wheat straw which, as the piece of matting below it showed, must have fallen from the roof. Among the straw there were stalks still retaining their grains in perfect preservation. There was no pony at hand like Turdi Khwoja's venerable animal at Dandan-Uiliq on which to try the value of the antique straw as a foodstuff. But my quaint old guide himself, the "Aksakal of the Taklamakan" as he was called in camp, just then turned up from Khotan. His arrival was greeted by me with joy; for instead of doubtful antiquarian spoil Turdi brought this time my long-expected mails, the postal accumulations of more than a month, and various much-needed stores.

It is impossible to refer here in detail to the ruins subsequently explored at this site. They were found scattered in small detached groups over a wide semicircular area, up to a distance of one mile and a half to the north of my second camp. Interesting as these excavations were, they yielded but a comparatively small harvest in written documents. The two dozen tablets brought to light comprised, however, an important find. In one of the houses belonging to the northernmost group I found the small tablet which furnished the unique specimen of Brahmi writing already referred to. In the same dwelling some fine specimens of architectural wood-carving (see p. 349) came to light in the shape of massive corbels, showing flower ornaments which are closely allied in style to those found in the Græco-Buddhist sculpture of ancient Gandhara. Less artistic but decidedly curious were the wooden boot-lasts we discovered in the same house; also a large cupboard had been left behind by its last inhabitants. A few hundred feet eastwards, close to some high sand dunes, the embankments of a small tank, 48 feet square, could be clearly made out. One of the poplars that once gave shade to its water still raised its gaunt, bleached trunk to a height of 12 feet, as seen in the photograph at the head of this chapter.

By the 13th of February I had completed the examination of every ruined structure that could be traced under the sand. From a high ridge rising about three miles beyond the northernmost ruins I searched the ground with field-glasses further towards the desert. But no indication of structural remains could be discovered over the great expanse where absolutely bare dunes alternated with equally denuded banks of loess. I was thus able to leave this fascinating site, which had yielded such precious antiquarian spoil, with a good conscience.

Almost the whole of my stay had been a succession of deliciously clear days with bitterly cold nights and mornings, the minimum thermometer usually showing temperatures from 6° to 9° F. below zero. It was striking evidence of the remarkable clearness of the air that early on the morning of the 11th of February the Sub-Surveyor's sharp eyes distinctly sighted the snowy mountains south of Niya, some 120 miles away. Yet I knew that such favourable conditions for desert work could not be expected to serve us much longer. I thought of the number of sites that still remained to be explored before the season of sand-storms would put an end to my explorations, and consequently realised the necessity of setting out for those fresh-fields of work as early as possible.

RUINED BUILDINGS WITHIN ENDERE FORT.

CHAPTER XXVII.

THE RUINS OF ENDERE.

On the 13th of February I once more started my caravan, back to Imam Jafar Sadik. As I passed one ruin after the other familiar to me from the incessant work of the last weeks, I took occasion to collect specimens of the various kinds of wood from the withered trees of ancient orchards. Where will it be next that I can walk amidst poplars and fruit trees planted when the Cæsars still ruled in Rome and the knowledge of Greek writing had barely vanished on the Indus?

I had already heard at Niya, of ancient remains in the desert near the Endere stream about half-way towards Cherchen, and subsequent information decided me to select them for my next explorations. It would have been difficult to take all my former labourers along to this new site, as the distance was great and the men were exhausted by the hard work of the last three weeks. The fresh set of men needed could only be secured from Niya. It was hence a welcome surprise when on arrival at that evening's camping-place I was met by the Deputy of the Beg of Niya, who brought not only a fresh Kashgar mail sent on by the thoughtful Amban of Keriya, but also assurance that all arrangements had been made for the timely dispatch of the fresh contingent. The next day's march to Imam Jafar Sadik was easy, and it rejoiced me to hear once more the rustling of the leaves in the luxuriant jungle that marks the end of the Niya stream. There was no sign yet of the approach of spring, but even in its winter sleep this living forest was a great change after the silent sands and ruins among which I had dwelt. At the Mazar hospice I enjoyed for one brief afternoon the cheerful warmth of a fireplace and indulged in that long-desired luxury, a thorough 'tub.' But there was plenty to do besides, as I despatched from there my mails to Europe and India with the first notice of my recent discoveries, and also settled all accounts with the labourers and the Sheikhs of the Mazar.

I had all along thought that the Endere ruins might be reached by striking straight across the desert to the east of Imam Jafar Sadik, instead of returning first to Niya and thence marching along the Cherchen road. At first all knowledge of such a direct route was stoutly denied, but in the end one of the shepherds from the Mazar acknowledged that he had more than once visited flocks grazing on the Yartungaz stream, the one flowing into the desert next east of the Niya River. So he and Abdurrahman, a half-crazy devotee of the shrine, who claimed to have paid a visit to those ruins, were engaged as guides, and the 15th of February saw us once more steering amidst the sand dunes. Two miles beyond the Mazar all vegetation was left behind. Then we crossed two steep Dawans rising to about 150 feet and toiled on through high sand-hills for about six miles until large patches of gravel soil were struck where camels and ponies marched with ease. A supply of ice brought along from the Mazar enabled us to camp that evening at a spot half-way to the Yartungaz stream, while low tamarisk scrub and some Kumush supplied fuel.

Marching south-eastwards on the following day over gravel-covered slopes and low sand-dunes, we crossed a wide belt of tamarisks and reeds which was said to be reached at times by a small stream known as the Suzüje Darya. Three miles west of the present course of the Yartungaz stream an older bed of it was passed, completely dry. It was at once succeeded by high sand-ridges, such as usually accompany these desert rivers, and I felt heartily glad for the sake of our tired animals when at last in the evening the glittering ice of the stream came in sight, which meant for them rest and water.

On February 17th we followed the Yartungaz River, which at our camping-place had a breadth of about thirty yards, down to the point where it is absorbed by the sands. It was a march of some eighteen miles, all through a belt of jungle which gradually widens out to a breadth of three or four miles. Everywhere we saw the tracks of sheep, but met no living creature until we emerged on the clearings which have been made by a small colony in the fertile area marking the furthest reach of the summer flood water. There is ample land and probably also irrigation water available for several villages. But only four families of agriculturists have established themselves here during the time of Niaz Hakim Beg; and though they are sufficiently well off to employ labourers, no more ground has been cleared than twenty to thirty hands are able to cultivate. Even thus, it was a strange feeling for me to ride once more past fields and irrigation channels. Our excellent Darogha had marched ahead. So Abdul Karim, the foremost 'Dehkan' of the little settlement, a fine-looking old man, was ready to welcome us. His father had come from Faizabad in Badakhshan on a pilgrimage to Imam Jafar Sadik, and on settling down received a grant of land here. Abdul Karim was evidently proud to air what little knowledge of Persian he retained and to do the honours of this forlorn outpost in the desert.

For the last five or six years the Yartungaz stream has shown a tendency to shift its final course westwards. Hence the present main channel loses itself in the sand some four miles to the west of the little colony. The water needed for irrigation is diverted into the old bed by a 'band' which I had passed some seven miles higher up. But even thus the supply is getting precarious, and as the labour available is quite insufficient to cope with the vagaries of the stream, the people of Yartungaz Tarim have started fresh cultivation at the new debouchure as an alternative in years when their old irrigation channel is likely to fail. Given an adequate supply of labour for the maintenance of dykes and canals, it is certain that the area of cultivation could be greatly extended. If fields were to replace the expanse of jungle, covering at present an area of at least twenty-five square miles, the terminal oasis of the Yartungaz River might well present the conditions we must assume to have once existed round the ancient site below Imam Jafar Sadik.

Here, too, it was impossible to obtain any clear information as to the ancient remains for which I was bound. But our energetic Darogha succeeded at last in hunting up reliable guides to the grazing-grounds of the Endere shepherds, and our supplies of foodstuffs and fodder could be replenished from the surplus stock of the little colony. Two long marches brought my caravan across the region of sand-dunes to the forest belt of the Endere stream. Immediately after leaving Yartungaz Tarim a formidable 'Dawan of sand, apparently about 180 feet high, gave trouble to the camels and ponies. But as usual the ridges further away from the river grew lower, and broad depressions between them covered with soda efflorescence offered easier ground. Ice brought from the Yartungaz and the contents of my water-tanks enabled us to camp half-way without the necessity of digging a well, and the quantity of dead tamarisk stems close at hand though scanty sufficed for the camp fires. After we left Yartungaz a fairly strong wind began blowing from the north or north-east, and the dust-haze it raised displayed an ominous persistence.

Late on the 19th of February we crossed the chain of high dunes which skirt the left bank of the Endere stream, and then continued to the south-east along what our guides called the 'old Darya' of Endere. Here, too, the river has in recent years been shifting westwards, so that we found quite a respectable sheet of ice, from ten to twenty yards in width, covering what previously had been a deserted, dry bed. On the other hand this return to the earlier channel has led to the abandonment of the little 'Tarim' or colony that had been formed some miles further east on the "new river," now in process of drying up. It was manifest that these constant changes in the river courses, just before the desert absorbs them, account for the many dry depressions we had crossed since leaving Imam Jafar Sadik.

On the following day we moved up the Endere stream for about ten miles to where a deserted shed of rushes marked the shepherd station of Kara-öchke-öltürgan ("Where the black goat sat"). From there our guides struck into the desert south-eastwards, and after another ten miles' march next morning across low dunes I arrived at what they called the 'Potai' of the 'Kone-shahr.' It was, of course, a brick Stupa, as I had assumed when this feature of the site was first vaguely mentioned to me at the Mazar. Nor was I surprised to find that it had been dug into, no doubt in the hope of treasure. All the same I pushed on with increased eagerness southwards, where the remains of old houses were said to exist. The eroded ground around the Stupa was thickly strewn with pottery fragments, many of them coloured; but no trace of structural remains appeared until I had arrived quite close to low dunes enclosing the ruins. The rows of wooden posts that rose above the sand were indeed a familiar sight. But the high brick walls of some large building, and the remnants of a massive rampart encircling the ruins, presented a novel feature.

The contingent of labourers from Niya had arrived just when I was nearing the Stupa. Considering the great distance, some 120 miles, from which the men had been brought, and the difficulty of communicating with them over wholly uninhabited ground, I felt not a little pleased at this well-managed concentration, which enabled me to start work at once. Going over the ground once enclosed by the circumvallation which had a diameter of about 425 feet, I noticed near the centre rows of wooden posts just reaching above the sand-dune which covered this part of the area. Their arrangement in two concentric squares at once recalled the temple cellas with enclosing passages I had excavated at Dandan-Uiliq. A little experimental digging at one of the corners of the inner square soon brought to light stucco fragments which had belonged to a large-sized image. So the whole of my little force, counting over twenty 'Madigars,' and supplemented by shepherd guides and other followers, was at once set to work here.

Within an hour I had conclusive proof that my surmise was correct. From the loose sand that filled the building more and more pieces of sculpture in stucco turned up, resembling in make and colouring the material used in the Dandan-Uiliq statues. My conclusion as to the approximate date of this shrine was soon verified by successive finds of portions of paper manuscripts. They comprised several leaves, broken in the middle, of a Sanskrit text in ancient Brahmi characters, as well as scraps of sheets written in that very cursive form of Brahmi which appeared so often in the non-Indian documents of Dandan-Uiliq. Here, too, the language for which this script was used was clearly not of Indian origin. The expectations roused by these first finds were not disappointed. It took nearly two days to clear the temple of the sand that had covered and preserved it. The shrine seen on p. 394 consisted of a cella, 20 feet square, having on each side a passage 5 feet wide, and was occupied in its centre by a large pedestal bearing originally four seated stucco images, presumably Buddhas. But of these only the legs and the lowest portions of the robes had survived. Life-sized statues in the same material, all broken above the waist, but retaining in part the vivid colouring of their robes, occupied the four corners.

At the feet of these statues and around the hexagonal base of the central pedestal our excavation revealed in rapid succession manuscript leaves on paper, evidently once deposited there as votive offerings. Among the finds made close in front of the central base the fragments of a Sanskrit text dealing with matters of Buddhist worship, apparently after the fashion of the Mahayana school, were particularly numerous. Judging from the palæographical features displayed by the very clear Brahmi hand this manuscript may well have been written as early as the fifth century. The manuscript, which had the shape of the usual Indian Pothi, must have been broken in the middle, either owing to folding or in the course of some previous digging by "treasure-seekers"; for among the separately recovered packets of leaves, right and left halves were represented in about equal numbers. The pagination numbers read by me ran up to forty-six, and probably about one-half of the original folia may yet be restored from these pieces.

Another very remarkable find was a closely-packed roll of

INTERIOR OF RUINED TEMPLE CELLA, ENDERE, AFTER EXCAVATION.

paper, about 4 inches high and half-an-inch thick, from which under the expert treatment secured in the British Museum the four large folia reproduced in my "Preliminary Report" have since been unfolded. The writing is Brahmi, of the well-known Central-Asian type, while the text is in a non-Indian language, perhaps identical with that represented by various manuscript finds from Dandan-Uiliq.

As the excavation proceeded on the other sides of the cella, curious evidence came to light of the various nations from which the worshippers of this shrine were drawn. Pieces of thin paper with a few Chinese characters and small coloured drawings were found at the pedestal of several images. Far more interesting, historically, was the discovery of numerous paper leaves with Tibetan writing. They are all written on a peculiar paper easily distinguished by its toughness and yellowish colour, and invariably on one side only. Already at the time of their discovery it was easy to recognise that, with the exception of three detached sheets showing very cursive characters, which have since been proved to contain Buddhist prayers and religious poems, all

TWO LEAVES IN CENTRAL-ASIAN BRAHMI, FROM PAPER ROLL (E. I. 7) FOUND IN ENDERE TEMPLE.

(Scale one-fourth.)

Tibetan leaves and fragments had formed part of a single Pothi. The manner in which the pieces of manuscript were found deposited before the various images and on the mouldings of the central pedestal leaves no doubt that they had been distributed purposely. In order to propitiate as many divinities as possible, the pious owner on his visit to this shrine seems to have first cut up the manuscript in the middle, and then proceeded to deposit the halved leaves all round the cella.

The careful examination since made of these *disjecta membra* by Mr. D. L. Barnett, of the British Museum, has proved that they belonged to an early Tibetan version of the Salistamba-sutra, a Buddhist treatise on philosophy, the Sanskrit original of which is known only from quotations. The great importance of the Tibetan text, of which about one-half has thus been recovered, has been lucidly discussed by Mr. Barnett in his "Preliminary Notice" of these discoveries published in the Royal Asiatic Society's *Journal* for 1903. Here it can be indicated only in the briefest outlines. The exceptional interest of the fragments rests not merely on the fact that they supply a valuable criterion for the comparatively modern version of the same text embodied in the Kanjur, and thus for the critical analysis of this great canon of Tibetan Buddhist literature. Being the oldest known specimens of Tibetan writing, they furnish a wealth of fresh material for the study of Tibetan palæo-

HALF-LEAF OF TIBETAN MS. ON PAPER, FROM ENDERE (E. I. 32).

(Scale three-eighths).

graphy and orthoepy. But still greater value must be claimed for them on account of the historical significance with which the place and circumstances of their discovery invest them.

There can be no doubt as to the political conditions with which we must connect the finds of Tibetan texts in this ruined temple, as well as the appearance of Tibetan graffiti that I found covering its stuccoed walls in several places. We know from the Chinese Annals of the Tang dynasty that, during the second half of the eighth century, Tibetan invasion seriously threatened, and towards its close actually destroyed, the authority of the Imperial Government in Eastern Turkestan. These records, of which Professor Chavannes has kindly communicated to me a series of very interesting extracts, indicate plainly that, though the Tibetan advance had already (about 766 A.D.) led to the isolation of those outlying provinces, the local Chinese administrators succeeded for a time in maintaining their authority, at least over part of their territories. In 781 A.D. they managed to transmit pathetic appeals for help to the Imperial court, from which, however, there came no succour, only grants of laudatory titles and liberal acknowledgments of official merits. In 784 A.D. their position appeared so desperate that the Central Government considered the advisability of their recall. Finally, from 791 A.D. onwards, the Tibetans possessed themselves of Turfan and the adjoining region, and nothing more was heard of Eastern Turkestan or the "Four Garrisons," as the Chinese then styled the territories controlled from Kucha, Khotan, Karashahr, and Kashgar.

It is a fortunate circumstance that a Chinese inscription scratched into the cella wall close to the image in the north-west corner (visible to the right in the photograph, p. 394) renders it certain that we must read the evidence of the Tibetan finds in the light of the Chinese records just summarised. From the photographs taken by me of this curious graffito, Professor Chavannes has been able to make out a considerable part of its contents, probably as much as the loosely scratched characters will ever permit to be read. It mentions the return of Tsin-kia-hing, a dignitary of the Chinese administration charged with official sacrifices, to his own district, apparently after the receipt of a report concerning the death of certain military officers with whom he was associated. Twice the 'Ta-fan' or Tibetans are mentioned, and a reference is also made to the "Four Garrisons." The date when this record was incised is given as the seventh year of a period which, owing to the defective preservation of the first character, may be read as Kai-yuen or Cheng-yuen, the year meant corresponding either to A.D. 719 or 791.

In the present state of our knowledge it seems hazardous to decide definitely between these two dates. The later one, 791 A.D., would singularly agree with that recorded by the Annals for the final subversion of Chinese rule, and seems to find some support also in the fact that the latest Chinese document of Dandan-Uiliq dates from 790. In favour of the earlier date,

719 A.D., it may be mentioned that only Han coins were found among these ruins, and also that the sculptural remains of the Endere temple seemed to me to bear a somewhat older character than those of the Dandan-Uiliq shrines. However this may be, it can be considered quite certain that the date when this Chinese graffito was scratched into the wall could not have preceded by many years the deposition of the various votive manuscripts and the subsequent abandonment of the shrine. The rough, and not very hard, plaster of these cella walls was not a material that could remain intact for a long period without repair, and with its renewal all these casual scratchings of pious visitors would no doubt have vanished. This consideration fixes the second half of the eighth century as the latest possible time for the production of the Tibetan as well as the other manuscripts found here. The same applies to the Tibetan graffiti which, owing to their very cursive writing, have not yet been fully deciphered.

The very numerous little rags which were found scattered in front of the various image bases are undoubtedly votive offerings of a humbler kind. They comprise shreds of many fabrics, from elaborately woven Chinese silks and printed cottons to the simple 'Kham,' a kind of buckram, mentioned in Hiuen-Tsiang's account of Khotan, and still worn by the common folk throughout this region. The variety of this collection vividly reminded me of the wonderful display of rags that graces the approaches to the resting-place of the holy Imam Jafar and other saints throughout Turkestan. Islam has indeed little changed the popular type of ex-votos which were in vogue during Buddhist times, and which in this case have provided for us a sample collection of ancient fabrics of no small archæological interest.

During the days following I had almost all the buildings within the enclosing ramparts cleared of sand. These excavations furnished interesting data as to the methods of construction employed, but failed to throw much light on the original destination of the whole of this ruined settlement. The large brick building to the east of the temple, of which a portion left exposed by the sand is seen on p. 388, occupies with its massive walls of sun-dried bricks three sides of a quadrangle over 100 feet square. The dimensions of its rooms suggest public use ; but as, with the exception of a walled fireplace or two, they were found completely empty, there was nothing to prove the true character of the structure. Were these the quarters of a well-to-do monastic establishment which found it advisable to protect itself by walls and ramparts ? Or do the latter mark a fortified frontier-post which sheltered also a Buddhist temple ?

LOWER FLOOR ROOM OF RUINED DWELLING-PLACE, ENDERE FORT.

In a row of small rooms built of timber and plaster, which stood to the north of the shrine, there was one that appeared to have served as a little chapel. Its wall on one side was occupied by an elaborate fresco, which seems to have represented a Buddha surrounded by his former epiphanies. The wall had been broken at five feet from the ground, but the colours and outlines of the remaining part were in very fair preservation. In the same little room we found a well-executed small painting on wood, showing the familiar figure of the elephant-headed Indian god of wisdom, Ganesha. To the south of the temple my excavations revealed a small double-storied building, of which, however, only the lower floor rooms remained. They had no doors, and were evidently underground apartments intended for use in the winter. The large fireplace found in one of them, with its elaborate mouldings, is seen in the photograph reproduced on p. 399.

The circumvallation, which originally consisted of a solid rampart of clay about 30 feet broad at the base and 17½ feet high, had survived only in parts of the south face, flanking a gate, and in much decayed segments elsewhere. On the top of the ramparts ran a parapet of brickwork 5½ feet high, and behind it a platform that seems to have been paved with bundles of brushwood, manifestly for the sake of greater consistency. There was nothing to tell of the attacks from Tibetans or other foes which this little stronghold may once have resisted. But its walls have certainly helped to ward off that worst danger of ancient remains in the desert region—the erosive action of winds and moving sands. Looking around from the ruined ramparts, it was easy to realise that the original level of the surrounding ground had been lowered at least ten feet by erosion. Inside the circumvallation the drift-sand, once accumulated, was less liable to be shifted by the winds, and thus provided a protecting cover for the ruins.

The extent of the erosion which the whole area has undergone was brought home to me by the closer examination I made of the Stupa already noticed. On surveying the structure I found that the lowest line of bricks in its foundation was about ten feet higher than the level of the ground in the immediate vicinity. Kept down by the weight of the masonry, the loess soil below the Stupa has resisted erosion and now appears like an additional base, making the structure look considerably higher than it is in reality. Though the outer casing of bricks has suffered a great deal, I succeeded with a little trouble in ascertaining the original proportions of this "memorial tower." On a square base, measuring 23 feet on each side and about 7 feet in height, there rose a solid dome 16 feet in diameter and approximately of the same height. Thus the total dimensions agree very closely with those of the little Stupa at the Niya River Site, though the arrangement there of a double basement introduces a marked difference in the detailed proportions. In Indian Stupas the increase of height relative to diameter may generally be considered a sign of later date, and a comparison of these two Stupas, the time of which can be approximately determined, seems to confirm this observation also for this northern region.

On the 26th of February my explorations at this site were completed, thanks to the energy with which the work of excavation had been carried on, from early morning until after nightfall by the light of bonfires. The interesting finds showed plainly that I had reached the border-line beyond which Indian influences yielded to Chinese. A move further east would have carried me beyond the limits of the territory with the archæological exploration of which I was concerned. Besides, the time that remained at my disposal seemed none too ample for the expeditions I had yet to make to ancient localities north of Keriya and Khotan. So I reluctantly decided that the time had come to set my face again westwards. There was consolation in the thought that it meant a start on the journey which was to bring me back to Europe and to dear ones not seen for long years.

CHAPTER XXVIII.

EXPEDITION TO KARADONG RUIN.

On the 26th of February I left the Endere ruins on my rapid march back to Niya. The river, which was crossed at a point some ten miles to the south-west of the old site, had through the warm sunshine of the last few days lost its coating of ice in the shallower parts; but over the main current of the stream, about 15 yards across, the ice was still strong enough to bear heavy loads. One by one our camels were got safely across. Then the water-tanks were filled once more for the passage of the broad desert belt towards the Yartungaz River. Marching along an old bed of the Endere River to the south, we passed through luxuriant Toghrak jungle for another ten miles, and late in the evening reached the deserted shepherd's hut of Tokuz-kol. The name means "nine lakes," but of water there was none.

On the morning of the 27th we still steered due south through a level plain covered with Kumush. All traces of the true sand desert for a time disappeared. The change of scenery was all the more striking as the distant mountain rampart of the Kuen-luen was clearly visible during the morning. Though sixty to eighty miles away from the range, we could distinguish a series of prominent peaks with the glaciers descending around them. They were duly recorded on the plane-table, but only just in time; for after midday, when we had struck the track which leads from Keriya to Cherchen, a strong north wind raised such a dust-haze that soon the mountain view vanished like a vision. Here the Endere shepherd guide was discharged, not until I had given him a little present for his children. I had met them, two sturdy little boys, on the way, but had then nothing to offer but bits of chocolate from my saddle-bag. This they could not be induced to try, though my little terrier, just to encourage them, readily swallowed some of it. I hope that the piece of a Russian sugarloaf I got out from the baggage and sent them was received with more confidence.

After reaching the Cherchen road, once the great line of communication to China, but now a lonely desert track with practically no traffic, we still had a long march to do that day. For over twenty miles we rode to the south-west, over hard-grained sand, with scarcely any dunes and bare of vegetation, until Yoke-toghrak was reached. There a small patch of tamarisks and Toghraks offered scanty fuel, and some brackish water was found in wells about 6 feet deep. The camels did not turn up until close on midnight, and dinner was accordingly an affair of the small hours of the morning. The next day brought, however, an easy march to the Yartungaz River, where men and beasts could be made comfortable. On the way I had the satisfaction to fall in with Tila Bai, my honest pony-man, who was now bringing mails and sadly wanted articles from the stores I had left at Khotan. It is always a pleasure to receive bags full of "home mails." But I enjoy the sensation most when it comes unexpectedly, and there is time to sit down by the roadside and pore peacefully over the contents, as I could this time. A look over the *Weekly Times*, nearly three months old, put me again in contact with the affairs of the far-off West and East.

The two long marches which brought me back again to Niya yielded pleasing variety in the little lakes and marshes we passed, They are fed by springs, the water of which, just released from the grip of frost, was flowing plentifully into the reed-covered lagoons. From the Shitala Darya, a watercourse similarly formed, at which we halted, there stretched an uninterrupted jungle to within some miles of the Niya River. Its eastern bank proved to be flanked, just like that of all the other rivers that flow into the desert east of Khotan, by a high range of sand dunes. This was crossed near the Mazar of Shitala Padshahim, a simple collection of posts with yak tails and fluttering rags, and at last, after a ride over much boggy ground, I again entered the little oasis. In the twilight it seemed like a return to civilisation. Since starting from Niya on the 23rd of January I had covered over 300 miles in a great oval loop. Yet when the positions indicated on the plane-table for the starting and closing points of our route came to be compared, the difference proved to be only three-fourths of a mile in longitude and a little over a mile in latitude.

Leaving my "goods train" of camels to follow behind, I covered the distance from Niya to Keriya, some eighty miles, in two stages. There I was busy at work with reports and letters, and with rearranging my baggage. The weather was rapidly getting warmer; hence all heavy winter clothing was to be left behind before the start for the ancient site I next intended to visit far down the Keriya River. As arrangements also had to be made for labourers to accompany us for excavation work, and for the supplies that men and animals needed, the two days, which were all I could allow myself, were indeed no time of rest for me or Ibrahim, my energetic Darogha.

Huang-Daloi, the kindly Amban, opportunely returned the day after my arrival from a little tour of criminal investigation. So I had the wished-for opportunity of thanking him personally for all the help which I had experienced at a distance. From the stores that had arrived from Khotan I had sent him the best selection of tinned goods I could offer. Everything seemed to be duly appreciated, and the return presents in the shape of fodder supplies, sheep, etc., were quite overwhelming. When the Amban, a few minutes after my departure, paid his return visit, I was able to satisfy his curiosity about my finds with specimens of ancient tablets, etc. With the historical sense which all educated Chinese seem to possess, he at once rightly surmised that the use of wood as a writing material indicated a period corresponding to that when split bamboos were employed in China previous to the invention of paper. Extravagant rumours as to my discovery of coffers full of gold, etc., seemed to have run through all the Bazars far away to Khotan and beyond. But I could see that Huang-Daloi had quite sensible notions of what I was looking out for, and of what I had found. So we parted once more in the friendliest fashion, and with mutual confidence.

Thanks to the Amban's energetic assistance, I was able to set out on the 7th of March for my next objective. It was the ruined site of Karadong, situated in the desert some 150 miles north of Keriya, to which Dr. Hedin had paid a short visit in 1896, on his memorable march down the Keriya Darya. I knew from the accounts given by Turdi, whose "treasure-seeking" expeditions had twice extended to this place, that the remains of this so-called "ancient city" (which he called Aktiken) were very scanty. Yet I felt that my duty demanded a personal examination of the ruins. For the loss of time which their great distance implied I decided to make up by hard marching.

With the baggage lightened and my camels partially relieved by the hire of fresh animals, I was thus able to push on in three days to the point where I had first struck the Keriya Darya from Dandan-Uiliq. The aspect of the river-banks was still as bleak and bare as two months before, but in place of the glassy sheet of ice there now rolled a muddy current, fed by the melting of the ice that had covered the marshes and pools about Keriya. It was a regular spring flood from the 'Kara-su,' ("black water") feeders of the river. while months would yet pass before the flood of 'Ak-su' ("white water") would bring down the melting snows of the mountains. At the Burhan-uddin Mazar I was cheerfully welcomed by the 'Sheikhs,' who evidently remembered the handsome offering made at my first visit; and I spent there pleasant hours, busily writing in the sheltered little loggia of the mosque. When I left to catch up my caravan, Ghazi Sheikh, the senior of the priestly fraternity, insisted on accompanying me. He was a jovial old man and quite looked the 'Bai,' or capitalist, which he was according to local notions, having at least a thousand sheep grazing along the river. He knew, of course, every living soul of the little community of nomadic herdsmen and the name of every grazing-ground. So it was easy for our Darogha to strengthen the band of labourers I had brought from Keriya by fresh recruits from among the shepherds. The men joined us readily enough; for uncouth and "jungly" as their appearance was, in rough furs and sandals made of goatskins, yet these supposed "semi-savages" were quite alive to the chance of earning a little hard cash that might come in useful on their periodical visits to Keriya and its Bazars. Thus my band kept swelling on the way like a small avalanche.

The route which we followed for three days from Kochkar Öghil downwards was new to me, but space does not permit more than a passing reference to one distinct change in scenery. The river, which down to this point had occupied a deep and narrow bed winding in rapid turns, now spread itself out in broad reaches. Though the channel actually filled with water was at the time only 80 to 100 yards wide, yet the clearly marked bed of the summer floods attained in places the imposing breadth of quite half a mile. The belt of vegetation, which accompanies the river on its course through the desert sand, did not spread out in the same proportion. But the increasing height of the Toghraks and the thickness of the Kumush beds showed that the moisture received from the river was plentiful wherever it reached.

On the 12th of March we crossed a high Dawan appropriately named 'Yoghan-kum' ("High Sands"), which juts out transversely into the river-bed, and is faced on the opposite eastern bank by similar high ridges of sand. But this obstacle once passed, wide room offered itself to the vagaries of the stream. From the height of the Yoghan-Kum I could make out no less than three dry beds spreading in different directions like the fingers of a hand. We followed the middle one—a wide, flat Nullah in which the yellow Kumush beds swayed by the breeze looked curiously like fields of ripe corn, down to where it met the actual river-course again near the shepherds' station known as Tonguz-baste. Here Ghazi Sheikh's flock was established for the time being. So hospitable offerings of sheep and milk turned up that evening. As usual, the end of the former bed was marked by a lagoon of fresh water communicating with the actual river-course, yet keeping its water clear of the mud which discoloured the latter. It seemed a favourite haunt of wild duck, of which hundreds were disporting themselves on this pretty sheet of water. That my camp was placed within 200 yards of its bank seemed in no way to disturb the birds. Their loud calls sounded strange to me after the stillness of my desert camps.

I knew from Dr. Sven Hedin's account that the ruins I had come in search of lay in the lesert, within a march to the north-west of Tonguz-baste. Mullah Shah, an experienced shepherd who was to guide us, turned up late at night, and after prolonged protestations of ignorance, acknowledged that he had twice visited Karadong. With him came another shepherd, Muhammad Shah, "the hunter" (Merghen), an active young fellow who had also once seen the place. He was to help Mullah Shah, his 'Ustad,' or master, in finding the track. This turned out no easy task. The morning was very hazy, and by the time the water-tanks had been filled and a depot made of supplies not immediately needed, a stiff north wind sprung up which by degrees developed into a regular 'Buran,' the first of the season. We followed for about seven miles a course almost due north, until we passed the westernmost of the former river-beds above mentioned, near a little pool, known as Toldama, retaining some flood water. Then our guides struck to the north-west.

So far we had marched in a whirl of dust. But now, with the increasing force of the storm, the air became so thick that it was difficult to see even for a hundred yards. The assurance with which Mullah Shah and his pupil continued to guide us was doubly welcome under such circumstances. With the sand driving into my face and accumulating under the eye-lashes in spite of goggles, it was difficult to see much of the route. But I noted that after a couple of miles the scattered groups of Toghraks were left behind and the sand dunes rose in height. After plodding on among them for another hour, our guides declared that we were near the tamarisk-covered copses that have given the site its name, Karadong ("the Black Hillocks"). But as in the blinding dust they could not make sure of the exact direction, I let them go on ahead while we sought shelter behind a tamarisk-covered cone. It was curious to watch how the sand was driven in a thick spray over the crest-line of the dunes, just as if they were storm-tossed waves. After half an hour Muhammad Shah returned with the reassuring news that the ruins were due west of us and not far off. In proof he brought a piece of old pottery he had picked up. So the march was resumed just as the force of the storm showed signs of abating, and after another two and a half miles, over fairly high dunes, we arrived at the ruins.

The remains of Karadong proved to consist mainly of a ruined quadrangle, which was formed by a mud rampart about 235 feet square, with rows of timber-built rooms over it. Within this quadrangle, which was crossed by two large dunes rising to about 20 feet above the original ground-level, I could just recognise the timber débris of a much-decayed structure sticking out from the deep sand. The photograph on p. 409 shows this ruin after excavation, together with the interior of the quadrangle as seen from the north-east corner. Excessive erosion had played havoc with the structures which once occupied the exposed top of the rampart, and the lines of walls could there be traced with difficulty. Potsherds, small broken pieces of glass and metal, shreds of felt and scanty refuse of a similar kind, were all that marked their former occupation.

The trying conditions under which I had reached this site curiously reminded me of what Hiuen-Tsiang tells of the sand-buried town of Ho-lo-lo-kia, which a local legend heard by him at Pi-mo (see p. 417), placed somewhere in the great desert to the north of Khotan. It was believed to have been covered up by a rain of sand in consequence of the curse of a holy visitor whom its king had treated with ignominy, and who foretold the destruction of the town after seven days. Only one pious man took warning and escaped to Pi-mo by means of an underground passage. "On the seventh day, in the evening, it rained sand and earth, and filled the city." Ho-lo-lo-kia, the pilgrim tells us, "is now a great sand mound. The kings of the neighbouring countries and persons in power from distant spots have many times wished to excavate the mound and take away the precious things buried there; but as soon as they have arrived at the borders of the place a furious wind has sprung up, dark clouds have gathered together from the four quarters of heaven, and they have become lost and unable to find their way."

I had not gone to the Karadong site to look for treasures such as old Hiuen-Tsiang's "persons in power from distant spots" sought; nor had the Buran that greeted me on the day of my

INTERIOR OF RUINED QUADRANGLE, KARADONG.

arrival made me lose the way. But the result was not very different if judged by the "finds" which rewarded the work here. I soon convinced myself that no other ruins of any kind could be traced in the neighbourhood besides those already briefly described. Even pottery fragments were scarce and limited to a small area. The natives may indeed call these remains a 'kone-shahr,' using the term which is applied throughout the country to old ruins of any kind. But to talk of an "ancient city" here would imply more imagination than an archæologist need care to take credit for.

The excavation of the ruined structures in the interior of the quadrangle kept my little force of diggers hard at work for two days, but there was little to reward their labour. Long prior to the accumulation of the present covering of sand, the buildings must have been exposed to the full force of erosion. The plaster of the walls had completely disappeared, and much of their wooden framework had also crumbled into loose débris. From the general arrangement of the rooms, however, which could still be made out, it was evident that these structures must have once served as dwellings.

Only Toghrak wood appears to have been used in the construction of these houses and of the enclosing quadrangle. This species of poplar grows plentifully in the jungles of all the rivers which lose themselves in the desert. But its twisted knotty trunks and branches by no means furnish as good a building material as the Terek or white poplar, the Jigda, and other trees planted in the cultivated areas. At Dandan-Uiliq and at the ancient site beyond Imam Jafar Sadik only timber of these latter trees seems to have been used for the framework of houses, which accordingly there bore a far more finished look than at Karadong. At those other old sites the dead trunks of Terek and other trees dependent on cultivation formed a conspicuous feature. But around Karadong I looked for them in vain. Dead trees rising from between the sand dunes were plentiful, but they were all old Toghraks, just as are still found growing luxuriantly along the recent river-beds a few miles to the east. I concluded from this observation that cultivation could not have existed to any extent in the vicinity of the Karadong site at the period from which its buildings date.

What then can have been the purpose of the latter, situated as they evidently were in the narrow belt of forest land between the desert and the river? Keeping in view the position and the peculiar plan of the ruined structures, I think the suggestion may be hazarded that we have here the remains of a fortified frontier post or roadside Sarai. A remark of Mirza Haidar, the Moghul leader and historian, makes it very probable that the

Keriya River reached the Tarim as late as the sixteenth century. Its old course across the desert can be followed even now without serious difficulty, and certainly forms the most direct route between Khotan and the ancient settlements of Kucha and further north-east. Karadong lies about half-way between the Tarim and the line of oases stretching to the east of Khotan, and a small post established here would have answered the purpose of guarding the route and protecting the approaches

WOODEN GATEWAY OF RUINED QUADRANGLE, KARADONG, AFTER EXCAVATION.

from the northern region. The age of the ruined structure is approximately indicated by the coins I picked up in its immediate vicinity, which were all copper pieces of the Later Han dynasty, showing long wear.

The best preserved portion of this ancient Sarai or post was the large wooden gateway which my subsequent excavations brought to light on the eastern face of the quadrangular enclosure. It formed a square of 22 feet, and its roof, perfectly intact, reached the top level of the rampart. Besides a broad central gateway, closed by a massive wooden door of two leaves, there were two narrower passages flanking it on either side. I noticed exactly the same arrangement in the gates of all Yamens I visited. As the whole of this gate was filled up with sand to its ceiling, 14 feet above the floor, it took two days' hard digging before we had cleared it. Above the gate there once rose another storey, but of this there remained only a few posts and a thick earth flooring. Embedded in the layer of rubbish that covered this we came upon a little store of remarkably well-preserved cereals. There were a couple of pounds of 'Tarigh,' a kind of pulse still cultivated about Keriya, together with small quantities of wheat, rice, oats, another sort of pulse, some roots apparently used as condiments, and a capful of large black currants dried perfectly hard. I had a small quantity of the 'Tarigh' boiled, and found the antique porridge made of it useful for glueing envelopes.

While this excavation was still proceeding, we had a return of the Buran that greeted us on our arrival. Though the force of the wind, this time from the south-west, was somewhat less, the driving sand made it decidedly uncomfortable both in and outside the tent. As the supply of sufficient water for my comparatively large number of men was also a serious difficulty, I felt heartily glad when by the evening of the 17th of March our work at this desolate spot was concluded. Next morning I left Karadong, just as I had reached it, in an atmosphere thick with dust and quite oppressive by its haziness. The look of the desert harmonised with the mournful news conveyed in the small mail sent on from Keriya which met me half-way that day. A short letter from home transmitted viâ Samarkand and Osh, and a communication from Mr. Macartney based on Russian intelligence, informed me of the death of our Queen-Empress. I could see that my two Indian followers, to whom I communicated the news, understood, and in their own way shared the deep emotion which filled me. There were no details to distract attention from the momentous main fact, the disappearance from this world-wide scene of the greatest ruler England has known since her expansion over the seas began.

CHAPTER XXIX.

THE SEARCH FOR HIUEN-TSIANG'S PI-MO.

My eyes were now turned to the south again, where a number of archæological tasks still awaited me in the vicinity of the inhabited area. First among them was a search for the site of the ancient town of Pi-mo. Hiuen-Tsiang had visited it on his way from Khotan to Niya, and its probable mention also by Marco Polo under the name of 'Pein' made me all the more anxious to identify its position. The distance and direction which the Chinese pilgrim indicated from Pi-mo, viz., three hundred Li (or about sixty miles) to the east of the Khotan capital, had long before made me look out for the place somewhere to the north-west of Keriya. I was hence much pleased when, on my last visit to the latter place, I heard from the Amban himself of a 'Kone-shahr' said to exist in the desert beyond Gulakhma, an oasis on the Khotan road some thirty miles west of Keriya. Ram Singh, too, had heard about the ruins, and in order to save time I decided to reach them now by striking across the desert south-westwards.

Of the series of rapid marches by which I endeavoured to effect my object, the briefest account must suffice. During the four days which saw us returning along the Keriya Darya as fast as camels and ponies could move, I still looked in vain for any sign of approaching spring in the vegetation of the riverine jungle. Small wonder, considering that after the windy days of Karadong the temperature showed a marked fall, down to a minimum of 14° Fahr. of frost on the 19th of March.

At the familiar shrine of Burhanuddin I picked up *en route* the two guides who, under the Amban's order, had been sent by the Beg of Gulakhma. They looked unusually reticent and stupid, but it was too late when we found out that they knew nothing of such a route as I wished to take. Too timid to aver their ignorance, they thought it safest to guide us further and further south, where at least there was no risk from the dreaded Taklamakan. Thus, after leaving the left river-bank and crossing a belt of high sand dunes, we found ourselves, on the 23rd of March, in a wide area of swampy jungle watered from the marshes of Shivul, west of Keriya. As the local knowledge of the guides quite gave out here, we had great difficulty in extricating our animals from the boggy marsh, treacherously covered with light sand, in which the Shivul stream ends. Though there were everywhere the tracks of flocks that had grazed here during the winter, we did not succeed in finding a single shepherd to help in guiding us. Fortunately we came at last upon firmer ground, where the Shivul Darya flowed as a limpid stream in a winding but well-defined bed, about fifteen feet broad. This helped once more to guide our "guides," and ultimately, after a long and tiring march through the dusk, we arrived at the solitary little shrine of Arish-Mazar. Though the rustic Sheikh living near the saint's tomb was at first greatly alarmed by the arrival of so large a party, fodder was soon forthcoming for the tired ponies, and big fires were lit to guide the belated part of the caravan.

After the experience I had gained of the value of our guides there was no alternative but to resign myself to letting them reach again familiar ground in the oasis itself before striking off into the desert. Accordingly we made our way south-westwards, through the sandy jungle in which the water of another marsh-fed stream, the Karakir Darya, finally loses itself. The track we followed led through a maze of tamarisk-covered sand-cones, standing closer together than I had seen them anywhere on the borders of the true desert. Unexpectedly we came in their midst upon the unmistakable remains of some ancient settlement, which the few shepherds whom our Darogha had succeeded in discovering called Aktaz or simply 'Tatilik' (ruins). On several small pieces of open ground, showing evidence of considerable erosion, pottery fragments abounded and foundations of mud-walled houses could be distinguished. But the latter had been levelled to within a few inches from the ground, and the few small objects, such as a ring of brass picked up by my men, gave no clear indication of date.

Ultimately we emerged on cultivated land at the village of Malakalagan, which had been formed about fifteen years ago by people from Domoko, the main oasis due south on the Khotan-Keriya route. The reclamation of desert soil going on here was a sight as cheering as it was instructive. Small irrigation cuts were seen winding along the old tamarisk-covered hillocks of sand that had not yet been levelled down, while between them extended carefully-fenced fields. Here and there the Toghraks of the desert jungle had been spared, particularly near the huts of the settlers. But it was clear they would soon disappear in a hopeless minority by the side of the avenues of young poplars, Jigda, and other fruit trees that were rapidly growing up along all irrigation channels.

My previous information had clearly indicated the ruined site I was in search of as being situated in the vicinity of the Mazar of Lachin-Ata. The people of Malakalagan, whom I closely questioned, did not deny their knowledge of this popular desert shrine, but none of them would acknowledge ever having visited the 'Kone-shahr' near it. Our wanderings of the previous two days had left me no illusions as to the capacity of our two worthy guides. Yet as better were not to be got and time was getting more than ever precious, I decided to set out with them on the morning of March 25th. Old Turdi, after a long absence on mail duty, had just joined me from Khotan, and I could rely on the old "treasure-seeker's" instinct and experience coming to the help of whatever local knowledge the Domoko guides might prove to possess. Turdi had brought along two more water-tanks previously left at Khotan, and as I took the precaution of having all six tanks filled before the start, we were safe from immediate risk. The three days' Odyssey which followed, and which is illustrated by the tortuous line of route, fully bore out my misgivings. Yet there was interesting experience to compensate for the trouble and fatigue.

The first couple of miles in a north-westerly direction had brought us to the limit of the newly irrigated land, when to my surprise I came upon unmistakable marks of earlier cultivation beyond. Old fields overgrown with tamarisk and thorny scrub could be clearly distinguished by the little embankments dividing them, as well as by the lines of dry 'Ariks' that once carried water to them. My guides explained that these were the fields of 'old Ponak' village, which had been abandoned "in their grandfathers' time," *i.e.*, forty or fifty years ago. Passing along a road still frequented by the people visiting the cemeteries of the deserted villages, I arrived some three miles further north-west at the southern end of the area known as 'old Domoko.' Here the ruins of mud-built dwellings, constructed exactly like the modern villages of this tract, seemed to extend, together with the interspersed orchards and cemeteries, for fully three miles from east to west. The mud walls, strengthened by the insertion of vertical bundles of Kumush, still often rose 4 to 5 feet above the ground, and the massive fireplaces were intact even to a greater height. The deserted homesteads had been stripped of all materials that could be of use, such as beams, wooden doorposts, etc.; and as scarcely any sand had accumulated about the crumbling ruins, their complete disappearance was only a question of time.

The villagers accompanying me, as well as the people I subsequently examined on my return to the oasis, all agreed in asserting that the gradually increasing difficulty of conducting the irrigation water sufficiently far had caused the cultivated area of these and some other villages of the Begships of Domoko and Gulakhma to be shifted as much as six to eight miles further south within the memory of living men. Local tradition, in fact, maintained that such shifts of the cultivated land, backwards and forwards, had occurred repeatedly in the case of these small oases along the road from Keriya to Chira. Evidence that cannot be detailed here seemed to support the belief that this tradition had some substantial basis, and I felt inclined to regard the gradual change of levels consequent on irrigation deposits as a possible explanation of these repeated shifts. It would need a prolonged investigation of local conditions, particularly those connected with the supply of irrigation water, which is here largely dependent on springs, in order to arrive at any safe conclusion. But anyhow, there could be no doubt that the ruins I saw here were the best illustration of the course of decay through which the 'Kone-shahrs,' or Tatis, found along the western route to Khotan and on the outskirts of the oasis, must be supposed to have passed once. There, too, villages were deserted owing to irrigation ceasing from one cause or other; and as they were so much further away from the desert centre than the terminal oases of Dandan-Uiliq or the Niya River site, the heavy drift-sand could not arrive in time and in sufficient quantity to give protection to the ruins.

For nearly three miles we traversed the desolate remains of these village homesteads, but it was not until some miles further north that the region of low sand dunes was entered near a little wooden tomb, worshipped as the supposed resting-place of a saintly associate of Lachin-Ata. The Mazar of the latter was not in view, nor could our guides give any clear idea where we should find the ancient site previously described as in its vicinity. As we plodded on amidst the gradually rising sand dunes, the villagers I had taken along for eventual excavations became more communicative. They professed never to have seen that site, but they were well aware ot its legend.

These same villagers had before shown a very matter-of-fact perception of the true cause which had led to the abandonment of their old lands. All the greater was my surprise to find that the legend they now proceeded to tell me of the 'Kone-shahr' in the desert beyond was in all substantial points the same as the one which more than twelve centuries ago Hiuen-Tsiang had heard at Pi-mo of the sand-buried city of Ho-lo-lo-kia, and which has been briefly quoted already in my account of Karadong. A holy man who had reproved the wicked inhabitants for certain offences, was treated by them with contempt. He thereupon cursed the town and foretold its approaching destruction. While they still mocked at his prophecy, sand began to rain from the skies and continued for seven days and nights until the whole of the buildings were buried. Only seven pious people who had shown respect for the holy one managed to save their lives, through a curious device which varies from Hiuen-Tsiang's story. The seven wise men are supposed to have clung to ropes fixed to a high pole after the fashion of a merry-go-round. Being whirled round and round by the raging storm they rose steadily higher above the ground while the sand accumulated, and thus escaped.

Similar stories, no doubt, are current throughout Turkestan of ruins buried in the Taklamakan; but it was of particular interest to note how the continuity of local traditions had here transferred the legend which Hiuen-Tsiang heard at Pi-mo of a still earlier site, to the remains of Pi-mo itself. For these I could safely recognise in the extensive débris-covered area, a portion of which we managed to trace in the course of the following day. The previous evening our luckless guides had dragged us aimlessly far out into the desert, until at last the weariness of animals and men and the difficulty of getting the caravan in the darkness over the rising dunes had forced us to pitch camp. During the night one of the guides deserted, having probably got bewildered by his own display of deficient local sense. The other, however, a timid young fellow whom Turdi, my desert factotum, kept under his eye and encouraged by advice drawn from his own lifelong "treasure-seeking" experience, recovered his bearings, and setting out before daybreak succeeded in finding the ruined area far away to the south-west.

Uzun-tati—"the distant Tati," as local tradition appropriately designates this site—proved to consist of several extensive patches of ground, one nearly half a mile square, thickly covered with pottery fragments, and other small débris. Owing to far-advanced erosion and the destruction dealt by "treasure-seekers," the remains of mud-built houses were too much decayed to permit of excavation or to offer clear indications as to their date. Yet such chronological evidence was needed before the identification of this site with Hiuen-Tsiang's Pi-mo, suggested as it was by every topographical consideration, could be definitely accepted. Pi-mo was undoubtedly, as already recognised by Sir Henry Yule, the same place as 'Pein,' which Marco Polo visited on his journey east of Khotan, and must thus have remained inhabited up to the close of the thirteenth century. The appearance of the bits of pottery, glass, china, small objects of brass and stone, etc., which turned up among the plentiful débris of Uzun-tati, entirely favoured this assumption. But it was only when myself picking up a Chinese copper piece of the Southern Sung dynasty (A.D. 1127–1278), that I secured conclusive proof that the site had been occupied up to the Middle Ages.

Our guides had previously spoken of a second 'Kone-shahr' which, from some supposed tombs of saints, they called Ulugh-Ziarat ("the shrine of the holy ones"). Though these remains were known to them as adjoining Uzun-tati, and in the end proved to be only about three miles distant in a direct line to the south-east, it took us nearly two days and very tiring marches and counter-marches in the sand, over an aggregate distance of some twenty-five miles, before this second site was discovered. Less extensive than Uzun-tati, it displayed débris manifestly of the same period. In addition I found not far from it the comparatively well-preserved remains of a small fort, built in the form of an oval of about 480 by 348 feet. The wall of stamped clay was some 11 feet thick at the base, and, including the parapet, rose originally to a height of about 14½ feet. No remains of any kind were found in the interior of this circumvallation, or around it, and consequently I was unable to form any definite opinion as to its date.

These days in the desert had convincingly demonstrated the serious difficulties which must always attend a search for scanty ruins hidden away among deceptive sand dunes if made without adequate guidance. The rapidly increasing heat and glare—on the 27th and 28th of March the air about midday was 88° Fahr. in the shade, though the minimum thermometer had for the corresponding nights still registered 28° and 30° Fahr.—rendered tramps through the sand very trying, and made us realise the limitations of the water supply carried in the tanks. Hence I felt as glad as my men when the satisfactory conclusion of my task allowed me to turn back southward to the inhabited area. Passing *en route* the desolate little shrine of Lachin-Ata and then the hamlet of 'New Ponak' on the fringe of the desert, I reached on the 29th of March the oasis of Gulakhma. There for the first time I caught sight of the young green of cultivated fields and orchards.

Gulakhma, which counts about 900 houses in its several villages and with the adjoining Begship of Domoko is undoubtedly the modern representative of the Pi-mo oasis, might have tempted me to give my caravan the short rest it had amply earned. But time would not permit. So on the 30th of March I sent on the main part of my camp under Ram Singh to reach Khotan by easy stages, while I myself with the minimum of impedimenta hurried back to Keriya to bid farewell personally to its kindly Amban. My rapid marches were made pleasant by noticing on all sides exuberant signs of spring, which seemed to have come over the land with surprising rapidity. Wherever the road passed through cultivated tracts the poplars and willows lining it showed plentiful young leaves in delicate bluish-green tints. At Yaqa-Langar, where I passed a night in the garden of a half-ruined Sarai built by Niaz Hakim Beg, my tent was pitched under blossoming plum-trees. The mild evening air and the picturesque neglect of the garden strangely recalled the surroundings of many a pleasant camp in the Punjab.

I found Keriya looking bright and cheerful in its setting of sprouting trees, and its whole population *en fête*, celebrating the festival known to the Muhammadans of India as the 'Bakri-Id.' Singing and feasting went all round the 'Topbashi's' garden where I camped. On the following morning, April 1st, I sent my last presents to Huang-Daloi, including a number of personal souvenirs, and then paid my farewell visit to his Yamen. In the course of our long confabulation I did not fail to emphasise the excellent services of Ibrahim, our energetic Darogha. So the Amban publicly lauded him and promised to reward him with a comfortable berth and good emoluments. It was already well known at Keriya that Pan-Darin on my recommendation had provided Islam Beg, for similar good services in the Khotan district, with a fat Begship at Kara-kash, and Huang-Daloi might well feel encouraged to follow the lead of his pious colleague. I myself felt pained by the thought of how little it was in my power to return the Amban's never-failing help with some substantial service, and how scanty the hope was of ever seeing his kindly face again. Yet when we exchanged our final goodbye outside my little camping-ground he seemed to realise the lasting gratitude I should retain for him and my sincere regret at the parting.

On the 2nd of April I started back to Khotan by forced

BOYS AND GIRLS AT KERIYA, IN HOLIDAY DRESS.

marches. The first brought me to Karakir Langar, a deserted roadside Bazar east of the Domoko oasis, where a curious illustration offered itself of the changes affecting cultivation in this tract. About ten years previously, I was told, abundant springs had unexpectedly appeared in the sandy jungle some miles to the south, fed, no doubt, by the Nura and other hill streams which higher up lose themselves on the pebble 'Sai,' that glacis of the mountains. The water supplied by these springs was so ample that land sufficient for 700 to 800 households has since been brought under cultivation in the desert tract to the north of Karakir Langar, with the result that the wayfarers' custom has been completely transferred to the new village of Achma. My second day's ride was to Chira, a large oasis counting some 3,500 households, and receiving its water from the river that comes from Hasa, and is fed by the glaciers north and north-east of the great Muztagh. My night's halt here was rendered enjoyable by the charming camping-place I discovered in a terraced orchard, where the white blossoms of the plum-tree ('ürük') covered the ground like fresh snow, while the air was scented with their perfume.

But already on the following morning we had to face a strong dust-storm blowing from the west, while we covered the forty odd miles across the dreary plain of sand and pebbles to the oasis of Sampula. The thick haze which enveloped us all day made me thankful for the guidance afforded by the rows of poles marking the road. Sampula, or Lop as it is also called from its chief village, is a thickly populated tract still included in the Ambanship of Keriya, though watered chiefly by canals from the Yurung-kash or Khotan River. I was struck by the thriving look of its villages, due largely to the flourishing carpet industry which is centred here. Its products, though unfortunately debased by the use of aniline dyes, are still much prized throughout Turkestan. There is little doubt that the manufacture of these famous silk carpets, and some other local industries connected with Khotan, are an inheritance from ancient days.

The fourth and last day of my journey to Khotan was utilised for a visit to the extensive débris area spreading on the outskirts of the desert beyond Hanguya, the northernmost large village of Sampula. It was a typical 'Tati,' just as Turdi's report had led me to expect, covering several square miles. Thanks to his expert guidance, I had no difficulty in tracing in the midst of it the much-decayed remains of a Stupa, known to the people of Hanguya as the Arka-kuduk Tim. The ruin itself showed no feature of special interest, but it was curious to note that, owing to deep erosion of the surrounding ground, the remains of the Stupa now stand on an isolated loess bank fully 20 feet high. In reality the lowest course of the brick-work marked the original level, and the mound on which it now appeared to be raised was but a witness or " Zeuge "—to use the geologist's term—indicating the remarkable depth to which the slow excavation of the loess soil had been carried by the force of the winds. Ancient coins, seals, and other small objects are frequently picked up on its site, and the specimens I acquired on the spot from one of Turdi's associates were as clear a proof of its antiquity as the extent of erosion.

The dreary expanse of the Tati looked doubly doleful in the yellow dust haze, and I felt quite relieved when in the evening,

VILLAGE CHILDREN, KERIYA.

after a long ride over much sandy waste interspersed with patches of young cultivation, I reached the edge of the Yurung-kash canton. There faithful Islam Beg, with the emblems of his new dignity, Badruddin Khan, the Afghan Aksakal, and a posse of local Begs and Yüzbashis were waiting to give me a cheerful welcome on my return to Khotan territory. Joined thus by old friends and an imposing escort, I rode on through shady lanes where the scent of the fruit trees and weeping willows, now in full bloom, was almost overpowering. When I reached my re-united camp in a pleasant old garden near the Madrasah of Yurung-kash town, 'Yolchi Beg' gave vent to his joyful feelings by the most sonorous of barks.

EXCAVATIONS PROCEEDING ALONG SOUTH-EAST WALL OF RAWAK STUPA COURT.

CHAPTER XXX.

AK-SIPIL AND THE SCULPTURES OF THE RAWAK STUPA.

On the 6th of April I halted in Yurung-kash, where fresh supplies and labourers had to be secured, and many repairs to be effected in our equipment. Increasing heat by day and recurring dust storms warned me that the season was close at hand when work in the desert would become impossible. Instead of taking the rest we all by this time felt much in need of, I hastened to set out for the ancient sites which still remained to be explored in the desert north-east of Khotan. So after discharging Ibrahim Akhun, our worthy Darogha, with a liberal reward in glittering gold roubles for himself and an ample supply of specially desired medicines for his Amban, the caravan was set in march again on the morning of April 7th.

The ruined site known to treasure-seekers as Ak-sipil (" the

White Walls"), and situated among high sand dunes, at a distance of nearly fifteen miles from the right bank of the Yurung-kash opposite Khotan, was my next objective. On the march, and close to the edge of the cultivated area, I examined with interest the site known as Tam-öghil, from an adjoining small hamlet, where ancient "culture-strata," yielding some leaf-gold, besides old coins, terra-cottas, etc., are worked under exactly the same conditions as those described at Yotkan. The extent of the excavations is, however, far more limited, as the available water supply is scanty and the proceeds are less remunerative. Here, too, the excavations, which now employ about a dozen people for one and a half to two months in the year, are said to have been started by the accidental discovery of gold in a small 'Yar' that had formed about twenty years ago through the overflow of an irrigation channel. I noticed that the banks of fertile earth overlying the ancient "culture-stratum" to a height of 10 to 18 feet, silt deposits as I take it, showed here and there distinct traces of stratification. Considering the short distance, less than three miles, which separates this site from the present right bank of the Yurung-kash, it appeared to me possible that these slight layers, 1 to 1½ inches thick, may, perhaps, be due to exceptional floods from the river. The fertile soil excavated is used by the villagers to improve gravelly fields in the vicinity.

As soon as we had passed the edge of the cultivated area, fragments of ancient pottery appeared on the bare loess, cropping up also in large patches between the low dunes over which our march led for the next four miles. There was ample evidence that the belt of villages and fields had extended much further to the north in ancient times. Then the dunes grew remarkably steep and high, up to sixty feet and more, the coarse, heavy sand unmistakably showing its origin from the gravel deposits of the river. Here the uniform direction of the dunes was also clearly marked, being N.N.W. to S.S.E. After five miles of these difficult dunes we reached open and in places much eroded ground near Ak-sipil, where I thought I could distinguish traces of little embankments dividing ancient fields, and of distributing 'Ariks' along them.

At Ak-sipil the most conspicuous remains are ruined portions of the rampart and parapet of an ancient fort. They have been visited before by several European travellers, and as some reliable data concerning them have been published by M. Grenard from M. Dutreuil de Rhins' notes, the briefest notice will suffice. The exact survey made by me showed that the extant ruins form a segment, about 360 feet long, of a circular wall which must have originally enclosed an area about 1,000 feet in diameter. Here, as at Endere, the lower portion of the circumvallation consisted of a rampart of hard stamped clay, rising about 11 feet above the original surface outside, which is still clearly distinguishable in places free of sand and uneroded. The rampart is surmounted by a parapet, 8 feet thick, which, by the large size of its sun-dried but fairly hard bricks (about 20 by 15 by 4 inches on the average), as well as by its solid construction, suggests considerable antiquity. The parapet, where in fair preservation, showed loopholes arranged in two uniform levels, one 16 inches, the other 5 feet above the base, but at irregular intervals. At two points of the extant segment the parapet is strengthened by solid brick platforms projecting about 3 feet on either side, which were provided with stairs, and probably served as watch-towers.

With the exception of the small segment facing due north, the circumvallation of this ancient fort, together with any buildings the interior might have once contained, has disappeared completely owing to erosion. The débris which covers the open ground between the low dunes for some distance around, has furnished to native "treasure-seekers" Chinese coins of the Han period, and plentiful small remains, such as seals, etc. All those acquired by me point to an early abandonment of this site.

A low mound, some 1½ miles south-west, to which Turdi conducted me, proved on excavation to mark the position of an ancient temple. Though the structure itself had been completely destroyed, no doubt through the operations of "treasure-seekers," there turned up among the loose débris of plaster and decomposed timber a considerable quantity of small relievo fragments in stucco of remarkable hardness. These fragments, among which pieces of draped relievo figures, as well as of decorative plaques are largely represented, display a style of modelling and a technical execution far superior to the stucco work of the Dandan-Uiliq and Endere temples, and recalling the best products of Græco-Buddhist sculpture in Gandhara. A feature as remarkable as the hardness of these small stucco relievos is their cracked and fissured surface, which in places looks as if scorched. The assumption that these stucco pieces received their present appearance in a fire that consumed the temple naturally suggests itself. But whether this accidental burning would also account for their exceptional hardness is a question still to be settled by a ceramic expert. "Treasure-seekers" call this place 'Kighillik,' from a large mound mainly composed of dry manure ('kighik') that rises quite close to the remains just mentioned. This huge refuse-heap, which measures, as far as exposed, some 70 by 50 feet, with a depth of at least 16 feet, has not escaped the attention of treasure-seekers. The regular galleries they have tunnelled through it enabled me to ascertain with comparative ease that its contents, besides manure (apparently horse-dung), were only small bits of bone, charcoal and fuel.

On the 10th of April I left Ak-sipil, and marching due north for about fourteen miles, partly over dunes of coarse grey sand, partly along a pebble-covered 'Sai' clearly recognisable as an ancient river-bed, arrived in the evening at the ruins called 'Rawak' ("High Mansion") by Turdi and the men of his craft. Here an unexpected and most gratifying discovery awaited me. Our honest old guide had spoken only of "an old house" to be seen there half-buried in the sand, but in reality the first glimpse showed a large Stupa with its enclosing quadrangle, by far the most imposing structure I had seen among the extant ruins of the Khotan region. Large dunes of coarse sand, rising over 25 feet in height, covered the quadrangle and part of the massive square base of the Stupa on the north-west and north-east faces. But towards the south the drift-sand was lower, and there great portions of the Stupa base, as well as the lines of masonry marking the quadrangular enclosure of the Stupa court, could be readily made out. Near the south corner of the enclosing wall fragments of the heads of colossal stucco statues, the spoil of casual diggings by "treasure-seekers," were lying on the surface. I realised at once that there was scope here for extensive excavations, and accordingly lost no time in sending back urgent orders for a reinforcement of labourers.

Fortunately the position of the ruin, within a day's march of the oasis, enabled me to secure a large number of willing workers from the nearest villages of the Jiya tract. A favourable factor

RAWAK STUPA, SEEN FROM SOUTH CORNER OF COURT.

of still greater importance was the relative ease with which the question of water supply for such a number of men was solved. For though the sand dunes surrounding us looked more formidable than at any ancient site previously explored, it was possible to dig a well in a depression within two miles of the Stupa, and there the labourers' camp was conveniently established. A look at the map shows that the distance from the Rawak site to the bank of the Yurung-kash is only about seven miles. In fact to this comparative proximity of the present river-bed were due both the forbidding height of the dunes and the slight depth of subsoil water.

The season of Burans had now fully set in, and the gales that were blowing daily, though from different quarters and of varying degrees of violence, carried along with them a spray of light sand that permeated everything. I noticed the frequency with which the wind would shift round to almost opposite directions on successive days, sometimes even between morning and evening—a feature of Burans well known to all natives living near the Taklamakan and observed also by former travellers. To the discomfort which the constant drifting of sand caused, and which we naturally felt in a still more irritating fashion while engaged in excavation, was added the trying sensation of glare and heat all through the daytime. The sun beat down with remarkable intensity through the yellowish dust-haze, and the reflection of its rays by every glittering particle of sand made the heat appear far greater than it really was. The quick radiation that set in as soon as the sun had gone down caused rapid and striking variations in the temperature at different portions of the day, and I have little doubt that the agues and fevers, from which all my own followers began to suffer after our start from Yurung-kash, were mainly brought on by these sudden changes. It was impossible for me to escape exposure to these adverse atmospheric influences; but luckily the chills I caught freely could be kept in check by liberal doses of quinine until my work at these fascinating ruins was done.

The excavations, which I commenced on the morning of the 11th of April in the inner south corner of the quadrangle, soon revealed evidence that the enclosing wall had been adorned with whole rows of colossal statues in stucco. Those on the inside face of the wall could still be expected to be in a fair state of preservation owing to the depth of the sand, which was in no place less than seven feet, greatly increasing towards the west and east corners. But I realised that great masses of sand would have to be shifted before these sculptures could be systematically unearthed and examined in safety. For the heavy earth-work implied by this task it was necessary to await the arrival of the reinforcements already summoned. But in the meantime I was able to utilise the dozen labourers already at hand for such clearings as the preliminary survey of the structural remains demanded.

The result of this survey showed that the Stupa court formed a great quadrangle 164 feet long from north-west to south-east, and 143 feet broad. It was enclosed by a solidly built wall of sun-dried bricks, a little over 3 feet thick, and rising to a height of over 11 feet at the exposed south corner of the court, but once probably higher. The centre of the quadrangle is occupied by the imposing Stupa base, which rises in two stories to a height of 20 feet above the floor. The photograph on p. 428 shows it as seen from the inner south corner of the court, before any clearing. Owing to bold projections on each face, originally supporting well-proportioned flights of steps, the ground plan of the base showed the shape of a symmetrically developed cross, each of the four arms of which extended to fifty feet on the lowest level.

The diameter of the Stupa dome, which was raised on a projecting circular drum and constructed like the rest of the structure of sun-dried bricks, measured a little over 32 feet. It seems to have had an inner chamber about 7½ feet in diameter, but this could not be exactly determined, as a large cutting had been made into the dome from the west. The top of the Stupa had also been broken long ago, the extant masonry reaching to a height of 33 feet above the level of the court. The dome had probably always been exposed to the attacks of "treasure-seekers" as well as to erosion, and the destruction thus caused made it quite impossible to determine its original height. The broad flight of steps which occupied the centre of each of the four faces of the base, and led up without a break from the court to the foot of the dome, must have been an imposing feature. The one on the south-east side, which faces the entrance gate of the quadrangle, could alone be cleared. The portions of the base flanking this flight of steps proved to be coated with a thick layer of white stucco which probably once covered the whole of the Stupa. It was here, sticking to the plaster under a bold moulding at the foot of the base, that I discovered four well-preserved copper-pieces of the Han period showing very little wear. Like subsequent finds of such coins, they had manifestly been deposited as votive offerings, and furnished me with the first indication of the probable age of the structure.

The great archæological interest of the ruins, however, does not centre so much in the Stupa as in the rich series of relievo sculptures decorating the walls of the Stupa court. These were brought to light by the systematic excavations which I commenced as soon as the bands of labourers, quickly collected and despatched by the Beg of Yurung-kash, had joined my camp in the early morning of the 12th of April. In order to avoid the risks of immediate damage to the friable stucco of the sculptures, and to get sufficient room for photographing them, it was necessary to open broad trenches at some little distance from the walls and then to proceed towards the latter, carefully clearing out the sand. Commencing at the inner south corner, the work of excavation was gradually extended along the south-west and south-east walls up to the furthermost points which the high dunes rising over the east and west corners permitted to be cleared. The photograph, p. 424, shows a portion of the south-east wall with the trenches in course of excavation, along both its sides, and also helps to convey an impression of the mighty ridges of sand immediately surrounding the ruins.

As the work of clearing proceeded, I soon recognised that the main adornment of the walls, both towards the court and outside, consisted throughout of rows of colossal statues in stucco. All the large relievos represented Buddhas or Bodhisattvas, but from the varying attitudes a number of groups could be distinguished, arranged apparently on a more or less symmetrical plan. Between the colossal images at frequent intervals were smaller relievo representations of attendant deities and saints. In numerous instances the walls were further decorated with elaborate plaques of stucco forming halos above and around the more important figures, as well as with small paintings in fresco. The whole of the relievo work had originally been coloured, but the layers of paint had peeled off except where well protected in drapery folds, etc. Thus the greatest portions of the stucco images presented themselves in their terra-cotta ground colour.

COLOSSAL STATUES WITH SEATED BUDDHA, IN SOUTH CORNER OF RAWAK STUPA COURT, AFTER EXCAVATION.

I found from the first that the excavation of this wealth of statuary was attended with serious difficulty. Owing probably to the moisture rising from the neighbourhood of subsoil water, the strong wooden framework which once supported internally the masses of stucco and fastened them to beams let into the wall behind, had completely rotted away. The cavities left by the beams, which were evidently about 5 inches square, and fixed at a uniform height of 8 feet above the ground, can clearly be seen in the photographs, pp. 432, 439, 440, while the round holes visible in the arms of the colossal statues (see pp. 432, 434) indicate the position once occupied by portions of the internal framework.

Deprived of this support, the heavy stucco images threatened to collapse when the protecting sand was being removed. The Burans greatly added to this risk. They carried away the fine sand which had filled the interstices between the statues and the wall behind, and thus placed the friable masses of stucco in danger of sliding down through their own weight to immediate destruction. Experience soon showed me that these risks could be obviated only by extreme care in clearing the relievos and by covering up again their lowest portions as soon as they had been photographed. Even so damage could not altogether be prevented. In some instances it was necessary to secure the upper portions of statues still intact by means of ropes held by my men, even during the few minutes required to obtain photographs. Our procedure in these critical cases is illustrated by the view on p. 434. It shows some of the minor statues excavated on the inner side of the south-west wall being thus held, and also helps to mark the true size of the colossal image seen to the extreme right by comparison with the labourers.

The conditions here briefly indicated, which rendered the excavation work so difficult and risky, are also a sufficient explanation why most of the colossal statues were found without their heads. Their upper portions, just like the top segments of the great halo seen on the left of the photograph reproduced on p. 432, had necessarily been left much longer without the protecting cover of sand, and had accordingly fallen away from the wall that once supported them. The heads of the smaller images were almost invariably found intact. I may here note that among all the sculptural decoration of the Stupa court I failed to trace any evidence of wilful destruction by human agency as distinguished from such casual damage as the spasmodic

RELIEVO STATUES OF RAWAK STUPA COURT, SOUTH-WEST WALL, AFTER EXCAVATION.

burrowing of "treasure-seekers" may have caused at some points of the more exposed outer face of the enclosing wall. This observation lends support to the belief, justified by other evidence, that this great shrine was already long deserted and the ruins of its court covered up by the time when Islam finally annexed Khotan.

It is possible that originally a wooden gallery or some similar structure projecting from the top of the enclosing wall offered shelter to the sculptures. But this, if it really existed, must have been systematically removed even before the sand had completely invaded the Stupa court, for only in one place near the inner south-east face did my excavations bring to light some pieces of timber, about four inches thick, that might have served for such a structure. Considering how comparatively expensive an article building timber is to this day in the immediate vicinity of a large Turkestan town, we could scarcely be surprised at the early removal of this, the most useful material the deserted shrine could offer.

The total number of individual relievos of large size, which were unearthed along the cleared portions of the south-west and south-east walls, amounted to ninety-one. In addition to these the finds included many small relievos forming part of halos, etc., or deposited as ex-votos before the main images. The position of all statues was carefully shown in the ground-plan and a detailed description of every piece of sculpture, with exact measurements, duly recorded. In addition, I obtained a complete series of photographs of whatever sculptural work appeared on the excavated wall faces, the aggregate length of which amounted in the end to more than 300 feet. It was no easy task to collect all these records with the needful accuracy while directing the successive stages of the excavation in atmospheric conditions trying alike to eyes, throat, and lungs. Though Ram Singh and Turdi rendered, each in his own way, very intelligent assistance, I had myself to remain in the trenches practically from sunrise until nightfall. I could judge from the dust-laden look of the men what an appearance I presented during those days. Needless to say that the notebook used at this site feels gritty with sand to this day!

It is impossible to attempt here a description of the mass of interesting materials which these excavations have yielded for the study of the ancient sculptural art of Khotan. While such a task must properly be reserved for the scientific Report on my explorations, it will be useful to offer brief notes on those relievos which are represented in the accompanying illustrations.

RELIEVO SCULPTURES ON OUTER SOUTH-EAST WALL OF RAWAK STUPA COURT, IN COURSE OF EXCAVATION.

Among the sculptural remains occupying the inner south-west wall nearest to the south corner, shown on p. 432, and partly reproduced also in the gravure of the frontispiece, the well-modelled figure of the seated Buddha and the elaborate halo of the larger standing image behind, filled with representations of teaching Bodhisattvas or Arhats, deserve special attention. The three-feet measure placed in front of the seated image, and visible also in the other photographs, indicates the scale of the sculptures. The statue of a richly-robed Bodhisattva, life-size, seen on p. 437, is of interest both on account of the elaborate drapery shown in the lower garment and of the carefully indicated strings of jewels which cover the breast and arms. Both in style and arrangement these jewels bear the closest resemblance to those displayed by many Græco-Buddhist sculptures from the ruined Stupas and monasteries of the north-west frontier of India.

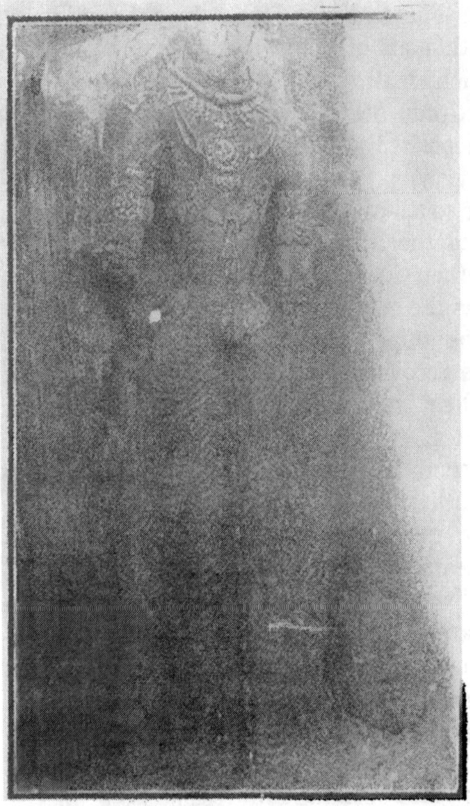

RELIEVO STATUE OF BODHISATTVA (R. IV.), ON SOUTH-WEST WALL, RAWAK STUPA COURT.

On the relievos of the outer south-east wall which the photograph, p. 436, represents just as they were found in the course of excavation, the careful execution of rich drapery and the elegant proportions of the hands and heads may be particularly noticed. The photograph opposite shows the grouping of colossal statues on the outer walls of the south corner. The images on the extreme right, which still reached with their shoulders to a height of eight feet, could not be completely cleared of sand, as the weight of the intact upper portions made a collapse imminent if the support of the mass of sand that enveloped the lower limbs were removed. The remains in the foreground belong to a kind of outer passage wall, decorated on both sides, which appears to have been added at this corner only. The relievos of this apex-shaped screen, which perhaps represents a later embellishment of the Stupa court, showed remarkably delicate work in the plaques of the halos, but had unfortunately suffered much damage owing to the thinness of the wall and its exposed position. The way in which small detached stucco representations of Buddha, in the attitude of teaching or meditation, mostly replicas, were found deposited at the feet of the larger images is illustrated by the view, p. 440, showing torsos of colossal statues along the inner south-east wall.

The entrance gate to the Stupa court leading through this wall was flanked on either side by two life-sized statues, which interested me greatly as the only figures found of a quasi-secular character. Though the upper portions of their bodies had broken away and were recovered only in fragments, there can be no doubt as to their representing the 'Dvarapalas,' or "Guardians of the gates," which Indian convention places at the entrances of all assemblies whether real or mythical. It is probable that the guardians of the Rawak Stupa court, like those sculptured at the approaches to many a sacred Buddhist shrine in India, were meant for Yakshas, a category of attendant divinities. But Buddhist iconography invariably gave to these a human appearance, and it was manifest that the figures here unearthed exhibit the customary dress of the period and of the country. The boots seen on the feet of the two guardians which stood inside the gate to the proper right (see p. 441) were wide at the top and showed remains of dark red colouring, with an ornamental border on their brim. Into them were tucked bulging trousers, hidden for the greater part by two large coats hanging down from the waist, one above the other. The bands

COLOSSAL STATUES ON OUTER WALLS OF SOUTH CORNER OF RAWAK STUPA COURT.

of embroidery running along the hems of the coats showed elaborate patterns with small circulets and crochets. These, as well as other details of ancient millinery, such as plaits, frills, etc., can still readily be made out in the original photographs.

Want of space does not permit further details about other

TORSOS OF COLOSSAL STATUES ALONG INNER SOUTH-EAST WALL.

remarkable pieces of statuary. But I may briefly mention the discovery of remains of gold-leaf stuck originally in small square patches to the left knee of the colossal image which is seen on the extreme left of the photograph on p. 441. I could not have wished for a better illustration of the quaint custom which Hiuen-Tsiang records of a miracle-working Buddha figure of colossal size he saw at Pi-mo. "Those who have any disease, according to the part affected, cover the corresponding place on the statue with gold-leaf, and forthwith they are healed. People who address prayers to it with a sincere heart mostly obtain their wishes." From the number of gold-leaf plasters of which the marks remain on this Rawak image, it would seem as if it

TORSOS OF STATUES (DVĀRAPALAS) AT GATE OF RAWAK STUPA COURT.

had enjoyed particular fame for healing power in affections of the knee.

But more important and fascinating than any such details was the very close affinity in style and most details of execution which every single find revealed with the so-called Græco-Buddhist sculptures of the Peshawar valley and the neighbouring region. Whether that sculptural art, mainly of classical origin, had been brought direct from the Indus or from Bactria, there can be no further doubt, in view of these discoveries, that

STUCCO HEAD OF SMALL BUDDHA OR BODHISATTVA, ORIGINALLY PAINTED, FROM RAWAK STUPA COURT.

at an early date it found a true home and flourished in Khotan. The close study of this wealth of sculpture is a task of great historical and artistic interest. I hope that it will be possible to facilitate it by the publication of adequate reproductions of all my photographs.

Our data for the chronology of Græco-Buddhist art in India are as yet too scanty to permit any safe conclusion as to the date of the Rawak relievos. No epigraphical finds of any kind were made in that part of the ruins which could be cleared, but I was fortunate enough to secure *in situ* numismatic evidence of distinct value. While cleaning the pedestals of various statues along different portions of the enclosure as well as while examining the wall where the wooden gate had once been fixed, we came again and again upon Chinese copper coins bearing the 'Wu-tchu' symbols and belonging to issues of the Han dynasty, just like the coins I had discovered below mouldings at the foot of the great Stupa. These coins were invariably found within small cavities or interstices of the plaster or brick-work, into which they must have been slipped as votive offerings. Subsequently, when a detached base only eight feet square, probably once surmounted by a small votive Stupa, was excavated near the inner south corner of the quadrangle, many more coins of the same type came to light between the masonry of the base and a much-decayed wooden boarding which encased it.

With this discovery the total number of such coins rose to close on a hundred. Most of them are in good preservation and do not show any marks of long circulation. Only current coins are likely to have been used for such humble votive gifts, and as no finds of a later date were made, there is good reason to believe that the latest known date of these issues marks the lowest chronological limit for the Rawak sculptures. The rule of the Later Han dynasty extended over the period 25–220 A.D., but the issue of some of its coin-types appears to have continued to the close of the fourth century So far as minor antiquarian indications, derived from the construction, the materials, etc., of the ruined Stupa and its adornments, permit us to judge at present, the date of its erection may well fall near the period to which the ruins of the ancient settlement beyond Imam Jafar Sadik have proved to belong.

I soon realised with regret that, owing to the extremely friable condition of the stucco and the difficulties of transport, the removal of the larger relievos was impracticable. Those pieces of the colossal images which were found already detached, such as portions of arms, projecting drapery, etc., usually broke when lifted, whatever care was used. An attempt to move the complete statues or torsos from their places would have meant only vandal destruction, unless elaborate appliances, including perhaps specially constructed coffin-like cases made to measure, as it were, could be provided. To improvise these I had neither time nor the technical means, and in any case it would have been a practical impossibility to arrange for the safe transport of such loads over the mountains, whether to India or Europe.

All that could be done in the case of these large sculptures was to bury them again safely in the sand after they had been photographed and described, and to trust that they would rest undisturbed under their protecting cover—until that time, still distant it seems, when Khotan shall have its own local museum. But of the smaller relievos and sculptural pieces already detached, I succeeded in bringing away a considerable number. I felt greatly relieved when I found on my arrival at Kashgar, and later also in London, that the great trouble and labour which the safe packing of these extremely fragile objects had cost me was rewarded by their having accomplished the long journey—some six thousand miles by camels, ponies, railway and steamer—without any serious damage. The two heads of saints in alto-relievo still retaining part of their colouring, which are shown on pp. 442, 445, illustrate types frequently recurring in this collection. Full-size reproductions of other sculptures have been given among the plates of my "Preliminary Report."

By April 18th those portions of the Stupa court which were not actually buried under sand dunes had been explored. The proper excavation of the other parts could not have been accomplished without months of labour and proportionately heavy expenditure. A careful examination of the surrounding area revealed no other structural remains; broken pottery found here and there on some narrow patches of ground between the swelling sand dunes was the only trace left of what probably were modest dwelling-places around the great shrine. The

STUCCO HEAD OF SMALL BUDDHA OR BODHISATTVA, RETAINING ORIGINAL COLOURING, FROM RAWAK STUPA COURT.

sand-storms, which visited us daily and the increasing heat and glare, had made the work very trying to the men as well as myself. It was manifestly time to withdraw from the desert.

Before, however, leaving the ruins I took care to protect the sculptures which could not be moved, by having the trenches that had exposed them filled up again. It was a melancholy duty to perform, strangely reminding me of a true burial, and it almost cost me an effort to watch the images I had brought to light vanishing again, one after the other, under the pall of sand which had hidden them for so many centuries.

Jumbe-kum, some four miles beyond Rawak to the north-east, was the only remaining desert site around Khotan from which occasional finds had been reported to me. I took occasion to visit it from Rawak and convinced myself that this débris-strewn 'Tati' contained no remains capable of excavation. Thus, when on the 19th of April I started back to Khotan, I had the satisfaction of knowing that the programme of my explorations in the desert was completed.

CHAPTER XXXI.

ISLAM AKHUN AND HIS FORGERIES.

THE eight days' halt that followed my return to Khotan passed with surprising rapidity. A severe cold, brought on by the exposure of the last weeks in the desert, developed into an attack of what looked like bronchitis. This obliged me to remain within doors for most of the time, and partly in bed. But the arrangement of my collections, their partial repacking, and the endless little agenda which accumulate after a long season of camp work, kept me so busy that this involuntary confinement was scarcely realised by myself. I could not have wished for a more pleasant shelter than that afforded by Nar-Bagh, the old country residence of Niaz Hakim Beg. The many-windowed lofty pavilion in the centre of the garden where I had taken up my quarters, as five years before me Dr. Hedin had done, secured quiet as well as fresh air. The trees along the four little avenues which radiate from this pavilion were still partly in bloom when I arrived, and even when the last blossoms had withered there was the fresh green of the leaves to please the eyes which had so long beheld only the yellow and grey of the sand dunes. Judged by the old Moghul gardens about Lahore, my cherished haunts in years gone by, Nar-Bagh would be thought a very plain villeggiatura of the Eastern type. But here in Chinese Turkestan, where even the cultivation of a field involves a serious struggle against sterile nature, real gardens are so few and far between that Niaz Hakim Beg's creation deserves grateful acknowledgment.

I was glad that, on the morning after my arrival, I still felt well enough to call on Pan-Darin, who received me at his Yamen like an old friend, and, as I imagined, somewhat like a fellow-scholar. Much I had to tell him of my excavations and the finds which rewarded them. When next day the old Amban came to return the visit, I had ready a little representative exhibition of my antiquities to satisfy his curiosity. Pan-Darin is undoubtedly a man of learning and versed in Chinese history. All the same I was surprised by the historical sense displayed in the questions which he put to me regarding the relative age, the import and character of the multifarious ancient documents I had discovered. When I attempted to explain by a reference to the plates in Professor Bühler's "Indian Palæography" how a study of the writing in the various manuscripts would enable us to fix their dates with approximate accuracy, Pan-Darin at once showed his appreciation of this evidence by writing down the modifications through which Chinese characters have passed in succeeding periods. I felt almost in company of a colleague, and forgot for a moment the irksome circumlocution and confusion which conversation through a not over-intelligent interpreter implies.

Only in one respect did the interest of Pan-Darin in my finds at first embarrass me. He dwelt on the fact of all these old records being carried away to the Far West. What could he show to the Fu-tai or Governor-General at Urumchi, who had been so inquisitive about the object of my excavations, and who undoubtedly would wish to hear of the results? I knew how sympathetically Pan-Darin had represented my case, and thanked him heartily for the support he had given to the cause of science. I assured him against the future curiosity of the Fu-tai by promising to send from Kashgar photographs of the various types of ancient documents. "But they should be in duplicate," was the cautious demand of my learned friend. For he seemed eager to retain for himself some samples of the strange records which the desert had yielded up after so many centuries. I feel confident that, of the copies of my "Preliminary Report" subsequently transmitted by the Indian Government for presentation to Chinese officials, his at least was duly appreciated.

My last stay at Khotan had to be utilised also for a curious semi-antiquarian, semi-judicial inquiry. Its success has been greeted with no small satisfaction by a number of fellow-scholars, besides greatly amusing me at the time. It enabled me to clear up the last doubts as to the strange manuscripts and "block-prints" in "unknown characters" which, as already mentioned, had during recent years been purchased from Khotan in remarkable numbers, and which had found their way not only to Calcutta, but also to great public collections in London, Paris, and St. Petersburg. The grave suspicions which my previous inquiries had led me to entertain about the genuineness of these "finds" was strengthened almost to certainty by the explorations of the winter. Ample as were the manuscript materials which the latter had yielded, and in spite of the great variety of languages and scripts represented among them (Kharoshthi, Indian Brahmi, Central-Asian Brahmi, Tibetan, Chinese), I had failed to trace the smallest scrap of writing in "unknown characters." The actual conditions of the sites explored also differed entirely from the conditions under which those queer "old books" were alleged to have been discovered.

There was good reason to believe that Islam Akhun, a native of Khotan and reputed "treasure-seeker," to whom it was possible to trace most of these manuscripts that had been purchased on behalf of the Indian Government during the years 1895–98, was directly concerned in the forgeries. He kept away from Khotan during my first visits. He had been punished some time before on account of other impositions which Captain Deasy and Mr. Macartney had brought to the notice of the Khotan authorities, and he evidently did not think it safe to attempt further deception in my case. I had no reason to regret the wide berth which Islam Akhun had given me while I was engaged in my archæological work about Khotan and at the ancient sites of the desert. But now when the antiquarian evidence as to the true character of those remarkable literary relics in "unknown characters" was practically complete, and my departure near at hand, I was anxious for a personal examination of that enterprising individual whose productions had engaged so much learned attention in Europe.

Pan-Darin, to whom I confidentially communicated my wish to get hold of Islam Akhun, readily granted his assistance. As an attempt on the part of Islam Akhun to abscond was by no means improbable, and as time was getting short, I took care to impress the learned Mandarin with the necessity of prompt and discreet action. Nor did he disappoint me in these respects; for on the morning of April 25th Islam Akhun was duly produced from Chira, where he had been practising as a 'Hakim' during the last winter. He scarcely anticipated being "wanted" now, as when passing through Chira some three weeks before I had purposely refrained from making any inquiries about him. The Beg who escorted him brought also a motley collection of papers which had been seized partly in Islam Akhun's possession and partly in his Khotan house, and which on examination proved rather curious. They were sheets of artificially discoloured paper, covered with impressions of the same elaborate formulas in "unknown characters" that appeared in the last batch of "ancient block-prints" which had been sold in Kashgar. A manuscript leaf, also in "unknown characters," had evidently remained over from the earlier manufacture when the forger was still content to work by mere writing.

ISLAM AKHUN.

Two large sheets of a Swedish newspaper, the *Svenska Morgonbladet* of July, 1897—I know how these got to Khotan, but "that is another story"—were relics of the imposture when Islam Akhun tried to make a living by representing himself among the ignorant 'Taghliks' south of Khotan and Keriya as an agent sent by Mr. Macartney to search out owners of slaves originally carried away by Hunza raiders from Indian territory. One of these newspaper sheets, nicely mounted on cloth, showed the portrait of a Swedish missionary in China, for which Islam Akhun pretended to have sat himself. The few Chinese characters printed below, giving the Chinese name of the reverend gentleman, were cunningly represented by him as containing his own name. Armed with these truly imposing documents, which he passed off as his official credentials, the clever rogue had managed to levy blackmail from innocent hillmen who feared to be accused of the retention of non-existent slaves. But after a short period of success he had been found out, and subsequently, on Mr. Macartney's representation, had received due punishment at the Khotan Yamen. When about 1898 the sale of "old books" fell off, owing to the growing suspicion attaching to them among the European residents of Kashgar, Islam Akhun had taken to the calling of a 'Hakim,' or medicine man. The leaves of a French novel (left behind perhaps by MM. Dutreuil de Rhins and Grenard) and the fragments of some Persian texts, which had been found on his person and were also duly produced, were said to have figured as part of his latest equipment. But whether he used the leaves of the French novel merely to read out imaginary charms from, or administered pieces of them for internal consumption, was, I regret, not ascertained at the time.

The examination of this versatile individual proved a protracted affair, and through two long days I felt as if breathing the atmosphere of an Indian judicial court. When first arraigned in my improvised "Cutchery," Islam Akhun readily and with contrite mien confessed his guilt in the above "personation case," and also to having in 1898 obtained money from Badruddin, the Afghan Aksakal, by a forged note purporting to be in Captain Deasy's handwriting. But in the matter of the "old books" he for a long time protested complete innocence. He pretended to have acted merely as the Kashgar sale agent for certain persons at Khotan, since dead or absconded, who, rightly or wrongly, told him that they had picked them up in the desert. When he found how much such "old books" were appreciated by Europeans, he asked those persons to find more. This they did, whereupon he took their finds to Kashgar, etc. Now, he lamented, he was left alone to bear the onus of the fraud—if such it was. Muhammad Tari, one of those who gave the "books," had previously run away to Yarkand; Muhammad Siddiq, the Mullah, had absconded towards Aksu; and a third of the band had escaped from all trouble by dying.

It was a cleverly devised line of defence, and Islam Akhun clung to it with great consistency and with the wariness of a man who has had unpleasant experience of the ways of the law. I had thought it right to tell him from the first that I was not going to proceed against him at the Amban's Yamen in the matter of these happily ended forgeries; for I was aware that such a step, in accordance with Chinese procedure, was likely to lead to the application of some effective means of persuasion, *i.e.*, torture. This, of course, I would not countenance; nor could a confession as its eventual result be to me of any value. Whether it was from Islam Akhun's reliance on these scruples of mine, or from his knowledge that direct evidence could not easily be produced within the time available, two long cross-examinations, in the interval of which I had Islam Akhun's wants hospitably looked to by my own men, failed to bring a solution. However, in the course of his long protestations of complete innocence, Islam Akhun introduced a denial which seemed to offer some chance of catching my wary defendant. He emphatically denied having seen any of the alleged find-places himself, in fact having ever personally visited any ancient site in the desert.

I had purposely refrained at the time from showing any special interest in this far-reaching disclaimer. Consequently I had no difficulty in inducing him to repeat it with still more emphasis and in the presence of numerous witnesses when he was brought up "on remand" for a third time. Whether encouraged by his apparent success so far or by the forbearing treatment I had accorded to him, it was evident that the sly, restless-looking fellow was for the time being off his guard. So I promptly confronted him, from the detailed account printed in Dr. Hoernle's Report, with an exact reproduction of the elaborate stories which he had told, in the course of depositions made on different occasions before Mr. Macartney, about his alleged journeys and discoveries in the Taklamakan during the years 1895–98.

The effect was most striking. Islam Akhun was wholly unprepared for the fact that his lies told years before, with so much seeming accuracy of topographical and other details, had received the honour of permanent record in a scientific report to Government. Hearing them now read out by me in re-translation, he was thoroughly startled and confused. He appeared also greatly impressed by the fact that, with the help of the exact information recorded by Mr. Macartney and reproduced by Dr. Hoernle, I could enlighten him as to what "old books" he had sold at Kashgar on particular occasions, what remarkable statements he had made about the manner of their discovery by himself, etc. He was intelligent enough to realise that he stood self-convicted, and that there was nothing to be gained by further protestations of innocence. He now admitted that he had seen manuscripts being written by his above-named employers (*recte* accomplices) at a deserted Mazar near Sampula. Little by little his admissions became more detailed, and ultimately, when assured that no further punishment awaited him, he made a clean breast of it.

Islam Akhun's subsequent confessions proved perfectly correct on many important particulars when checked from the records kept at Kashgar, as well as from the evidence of a number of independent witnesses. He showed himself to be possessed of an excellent memory, and readily recognised among the numerous photogravure plates accompanying Dr. Hoernle's Report those representing specimen pages from the "block-printed" books in "unknown characters" which formed his own manufacture. He had, previous to 1894, been engaged at times in collecting coins, seals, and similar antiques from Khotan villages. About that time he learned from Afghan traders of the value which the 'Sahibs' from India attached to ancient manuscripts. Genuine scraps of such had indeed been unearthed by Turdi and some other "treasure-seekers" at

Dandan-Uiliq. But the idea of visiting such dreary desert sites, with the certainty of great hardships and only a limited chance of finds, had no attraction for a person of such wits as Islam Akhun. So in preference he conceived the plan of manufacturing the article he was urged to supply the Sahibs with.

In this enterprise he had several accomplices, among whom a certain Ibrahim Mullah was the leading man. This person appears to have made it his special business to cultivate the Russian demand for "old books," while Islam Akhun attended chiefly to the requirements of British officers and other collectors. Ibrahim Mullah, from whom the Russian Armenian I met on my first arrival at Khotan had purchased his forged birch-bark manuscript, was credited with some knowledge of Russian, a circumstance which explains the curious resemblance previously noticed between the characters used in some of the "block-prints" and the Greek (*recte* Russian) alphabet. Ibrahim Mullah gave proof of his "slimness," as well as his complicity, by promptly disappearing from Khotan on the first news of Islam Akhun's arrest, and could not be confronted with him.

The first "old book" produced in this fashion was successfully sold by Islam Akhun in 1895 to Munshi Ahmad Din, who was in charge of the Assistant Resident's Office at Kashgar during the temporary absence of Mr. Macartney. This "book" was written by hand, and an attempt had been made, as also in some others of the earliest products of the factory, to imitate the cursive Brahmi characters found in fragments of genuine manuscripts which Ibrahim was said to have secured from Dandan-Uiliq. Though the forgers never succeeded in producing a text showing consecutively the characters of any known script, yet their earliest fabrications were executed with an amount of care and ingenuity which might well deceive for a time even expert scholars in Europe. This may be seen by referring to the fac-similes which are given in Dr. Hoernle's Second "Report on Central-Asian Antiquities," from "codices" belonging to the early output, now deposited with so many other products of Islam Akhun's factory in the "forgery" section of the Manuscript Department of the British Museum. The fac-simile of an "ancient Khotan manuscript" which appears in the German edition of Dr. Sven Hedin's work, "Through Asia," is a conveniently accessible illustration of the factory's produce in a somewhat later and less careful phase of its working.

Seeing that remunerative prices could be obtained for such articles at Kashgar and, through Badruddin's somewhat careless mediation, also from Ladak and Kashmir, the efforts of the forgers were stimulated. As Islam Akhun quickly perceived that his "books" were readily paid for, though none of the Europeans who bought them could read their characters or distinguish them from ancient scripts, it became unnecessary to trouble about imitating the characters of genuine fragments. Thus, apparently, each individual factory "hand" was given free scope for inventing his own "unknown characters." This explains the striking diversity of these queer scripts, of which the analysis of the texts contained in the "British collection" at one time revealed at least a dozen—not exactly to the assurance of the Oriental scholars who were to help in their decipherment.

The rate of production by the laborious process of handwriting was, however, too slow, and accordingly the factory took to the more convenient method of producing books by means of repeated impressions from a series of wooden blocks. The preparation of such blocks presented no difficulty, as printing from wooden blocks is extensively practised in Chinese Turkestan. This printing of "old books" commenced in 1896, and its results are partly represented by the forty-five "block-prints" which are fully described and illustrated in Dr. Hoernle's First Report. These, too, showed an extraordinary variety of scripts in their ever-recurring formulas, and were often of quite imposing dimensions in size and bulk.

Islam Akhun, when once his defence had collapsed, was not chary about giving technical details about the forgers' methods of work. In fact, he seemed rather to relish the interest I showed in them. Thus he fully described the procedure followed in preparing the paper that was used for the production of manuscripts or "block-prints," as well as the treatment to which they were subjected in order to give them an ancient look.

The fact of Khotan being the main centre of the Turkestan paper industry was a great convenience for the forgers, as they could readily supply themselves with any variety and size of paper needed. The sheets of modern Khotan paper were first dyed yellow or light brown by means of 'Toghrugha,' a product of the Toghrak tree, which, when dissolved in water, gives a staining fluid.

When the dyed sheets had been written or printed upon they were hung over fireplaces so as to receive by smoke the proper hue of antiquity. It was, no doubt, in the course of this manipulation that the sheets occasionally sustained the burns and scorchings of which some of the "old books" transmitted to Calcutta display evident marks. Afterwards they were bound up into volumes. This, however, seems to have been the least efficiently managed department of the concern, for the coarse imitation of European volumes which is unmistakable in the case of most of the later products, as well as the utter unsuitability of the fastenings employed (usually pegs of copper or twists of paper), would *à priori* have justified grave suspicions as to their genuineness. Finally the finished manuscripts or books were treated to a liberal admixture between their pages of the fine sand of the desert, in order to make them tally with the story of their long burial. I well remember how, in the spring of 1898, I had to apply a clothes brush before I could examine one of these forged "block-prints" that had reached a collector in Kashmir.

All the previously suspected details of this elaborate and, for a time, remarkably successful fraud were thus confirmed by its main operator in the course of a long and cautiously conducted examination. It was a pleasure to me to know, and to be able to tell fellow-scholars in Europe: *habemus confitentem reum*—and that without any resort to Eastern methods of judicial inquiry. Yet possibly I had reason to feel even keener satisfaction at the fact that the positive results of my explorations were sufficient to dispose once for all of these fabrications so far as scholarly interests were concerned, even if Islam Akhun had never made his confession. In the light of the discoveries which had rewarded my excavations at Dandan-Uiliq and

Endere, and of the general experience gained during my work in the desert, it had become as easy to distinguish between Islam Akhun's forgeries and genuine old manuscripts as it was to explode his egregious stories about the ancient sites which were supposed to have furnished his "finds." Not only in the colour and substance of the paper, but also in arrangement, state of preservation, and a variety of other points, all genuine manuscripts show features never to be found in Islam Akhun's productions. But apart from this, there is the plain fact that the forgers never managed to produce a text exhibiting consecutively the characters of any known script, while all ancient documents brought to light by my explorations invariably show a writing that is otherwise well known to us. There is, therefore, little fear that Islam Akhun's forgeries will cause deception hereafter.

This consideration, as well as the fact of the forgers' work having ceased some three years earlier, had decided me not to press for Islam Akhun's punishment on the score of this fraud. I knew besides that my kind-hearted friend Pan-Darin was not without reason popularly credited with a pious proneness for pardoning sinners. In fact, I had noticed during our interview how relieved the old Amban looked when I told him that I did not consider it a part of my business to demand Islam Akhun's punishment for antiquarian forgeries, of which Chinese criminal justice might perhaps take a view very different from ours. There was also the manifest difficulty of bringing the other members of the firm to book, not to mention the "extenuating circumstances" connected with the way in which encouragement had been afforded to the fraud by undiscriminating purchasers. Nevertheless, when I remembered the great loss of valuable time and labour which the fabrications of Islam Akhun and his associates had caused to scholars of distinction, it was a satisfaction to know that this clever scoundrel had already, on one count or another, received from Chinese justice his well-deserved punishment. For fraudulently obtaining from Badruddin a sum equivalent to about Rs. 12 on the strength of a scrawl which he pretended to be Captain Deasy's order, he had been made to wear the wooden collar for a good time;

for the imposture practised as Mr. Macartney's Agent he had suffered corporal punishment as well as a term of imprisonment.

I had ample opportunity in the course of these prolonged "interviews" to convince myself that Islam Akhun was a man of exceptional intelligence for those parts, and also possessed of a quick wit and humour, equally unusual among the ordinary 'Khotanliks.' He was of slender build, with a face and eyes expressing sharpness as well as sly restlessness. Something in his looks I thought suggested Kashmiri descent, but this I was not able to ascertain. He greatly amused me by his witty repartees to honest old Turdi, whom with humorous impudence he adduced as a living demonstration of the fact that "there was nothing to be got out of the desert." He was greatly impressed by seeing his own handiwork so perfectly reproduced in the photogravure plates accompanying Dr. Hoernle's Report, and was very anxious to learn how this feat could be accomplished I had no doubt he was fully alive to the splendid opportunities for fresh frauds which this 'Wilayeti' art might provide. How much more proud would he have felt if he could but have seen, as I did a few months later, the fine morocco bindings with which a number of his block-printed Codices had been honoured in a great European library!

I represented to Islam Akhun that, willing as I was to credit him with a reliable memory concerning the methods and materials employed in his factory, it would still be desirable for me to obtain some tangible memento of them. So he at once volunteered to furnish one or more of the blocks employed in printing those precious "books." As all information had by that time been duly recorded, I allowed him to be set free conditionally from the lock-up of the Yamen, and on the following morning he turned up in due course with one of the promised blocks from his own house. The news of his arrest had of course long before spread through the town, and hence it was difficult for him to gain access to the homes of his former associates, where more of these materials may have been retained.

Whether it was from a right perception that his *rôle* was now completely played out, or because he felt that his ignominious collapse in the course of the inquiry had rendered him ridiculous before his old friends, Islam Akhun looked far more cowed in the end, though free, than when first brought up as a prisoner. I had told him before in jest that I thought him far too clever a man to be allowed to remain in Khotan among such ignorant people. A curious incident showed that the remark had not passed unappreciated. Shortly before my departure Islam Akhun presented himself with a petition, evidently meant to be serious, praying that I might take him along to Europe. It was not quite clear in what capacity he expected me to utilise his services *en route.* But I think there could be no doubt that the strange request was prompted by the hope of finding in distant 'Wilayet' a wider sphere for his forging abilities! So I need not regret, perhaps, having shown myself obdurate.

IN A KHOTAN BAZAR.

CHAPTER XXXII.

LAST DAYS IN KHOTAN OASIS.

ON the 27th of April I paid my farewell visit to the Khotan Yamen with sincere regret. It meant good-bye to Pan-Darin, who had proved in every way a true friend to me. He was unmistakably a man of the old school, not over fond of Western notions and influences. Yet from my first visit I felt that he understood my scientific aims and was ready to further them. I soon grew fond of his quiet, unaffected ways, which seemed to express so plainly his personal character. As an administrator this learned old gentleman may have his shortcomings. But all my native informants were unanimous in praising his integrity and genuine kindness. So I hoped that the literary attainments of my Mandarin friend would carry weight at Urumchi, whither he was shortly to retire, and would secure him some comfortable appointment, maybe the Taotai-ship of Kashgar.

On my way back I treated myself to a last long ride through the Khotan Bazars. It was the Saturday market of the "Old Town," and its long central street was overflowing with buyers and sellers. A glorious sunshine, pouring through the shaky tattered awnings that connect the houses and shops flanking the street, gave brilliancy to all the gaudy wares exhibited in the booths from which I selected mementoes. The old skill of the Khotan workmen still shows itself in the quaint articles of dress which form a prominent feature of the Bazar stores. But the universal use of aniline dyes seems, here as elsewhere in the East, to have destroyed the old sense of colour harmony. The capital of Khotan is indeed a small place, and in the course of my ride I revisited almost every picturesque lane and quaint mosque I knew from my stay in the autumn. After the long months in the desert I found a strange pleasure in seeing humanity again surging around me. But more than anything else the beautiful green of the young foliage which intruded everywhere into the lanes and the deep blue sky helped to throw lustre on my last impressions of Khotan.

On the following morning I said good-bye to Nar-Bagh. I had started off my heavy baggage under Ram Singh's charge four days earlier for Yarkand. So the final departure was not so troublesome an affair as starts on new journeys usually are in Turkestan. All the same I was kept hard at work with leave-taking from local acquaintances who came to see me off, with the distribution of medicines for cases actual and prospective among my friends' families, and—last but not least—the dispensing of "tips." Chinese Turkestan is a country where services whether large or small must be compensated by "tips" just as much as in the best conducted hotels of European centres of civilisation. Attendants of the Yamen who had been deputed to look after my camp; visitors who had helped in collecting information or antiques; Yüzbashis who had arranged for supplies, *et hoc genus omne*, had to receive appropriate tokens of my satisfaction. Expensive in a way as this system is, it saves needless circumlocution and *gêne*. There is no need to disguise one's "tips" in the form of presents, or to press them into hands that for the sake of appearances pretend to refuse them. Silver or gold, as the case may be, is accepted with the same unblushing readiness which seems to have been the proper style at Indian courts before European notions effected a change—on the surface. Of course, little souvenirs are not rejected by one's Turkestan friends. But what marks the value of services rendered, and is mainly looked for, is hard cash.

My march of the first day was only a short one. I did not wish to leave Khotan without a farewell visit to the site of the ancient capital, Yotkan. The road I followed was the same by which I had returned from that spot on a gloomy and cold November day. But what a glorious change in the landscape! Riding through the hamlets clustering in the fertile cantons of Tosalla and Borazan, there was nothing but deliciously green fields and orchards to rest one's eyes on. The first crop of lucerne was already standing high; the avenues of poplars, mulberry-trees, and willows had decked themselves with the richest foliage, and since the unusual rain that had fallen during my stay in Nar-Bagh scarcely any dust had had time to settle on the young leaves. It was a delightful ride which showed me the oasis under its prettiest aspects. When more open ground was reached beyond Halalbagh, the whole range of the great mountains burst into view. Quite clearly I saw the heights of Ulughat-Dawan and Kauruk-kuz where we fixed our triangulation stations. Beyond them, to my surprise, the icy ridges which form the watershed towards the sources of the Karakash showed themselves in rugged splendour. The inhospitable mountains through which I had toiled in November seemed thus to send me a farewell greeting. Their grand panorama was the finest setting for the last views I carried away with me of this strange little world between the desert and the mighty Kuen-luen.

At Yotkan, where I pitched my tent once more in the pretty orchard below the Yüzbashi's house, I was busy collecting samples of soil from the different strata which contain the ancient deposits and the silt that has buried them. I was, also, able to acquire an additional number of ancient coins, seals, terra-cottas, etc., the owners of which had not come forward on the former occasion. The most notable of these antiques was a tiny statuette in solid gold, representing a sitting monkey of exactly the same style and attitude as frequently found among the terra-cotta figurines from the same site.

On the morning of the 29th of April I left Yotkan for the canton of Kara-kash, which forms the north-western edge of the oasis. I had not found a previous opportunity to visit it, and had now an additional reason to look it up before my final departure. Islam Beg, my faithful 'Darogha' of the days of Karanghu-tagh and Dandan-Uiliq, had since been appointed one of the Begs of Kara-kash. Rightly or wrongly, he attributed his good fortune to my recommendation with the Amban. So he was anxious to show me Kara-kash, both as his native place and the present sphere of his official functions. Both he and Badruddin Khan, the Afghan Aksakal, had followed me from Khotan and claimed the privilege of keeping me company up to the very border of the oasis.

BADRUDDIN KHAN AND AFGHAN TRADER, KHOTAN.

The weather kept bright and clear, and made the day's ride most enjoyable. In the early morning we passed through Bizin, the market-place of the Borazan tract, on the high-road that leads from Zawa to Khotan. It was Monday, the local market-day, and the long rows of booths and shops were already thronged with villagers. But a sight more curious to me was the long stream of petty traders whom we passed along the country tracks leading from Kara-kash to Bizin. The weekly market of Kara-kash had been held on the preceding day, and the same traders who had then exhibited their wares there were now hurrying on to Bizin. Badruddin Khan, who usually himself shares these migrations, explained to me the system by which the week-days are divided between the seven main Bazars of the oasis. The "Old" and "New" towns of Khotan, Yurung-kash, Sampula, Imam Musa Kasim, Bizin, and Kara-kash have each a weekly market day, and as the distances are not great and the succession of the several local markets is conveniently arranged, the traders make it a point to attend all these markets in turn. Ponies carry the bales containing the migratory "shops," and, balanced on the top of the loads, their owners and assistants. Thus that morning the greater part of the petty trading community of Khotan passed me as it were on review. Badruddin Khan knew them all well, goods, ponies and men, and had much to tell of their financial fortunes and personal characters.

I was surprised at the number of foreigners whom we met among these hurrying traders. There were Kabulis and Bajauris, men from Pishin in Baluchistan, and plenty of Andijanis. A few Kashmiris, too, I saw in the straggling procession, but the greeting I addressed to them in familiar 'Kashür kath' (Kashmiri) met with no response. They were the sons of emigrants settled in Yarkand, and had forgotten their fathers' tongue. Among the Afghans, too, it is rare that the children know anything of Persian or Pushtu. Once more I had occasion to reflect on the great power of assimilation exercised by the Turki-speaking population throughout Turkestan. It quickly absorbs races which on Indian soil would retain their well-marked individuality and difference of speech for generations. Whatever the causes may be, this rapid amalgamation at centres like Yarkand and Khotan always presents itself to me as an apt illustration of the historical process by which Turki tribes far away to the west have peacefully absorbed foreign elements more numerous and cultured than themselves.

I reached Kara-kash town in the afternoon, after crossing the wide bed of the river from which it is named, and found it a comparatively lively and well-built place. The garden of one of Islam Beg's relations had been hospitably prepared for my reception, and there I was busy until a late hour with the measurement of many heads for anthropological purposes and the record of interesting details about local administration, taxes, etc., for which I had in Islam Beg a first-hand authority.

April 30th was to be my last day within the territory of Khotan. I used it for a long excursion to a 'Tati' site called Kara-döbe ("the Black Mound"), of which Islam Beg had obtained information, away to the west on the edge of the desert. In order to reach it we had to traverse in succession the remarkably fertile tracts of Bahram-su, Kayesh, Makuya, and Kuya, all stretching in long strips of highly cultivated ground with shady orchards and lanes along their own separate canals fed by the Kara-kash. No more pleasing picture could I retain as a souvenir of rural Khotan. The day was hot and close, and the vision of the mountains had already vanished in the usual haze. So I was quite glad when, after passing for some seven miles over a scrub-covered sandy plain and then through low dunes, Kara-döbe was reached. I found the ground for about a square mile covered with ancient pottery, and in the midst of this débris a small mound of broken masonry. The brick-work was undoubtedly old, and might well have belonged once to the base of a Stupa. Elsewhere broken pieces of hard white stucco with relievo ornament possibly represent the last remains of some long-decayed shrine. Heavy dunes of coarse sand, very trying to our ponies, had to be crossed for some four miles before we struck the western bank of a broad marshy Nullah in which the stream of Yawa expands among reed-covered lagoons. And when by nightfall I arrived at my camp pitched near the village of Zawa, I might feel as if, by these changes of rich village land, sandy jungle, high dunes and marsh, Vaisravana, the divine *genius loci* of Khotan in Buddhist legend, had wished to let me once more see, as a parting favour, every type of scenery I had beheld in the land over which he presided.

By daybreak of the 1st of May I set out for my long journey westwards. Cheered as I was by the thought of the road that

30

now lay clear before me to Europe, I felt the sadness of saying farewell, probably for ever, to a fascinating field of work and to the last of my faithful local helpmates. At Zawa itself I had to take leave of Turdi, my honest old guide, whose experience and local sense never failed me in the desert. I liberally rewarded his services with more "treasure," *i.e.*, cash, than he had ever brought back from his wanderings in the Taklamakan. He had also the expectation of seeing himself, through Pan-Darin's favour, installed as 'Mirab' or steward of irrigation for his native village near Yurung-kash. It was a snug though modest post to which our 'Aksakal of the Taklamakan' fondly aspired, since he thought he was getting too old for the desert, and in view of his proved honesty I had been able to recommend him with a good conscience. Yet with this comforting prospect before him, I could see how genuine the tears were that at our parting trickled over the weather-beaten face of the old treasure-seeker.

It was easier to leave behind Niaz Akhun, my Chinese interpreter. He had fallen into a matrimonial entanglement with a captivating Khotan damsel of easy virtue, and had decided to remain, against the emphatic warnings of the old Amban, who plainly told him that, as a confirmed gambler and without a chance of employment, he would soon be starving. He had taken the earliest opportunity to divest himself of all further responsibilities for his wife and children at Kashgar by divorcing her "through letter post" as it were, the necessary document from a Khotan Mullah costing only a few Tangas. With such remarkable ease of divorce throughout the country, as illustrated by this typical case, the organisation of Turkestan family life has always appeared to me rather puzzling.

Islam Beg and Badruddin Khan, who had reason to be satisfied with the rewards their efficient services had earned them, would not leave me until we reached Tarbugaz, the lonely Langar on the desert edge where I had passed my first night on Khotan soil. When they too had bidden me farewell and I was riding on alone by the desert track to the "Pigeons' Shrine," my thoughts freely turned to a more cheerful theme—the results I was bringing back from Khotan. When I had passed here nearly seven months before, there was little to give me assurance that I should ever see the hopes fulfilled that had drawn me to this distant land. But now my task was done and I could rejoice in the thought that my labours had been rewarded far beyond those long-cherished hopes. Again there came into my mind a remembrance of the pious custom which Hiuen-Tsiang had recorded at this very site, of the sacred rats that once enjoyed the honour now paid to the sacred pigeons. "On passing the mounds they descend from their chariots and pay their respects as they pass on, praying for success as they worship. . . . Most of those who practise these religious rites obtain their wishes." It was true, the sacred birds had not seen me worship; for success too I had not prayed, but only worked. Yet as success had come, I felt justified in offering to the birds a liberal treat of maize and corn as my grateful ex-voto on leaving Khotan.

HALT ON THE MARCH DOWN THE GULCHA VALLEY, FARGHANA.

CHAPTER XXXIII.

FROM KHOTAN TO LONDON.

THE story of the journey which, within two months of my start from Khotan, brought me back to Kashgar and thence through Russian Turkestan to Europe, can be told here only in the briefest outlines.

Six rapid marches, diversified by Burans and that almost forgotten experience, a "Europe day" with real rain clouds, carried me to Yarkand, where my caravan had safely preceded me. The short halt I was obliged to make there, mainly to settle accounts and to adjust the debts which my several Yarkand followers owed to Hindu money-lenders, coincided with an abnormal burst of rain such as this region had not seen for long years. The downpour continued with short breaks for two days and two nights, until all roads in the oasis were turned into quagmires and the mud-built walls of many houses in town and villages collapsed. In Yarkand city much distress prevailed; and even in the palatial halls of Chini-Bagh, which I again occupied, the mud roofs were soon leaking so badly that I felt serious concern about the safety of my antiquities. However, the heavy downpour had delightfully cooled the air, and thus the 140 odd miles to Kashgar, which I covered in less than three days, was a thoroughly enjoyable ride.

The morning of May 12th, a brilliantly clear day and full of the sensation of spring, saw me once more at Chini-Bagh under Mr. Macartney's hospitable roof, which I had left almost exactly eight months before. The warmest welcome greeted me there, and in the company of such kind friends I found it difficult to realise how long I had been cut off from personal touch with Europe. I might have feared to tire my hosts by a pent-up torrent of talk, had I not been assured by so many proofs of the constant interest with which Mr. Macartney had from afar followed my explorations. It was a source of keen pleasure to me to be able to show him what ample results had attended my work, and how much I owed to that local help which his influence and care had mainly assured me.

The kind hospitality I enjoyed made my stay at Kashgar a period of welcome physical rest, notwithstanding the multifarious preparations that kept me constantly at work. The Government of India in the Foreign Department, in accordance with the request I made before my start from Calcutta, had obtained for me permission from the authorities in St. Petersburg to travel through Russian Turkestan and to use the Trans-Caspian Railway for my return to Europe. I had also been authorised to take my archæological collections for temporary deposit to England, where alone convenient arrangements could be made for their scholarly examination. It hence became necessary at Kashgar to repack all my antiquarian finds with special regard for safe transport on this long journey, while all surveying instruments and other equipment, together with the records of our survey work, were to be sent back to India viâ Hunza in charge of the Sub-Surveyor.

While the fresh transport arrangements thus necessitated by

our different routes demanded much careful attention, I was also kept busy with the "demobilisation" of my old caravan. The camels and ponies, which had served us so well during the journeys of the preceding eight months, could not be taken any further, and as a not insignificant portion of the grant allotted for the expenses of my journey was invested in the animals, their satisfactory disposal was a matter of some concern. After a good deal of bargaining, which, in view of the trade customs of the Turkestan 'Kirakash,' or carriers, could scarcely be wondered at, I succeeded in this quasi-commercial task far better than I had ventured to hope at one time. The ponies sold practically without any loss, while in the case of our eight camels I realised not less than three-fourths of the purchase price. If I could have afforded the time to await the proper season of caravan traffic northward into Russian territory, I should probably have recovered for Government the whole of the original outlay on my Turkestan transport. That, after all the hard marching and exposure of our winter campaign in the desert the whole of the transport had been safely brought back, in a condition which allowed of its sale with such small loss, may justly be claimed as a proof of the care we had taken of our animals.

The arrangements for my onward journey were greatly facilitated by the kind help of M. Petrovsky, Imperial Consul-General of Russia at Kashgar, whose acquaintance I was fortunate enough to make on this occasion. During a long official career in Turkestan M. Petrovsky has devoted a great deal of scholarly zeal to the study of the history and antiquities of the country, as I had ample occasion to note in the course of the instructive interviews with which I was favoured within the Russian Consulate. He now did all in his power to ensure the safe transit of my archæological finds to England, and to secure for me the friendly assistance of the authorities in Russian Turkestan. For the help thus accorded I may be allowed to express here my grateful acknowledgments.

During my stay at Kashgar I had repeated occasions to meet again Huang-Kuang-ta, the kindly old Tao-tai, and to assure him of my gratitude for the most effective co-operation which

I had received from the Chinese officials wherever my explorations took me. The amiable old administrator did not deny the genuine interest and goodwill with which he had followed my work. But he politely insisted on attributing all the sympathy and support I had enjoyed from him and his Ambans to the benediction of my patron saint, 'Tang-Seng.' He even suggested as an explanation that we might both, in some previous birth, have been together under the direct spiritual influence of the great Buddhist monk! The Tao-tai talked of an early retirement to Hu-nan, and of his wish to end his days peacefully in a famous Buddhist convent near his home. This pious hope was not fulfilled; for illness and age caused him to pass away at his post within a year of my departure.

After a fortnight of busy work the demobilisation of my camp was completed, and all my antiquities safely packed in twelve large boxes. They were duly presented at the Russian Consulate for purposes of customs examination (a most gently conducted one), and then received their seals with the Imperial eagle, which I succeeded in keeping intact until I could unpack my treasures in the British Museum. I may mention the fact of my personally taking these boxes unopened over the various land frontiers from China to England as an indication of how much civilisation has done to obliterate in some respects the great barriers between Kashgar and London.

At last the day came when I had to say farewell to my hosts, whose unceasing kindness had made this first and practically only rest after my desert wanderings an experience of which the pleasure will not easily fade from my recollection. On the morning fixed for my own departure I saw Sub-Surveyor Ram Singh, the faithful companion of my travels, set out for the return journey to India. He had rendered excellent services in accurately surveying the whole of the ground covered by my journeys, and had in addition to his proper duties been always eager to make himself useful in connection with my archæological work. He had at all times cheerfully borne the fatigues inseparable from rapid travelling over difficult ground and often under trying climatic conditions, and had given me valuable help in the management of my camp. I had indeed every reason to feel grateful to the Survey of India Department, and in particular to its present head, Colonel St. G. Gore, C.S.I., for having provided me with so willing and well trained an assistant. With Ram Singh there left also Jasvant

RAM SINGH AND JASVANT SINGH, WITH 'YOLCHI BEG,' IN MR. MACARTNEY'S GARDEN, KASHGAR.

Singh, the wiry little Rajput who had looked after the Surveyor's bodily comforts with exemplary care and devotion. Cheerful and contented, however long the march or bleak our camping-ground, Jasvant Singh could indeed serve as a model to every one of my followers.

Knowing how great a favourite 'Yolchi Beg' was with both my Hindus, I could safely entrust the genial little fox-terrier to their care for the journey back to India. To take him along with myself to Europe was out of the question. Equal as my little companion had proved to all hardships of mountains and desert, it would have been cruel to subject him to weeks of a wearisome journey by rail merely to leave him in the end to the confinement of quarantine on reaching England. Yet I confess I felt the separation from the devoted comrade of all my travels, until we joyfully met again one November night on a Punjab railway platform. He had ailed a little before my return, but soon picked up his spirits again—only to pine away in the end when my scientific task had forced me once more to proceed to England. Fate favoured him in the place of his death, for he breathed his last in Alpine Kashmir, which he loved like his master.

On May 29, 1901, exactly a year after leaving Srinagar, I started from Kashgar for Osh, the nearest Russian town in Farghana. My caravan was small, six sturdy ponies carrying my antiquities, while two more sufficed for a *tente d'abri* and my much reduced camp outfit and personal baggage. Besides the men attending to the hired animals only Sadak Akhun accompanied me. Safely removed from the evil spirits of the desert (*recte* the temptation to take too large doses of 'Charas') he had become again a fairly sober character. The caravan route from Kashgar to Osh, across the Alai mountains, is reckoned at eighteen marches. Anxious to save time, I managed to cover it in ten days, keeping in the saddle or on foot from early morning until nightfall.

Owing to the exceptional rain of the previous weeks and the rapid melting of the snows, the feeders of the Kizil-su, which the route crosses repeatedly before reaching the Russian frontier towards the Alai, were all in flood. The passage of my precious loads of antiques across the swollen streams was hence a daily anxiety. However, with care and some good fortune we managed to negotiate each of these obstacles without a single box getting drenched, and on the evening of the fifth day I arrived at Irkeshtam, the Russian frontier post. Never have I felt so much the significance of a political barrier. For it seemed Europe indeed into which I stepped when, a few hundred yards from the Chinese frontier, I entered the well-built, comfortable house, nestling below the Cossack garrison's fort, where M. Dochenko, the hospitable officer in charge of the Russian Customs, gave me a warm welcome.

The scenery next morning showed an equally marked and pleasant change. The barren rock and detritus of the valleys at the head-waters of the Kizil-su gave way to grassy alpine slopes soon after I left Irkeshtam. The usual route over the Terek Pass was closed by the depth and softness of the snow. So I had to take the more circuitous route over the Alai. On the Taun-murun Pass (close on 12,000 feet above the sea), which crosses the water-shed between Tarim and Oxus, and on which we had to spend a comfortless night, the deep snowdrifts and inclement weather caused much trouble. The sky did not clear next day when I rode down the broad rolling 'Margs,' as we should call them in Kashmir, of the head of the Alai Valley, and consequently I lost the chance of sighting Mount Kaufmann and other high peaks of the Trans-Alai range towards the Pamir.

The Kirghiz had not yet ventured up to these splendid summer grazings which would force even the most stolid of Kashmir Gujars to admiration. The consequent want of shelter and supplies forced us to attempt the same day the crossing of the Taldik Pass in order to reach less exposed ground northwards. We were now indeed on the good bridle road that leads from Gulcha to the 'Pamirski post,' the well-known Russian fort on the Pamirs; but it was completely obliterated higher up by deep snow, and a blinding snowstorm came on while we toiled up to the Pass. But for the excellent guidance of our plucky 'Jigit,' a Nogai or Russified Muhammadan from Kazan whom the obliging Customs officer of Irkeshtam had provided as an escort, we might have fared badly. It was late in the night before we struggled through to the deserted Kirghiz blockhouses of Öch-töbe at the northern foot of the Pass. It was a wretched shelter, but all my boxes were safe.

After this experience, the rapid marches of the next three days, which carried me down the valley of the Gulcha River, were doubly delightful. The Alpine scenery, the luxuriant growth of herbs and flowers, as well as the abundance of pine forest in the higher side valleys, reminded me at every turn of familiar views in Kashmir. We met plenty of Kirghiz with their entire household on camels and ponies, slowly moving up for their summer 'Yailaks' on the Alai. The fine carpets

IN THE BAZAR OF OSH, FARGHANA.

displayed on the camels which the women-folk rode gave to these caravans quite an air of splendour.

I cannot pause to describe the many signs of prosperity and rapid material development which met the eye everywhere as soon as I had entered, on the 7th of June, the open fertile parts of the great Farghana Valley. Through carefully cultivated fields and substantially built villages, where there was much to indicate the beneficial results of a well-ordered European administration combined with great natural resources, I rode that evening into Osh, the prettily situated headquarters of the district. Its cantonment, founded by General Skobeleff on the conquest of Farghana only some twenty-five years before, looked, with its clean streets of Russian houses and its fine park along the broad, tossing river, like a favoured spot of Eastern Europe. Yet at the same time I was curiously reminded by many a pleasant feature of Indian "stations" I knew well along the foot of the Himalayas.

Colonel Zaytseff, the Chief of the District, and an officer of distinguished attainments, received me with the greatest kindness. His office, with picturesque Ming-bashis and Kirghiz headmen in attendance outside, still suggested the "Cutchery" of an Indian Frontier District. But at the charming villa where I enjoyed his hospitality, together with a glorious view of the snow-covered Alai range in the distance, everything breathed the air of Europe. The telegraph, which enabled me here to get into touch with home, still further strengthened the illusion that I had reached the confines of the West.

A short halt at Osh gave much-needed rest. I here discharged Sadak Akhun, whose open-air kitchen arrangements had aroused as much interest in the Russian household of my host, the local postmaster, as if they had been carried on in the back garden of a London suburb. I also disposed there of my remaining Indian camp furniture. I had reason to compliment myself on the lucky inspiration which prompted this last step. For when, after a four-hours' drive by the well-shaded road that traverses the open fertile plain towards Andijan, I reached this great town and with it the terminus of the Trans-Caspian Railway, I found myself in full Europe for all practical purposes. In the comfortable hostelry of the "Moskwiya Numer" my camp-bed and camp-chair would have been as much out of place as if set up in the inn of an English country town.

The Russian part of Andijan, stretching with broad and well watered roads to the east of the railway head, presented in all respects the appearance of a thriving commercial town of Eastern Europe. There were numbers of well-stocked shops, offices full of

Russian clerks, and, in the evening, a large gathering of European *employés* listening to the military band that played in the public gardens surrounding the fine church. The large native city some miles off bore the same air of bustling life and prosperity. Andijan was an important centre long before the Russian occupation, and the great impetus given by the latter to the material progress of Farghana had only added to the wealth of its traders, particularly since the extension of the Trans-Caspian Railway. While walking through the broad, well-kept Bazars, stocked with all kinds of European manufacture, as well as the produce of home industries in Russian and Chinese Turkestan, how little could I think of the terrible doom awaiting Andijan in the earthquakes of the last year! Every Central-Asian race seemed to be represented in the busy multitude that thronged the Bazars. Curiously enough I was greeted here by a Kashgar 'Haji,' who a little over a year before, while on his way to Bombay, had met me at the Turki Sarai of the Kashmir capital. Since performing the pilgrimage to Mecca, he had seen Egypt and Constantinople, and had chosen for his homeward journey the convenient railway route from the Black Sea and the Caspian. Our meeting here seemed a striking illustration how small the "world" is growing, even in Central Asia.

On the 11th of June I left Andijan by the Trans-Caspian Railway, which was now to carry me and my antiquities in comfort and safety towards real Europe. This journey, however hurried it had to be under the circumstances, enabled me to obtain many interesting glimpses of a part of Central Asia, which by its historical associations and its ancient culture, has had a special fascination for me ever since my Oriental studies began. Though luckily now under a civilised power and hence fully accessible, how much it still offers to the historian and archæologist to explore! I made short halts at the provincial capitals of Margilan and Samarkand, where I was favoured with much kind attention by Generals Tchaikowsky and Medinsky, the respective governors, and offered special opportunities for examining the antiquities collected in the local museums. I may add here that, though my knowledge of Russian is as scanty as it could be, I met nowhere with anything but courtesy and goodwill among Russian fellow-passengers and local officials. The impressions of the delightful days I spent at Samarkand, mainly in visits to the incomparable monuments of architecture of Timur's period which mark the height of Muhammadan power and art in Central Asia, could not be surpassed even by the combined reminiscences of Lahore. Delhi, and Agra. It was. in truth, another ex-

AT SAMARKAND : MARKET WITH RUINED MOSQUES IN BACKGROUND.

hibition of Moghul grandeur, but under a sky and in a climate that even in June recalled Kashmir.

A brief stay at Merv allowed me to touch ground full of great memories of ancient Iran. It was a tantalising pleasure, perhaps, seeing how little chance there seems for me to follow up my early historical studies in this field, yet I feel grateful for it. Then past the ruins of Gök-tepe, an historical site of more recent memories, the railway carried me to Krasnowodsk;

From there I crossed the Caspian to Baku, and finally, after long and tiring days in the train (viâ Petrovsk, Rostoff, Podwoloczyska, Cracow, Berlin) I arrived in London on July 2, 1901.

There I had the satisfaction of depositing the antiquities unearthed from the desert sands in the British Museum as a safe temporary resting-place. Neither they nor my eight hundred odd photographic negatives on glass had suffered by the long journey. It was for me *finis longæ chartæque viæque,* but also the commencement of a period of toil, the more trying because the physical conditions under which it had to be done were so different from those I had gone through.

* * * * * *

Owing to the great extent of the collections I had succeeded in bringing back, the task of arranging and cataloguing proved a very exacting one. As the period of six weeks' deputation in England originally sanctioned by the Government of India for this purpose proved wholly insufficient, the Secretary of State for India was pleased to extend it by another period of six weeks. I had every reason to feel grateful for this concession; but it was only at the cost of great exertions and through the devoted help of my friend, Mr. F. H. Andrews, that I succeeded in accomplishing the temporary arrangement of my collection and the preparation of a "Preliminary Report" during the allotted period.

When this urgent task was concluded by the close of September, I felt glad that my impending return to India for ordinary duty as Inspector of Schools in the Punjab promised at least a change and temporary respite. The busy weeks spent mainly in the basement rooms which the authorities of the British Museum had very kindly offered for the first accommodation of my collections, seemed to me a time of immurement for the sake of science. How often have I not, then and since, wished myself back in the freedom and peace of the desert !

KIRGHIZ FAMILY ON THE MARCH.

INDEX.

NOTES.—TRANSCRIPTION. The spelling of Oriental names and terms in the text and Index conforms to the system of phonetic transliteration approved by the International Congress of Orientalists and adopted, in a simplified form, for Indian Government publications. No use, however, has been made of diacritical marks which would appear out of place in a book intended for the general reader.

In the Index an endeavour has been made by a uniform use of hyphens to distinguish the component parts of Turki words whenever clearly traceable. In the text the use of such hyphens has been restricted.

ABBREVIATIONS. The following abbreviations have been employed to mark, where desirable, the derivation of Oriental words: A. Arabic; Ch. Chinese; I. Indian; P. Persian; Pr. Prakrit; S. Sanskrit; T. Turki.